D0152813

STUDIES ON CHINA

A series of conference volumes sponsored by the Joint Committee on Chinese Studies of the American Council of Learned Societies and the Social Science Research Council.

1. Origins of Chinese Civilization
edited by David N. Keightley,
University of California Press, 1982

2. Popular Chinese Literature
and Performing Arts
in the People's Republic of China
1949–1979
edited by Bonnie S. McDougall,
University of California Press, 1984

Popular Chinese Literature and Performing Arts in the People's Republic of China 1949–1979

Popular Chinese Literature and Performing Arts

IN THE PEOPLE'S REPUBLIC OF CHINA 1949–1979

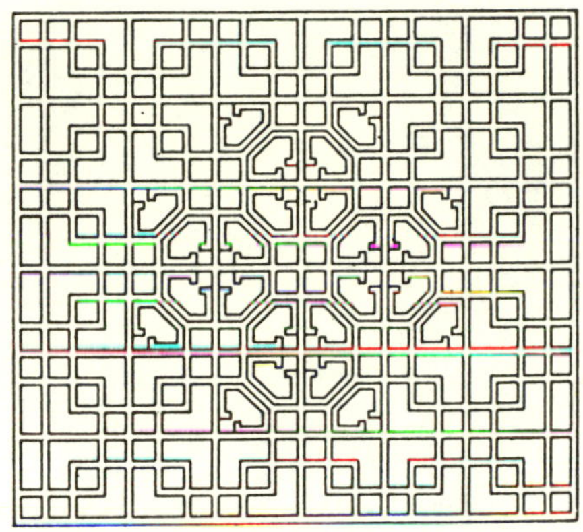

EDITED BY

Bonnie S. McDougall

CONTRIBUTORS

Paul Clark · Michael Egan · Edward Gunn
Robert E. Hegel · David Holm · Kai-yu Hsu · T. D. Huters
Perry Link · Wai-fong Loh · Bonnie S. McDougall
Isabel K. F. Wong · Bell Yung

UNIVERSITY OF CALIFORNIA PRESS
Berkeley · Los Angeles · London

Randall Library UNC-W

To Cyril Birch

Whom neither Ocean, Desarts, Rockes nor Sands
Can keepe from th' intertraffique of the minde

UNIVERSITY OF CALIFORNIA PRESS
Berkeley and Los Angeles, California
University of California Press, Ltd.
London, England
© 1984 by
The Regents of the University of California

Library of Congress Cataloging in Publication Data
Main entry under titles:
Popular Chinese literature and performing arts in the People's Republic of China, 1949–1979.
Based on papers presented at a workshop held at Harvard University, June 1979.
Bibliography: p.
Includes index.
1. Arts, Chinese—Addresses, essays, lectures.
I. McDougall, Bonnie S., 1941– II. Social Science Research Council (U.S.) III. Joint Committee on Chinese Studies.
NZ583.A1P66 1984 790.2'0951 82-21942
ISBN 0-520-04852

Printed in the United States of America
1 2 3 4 5 6 7 8 9

NX
583
.A1
P66
1984

CONTENTS

PREFACE

The state of literature and of its writers and audiences in contemporary China has attracted much Western attention in recent years.[1] The novels and short stories of "socialist realism" written in the 1950s and early 1960s, the "model revolutionary theater" of the Cultural Revolution and its aftermath (1966–1976), and the second Hundred Flowers after the fall of the Gang of Four have all been described by journalists and scholars. Most of their studies, however, whether descriptive or analytical, have focused on the content of the literature and on the way it has reflected changes in Party or government policy.[2] In this they have echoed the concern for the content of literary works that has been the major preoccupation of the Chinese Communist Party. All but a handful of these studies, moreover, concentrate on written literature: films, operas, or dramas are considered, when they are considered, more often as written scripts than as performing arts. Designed to complement existing studies, the present volume goes beyond content and policy analysis of these cultural products to literary-artistic methods of analysis. In this way, we hope to give a fuller picture of the literature and arts of today's China—how they might seem to China's audiences, how they relate to China's past traditions, and how a modern Western reader might best appreciate their merits and shortcomings.

As well as examining the conventional written literature of poetry, fiction, and modern drama, this volume pays particular attention to oral and performing literature. Since the circulation of almost all written literature was suspended during the three years of the Cultural Revolution proper

[1] For a selection of books and articles on contemporary Chinese literature and performing arts, see the Bibliography at the end of this volume.

[2] See, for example, Howard L. Boorman, "The Literary World of Mao Tse-tung," in Cyril Birch, ed., *Communist Chinese Literature* (New York: Praeger, 1963), p. 15.

(1966–1969), only the performing arts, chiefly in the shape of "model revolutionary theater," provide any continuity in the cultural history of the period. The performing arts are also a necessary complement to written literature because of the two forms' constant interaction in theory and practice. Finally, the performing arts are part of Chinese cultural history in their own right: such genres as film and song probably reach a wider audience than any written literature, and are objects of serious attention for writers and performers as well as for the cultural authorities.

This collection of essays covers contemporary Chinese literature and performing arts through the end of the 1970s, at a particularly propitious moment for looking back on the achievements and vicissitudes of the post-1949 period. The Cultural Revolution has given us a perspective on the Hundred Flowers campaign of the late 1950s and the relaxation of the early 1960s, especially into the personal relationships among cultural workers, which was not available to Western observers at the time.[3] The dismantling of the Cultural Revolution policies in the 1970s gave, in addition, a promise of new possibilities for cultural life in a socialist state and raised new questions about the strength of the various traditions that make up the cultural scene.

The first three essays (Part I) in this volume show how the ground was prepared for the development of popular and elite forms of literature and performing arts in the late 1930s and the 1940s. Holm discusses the transformation of the rural song-and-dance *yangge,* as effected through political directives from Communist headquarters in the remote Northwest. In contrast, Gunn discusses the popularization of a modern urban elite form, the *huaju* (spoken drama), by the injection of elements from traditional drama as a commercial response to wartime conditions in occupied Shanghai. Finally, Huters discusses the gradual undermining of the modernist May Fourth writers in the late 1940s by political and social forces beyond their apparent control.

The core of the volume (Part II) deals with the fate of the different written and performings arts in the first three decades of the People's Republic of China, from its establishment in 1949 through its radical transformation in the 1970s. Three essays in this center section survey, respectively, the historical development and contemporary condition of *xiangsheng* (comedic monologues or dialogues), *geming gequ* (revolutionary songs), and poetry. Link and Wong discuss the origins of *xiangsheng* and *geming gequ* in the nineteenth century, the former as a popular urban

[3] For example, the contributors to *Communist Chinese Literature,* whose articles were originally prepared for a conference in summer 1962 and published in 1963, showed little belief in the "relaxation" of 1959–1962 (pp. 115, 159), though one contributor notes a slight relaxation (p. 204). From the mid-1960s, the early 1960s looked quite different: see D. W. Fokkema, "Chinese Criticism of Humanism: Campaign against the Intellectuals, 1964–1965," *China Quarterly* 26 (1966): 70, 77.

form that sometimes directed its satire against the authorities and the latter as a propaganda medium that was intentionally developed by organized rebellious forces. Whereas *xiangsheng* is a genuinely popular form that was adapted to meet the needs of the state after 1949, *geming gequ* is an example of a so-called popular form created from above. Hsu's essay on poetry charts the form's vicissitudes from the 1950s through the 1970s, showing the sometimes uneasy balance that existed among classical, folk, and modernist forms.

Two further essays analyze in detail the production of particular works: Loh, the musical film, *Liu Sanjie,* and Yung, the "transplanted" revolutionary opera *Sagabong.* These contributors demonstrate the processes by which writers and composers handled the task of creating new mass works on the basis of popular myths and performing traditions. Yung, like Holm, takes us beyond the centers of Peking and Shanghai to show the variety in provincial or regional forms. In the first of two essays on fiction, Egan describes how a self-professed peasant writer, Hao Ran, progressed from using a genuine folk idiom in narrative to develop a more purified, politicized style in the 1970s. In the following essay, Hegel examines the part of the tradition mined for the mass fiction of the 1950s and 1960s, and how that fiction was itself mined for the "model operas" of the 1960s and 1970s. Clark's essay on film in the 1970s describes the gradual reemergence of film personnel before as well as after the fall of the Gang of Four, and shows also their continuity with the film world of the 1960s (a situation also broadly true of the other arts).

The volume concludes (Part III) with a survey of writers and performers, their works, and their audiences over the three decades from 1949 through the 1970s, pointing to the complexities and changing relationships within literary and art circles, their overlap with political groups, and their mutual relations. Taken as a whole, the essays cover the major time periods and literary genres of the People's Republic of China and offer a comprehensive view of its problems and achievements in the field of popular culture.

THE STUDY OF CONTEMPORARY CHINESE LITERATURE AND PERFORMING ARTS IN THE WEST

The essays in this volume came out of a workshop on contemporary Chinese literature and the performing arts held at Harvard University in June 1979.[4] In the sometimes heated discussions that followed the presen-

[4] The workshop was sponsored by the Harvard University Council on East Asia, the John K. Fairbank Center for East Asian Research, and the Department of East Asian Languages and Civilizations. We gratefully acknowledge the support of the Mellon Foundation, the American Council of Learned Societies, and the Social Science Research Council. I should also like to express my appreciation of the contributions made by the more than fifty scholars who took part in the workshop.

tation of the papers, the problems facing students and researchers in this new subfield became only too evident. Many of these problems are raised in the essays included in this volume; the major ones are outlined below.[5]

Informational Problems

The difficulty in obtaining adequate information about our material poses a serious problem, as it does in other kinds of contemporary Chinese studies. Over most of the past three decades, we have been largely restricted to a small selection of the official cultural products emanating from the center and approved for foreign distribution. Failure to secure even these limited materials immediately upon release often results in their permanent absence from Western collections. Some additional materials can be obtained without official sanction, but these may have drawbacks such as unsystematic supply and unconfirmable authenticity. Our information about literature and the arts, and about the people who practice them and about their audiences, may be misleading, whether it comes from official or nonofficial sources; more often, it is the simple lack of information that hinders our better understanding.

Disciplinary Problems

First, in addition to the problems we share with political scientists, historians, and so on, we lack a tradition in Western literary sinology for the study of literature as it is produced. Before World War II, the study of Chinese literature in the universities was largely confined to the traditional classics in the literary language. Perhaps because of its obvious westernization and seeming lack of continuity with the past, May Fourth literature did not receive sustained and detailed study until the 1960s. The heavy politicization of Chinese literature that took place in the 1940s and after alienated a great many scholars, including those who had developed strong interests in May Fourth literature. The overt nature of the political content, which embodies an ideological stand not shared by most American scholars and students, remained a serious obstacle to contemporary literary studies throughout the 1960s and 1970s.

In the case of Western or Japanese literature, the effects of literary conservatism are usually limited, as modern information-collecting systems continue to collate and store the material for future research. In contemporary China this has simply not been the case, given the stormy political conditions of the past three decades. For the period 1966–1973, a single person resident in China could be confident of having read all the literature and seen all the productions created centrally in China. Since then, the

[5] For this section I am greatly indebted to the ideas expressed by John Berninghausen in "The State of the Field and Future Directions," paper at the workshop on Contemporary Chinese Literature and Performing Arts, Harvard University, June 1979.

picture has changed rapidly—especially since 1978—and it is now necessary to exercise selectivity in studying the total production. Instant literary judgments pose substantial hazards to scholarly reputations—but if not to literary scholars, then to whom should we turn?

Second, most Western studies of Chinese literature are undertaken from a background in sinology rather than literature. Scholars of traditional Chinese literature have recently paid more attention to the literary nature of the texts, but this perspective has not yet carried over into modern studies. Most Western discussions of May Fourth literature still dwell on the external circumstances of the text—its author, the social and intellectual background, and its impact on its audience—rather than on its structure and internal coherence. In contemporary Chinese literature, where the content has seemed so alien and the literary value so slight, a large part of the research has been undertaken by political scientists rather than by literary scholars. Fortunately, new developments in literary analysis, such as structuralism, have made possible a more systematic study of China's new literature in terms of its own needs, structures, and traditions. Nevertheless, the general lack of information about contemporary China has led to an abnormally heavy Western demand on Chinese literature to serve as documentary material, and studies of the literature by literary scholars have also been influenced by this demand. Further, since political and social forces have exerted such strong control over literary products, the literary scholars must give more than usual weight to the external circumstances of literary production and consumption, a focus that inevitably detracts from autonomous textual studies.

Third, until very recently, literary sinology concerned itself only with the written genres such as poetry and the great vernacular novels, and ignored nonwritten, oral literature. In studies of modern Chinese works, the practice resulted in a very narrow and biased view of the contemporary cultural scene, since in some ways the conventional written literature is one of its most rigid and unattractive cultural forms. This limitation is now disappearing, due to changes in social thinking and recent advances in scholarly analysis of oral and popular works. These essays reflect some of the first efforts to extend this broader analysis to the contemporary performing arts.

Attitudinal Problems

Our most serious problem is the attitudes or values with which we approach the literature and arts of contemporary China. Literature has traditionally been a very value-conscious discipline, and in literary criticism and theory even the term "literature" is often synonymous with "good literature." The choice of a literary topic for study often implies approval of the quality of the work or works involved, and it becomes taken for granted that only "good literature" is genuinely worthy of study. In consequence, bad or merely indifferent literary works are either ignored or are written about with indifference or hostility. Most written contemporary Chinese literature has been perceived by Western scholars as bad or indifferent, and the study of contemporary Chinese culture has suffered accordingly. The Tolstoyan distinction between literature/nonliterature and good/bad literature has only marginally affected Chinese literary studies, but at least it points to the theoretical possibility that bad literature also has literary devices, structures, and genre requirements, for example, and can thus be of interest to literary scholars. It would clearly be absurd if political scientists and historians were to study only societies or institutions of which they approved—and, in fact, the reverse has often been true. It therefore seems academically indefensible for literary scholars to avoid or dismiss material that offends their sensibilities, solely on these grounds.

Is the study of contemporary Chinese literature and art, then, to be value-free? Again, the analogy of history and political science seems valid. It is important that we do not allow our values to distort our perceptions of contemporary Chinese culture, and also that we do not confuse our values with those of the society that produces and consumes that culture. But this in no way implies that we must discard our values in our assessment of that culture. Evaluation is both an extremely useful tool in intellectual analysis and ultimately the justification for any literary criticism. Equally, we must avoid adopting a double standard (with its patronizing overtones) toward contemporary Chinese culture, since our position as Western scholars in regard to both Western and Chinese studies depends on our integrity as outside observers. Above all, we must remain conscious of our own identities and not pretend to be speaking on behalf of the whole or of any section of the Chinese people.

Possibilities for Future Studies

There was considerable agreement at the workshop that studies of both written and oral literature should take as their starting point the texts themselves. In the past, most studies on modern and contemporary literature and art have focused on the biographies of writers and performers, their contribution to intellectual history, the sociopolitical context of their works, and content analyses of works for studies of policy changes. All of these are valid approaches, but they are not the concern of literary studies per se. The information gained from such undertakings is generally available from other sources (perhaps more reliably), and the special qualities of literary works are ignored. If on the one hand, our ultimate aim is to understand the society through the works of culture it produces, then a more valid approach is first to understand the internal logic of that culture: its forms, its traditions, and its styles. A whole range of analytical techniques can help in that understanding: those of mythic, structural, semiotic, formalist, comparative, and genre analysis, to name some represented at the workshop. Once made more accessible through literary and artistic analysis, the material can be more readily drawn on for different scholarly or humanistic purposes.

If, on the other hand, we wish to focus on the literary text itself, we may use sociological analysis to study patterns of cultural production and consumption. The material conditions of writers, performers, and audiences may be directly relevant to the literary work. It can readily be established that, in China, neither the Party nor the literary bureaucracy, nor writers, performers, and audiences constitute monolithic and static blocs. Beyond that negative assurance, however, we possess very little reliable and systematic information about the sociological dimensions of Chinese creativity.

The cultural scene as a whole consists of a wide variety of genres and forms. When performing arts are studied alongside written literature, and popular arts are given the same depth of analysis as elite forms, phenomena such as the strength of the traditional heritage in contemporary Chinese culture become more apparent. The broader perspective also allows the study of genre transposition: when a story or theme is shifted from one genre to another (e.g., from novel to opera, or from opera to film), we have an opportunity to observe what is common to both—i.e., not genre-specific, but perhaps imposed by political necessities. The picture of contemporary Chinese literature and performing arts that emerges when these two factors are studied in conjunction with each other shows more variation, in range and in quality, than has perhaps generally been assumed. By no means have all previous judgments been overturned. Some have been confirmed. But comprehensive studies similar to those undertaken here should lead to a better understanding of what was produced in these three decades and of why it was produced in just these ways.

Finally, many workshop participants drew attention to the need for contemporary scholarship to develop a readiness to tackle the ongoing literary and artistic scene in China, despite the high risks of mistakes in judgment involved. The alternative is to leave the field to journalists or other nonspecialists, whose mistakes and misinformation would be at least as great as any we might be guilty of. Even more importantly, our ignorance of the contemporary cultural products may preclude a full and accurate gathering of information and material that later generations may never have the opportunity to acquire. A more attractive reason for studying the present scene is that just now, at the turn of the decade, it is probably more lively and varied than at any time since the 1930s and 1940s.

The preparation of a manuscript as lengthy and diverse as this is not an easy task, nor is the process of submitting it for publication and shepherding it into final book form a simple one. I should like to thank all the contributors to this volume for their patience, goodwill, and cooperation over a period of several years. I should also like to thank the following people without whose advice, encouragement, and active assistance I doubt that the transformation of manuscript to book could have been achieved: Cyril Birch, Perry Link, T. D. Huters, Edward Gunn, Patrick Hanan, Rulan Chao Pian, John Berninghausen, Merle Goldman, Ezra Vogel, Anders Hansson, and Sophie Sa. I am also most grateful to Virginia Mayer Chan, who typed the manuscript and shared many unrewarded hours on the index. Finally, on behalf of the contributors, I want to express our very deep appreciation to Mary Lamprech of the University of California Press, our capable production editor, and to Joyce Coleman for her highly skilled and infinitely patient copyediting of an unusually intractable text.

BONNIE S. MCDOUGALL
Harvard University

NOTE ON ROMANIZATION

The romanization used in this book is based on the *hanyu pinyin* system now in use in the People's Republic of China; it replaces the Wade-Giles system formerly in common use in English-language material. Some place names and personal names not formerly spelled according to Wade-Giles are kept in their more familiar form; for example, place names in post-office or older spellings (Peking, Canton) and personal names spelled idiosyncratically or according to non-northern dialects (Y. R. Chao, Chiang Kai-shek).

Conversion Table
from Wade-Giles to *hanyu pinyin*

Chiang Ch'ing	Jiang Qing
Chou En-lai	Zhou Enlai
Chou Yang	Zhou Yang
Ch'ü Ch'iu-pai	Qu Qiubai
Ch'ü Po	Qu Bo
Ho Ch'i-fang	He Qifang
Ho Ching-chih	He Jingzhi
Hsü Chih-mo	Xu Zhimo
Kuo Mo-jo	Guo Moruo
Lu Hsun	Lu Xun
Mao Tse-tung	Mao Zedong
Pa Chin	Ba Jin
Teng T'o	Deng Tuo

Tsang K'o-chia	Zang Kejia
Ts'ao Yü	Cao Yu
Wen I-to	Wen Yiduo

PART I

The Ground Prepared, 1937–1949

ONE

Folk Art as Propaganda: The *Yangge* Movement in Yan'an

David Holm

The year 1942 is widely regarded, both in China and by scholars in the West, as a watershed in the history of modern Chinese literature and the arts. After the delivery of Mao Zedong's "Talks at the Yan'an Forum on Literature and Art" and the literary rectification campaign of the same year, nothing was ever quite the same for the writers and artists working in the Chinese Communist Party's wartime base areas. Since then, literary and artistic production has been subject to Party control and direction, and professional writers and artists have been recruited periodically into popularization work for various mass campaigns. The negative effects of this system on the quantity and quality of serious literature produced since then, and particularly after 1949, have been much discussed; until recently, however, the active implications of Party policy and the effects of this policy on less exclusive, more popular genres have received little attention. Even for the study of prose fiction, however, the close connection between art and politics in China is bound to present the scholar and student with a special and peculiar range of problems. How do we assess works that, whatever else they are, are propaganda for an official point of view or that at least stand in close relationship to the views of some section or other of the political and cultural apparatus? How useful under these circumstances are the usual methods of evaluation developed by literary critics in the West?

It has been suggested a number of times in recent years that, rather than evaluate Chinese literary production solely in terms of our own values and in light of our own ideas about literary excellence, we should also measure it against the yardstick of the rather different values professed by the Chinese. Well and good, but there are a number of pitfalls apart from the obvious one of mistaking the official Chinese position for unofficial opinion at various levels. We must seek to understand something about Marxism-Leninism—not just in the abstract, as a system of beliefs or set of sacred texts, but also as it functions in Chinese society as an ideology. If we take, say, a contemporary novel, read it through, and analyze it, we will no doubt find that it propounds in some way or another the various tenets of Marxism-Leninism and Mao Zedong Thought. This is not very surprising, or very interesting, either. Such an analysis would tell us virtually nothing about how that particular work is intended to function in society, or about the actual effects of the work on a readership or audience. These are important considerations, since the whole rationale of revolutionary literature and art, in practical terms—and an important strain in the Chinese Communist Party's literary ideology—was that literature and art should contribute to a liberation of mass energies and provide correct motivation for revolutionary action. To make any serious attempt to gauge these effects, however, we would have to go much further than we have been accustomed, not only in our reading of texts but also in relating the ideological formulations in those texts to wider phenomena. These phenomena would include traditional notions and motifs, fragments of popular discourse, and the salient events of recent history both official and unofficial.

This kind of approach is particularly appropriate for the study of mass movements. Cultural mass movements are generally very difficult to assess, if only because of the sheer amount of activity involved, yet their importance in the cultural life of millions of Chinese can hardly be ignored. One of the most distinctive phenomena of contemporary Chinese culture since 1942 is the officially sponsored mass movement based on a single literary-artistic genre. The *yangge* movement, launched in 1943, was the first of these and, as such, the forerunner of the revolutionary folksong of the Great Leap Forward period and of the revolutionary model Peking opera of the Cultural Revolution years. A study of it will shed light not only on Mao's "face-the-masses" orientation in literature and art and on how it came to be interpreted in practice during a formative period in recent Chinese history, but will also highlight the continuing tension between populist and "elevating" perspectives, both within the Party's own cultural apparatus and in the Party's artistic ideology.

ART AND PROPAGANDA

A concern with the "educative function" of art runs like a red thread through the whole range of the new art and literature produced under Party guidance after 1942. Yet for a number of reasons Western scholarship—most notably in the favored field of prose fiction—has chosen to ignore this aspect of Chinese art or to deal with it in a simplistic manner. It will help, for a start, to draw some elementary distinctions between art and propaganda. The general feeling is, of course, that propaganda is lies—in the words of Dr. Goebbels—and that therefore a study of propaganda will yield nothing of value except perhaps a moral lesson on the wickedness of totalitarian regimes. I would suggest that, on the contrary, propaganda is interesting—and revealing—precisely because it is an attempt to manipulate and persuade.[1] Of course, in recent Chinese history propaganda has sometimes been formulated less with a view to persuading the target population than with respect to various internal considerations, such as pleasing the heads of propaganda departments or presenting a particular ideological position in a "pure" and uncompromising fashion. Such, however, was far from the case in the years before 1949, when the Party was fighting for survival and pursuing a strategy of maximizing its friends in order to isolate its enemies.

Propaganda, unlike literature and art, is generally thought of as emanating from organized political groups and is evaluated by the sponsor primarily on how effectively it changes patterns of thinking and behavior in a target population—or, put more negatively, on how it prevents people from thinking and acting in certain ways. Artistic criteria may of course play an important secondary role as a source of appeal; thus, works of propaganda of a high artistic quality may be more effective, as propaganda, than works that are, for whatever reason, less satisfactory artistically. This is particularly so when the target population is a section of society that sees its traditional role as guardian of cultural values. Nevertheless, in the eyes of the agencies commissioning or producing the propaganda, artistic quality is a means to an end rather than an end in itself.

Moreover, propaganda, unlike most literature and art, is designed explicitly with a specific audience in mind—a "receptive object" (*jieshou duixiang*), as Mao put it in the Yan'an "Talks."[2] Of course, literature too may be written for specific sections of society—children's literature, for instance, is literature nonetheless. But at least in the West there has been historically a strong tradition that literature of quality is intended—to the extent that the audience is envisioned at all in the process of creation—for all humankind. Chinese writers in the early years of this century were very strongly influenced by this idea of the universality of literature.

[1] For an interesting account of propaganda in general, see Jacques Ellul, *Propaganda: The Formation of Men's Attitudes* (New York: Knopf, 1965). This work is mainly concerned with industrial societies but also gives some account of propaganda in China.

[2] See the original text in *Jiefang ribao* [Liberation Daily], 19 October 1943, reprinted in Takeuchi Minoru, ed., *Mō Takutō shū* (Tokyo: Hōkubo sha, 1970–1974), 8:115. This and a number of other "technical" terms were later removed from the text for the *Selected Works* version.

A corollary of this belief was the idea that literature—good literature at least—is valid for all time. There has been much discussion in the field of esthetics about why the literature of ancient Greece and Rome, for instance, should still have meaning for readers living in a vastly different society over two thousand years later. The idea of writing or creating a work of art for posterity, however, is in fact a specific historical phenomenon. Premodern China had a strong tradition of the universality of art, but many modern Chinese writers had lost contact with this native tradition. Its modern Chinese incarnation can be traced back to the European Enlightenment and the early Romantic movement. Modern Chinese writers and artists were heavily infected with this idea when they first came into serious contact with the culture of the modern West. Propaganda, on the other hand, is not ordinarily produced with eternity in mind. Rather, it is intended to operate within a restricted time span and to retain relevance for short periods only, varying from the medium term (several months or several years) down to the very short term (one day or even several hours).

These general points also form the basis of the approach to propaganda policy that the Chinese Communist Party developed during the early years of the Red Army. As early as 1929, at the Gutian Conference, Mao and other advocates of "political warfare" developed a sophisticated and highly articulated set of ideas on propaganda, which are set out in the draft resolution of the conference.[3] The resolution recognized that propaganda work, in order to be effective, should have "time quality" (*shijianxing*) and "local quality" (*difangxing*). Two separate notions are involved in time quality. First is the idea that propaganda should be appropriate for the time of year; this was particularly important with propaganda directed at peasants, who are involved in an annual round of activity. Secondly, there was the stipulation that propaganda be up to date and reflect current events. To the extent that it does so, of course, propaganda tends to become out of date very quickly; when the situation changes it loses its value as propaganda and has to be replaced. In the Gutian resolution the problem is mentioned specifically in connection with written media like pamphlets and announcements, but it affected all media to some degree. Obviously a great deal of variation was possible: in any well-organized propaganda machine there would be a continuum between propaganda pieces intended for general distribution over a long period of time and those directed more specifically at a particular situation.

"Local quality" was also used in two senses, first that propaganda

[3] Text in *Mō Takutō shū,* 2:77–126. See especially section 4, "Hongjun xuanchuan gongzuo wenti" [Problems of propaganda work in the Red Army], pp. 103–116. The whole text was reissued during the Yan'an period for study by army officers and was subsequently included in the standard collection of rectification documents for study by all Party cadres: see Stuart Schram, *Mao Tse-tung* (Harmondsworth: Penguin, 1968), p. 233.

should be couched in terms of local issues and local personalities, and second that it should make use of local dialects and should be put into words that local people without a high level of education could understand. Both aspects of this concept were of cardinal importance in China, with its patchwork of local cultures and dialects, where the horizons of the mass of the population were generally very limited. In practice, however, the desirability of propaganda adapted to the local level had to be balanced by administrative costs as well as by the abilities of the available propagandists: in the transition from a general to a locally specific form, propaganda lost much of its relevance and effectiveness in other locations, and new versions had to be prepared for each locality. The result was that propaganda was produced with varying degrees of local quality: different media worked on different levels, some with broad regional coverage and others at the level of the county, parish, or village.

The Gutian resolution also embodied the recognition that propaganda increased in effectiveness the more it was directed specifically at particular sections of the population. Party propaganda was henceforth to be produced and directed not just at the masses "in general," but at a range of distinct social groups with different cultural backgrounds, occupations, and levels of education. It is interesting to note that social class, as usually defined in Chinese Communist writings, was regarded, implicitly, as much too coarse a filter for the organization of effective propaganda work. For example, the resolution urged that propaganda not only be directed at vagrants (*liumang*) separately, but also that differences in the lifestyle and character of different occupational groups within this classification (gamblers, beggars, watervendors, and so forth) be taken separately into account. I shall be dealing in this paper mainly with the Party's attempt to reach the peasantry, but it must be borne in mind that neither Chinese rural nor town society was as simple as the formula "workers, peasants, and soldiers" would lead us to suppose. Since the Maoist strategy for revolution was basically to form the broadest possible alliance among the people while picking out enemies, both domestic and foreign, one by one, the above guidelines implied that the Party's propaganda apparatus should direct propaganda at virtually every group and stratum of Chinese society. Taken to its logical conclusion, this policy meant, in effect, replicating all the ideological complexities of that society.

For another point raised in the Gutian resolution was that all targets of propaganda were to be addressed in terms of their own specific psychology and within the terms of their own experience, not merely in terms of general political issues: the general was to be linked with the particular. "Propaganda must fit in with the emotions of mass struggle, but apart from issuing general slogans for an uprising, there must also be slogans appropriate to the daily lives of the masses at a level below that of the emotions of mass struggle." The implications of this proclamation are of utmost importance for later developments. All pre-existing values, world-views, and modes of expression, all the forms of China's "old culture" as they existed in the minds and collective experience of the Chinese people within particular social milieux, were potentially, at least, grist for the mill and could be linked to the new political ideals and manipulated for the furtherance of revolutionary aims. The use of "old forms" of literature and art, then, was simply a particular manifestation of a much more fundamental strategy in the Party's political work.

This, then, was the tradition of propaganda and political work brought to the wartime Border Region of Shaan-Gan-Ning (Shaanxi-Gansu-Ningxia) by the Red Army. During the Yan'an period (1937–1945), large numbers of writers and artists from the metropolitan cities and treaty ports came into contact with this tradition for the first time. The complex and convoluted character of developments in cultural policy during the Yan'an period before 1942 largely stems from the interactions between the Red Army tradition and the very different left-wing ethos of prewar Shanghai.

This is not to suggest that the urban wing of the Communist movement in China was entirely unfamiliar with the principles outlined above. The call to "make use of old forms" was heard repeatedly throughout the 1930s, and indeed the policy documents of the League of Left-Wing Writers made specific reference to the use of old forms as a means of making contact with the urban masses.[4] The idea can be traced back to the instructions and techniques communicated by Soviet advisers in China in the early days of collaboration between the Communist and Nationalist parties. In Shanghai, however, by common admission, there was a great deal of debate about literary popularization (that is, the popularization of prose fiction) and very little actual experiment or practice. Nevertheless, it is important to review briefly the terms of the debate, for these were later to provide the theoretical basis for the *yangge* movement in Yan'an.

THE DIALECTIC BETWEEN OLD AND NEW FORMS

One of the foremost advocates of the use of the old forms in the years before the war was Lu Xun, a man with a much wider experience of Chinese culture and society than many of the literary youths he sought to advise, who were largely products of a new Western-oriented education in

[4] Zuolian zhiweihui [Left-Wing League Executive Committee], "Zhongguo wuchanjieji geming wenxuede xin renwu" [The new tasks of Chinese proletarian revolutionary literature] (1931), in Beijing shifan daxue zhongwen xi xiandai wenxue jiaoxue gaige xiaozu, ed., *Zhongguo xiandai wenxue shi cankao ziliao* [Reference materials on the history of Chinese modern literature] (Peking: Gaodeng jiaoyu chubanshe, 1959), 1:290.

the arts. Lu Xun argued, along with the Party spokesmen Qu Qiubai and Zhou Qiying (Zhou Yang), that old forms of art, if used selectively in the service of the revolution and combined with new content, were capable of giving rise eventually to new and distinctive forms of art. His expression of this point in a 1934 essay was later adopted by Party spokesmen as the classic formulation of the official Party viewpoint:

> To work on behalf of the masses and strive to make things easy for them to understand—precisely this is the correct area of effort for the progressive artist. If we select from old forms, there will necessarily be parts we have to delete. And because of these deletions, there will necessarily be parts we have to add. This will result in the emergence of new forms, and will itself be a transformation.[5]

This essay was addressed to an audience more concerned about literature, and especially new forms of literature, than about effective communication with the masses. Lu Xun was clearly prepared to argue that form and content were separable, that new wine could be put in old bottles. Other writers were much less positive, and were quick to point out that the musty smell of old bottles would almost certainly taint the new wine with which they were filled. The truths of Marxism-Leninism, in other words, or of modern science and democracy, would be distorted in the process of transmission if expressed via literary-artistic forms more appropriate to a semifeudal and semicolonial stage of social development.

The idea behind Lu Xun's suggested transformation of old forms into new forms, however, was eminently respectable in terms of Marxist-Leninist philosophy, where operations involving the categories of form and content were a part of the tradition of dialectical materialism then current and popularized in China during the 1930s by Ai Siqi in his best-selling book *Dazhong zhexuė* [Philosophy for the masses].[6] In dialectical terminology, the contradiction between old form (thesis) and new content (antithesis) gave rise to new form (synthesis) on a higher level. This process, which involved the simultaneous transcendence and annulment of the old form, was referred to as "sublation" (*Aufhebung* or, in Chinese, *yangqi*). A corollary of this view was that, in the last analysis, it was changes in content, and indirectly in social life, which gave rise to changes in form; content, in other words, determined form. The implications of this conclusion for the use of old forms were double-edged, since it could be argued

[5] Lu Xun, "Lun jiu xingshide caiyong" [On the use of old forms], *Qiejieting zawen* (May 1934), reprinted in *Zhongguo xiandai wenxue shi cankao ziliao,* 1:305.

[6] First published in 1934, it went through numerous editions both before the war and after; it has recently been reprinted. Ai's book was basically a simple exposition of dialetical materialism as it was taught in the Soviet Union at the time. The following summary is based on his section on the categories "form" and "content."

that new content simply required new forms—the genres of art and literature, that is, introduced from the modern West.[7]

Given the widespread dislike of the old Chinese forms among the urban intelligentsia, the cultural policy that grew out of this type of dialectical analysis in the early years of the War of Resistance was essentially an eclectic one. In line with the forced pace of cultural change demanded by the Party, writers and artists experimenting in the use of old forms were expected to retain those features of the old form that fitted in with the new political content while "courageously" discarding features that openly conflicted with it. Any resulting gaps were to be made good by borrowing techniques from the new forms of art imported from the West. Similarly, writers and artists using the new European forms were asked to incorporate gradually more techniques and motifs from Chinese popular tradition.[8]

This at least was what was supposed to happen. Owing to a number of factors, however, it was only after the literary rectification of 1942 that the policy was really applied consistently to professional writers and artists. One of the main reasons for the delay was the widespread opposition to any "use of old forms." The beginning of the war in 1937 saw the use of old forms of art for "Save the Nation" propaganda on a very considerable scale, not only by dedicated Communist writers and by writers of the May Fourth tradition, but also by rural populists, opera companies, *dagu* ("drum") singers, and the like. Many of these productions were extremely crude, artistically speaking, and it was soon discovered that the attempt to reach a mass audience in one particular area often rendered the work of art unintelligible both to a nationwide audience and to mass audiences in other areas. Inevitably there was a revulsion against activity of this type.[9]

It was partly in order to stem the tide and change the terms of debate in

[7] Support for this viewpoint was widespread if not predominant in intellectual and artistic circles, and advocates of it included such people as Hu Feng, Ai Qing, Lao She, and Wang Shiwei. See on this point D. L. Holm, "Art and Ideology in the Yenan Period, 1937–1945" (D.Phil. dissertation, Oxford University, 1979), pp. 17–36. On Wang Shiwei in particular see D. L. Holm, "The Literary Rectification in Yenan, 1942–1943," in Kubin and Wagner, eds., *Essays in Contemporary Chinese Literature and Literary Theory* (Bochum: Brockmeyer, 1982).

[8] Such a two-pronged approach to sinification had many adherents, since it allowed everybody to continue what they were doing already (more or less). During the national form debates it was developed theoretically by the writers and critics of the Lu Xun College, led by Zhou Yang. A particularly clear example of the approach is Zhang Geng's essay "Xiju minzuhua yu jiuju xiandaihua" [The sinification of drama and the modernization of old opera], in Hu Feng, ed., *Minzu xingshi taolun ji* [Collected discussions on national form] (Chungking: Huazhong tushu gongsi, 1941), pp. 66–68.

[9] Lao She, for instance, who was very actively using old forms for mass propaganda in the first year or so of the Resistance War, later came to the conclusion that new wine could not be put in old bottles. See Holm, "Art and Ideology," pp. 35–36.

favor of the use of old forms that Mao issued his famous statement of October 1938 on "national form" (*minzu xingshi*).[10] This was only partly successful, however. Neither on that occasion nor in the more extended treatment he gave the subject in "On New Democracy" did Mao point out exactly which aspects of the folk tradition were "fine flowers" and which were "feudal dross":[11] the choice was regarded either as self-evident or else as a question to be solved on the level of artistic practice. The result was, however, that theory never became in any real sense a guide to practice; rather, it remained a general framework to bridge over wide differences of opinion inside and outside the Party. Moreover, the revulsion against old forms was much too strongly and deeply felt to be seriously deflected by political speeches.

This was particularly the case because certain strands of argument in the tradition of Marxist-Leninist esthetics provided ample justification for such prejudice. According to this view, art was a product of the stage of society that produced it. Old forms—that is, traditional Chinese folk and popular genres—were products of a feudal or semifeudal society, while the new forms of art imported from the West were the reflection of a society at the higher, capitalist stage in human history. Old forms were therefore inferior to new forms, which were more "scientific" and "advanced" in every respect. Thus, with the inevitable advance of human society, old forms were bound to be replaced completely, sooner or later, by new forms. In spite of the many logical inconsistencies in this argument (the Chinese forms labeled "old" were frequently more recent in origin than the European "new" forms), it was one that not even the foremost advocates of cultural populism were prepared to challenge.[12] Thus, by the early 1940s the use of old forms came to be regarded almost universally among literary youth and Party writers and artists in Yan'an as a temporary expedient only—an artistic dead end.

THE RECTIFICATION

It was against this background that Mao and the cultural populists launched the rectification of 1942. As is well known, Mao in his "Talks" of May 1942 dealt mainly with the political issue—the right of the Party to "lead" literature and art—but he also took the opportunity to launch a

[10] Holm, "Art and Ideology," pp. 54–55. For the original text see *Mō Takutō shū,* 6:260–261.

[11] Mao Zedong, *Selected Works,* 2:339–384, esp. pp. 380f. Cf. *Mō Takutō shū,* 7:201f. For discussion, see Holm, "Art and Ideology," pp. 54–55.

[12] See, for instance, Ai Siqi, "Jiu xingshi yunyong de jiben yuanze" [Basic principles of employing old forms], in *Wenyi zhanxian* [Literary battlefront] 1:3 (April 1939): 17–20. Reprinted in *Zhongguo xiandai wenxue . . . ,* 1:740–748.

counterattack against the prevailing unwillingness to experiment with folk forms by unveiling and providing theoretical backup for his "face-the-masses orientation in literature and art." Though Mao underplayed the issue of national form, and preferred to allow the implications of his policy to sink in gradually, his formulations were intended to encourage the use of the local North Shaanxi performing and visual arts. They also allowed, however, an eclectic approach that combined native with European forms. Mao presented the same ideas in a more clear-cut, less theoretical way a few days later in a speech he made at the Lu Xun Academy of Art and Literature (Lu Xun yishu wenxue yuan; usually referred to as "Luyi") outside Yan'an. No text of this speech has ever been issued, but the contents and key phrases are known in outline from a number of reminiscences.[13] Speaking allegorically, Mao recalled how impressed he had been with the majestic pine trees he had encountered high in the mountains during the Long March, and observed that they had all started life as seedlings no bigger than beansprouts. Writers and artists, he said, were not to despise the "beansprouts" of the popular and folk tradition, for these too were pine seedlings and could in the future grow to be majestic pine trees. The folk arts, in other words, could give rise to great art of a world standard.

The literary rectification campaign that followed in the summer and autumn of 1942, when writers and artists in Yan'an were set to work studying policy documents and discussing them in light of their own experience, was intended to reinforce these points and to prepare both professional writers and artists and the literary youth for mobilization on an unprecedented scale as a "cultural army." This goal entailed their transfer from Yan'an down to the countryside to take part in basic-level work in the villages, often to serve as village schoolteachers or *xiang* (parish) secretaries while organizing "literary amusements" (*wenyi yule*) in their spare time. Mao's policy also envisaged the potential participation of millions of peasants and soldiers in locally organized cultural activities. As a focus for these efforts, the *yangge* movement was launched in Yan'an during the Spring Festival of 1943—ostensibly to celebrate the abrogation of the "unequal treaties" by China's allies but clearly also to herald the beginning of the "age of the new masses" proclaimed by Mao at the Yan'an Forum.

[13] See He Qifang, "Mao zhuxi zai 'Luyi' de tanhua yongyuan guwuzhe women" [Chairman Mao's speech at Luyi will always inspire us], *Renmin xiju* 9 (1977): 7–11. Also Ba Zhi, "Zui zhenguide yike" [A most valuable lesson], *Beijing wenyi* 6 (1962): 16–17. It was also in this speech that Mao made reference to "Big Luyi" and "Little Luyi"—a distinction between the narrow confines of the art college and the world outside that was meant to reinforce the mentality suitable for *xiaxiang*.

THE OLD *YANGGE*

"Yangge" was the name given in North China to the dances, songs, and variety acts performed by amateur, peasant artists during the New Year, and especially during the Lantern Festival. The Party's decision to adopt *yangge* as the basis for its new direction calls for some comment. Like other mass movements launched in early 1943, the *yangge* movement was based on pre-existing social formations—"old forms," that is—and also on precedents culled from earlier Chinese history.[14] The use and adaptation by Chinese rulers of songs and dances current among the people, both for court ceremonial and for purposes of public instruction, has a long history in China, dating back at least as far as the *Shijing* [Book of songs].[15] More specifically, the staging of large-scale public spectacles of a kind not unlike *yangge* has been an act characteristic of newly established, strong dynasties; it is meant to signal a return to correct government and an era of Great Peace (*taiping*). Such, for instance, were the Great Rejoicings (*dapu*) held at the beginning of the Song dynasty.[16] Against this background, the Party's decision to mount large-scale celebrations of *yangge* in 1943 amounted to a claim on the Mandate of Heaven.

There were also other reasons, both ideological and practical, for the choice of *yangge*. In the first place, the songs, dances, and short plays performed during the New Year were the most highly developed and conspicuous form of cultural life in the villages of many areas of North China. As the basis for a Party-sponsored village drama movement, *yangge* had a number of advantages over other dramatic genres. Unlike Peking opera, *Qinqiang* (Shaanxi opera), or even the local forms of little opera, *daoqing* and *Meihu*,[17] *yangge* was performed largely by amateurs. *Yangge* troupes were also found in far greater numbers than were opera companies; statistics collected in 1944 indicate that for twenty companies performing old opera in the Shaan-Gan-Ning Border Region, and sixty-two putting on shadow shows, there were nine hundred and ninety-four active

[14] Mark Selden, *The Yenan Way in Revolutionary China* (Cambridge: Harvard University Press, 1971), pp. 208–274.

[15] See on this point Yang Yinliu, *Zhongguo yinyue shigang* [A draft history of Chinese music] (Shanghai: Wanye shudian, 1953), passim.

[16] Piet van der Loon, "Les origines rituelles du théâtre chinois," *Journal asiatique* (1977): 149.

[17] On *daoqing* and *Meihu* see Holm, "Art and Ideology," pp. 219–226. These genres were performed by semiprofessional troupes from the villages and their repertoires included many numbers that portrayed everyday life in a burlesque or farcical manner. They were thus quite different from the hereditary professional genres, with their highly elaborate music and repertoire of historical plays and court scenes. See further Wu Junda, "Shan'ge xiaodiao dao xiqu changqiang de fazhan" [The development of hillsong and popular ballads into opera singing], *Yinyue yanjiu* 1 (1958): 78–106.

yangge troupes.[18] Then, too, there was the collective nature of the *yangge* dance itself: troupes often numbered sixty to one hundred dancers, and included most if not all of the able-bodied men and boys of the village. It was this characteristic, together with the peculiar density of *yangge* troupes in the countryside, that led specialists in the 1950s to describe *yangge* as "intimately connected with the lives of the people."

Another attraction was the name "*yangge*" itself. As usually written ("rice-sprout song"), it suggested that this was a form that developed from songs sung by peasants while transplanting rice seedlings.[19] As an account of the origins of *yangge* this is highly questionable. There is no doubt, however, that it was ideologically a very useful notion, because *yangge* could then be used to "prove" the Marxist theory of the origins of art in the rhythms of productive labor. This theory had been given its fullest expression by the Russian Marxist Plekhanov in his *Unaddressed Letters*—a text well known in China through Lu Xun's translation of 1930.[20]

Equally important, however, was the fact that *yangge* was already well known among the Chinese intelligentsia through the efforts of earlier, non-Communist rural reformers. Particularly important here was the Baptist Mass Education Society and its model *xian* (county) project in Dingxian, Hebei. Publication of the society's *Dingxian Yangge Collection* of 1933—a collection of forty-eight playscripts from the repertoire of local *yangge* societies—set in motion a minor fashion for *yangge* and similar types of folk music among the urban intelligentsia.[21] The editors of the collection, Li Jinghan and Zhang Shiwen, were not slow to point out the

[18] Shaan-Gan-Ning yizu, "Zileban," *Jiefang ribao* [Liberation daily], 12 December 1944, p. 4; reprinted in Zhou Yang et al., *Minjian yishu he yiren* [Folk art and artists] (Zhangjiakou: Xinhua shudian Jin-Cha-Ji fendian, 1946), p. 67.

[19] This was a view popularized by Li Jinghan and Zhang Shiwen in their introduction to *Dingxian yangge xuan* [Dingxian *yangge* collection] of 1933 (repr. Peking: Guoli Beiping daxue Zhongguo minsu xuehui, 1937), and later by Sidney Gamble. Li and Zhang noted the locally current story that Su Dongpo, while serving as magistrate of Dingzhou, invented *yangge* for the consolation of peasants transplanting rice, but they reserved judgment on the substance of this tradition (p. 2).

[20] See the publisher's introduction to Puliehannuofu, *Lun yishu* (*meiyou dizhi de xin*) [On art—unaddressed letters], trans. Cao Baohua (Peking: Shenghuo dushu xinzhi sanlian shudian, 1973), for details of the first Chinese edition. For an English translation, see G. Plekhanov, *Unaddressed Letters on Art and Social Life* (Moscow: Progress Publishers, 1957). Plekhanov's work, based largely on the work of late nineteenth-century anthropologists in the South Seas and other areas, made possible a comparison between *yangge* and other Chinese folk performances and the "primitive" rites of tribes at a "primeval" stage of development.

[21] There were commercial gramophone recordings of *yangge* in the 1930s—by, e.g., RCA Victor. *Dingxian yangge xuan* was originally published by the Mass Education Society in 1933, and was reprinted in Guoli Beiping daxue Zhongguo minsu xuehui minsu congshu, vols. 37–40, 1937. For an English translation of these plays see Sidney D. Gamble, *Chinese Village Plays from the Ting Hsien Region* (Amsterdam: Philo Press, 1970).

potential of *yangge* as a basis for social education and for the reform of old customs in the countryside. The Dingxian project was brought to an abrupt end by the Japanese invasion, but many of its methods and rural reform programs were later adopted by the Communist Party for use in its own base areas.[22]

By 1939 *yangge* had become the centerpiece of a flourishing village drama movement in West Hebei, a base area immediately to the west of Dingxian. There, for Women's Day of 1940, for instance, "a big congress of over ten thousand women was held in Pingshan *xian,* and participants witnessed a large-scale performance by women's *yangge* troupes from several tens of villages—a total of one or two thousand performers."[23] Such activities were much more highly developed in West Hebei at this time than they were in Shaan-Gan-Ning. A detailed knowledge of these developments finally reached North Shaanxi in the latter half of 1942, when a professional drama troupe from the area was transferred to Yan'an for discussions with Party leaders and cultural personnel.[24]

All of this is not to suggest that North Shaanxi *yangge* was an ideal medium for Communist Party propaganda or for its efforts in mass education. Reports from observers visiting Yan'an in 1944, and accounts by other apologists for the Party, have given the impression that the Party's reform of *yangge* was somehow straightforward and unproblematic.[25] Such was not the case, as will become apparent from an examination of the basic character and features of *yangge* as it existed before the Communist Party's reform. *Yangge* was, we should remember, an observance both religious and secular in nature. Typically, *yangge* included a procession through the streets and from door to door, a large-scale figure dance with or without lanterns, stick dances and mock combats, a hobby horse (*zhuma*), a boat on dry land (*hanchuan*), wheelbarrows (*tuiche*), donkey dances (*paolü*), a lion dance, a dragon-lantern, and a number of short, obscene skits of the one-*dan* one-*chou* (one-female one-clown) type.[26] Most of these numbers are of great antiquity in China, and parallels for

[22] Claire and William Band, *Dragon Fangs: Two Years with the Chinese Guerrillas* (London: Allen and Unwin, 1947), p. 134. The Dingxian collection was also available in Yan'an during the war and was well known to the cultural leadership. See, for instance, Zhou Yang's 1944 essay "Biaoxian xinde qunzhong de shidai" [Portraying the age of the new masses], in Ai Siqi et al., *Yangge lunwen xuanji* [A selection of essays on *yangge*] (Dalian: Zhong-Su youhao xiehui, 1947), p. 11.

[23] Kang Zhuo, "Nongminde guanghui" [The glory of the peasants], *Wenyi bao* 2 (20 May 1949): 5.

[24] This was Zhandou jushe ("The Battle Theatre Troupe"), a professional troupe attached to the 110th Army under He Long. See Holm, "Art and Ideology," pp. 235–238.

[25] See, for instance, Gunther Stein, *The Challenge of Red China* (London: Pilot Press, 1945), pp. 173–177.

[26] A list of the genres performed in Yan'an is given by Zhou Yang, "Biaoxian xin," p. 7.

many of them can be found in European folklore.[27] Not all were performed in every locality, and in North China the emphasis varied considerably from place to place. In Dingxian, for example, the dramatic element in *yangge* had undergone considerable development under the influence of local varieties of opera, and the dances and variety acts had been divided among separate organizations. In other areas the dramatic element was minimal and various forms of dance predominated.

The name of *yangge* also varied. For one thing, the word "*yangge*" itself was written in a variety of different ways: "rice-sprout song" in Dingxian (hence standard modern usage); "elevated song" in Peking, where stilt-walking was the main form of performance; "*yang* song" (as in *yin* and *yang*) in Jiaxian, North Shaanxi; "brave elder brother" in Chaozhou; and "cockatoo" in Guangdong.[28] This variation in itself is enough to suggest that the "rice-sprout song" theory of the origins of *yangge* may be no more than a folk etymology. The problem is too complex to go into here, but it is interesting to note that even some of the Party critics preferred to reserve judgment on the etymology and to look more closely at the performance and its context. Zhang Geng, for instance, was led to observe that *yangge* was essentially a religious ritual, and one whose basic ritual function could be traced back to the Great Exorcism (*Nuo*) of Han times.[29]

There is in fact a great deal of evidence for this view: if in some areas any original meaning had been forgotten by the participants themselves, and the performance of *yangge* carried on simply as a customary observance, in other areas *yangge* retained its significance as a ritual well into the twentieth century. In Huimin *xian*, Shandong, on the fifteenth of the first month, performers gathered in the village temple to burn incense and make offer-

[27] Notably the hobby horse, large-scale carnival figures, stick dances, and the boat on dry land; for the latter see Van der Loon, "Les origines rituelles," pp. 148–150. The folk play is similarly characterized by its quality of obscene buffoonery, and includes such characters as the Dragon, the Quack Doctor, the Turk, and the Old Man and Old Woman clowns who beat each other with sticks. See E. K. Chambers, *The English Folk Play* (1933; reprint ed., Oxford: Oxford University Press, 1969).

[28] For the Peking *yangge* see Li Jiarui, *Beiping suqu lüe* [A sketch of the popular airs of Beiping] (Beiping: Guoli Zhongyang yanjiuyuan lishi yuyan yanjiusuo, 1933), p. 182. For the Jiaxian transcription see *Shanxi sheng Jiaxian xianzhi* (1933 edition), 2:17a. For Chaozhou, see Moubu wengongtuan wudao yanjiuzu, "Yingge," in Zhongguo wudao yishu yanjiuhui, ed., *Zhongguo minjian gewu* [Chinese folksong and dance] (Shanghai: Wenhua chubanshe, 1957), pp. 103–107. For Guangdong, see Xu Ke, *Qing bai lei chao* [Classified transcriptions of Qing trifles] (Shanghai: Shangwu yinshuguan, 1918) 78:74. The problem of nomenclature is further complicated by the fact that *yangge* was not always called "*yangge*": in general *yangge* in the North corresponds with *huagu* ("flower drum") in the South, but even in the North there are local and regional variations.

[29] Zhang Geng, *Yangge yu xin geju* [*Yangge* and the new opera] (Dalian: Dazhong shudian, 1949), p. 2. For the *Nuo*, see Derk Bodde, *Festivals in Classical China* (Princeton: Princeton University Press, 1975), pp. 75–127.

ings, and danced *yangge* after the completion of the sacrifice. The purpose of the dance, as explained to Party cultural workers by an old dancing master, was "to draw in the souls of the dead and ensure that they pass the New Year in peace and happiness; otherwise, the dead would take offense, demon fires would fill the land, and there would be such an uproar that the living would not be able to pass the New Year peacefully."

Here, at least, the "target audience" was not so much a particular social stratum or even living humanity, but rather the inhabitants of the spirit world—that is, the souls of ancestors and wandering ghosts.[30] Indeed, we can discern in *yangge,* as in other rituals connected with Chinese popular religion, two partially overlapping functions: exorcism and placation. The idea of exorcism—driving out evil spirits, and especially plague demons, beyond the confines of the village—is uppermost in the lion dance and in the displays of martial arts,[31] while that of placation and entertainment is predominant in *yangge* dances and folk plays. In *yangge* dances particularly the basic concept seems to have been to lay before the spirit audience a panorama of peace, prosperity, and reproductive vigor, and by this means to obtain their blessing and assistance for the coming year. The expense of the various productions and spectacles put on during the New Year was part of this display, as were also the eroticism and energetic activity of the *yangge* dance and folk play, the avoidance of inauspicious words and actions, and the recurrence of Great Peace (*taiping*) and other traditional motifs.

Let us take a closer look at various aspects of the performance. The traditional celebration of *yangge* took the form of a procession from door to door, called *pai menzi* in North Shaanxi. It was rather like trick-or-treating: the troupe would be welcomed into a courtyard, would perform songs and dances for the benefit of the household, and would ask for gifts of money. Generally the troupe visited only the more prosperous families in the village or performed numbers only when gifts of money were forthcoming. While in the courtyard they would also make offerings before the shrine to the Lords of Heaven and Earth and the "Hundred Offices" of the pantheon on the family's behalf. The troupe, it was supposed, thus brought spiritual favor on the household.[32] *Yangge* was also performed in

[30] Li Zhijun, "Shandongde daguzi yangge" [The Big Drum *yangge* of Shandong], *Wudao* 2 (1960): 19. Li interprets this ritual function, however, as a recent accretion and a distortion of the original meaning of *yangge*.

[31] Van der Loon, "Les origines rituelles," pp. 152–154.

[32] (Sun) Jingshen, "Shanbei Jiaxiande yangge" [The *yangge* of Jiaxian in North Shaanxi], in *Zhongguo minjian gewu,* p. 83, on *pai menzi.* For the offerings performed in the courtyard see P. J. Dols, "La vie chinoise dans la province de Kan-sou (Chine)," *Anthropos* 12–13 (1917–1918): 1008, and *Jiefang ribao,* 18 February 1945. For a description of the altar see Albert Nachbaur and Wang Ngen Joung, *Les images populaires chinoises* (Peking: Na Che Pao, 1926).

cities. Upon entering the city of Chengde in Rehe (Jehol) troupes from outlying villages went first to the temple of Guandi and the Founder's Temple (*Zushi miao*) to greet the gods, then to the yamen, and finally through the big streets of the city, performing at merchant houses.[33]

Performance of the big *yangge* dance (*da yangge*) was usually followed by a series of *yangge* songs, led by the "umbrella dancer" with the rest of the troupe responding in unison; this type of song was called *lingchang*. After this came the performance of "little dances" (*xiao changzi*) performed by two, three, and sometimes six or eight dancers, variety acts like the boat on dry land, and folk plays like *Zhang sheng xi Yingying* [Scholar Zhang flirts with Yingying]. During these numbers the rest of the troupe sat in a circle around the outside. The performance ended with another big *yangge* dance, during which the Umbrella leader sang a few verses, usually improvised, thanking the hosts for their generosity, and the troupe then moved on to another location.[34]

The leader of the procession in North Shaanxi was called "the Umbrella" (*santou*) because he wielded an open umbrella which he used to direct the movements of the other dancers in the troupe. In one early description from Zhenzhou (present-day Yizheng in Jiangsu), this character is identified as Wang Kuazi the Seller of Quack Medicine; there he wore a high white felt hat and a white goatskin riding jacket turned back-to-front, shook a horsebell in one hand, and held up an illuminated umbrella-lantern in the other. The same character is found in many other areas of China, in Peking *yangge,* in the *huagudeng* of the Bangbu-Fengtai area in Anhui, and in several regional systems of Shandong *yangge* as well. Among North Shaanxi peasants the original significance of the umbrella seems to have been forgotten, and people interpreted it as a prayer for rain.[35]

Many other comical characters in bizarre and colorful costume made their appearance in the procession and dance, including the Big-Headed Priest (*Datou heshang*) and the coquette Liu Cui—both of whom wore masks—an old woman clown and an old man clown, a fisherman, a firewood gatherer, the innkeeper's boy (*xiao erge*), the Eight Immortals, and Scholar Zhang and Yingying. Many of these characters are of considerable antiquity: the Big-Headed Priest and Liu Cui are first mentioned in Song sources. They, and other characters as well like the Tinker (*bugang jiang*) and Lady Wang (*Wang daniang*), appeared not only in the procession but also separately in "little dances" performed by two or three people.

[33] Karel de Jaegher, "Customs and Practices," *Folklore Studies* 6, 2 (1947): 91.

[34] Wei Tianxi, "Shanbei gongzuo sanji" [Random notes on work in North Shaanxi], *Wudao* 4 (1959): 22.

[35] (Sun) Jingshen, "Shanbei Jiaxian." For Zhenzhou see Li Xiufang, *Zhenzhou zhuzhi ci* [Occasional poems on Zhenzhou] (1857; reprint ed., Taiwan, 1958), pp. 26–27.

The most prominent part of *yangge* in North Shaanxi, as elsewhere, and the first item in the performance, was the big *yangge* dance.[36] This was a large-scale number, performed by the whole troupe, in which lines of dancers were led by "the Umbrella" through a series of dance figures. The first of these figures was almost invariably a simple circle around the dancing arena—a lustration, as it were, to set the boundaries of the enclosure. This was called "running the perimeter" (*pao dachang*). It was followed by a succession of other, more decorative figures such as "Scissors handles," "Dragon thrashes its tail," "Serpent coils round nine eggs," "Double lotus lantern," "Cabbage heart," and so on. Some figures bore reference to popular mythology, like "Erlang shoulders a mountain," while others like "Coiled rhombus" (*panchang*) were traditional symbols of good luck in the decorative arts and thus had a votive function. While the repertoire of these dance figures varied somewhat from locality to locality, many of them were standard all the way across North China. The troupe accompanied these dances with songs wishing good luck and happiness to their hosts.[37] Another form of dance common to big *yangge* was paired dancing, in which troupe members performing male and female roles danced opposite each other and sang in turn songs of the question and answer type, like "Duihua" [Guessing flowers]. The poet Ai Qing observed a dance of this kind in Yan'an before the Party's reform of *yangge;* he noted that its character was essentially erotic.[38]

Closely related to the "little dances" but more dramatically developed were the folk plays of North Shaanxi. These went by various local names; in the Yan'an area they were commonly called "little dance plays" (*xiao changzi xi*).[39] This was the genre that the Party adopted after 1943 as the traditional prototype for its new form *yanggeju*—the *yangge* play. In North Shaanxi, however, these plays were relatively simple and short, compared with the elaborate stage plays of big opera genres or even the plays of Dingxian *yangge*. They were usually performed on the ground rather than on a stage, and in musical and dramatic form were not all that

[36] The characters vary somewhat from locality to locality. Some, like the Big-Headed Priest and Liu Cui, are found all over China. For a review of early references see Dong Xijiu, "Songdaide 'wudui' ji qita" [Song dynasty 'dance troupes,' and other matters], *Wudao* 4 (1979): 49–51.

[37] For dance figures see Hu Sha, "Huiyi Yan'ande yangge" [Reminiscences of *yangge* in Yan'an], *Wudao* 4 (1959): 29. For Manchurian *yangge* see He Jian'an, "Dongbei yangge," in *Zhongguo minjian gewu,* p. 75.

[38] Ai Qing, "Yanggejude xingshi," in Ai Siqi et al., *Yangge lunwen xuanji,* pp. 23–24. Translated by D. Holm in John Berninghausen and Ted Huters, eds., *Revolutionary Literature in China* (White Plains: Sharpe, 1976), p. 72.

[39] Hu Sha, "Huiyi Yan'an." In Jiaxian they were called *xiao huihui* ([Sun] Jingshen, "Shanbei Jiaxian"); in East Gansu *xiao gushi* ("little stories"), *di taizi* ("stage on the ground"), or *zhuanzhe* ("excerpts"): *Jiefang ribao,* 18 February 1945.

different from song and dance. They were generally performed by two or three characters only, and the dramatic action was conveyed in the lyrics by means of a combination of narrative and indirect dialogue (*daiyanti*), usually interspersed with riddling songs of the question and answer type. Such, for example, was the level of dramatic form in the play *Xiao fangniu* [The little cowherd], a play mentioned in Mao's "Talks."

In the plot of this play, a young village girl loses her way and asks a young cowherd for directions; he teases her rather than give her a direct reply and she, not to be outdone, returns his banter and makes fun of him. The play ends with the couple plighting their troth, and the dance, we may suppose, was also erotic. Available texts of the play, however, suggest that the story line was really only a peg on which to hang a series of riddling songs whose lyrics were not necessarily connected with the plot.[40] The songs in these plays are close to, if not indistinguishable from, folksong both in style of delivery and in musical form: that is, they are delivered in a simple style without a great deal of ornamentation and without the elaborate instrumental interludes characteristic of more highly developed dramatic forms. Lyrics were in stanzas of two, three, or four lines and were characterized by rhythmic freedom and large numbers of "padding words" (*chenzi*) and nonsense syllables.

The subject matter of *yangge* plays in North Shaanxi was also quite different from that of big opera. Unlike opera, with its emphasis on historical themes, court scenes, and battles, *yangge* plays were particularly strong on scenes from everyday life, presented in a farcical manner. These included domestic quarrels, as in *Tan qin* [Visiting relatives] and *Xiaogu xian* [The virtuous daughter-in-law]; fortune tellers and geomants, as in *Xiazi suanming* [A blind man tells fortunes]; child marriages, as in *Tuzi niao chuang* [Baldy wets his bed]; and henpecked husbands, as in *Dingdeng* [Carrying a lantern on the head]. Like folk plays elsewhere in the world, many of these were obscene in both lyrics and dance movements.

It can be readily seen that some of the songs, dances, and skits included under the general heading of "*yangge*" were of more use to the Party than others. Flexible numbers with some dramatic content were held to be more promising than dances for the display of technique or set ceremonial pieces. Clearly, a successful effort to supplant the old *yangge* in the villages would have to produce a new version for every significant item in the repertoire. Yet even with the most favored genres—the big *yangge* dance and the *yangge* play—considerable modification of the old forms was required before they could serve as the basis of a mass movement spon-

[40] Zhang Geng, *Yangge yu xin geju,* p. 6. For text with music see Zhongguo minjian yinyue yanjiuhui, ed., *Yangge quxuan* [A selection of *yangge* songs] (Yan'an: Yingong hezuoshe, 1944), nos. 76–78.

sored by the Party. How then did the Party set about the reform of *yangge*? Which elements of form did cultural workers retain, as the valuable "essence," and which were eliminated as feudal "dregs"?

THE MODEL *YANGGE* TROUPE: LUYI IN SPRING 1943

The initial reform of *yangge* was undertaken in Yan'an for the Spring Festival of 1943 by the Propaganda Troupe of the Lu Xun Academy of Art and Literature. This was a group of musicians and dramatists formed originally for the purpose of putting on a New Year's evening party for the staff and students of the Academy. The original performance is said to have consisted entirely of locally current folk forms, including *yangge,* a boat on dry land, a wheelbarrow dance, *shulaibao* recitations, and a song-and-dance flower drum.[41] Such were the humble and informal beginnings of what soon became a very big propaganda troupe, involving the mobilization of a large part—perhaps a majority—of the staff and students of Luyi.

The process of reform was later described by Party spokesmen as "from the masses, to the masses." As in other areas of political action to which the rectification work-style was applied, the first step was local investigation (*diaocha yanjiu*). The first performances by the Luyi troupe were based closely on the *yangge* as it was performed in Qiaoergou, the village where Luyi was located, ten *li* east of Yan'an. These performances were almost entirely traditional. Thus the procession and dance included many colorful characters of a traditional type: a priest in a yellow-tasseled robe, wearing comic makeup and a small red pigtail; an old woman clown with chili peppers dangling from her ears, who carried two clubs of the kind used for washing clothes; an old man clown; and a character dressed in white trousers and a white jacket—probably the stupid young gentleman (*sha gongzi*)—with red circles under his eyes and his hair done up in a pigtail. The troupe also included, however, more modern types like Eighth Route Army soldiers, workers, students, and even Japanese generals and "Chinese traitors."[42]

After performances in early February 1943 before audiences that included Mao and other members of the Party leadership, however, there was a radical change in the character and tone of the troupe's performances of *yangge.* The traditional characters were abolished and their place taken by "a column composed of a great alliance of workers, peasants, soldiers, students, and merchants." The role of the Umbrella dancer was likewise abolished, on the grounds that it served a superstitious func-

[41] Ren Ying, "Huiyi Wang Dahua," *Beijing wenyi* 5 (1962): 14.

[42] Li Bo, "Yan'an yangge yundongde pianduan huiyi" [Fragmentary reminiscences of the *yangge* movement in Yan'an], *Beijing wenyi* 5 (1962): 22.

tion, and his place at the head of the troupe was taken by a worker wielding a hatchet and a peasant bearing a sickle. Not only the makeup of the clowns but also the clowning disappeared: actors were expected to make their characterizations entirely positive, and a serious and conscientious attitude became essential. Negative types like Japanese generals and Chinese puppet troops also disappeared, on the grounds that the big *yangge* dance symbolized the unity of the people and could not include the enemies of the people.[43]

Basically, in this "protestant reformation," as it were, of the *yangge* dance, the *yangge* troupe was taken to symbolize the "new people." From this all else followed: the ideology of New Democracy and rectification was read out into artistic form and content. Thus, characters appeared in this new *yangge* as representatives of social classes and strata in the New Democratic four-class bloc. They appeared, moreover, in order of their relative ideological importance in the Party's mass base, with the working class in the lead, followed by the peasants, the army, and so forth. One might well wonder whether the new characters should be regarded as characters at all: as personifications of whole social classes, they were closer to allegorical figures.

During later stages of the *yangge* movement, however, writers and artists realized that this initial reform had deprived the form of much of its traditional color and appeal, especially with peasant audiences, and they took steps to reintroduce variety into the characters and dances. For the Spring Festival of 1944, the big *yangge* performed by the Public Security Office troupe included the following types, all dancing in different styles and carrying props that identified them to the audience: an old man with a tobacco pipe, an old woman carrying a basket, a young married woman clutching a baby, a little boy carrying a big sword blade of the kind used for sentry duty, a militiaman holding a red-tasseled spear, an Eighth Route Army soldier with a rifle, and a peasant shouldering a mattock. The selection of colors for the costumes was also meticulous and reflected local custom. The young married woman, for instance, wore a pink shirt and trousers, with a skirt tied round the waist, and had her new-born baby wrapped up in a coverlet of red silk; the old woman wore a wide jacket of blue cloth and a dark brown waistcoat with a wide border on it. Although negative characters were still banned from participation in the big *yangge* dance, and the comic element was not restored to its former place, many additional aspects of the original folk performances were reintroduced. We see here the emergence of a new set of village stereotypes, corresponding to and replacing the old stock characters of traditional *yangge*. Subsequently,

[43] Ibid.

it was this type of *yangge* dance, rather than the more severe Luyi model, that became the basis for the new *yangge* in North China.[44]

Let us also consider briefly some of the other formal aspects of the transformation of *yangge*. Musically, the performances of the Luyi troupe represented a combination of Western elements and the native folk tradition. The orchestra accompanying the troupe, for a start, was composed not only of the traditional Chinese flutes (*dizi*) and percussion section—big drums, big gongs, and cymbals—but also included seven violins and, according to one account, a cello. The violin was the most popular Western instrument in China at this time and, before 1942, had featured in concerts of Western music at Luyi that included such numbers as "Viennese Rhapsody," performed by musicians dressed formally in ties and tails.[45] The *yangge* movement marked a break with this style of performance, but the music played by the propaganda troupe was still Western in style, in spite of the fact that most of the melodies were taken from local folksong. This was not surprising, considering that the musicians at Luyi were trained in the Western manner; only in the latter half of 1942 was the study of folksong and local opera made an essential part of the curriculum.[46]

Apart from locally current folksong—like the tune "Da huangyang" [Beating the yellow sheep] used for the number "Support-the-Army Drum Song"—the Luyi troupe also borrowed melodies from the revolutionary songs of the Red Army, early-war National Salvation songs, and *Meihu*, a genre of little opera popularized in the Yan'an area by the Popular Masses Drama Troupe (*Minzhong jutuan*), led by Ke Zhongping.[47] New words were set to all of these "old tunes"—in keeping with the propaganda tasks laid down by the Party leadership—celebrating the abolition of the unequal treaties, the return of foreign concessions, and recent victories by the Soviet Red Army and publicizing the deeds of labor heroes and the Party's Great Production movement. In many cases, however, the new lyrics were composed in a way that closely followed the format and style of traditional *yangge* songs: for example, a song of the "Guessing Flowers" type with lyrics composed by the poet He Jingzhi. Like its traditional counterpart, it was meant to be sung antiphonally:

A: Which kind of flower blooms facing the sun?
Which kind of men support the Communist Party?
B: The sunflower it is that blooms facing the sun.
The common people support the Communist Party.

[44] Hu Sha, "Huiyi Yan'ande yangge," *Wudao* 7 (1959): 34.

[45] Hu Sha, "Huiyi Yan'ande yangge," *Wudao* 6 (1959): 33.

[46] Holm, "Art and Ideology," pp. 81–84.

[47] See Ding Ling, "Minjian yiren Li Bu" [The folk artist Li Bu], in Zhou Yang et al., *Minjian yishu he yiren*, pp. 11–18.

A: Which flower blooms and is on the body worn?
Which the man whose words are engraved in our hearts?
B: Cotton flowers bloom and are on the body worn.
It's Chairman Mao whose words are engraved in our hearts.
A: Which kind of flower blooms obstructing the road?
Which are the demons that should be rooted out?
B: Gorse it is that blooms and obstructs the road.
It's the fascist demons that should be rooted out.[48]

Many of Luyi's efforts were admittedly rather crude—much more "crude and simple" both musically and thematically than the performances by local troupes—but they were first efforts of people who had for the most part very little previous knowledge or experience of working with folk forms.

In the dance, too, the first step in the reform of *yangge* was a radical simplification. This was necessary if *yangge* was to become the basis for the Party's cultural mass movement and accessible to amateurs with little previous experience. The traditional *yangge* dances of North Shaanxi, though performed by uneducated peasants, were anything but simple. Though no detailed or even adequate descriptions exist, recently published materials and information on the dance in other areas would suggest that there were perhaps as many as a hundred different dance steps.[49] Traditional *yangge* was highly organized; troupes trained for the forthcoming New Year throughout the winter months, under the guidance of a *yangge* dancing master (*bashi*). The Luyi reform seems to have reduced the number of basic dance steps in the big *yangge* dance to about three to four, including the well-known three-steps-forward, one-step-back method. This style of dancing *yangge* was called "twisting a *yangge*" (*niu yangge*): the shoulders of the dancer moved in the opposite way from the legs and hips, thus inducing a twist at the waist.

Within these limits the new *yangge* was choreographically conservative. There was little change in the dance figures performed in the big *yangge* dance; only one major innovation was made: the "five-cornered star" formation, hailed by Zhou Yang in 1944 as a new creation.[50] The most important difference between old and new, however, was the elimination of sexuality. As one later dance pamphlet put it: "There used to be many degenerate elements in performances, like sexual love, and the postures of

[48] "Qizhi hua" [Seven flowers], with lyrics by He Jingzhi and music by Du Shijia, *Jiefang ribao*, 23 March 1943.

[49] Lü Feng and Wang Changfeng, "Shanbei yangge," *Wudao* 4 (1978): 51–55, and *Wudao* 5 (1978): 43–47, describe seventeen separate steps, but this is clearly a selection from a much larger number. For Shandong see Liu Zhijun and Zhou Bing, "Shandong minjian wudao xuanjie" [Selected introductions to Shandong folk dances], in *Wudao* 1–3 (1977).

[50] Zhou Yang, "Biaoxian xinde qunzhong de shidai," p. 10.

the dance were also very lascivious, full of raised shoulders and flashing waists. We have thoroughly reformed these aspects of the dance."[51] After 1943, the movements of the dance were variously interpreted as ordinary walking movements, exaggerated and set to rhythm, or else as a development from the movements of manual labor. In one new style the dancers threw their arms out sideways, imitating the broadcast sowing of grain.

The crowning achievement of the Luyi Propaganda Troupe, however, was the reform of the folk play and the development of a new hybrid prototype that would serve as a model for the subsequent village drama movement. This was the play *Xiongmei kaihuang* [Brother and sister clear wasteland], afterward hailed as one of the first fruits of Mao's "face-the-masses orientation."[52] It was created collectively by the leading members of the Luyi troupe and, like the troupe's other productions, was a hybrid on every level of form. The music, for instance, was specially composed for the occasion, but was based closely on the hexatonic scale used in *Meihu* and retained the characteristic intervals and rhythmical patterns of this genre. Onstage, the new form contained the elements of *yangge* dance steps and *yangge* "little dances," combined with dances portraying physical labor, and elements of spoken drama (*huaju*) were also combined with some of the symbolic techniques of the old opera.

The plot of this short play is very simple and serves to illustrate the contradictions underlying the Party's reform of the old genre. At the beginning, Elder Brother comes on stage with a mattock over his shoulder, tells us how good life is now in the Border Region, and then starts clearing hilltop land. When he hears his younger sister coming with his breakfast, he decides to play a trick on her and pretends to be asleep. In the dialogue that follows, she chides him for his laziness, while he makes excuses. Finally she threatens to go to the district government to have him "struggled" (publicly criticized) as a layabout. Realizing that things have gone too far, Elder Brother is forced to admit his deception and the play ends as the two are reconciled and return with renewed vigor, mattocks flailing, to the task of clearing wasteland. The high point of the play is the song and dance portraying the activity of labor.

Zhang Geng, then head of the drama department at Luyi, gives us the inside story of how this plot took shape:

> With *Brother and Sister Clear Wasteland* we first studied the one male–one female form of folk *yangge*. Now with this one male and one female there must be a plot and a few flirtatious incidents. But several points here are fundamentally different from the old *yangge*. Old *yangge* describes the old

[51] Gao Geng, *Yanggewu* [*Yangge* dance] (Shanghai: Xinfeng she, 1950), pp. 5–6.

[52] Ai Siqi, "Cong chunjie xuanchuan kan wenyide xin fangxiang" [A look at the new orientation in the arts from Spring Festival propaganda], *Jiefang ribao,* 25 April 1943.

> society and old personalities, while this play portrays the new society and new personalities. In old *yangge* there is a heavy atmosphere of sexuality; here that cannot obtain. Old *yangge* was entertainment pure and simple; here we must have educational significance. There are also several points in common: both require a lively, happy atmosphere; both should be short and simple and resolve themselves within a short space of time. Hence, in order to drop the sexual element, we took the man and wife—a male-female relationship that could give rise to rather a lot of sexuality—and changed it into one which absolutely could not elicit sexual responses, the brother-sister relationship. And again, if we were to start up some kind of plot, the best way of doing this would have been to have a confrontation between one advanced person and one backward person. We must, however, portray the new personalities of the new society: if out of two people we make one backward, surely this is fifty percent? Now that is just not true, and not realistic. If both of them are positive characters, however, how do we develop a story line? The result was that we thought up a way of dealing with it, by having one character deliberately play a joke on the other. In this way the activism of both people is brought out.[53]

Two points in this passage require particular comment. First, Zhang Geng confirms that male and female roles (originally one *dan* and one *chou*) were cast as Elder Brother and Younger Sister in order to try to prevent the peasant audiences from seeing the play, out of habit, in the traditional way—as a flirtation skit. It is hard to say to what extent this stratagem succeeded: in the peasant speech of the North Shaanxi area *gege* ("elder brother") and *meimei* ("younger sister") are the common terms of address between husband and wife and between lovers. Secondly, the artistic difficulties that result from too literal an interpretation of the Marxist theory of reflection are particularly apparent here. The official, rather sanguine view of Border Region society leads to the construction of a play in which the characters are one hundred percent positive and in which plot development results only from one of the characters assuming a false, "backward" identity. On the one hand, the plot is quite literally a joke; thus there is clowning in the play, but no clowns. The contradictions between "old form" and "new content" are, as it were, encapsulated within the structure of the play, resolved only by artistic sleight of hand. In this strict sense *Brother and Sister Clear Wasteland* was of limited use as a model play, since the formula it embodied could not really be applied over and over again to the creation of other plays without risk of becoming very stale. On the other hand, even if the ideological justifications for it were rather tortuous, the formula adopted did provide a way of preserving within the play the traditional elements of banter and argument. At least in

[53] Zhang Geng, *Yangge yu xin geju*, pp. 16–17.

this respect, *Brother and Sister Clear Wasteland* was better than some of the plays that came after it, which lost the comic element entirely. The ideological situation, in any case, was later relaxed.

This, then, was a play that could be seen in different ways by different strata of society. Some indication of the persistence of traditional preconceptions is to be found in a report on a slightly later New-Year print (*nianhua*) of the play:

> *Brother and Sister Clear Wasteland* was seen by the illiterate peasantry as "man and wife clear wasteland" (*fuqi kaihuang*). Even though it was explained to them, they persisted in thinking that "brother is being lascivious with sister" (*gege xiang meimei saoqing*). This was in direct conflict with the artist's intention to portray activism in production. The "misunderstanding" thus elicited was a result of not having carefully considered whether or not the image itself was enough to convey enthusiasm for labor. Here we see merely exaggerated and lively gestures that have no connection with the social position of the characters.[54]

Brother and Sister Clear Wasteland was soon hailed as a new form of drama, the *yanggeju* ("*yangge* play"), also known as the *jietou yanggeju* ("street *yangge* play"). This form, it was claimed, had been developed directly from the more inchoate, subdramatic forms of North Shaanxi folk *yangge;* it thus represented "elevation on the basis of extension" and was a concrete case of artistic evolution in action. As was also the case with *yangge* dances, the central plank in this reform of the *yangge* play was the elimination of sexuality. This development was of the utmost importance, because it changed fundamentally the basic character of the folk play. It would also have implications for the Party's treatment of a wide range of other traditional performing genres in the years ahead.

In the Party's ideology, the presence of sexuality in the old *yangge* was ascribed to the distorting influence of the landlords. Zhou Yang noted in an influential essay that, on the one hand, the flaunting of sexuality was the peasants' way of resisting and sabotaging the feudal order and feudal morality in a society where other paths of expression were blocked; with the overturn of the feudal order in the countryside, he argued, such a mechanism was no longer needed. On the other hand, the erotic element was also explained as a means of "titillating the landlords" (*saoqing dizhu*). With an end to feudal oppression in the villages, of course, tenant farmers would no longer be forced to participate in *yangge* against their will, and there would no longer be a need to cater to the tastes of a decadent local elite. The important point about both these explanations is that sexuality could thus be decried as a later and alien accretion, due not

[54] *Jiefang ribao,* 18 May 1945.

to the people themselves but rather to the patterns of dominance and subordination in feudal society.[55]

Much the same kind of argument was used to justify the abolition of the clown roles and their replacement by serious characters. Zhou noted that, in the old *yangge* procession, improvised jokes and clowning were often directed at social superiors and at the existing order: a parallel, Zhou noted, with the plays of Shakespeare, where the common people often appeared onstage in comic roles. "However," he went on to say, "under the conditions of the new society, the status of the little clown is entirely changed. The Border Regions and base areas find themselves under a dynasty where power is in the hands of the workers, peasants, soldiers, and popular masses: the people are masters—they are the emperors—and are no longer little clowns."[56] Thus the clown roles, too, were declared obsolete and redundant in the new society. While there were important positive reasons for this decision—the Party was anxious that the new *yangge* should perform a serious educational function—there must also have been a concern with problems of control, since the sharp wit and ridicule could also have been turned against the Party.

In artistic circles, within Luyi and elsewhere, the problem of how much of the original character of the *yangge* play was to be retained remained a contentious issue throughout the rest of the Yan'an period. In 1943 this was discussed largely in terms of *quwei,* "appeal" or "amusement." It became an issue partly because Mao had warned against "low appeal" (*diji quwei*) at the Yan'an Forum the previous year, and partly because the Luyi troupe had introduced humorous and burlesque elements into its performances. After the Spring Festival of 1943, it must have seemed to many literature and art workers that the new drama movement was in danger of going the same way as the *wenmingxi* (modern drama) of the early twentieth century—that is, of drifting from serious-minded reform towards vulgarization and an abdication of artistic and moral standards.[57] By 1944 two schools of thought had arisen in Luyi, with one group in favor of longer plays with more *huaju* elements and less folk coloring, and another, smaller group in favor of short song-and-dance plays that remained close to the style and flavor of the original folk plays. Ma Ke's *Fuqi shizi* [Man and wife learn to read] and He Jingzhi's *Zaishu* [Planting trees] are products of the latter school.[58]

[55] Zhou Yang, "Biaoxian xin," p. 11.

[56] Ibid.

[57] (Cheng) Anbo, "You Luyide yangge chuangzuo tandao yanggede qiantu" [The future of *yangge* on the basis of Luyi's *yangge* creations], *Jiefang ribao,* 12 April 1943.

[58] Zhang Geng, "Huiyi Yan'an wenyi zuotanhui qianhou 'Luyi' de xiju huodong" [Reminiscences of dramatic activities at Luyi before and after the Yan'an Forum on Literature and Art], *Xiju bao* 5 (1962): 10.

1944 AND AFTER

These, then, are some of the complexities and contradictions that lay at the heart of the Party's reform of *yangge*. Internal disagreements about the level of artistic form are, of course, important for an understanding of Party policy toward the folk arts as it evolved in the years ahead. It is equally important, however, to note how the model was adapted and changed in the subsequent stages of the *yangge* movement. Here the positive aspect of Luyi's reform of *yangge* came into play; the hybrid nature of the new *yangge,* while felt to be a problem by professional artists and dramatists, was intended to facilitate ad-hoc combinations of amateur talent. The form of the new *yangge,* in other words, was not a set formula, but rather open-ended and all-embracing—provided certain essential features of the reform were observed. Thus, for example, amateur troupes were expected to make use of whatever musical talents were available and to perform in whatever genres were current and appropriate for local conditions. Hence, also, the emphasis on portraying contemporary scenes from everyday life, which meant that expensive costume chests were no longer a prerequisite for performance, since actors could borrow from neighbors and relatives any items of clothing they required.

The second, wider stage of the *yangge* movement got under way in earnest during the Spring Festival of 1944, when professional drama troupes from Yan'an were sent out on tour to the outlying areas of the Border Region, and celebrations in Yan'an itself were arranged on an unprecedented scale using the resources of amateur troupes alone. If the tours by the professional troupes were intended to provide models for *yangge* troupes in the countryside and in the subregional capitals, and thus to spark off a *yangge* movement in the villages, the celebrations in Yan'an, in which some thirty troupes participated, were intended to give Party cadres and office personnel experience in the creation and production of short plays and song-and-dance numbers. The scale of the latter movement was impressive. One report estimated that there were over two thousand participants, and given that the total number of public personnel in Yan'an was around twelve thousand, this indicates that roughly one person in six was mobilized to take part in *yangge* performances.[59] This effort was worthwhile not only for its immediate effects but also because it paid dividends later on. Foreign correspondents visiting Yan'an in later 1944 were suitably impressed by the *yangge* performances they saw and, as a result, the Border Regions gained favorable international publicity when the visitors' reports were published. More important, the movement bore fruit domestically in the years after 1945, when thousands of trained cadres from Yan'an were deployed in the Party's base areas throughout

[59] Holm, "Art and Ideology," pp. 275–277.

North China and Manchuria. The *yangge* movement ensured that many of them had had experience in organizing the production of propaganda plays based on locally current genres.

Let us then examine some of the characteristics of the *yangge* movement as it unfolded in these later stages. The same thinking that led the Party to emphasize flexibility of form and adaptation of performances to local conditions and locally available talent also led to an overall policy summed up in three important slogans: "Short and snappy" (*Duanxiao jinghan*), "Self-composed and self-performed" (*Zibian ziyan*), and "Real people and real events" (*Zhenren zhenshi*). The first was meant to encourage troupes to avoid undertaking the production of lengthy, "elevated" plays of the kind to which professional playwrights aspired and to aim for maximum energy and pace within a less ambitious framework. The second slogan was promulgated as part of a general strategy of encouraging the creation of plays by amateurs at the local level. This was in part intended to avoid a repetition of the playscript famine that had beset the Party's village drama movement in the early years of the war. Even using mimeograph methods and printing scripts at the county or subregional level, the Party had found it hard to ensure an adequate supply for a mass movement because of paper shortages and lack of sufficient skilled personnel. If, under suitable guidance, local troupes could be encouraged to produce their own new plays or to produce new versions of old ones, these problems could be kept to a minimum: literacy and paper would not be necessary.

Moreover, in urging local troupes to produce their own plays, the Party hoped to increase the relevance of the subject matter for local conditions. This is where "real people and real events" came in: the Party cultural authorities argued that mass creativity could best be fostered by encouraging people in local units to produce plays based on either their own experience of work within the unit or locality or on the experiences of well-known local personalities, particularly labor heroes. Since labor heroes were selected for every occupational group—and, in the countryside, for every county and local district—as part of the Great Production Movement of 1943, there was no dearth of this kind of subject matter. In this way, it was hoped, plays would be produced that would reflect and publicize local and near-contemporary events, rather than relying on second-hand information or historical themes. The result of this policy was to produce a kind of documentary drama, in which, not infrequently, the "real people" themselves took part in a dramatic reconstruction of events in which they had recently participated.

Such, for example, was the case with the play *Zhong Wancai qijia* [Zhong Wancai establishes his household], performed in 1944 by the

Army Legal Office Troupe in Yan'an.[60] Zhong Wancai was a prominent ex-layabout from a nearby village who had reformed himself and become a labor hero; the play, divided into three acts, portrayed Zhong before, during, and after his reformation. Zhou Yang, who singled the play out for special mention, noted that Zhong had not only supplied "comprehensive materials" to the troupe but had also attended rehearsals and, when the troupe performed in his own parish, was present in the audience at almost every performance.[61] Both these points are confirmed by a report on the play compiled by the Army Legal Office Correspondents' Group, which also makes clear that the intended audience for the play was very localized—in fact, confined to a single district on the northwest side of Yan'an municipality. In performance, also, the play was locally specific—much more so than one would imagine from reading the text. The actors systematically consulted with Zhong and his wife, after every performance, about any points where diction or gesture may have departed from realistic portrayal or strict authenticity. What is even more interesting, though, is that the report also gives us a glimpse of how this type of documentary theater interacted with village society:

> The many opinions from the masses prove that this [documentary] direction was correct. Zhong and his wife even called lots of neighbors over to watch the play together. When they were performing the first and second acts the pair hung their heads in shame, but when it came to the third act he was laughing out loud and taking cigarettes out of his belt and offering them round. Afterward they saw it over again two or three times, and we repeatedly sought their opinions. He would always say: "What you perform is all true—it was just like that, from bad to good! It's always best to make an effort—otherwise how can you call it a transformation!" We questioned him repeatedly . . . but he would smile and say: "It's all real. Now that the public households have raised me up in this way, we must work hard." Because the characters and the events were well known to the masses, they felt unusually familiar with them. For instance, when the locals of West District saw the play, they started smiling as soon as they heard the names of the characters, and were soon heard discussing it: "Zhong Wancai's turned good, but he'd better work hard—if he doesn't, this play will turn false, won't it?" Without knowing it they had begun to assume the role of encouraging and watching over Zhong Wancai. At the same time the play educated the masses (and especially the layabouts) more directly; the parish head of Third Parish, Wang Si, specially called together all the layabouts [*erliuze*] in the parish to go and see it. After the Houjiagou layabout Li Mantang had

[60] Text in Zhang Geng, ed., *Yangge juxuan* (Peking: Renmin wenxue chubanshe, 1977), pp. 79–122. Original text published in *Jiefang ribao,* 19 March 1944, where it was subtitled *jietou baodaoju* [A street reportage play].

[61] Zhou Yang, "Biaoxian xin," p. 8.

> seen the play, he made a resolution then and there to transform himself and resolutely declared to the village head: "I'm going to work hard this year. I will plant twelve to thirteen *shang* [36–39 *mou*] of land, with my one labor-power, and I'll even dare to compete with Zhong Wancai!"[62]

It is clear from this account that the close connection of the artistic representation with local society in effect changes the whole relationship between art and reality, and with it the whole meaning, in this context, of a term like "realism." One possibility for hypothesis is that drama troupes could become indebted to and perhaps even subject to manipulation by the local society and "real people" they attempted to portray. Plays of this kind celebrating the deeds of local heroes could be counters in more than one game, played out by a number of parties each with something to gain: the labor heroes themselves, local cadres in search of concrete results to show to their superiors, or whole local communities, seeking favored status as "model villages." More important, however, is that this type of play was explicitly intended by the Party to have a direct educative effect on the target audience; from the account quoted above and a host of other materials, it is clear that audiences generally recognized this and responded to the Party's expectations in an overtly positive manner. That is, they may or may not have been deeply moved, but they certainly said what they thought the authorities wanted to hear, and ascribed great educative and persuasive powers to the stage action.

Particularly noteworthy is the importance attached to participation in the rituals of public confession and public oath-taking that followed the performance. This is part of a much wider general pattern, for, during the middle and later 1940s, *yangge* and other plays were not simply performed on their own, as a form of entertainment: they were more often than not performed as an integral part of mass meetings and other public occasions of an actively political nature. In fact, the period after 1942 saw in the Party's base areas a very rapid development, as the Party intensified its efforts to penetrate village society, of a range of new rituals and ritual-like observances designed to involve the masses as participants in public life and to give expression to the values of New Democracy. Such, for example, were the exchanges of gifts during the Spring Festival between the army and the civilian population for the "Support the Army" and "Support the Government and Cherish the People" campaigns. The standard gifts were pork and mutton, cloth shoes, and agricultural produce on the one hand and help with spring plowing on the other—but it is interesting to note that mutual visits often included the performance of plays, with army troupes performing for nearby villages and villages performing for

[62] "*Zhong Wancai qijia* de chuangzuo jingguo" [On the process of creating *Zhong Wancai Establishes His Household*], *Jiefang ribao*, 28 January 1944.

troops in nearby barracks.[63] Such exchanges were intended to symbolize solidarity between these two sections of New Democratic society.

Other observances were intended to invoke the support of the public, or the pressure of local opinion, for individual transformations. Such was the case in *Zhong Wancai* for layabouts, but mass meetings that included the performance of *yangge* plays and culminated in acts of public confession and resolution were also of major importance in the campaign against secret agents of the Nationalist Party within the Border Region (the "confession movement" of late 1943 and 1944) and in the campaign against witch doctors (*wushen*) launched in mid-1944. Ding Ling, reporting on the horse and mule fair in Zhuanyaowan, described a meeting of the *wushen* campaign; it included the performance of an antisuperstition play that was followed by denunciations and confessions from the audience.[64] Similarly, at public meetings to promote the production movement, performances were often followed by "declarations of war" from peasants resolved to overtake the production record of the local labor hero. Frequently the public declaration of such a "production plan" included a specific target—either the amount of land to be cleared for cultivation, as in the account above, or the amount of grain to be harvested. Great weight seems to have been attached to these acts of public confession and oath-taking, and one may well imagine that they would result in considerable pressure on individuals to live up to their promises.

A word of caution, however, is necessary. The difficulty posed by all such highly formalized patterns of political action is, of course, that they do not necessarily bear any relation to what goes on privately or internally, "offstage" as it were, and may indeed serve to mask the true situation from the eyes of the authorities. In other words, the Party was faced with a problem of form and content: the ritualistic character of the peasantry's response to Party policy created a complex pattern of interaction in which dramatic art and social life imitated each other and became increasingly difficult to disentangle.

These, then, are some of the ways in which the performance of *yangge* plays operated within the villages as propaganda for the "new society" during the peak of the *yangge* movement in Shaan-Gan-Ning. Much more research will be needed before the picture is complete. Thanks, however, to the Party's insistent emphasis on basic-level investigation of audience reactions, there is a wealth of material waiting to be tapped in base-area newspapers and literary magazines. Even this preliminary investigation has indicated fairly clearly that the new *yangge*—within certain limitations,

[63] These gatherings were called *lianhuanhui* ("linked enjoyment meetings" or, rather, "parties"). See Holm, "Art and Ideology," p. 298, and *Jiefang ribao,* 28 January 1944.

[64] Ding Ling, "Ji Zhuanyaowan luoma dahui," in her collection *Shaanbei fengguang* [North Shaanxi scenes], 2d ed. (Peking: Renmin chubanshe, 1951).

and together with other modes of political action—was instrumental in the development of a new pattern of formalized public sentiment and deportment among the peasantry.

GENERAL PERSPECTIVES

What can we say then, on the basis of this study, about the relationship between the old and new forms in *yangge*? What, on the level of artistic form, were the continuities and discontinuities? No easy answer that covers all cases can be given. Genres like *yangge* that were singled out for promotion to the national level, as it were, existed in a multitude of different versions at different levels in society. With *yangge* the performances at the local level remained close to the original "old form," while the model "new *yangge*" was elevated a considerable distance away from it. In Luyi the method used to obtain this elevation was the elimination of politically undesirable features, considerable simplification, and the reorganization of traditional music and dance material in accordance with a "modern, advanced, scientific outlook." The effect, moreover, of the policy of "walking on two legs" was to create an art that was a hybrid on every level of form. Zhang Geng observes that many artists had trouble in combining Western methods of voice production (the so-called "foreign throat," *yang sangzi*)[65] with the open-throated Chinese style of singing: to such lengths was the policy taken.

The trouble was, however, that these compromises between Chinese and Western artistic conventions were always very unstable. They were by their very nature eclectic, and therefore there was no synthesis between European thesis and Chinese antithesis except at the level of artistic practice. That is to say, the decision, for instance, whether to use the "symbolic" acting methods of old opera—and if so which ones—had always to be made afresh for every new play and was often the subject of bitter disputes. This instability arose not from any merely formal consideration—though there are certainly points of genuine incompatibility between Chinese artistic conventions and the very different European ones—but from deep-rooted social causes. Not least of these was the antipathy felt by most intellectuals (including art workers) for forms of art closely connected with religious observances and feudal superstition. In spite of rectification study and the face-the-masses orientation implemented after 1943, the gulf between the urban intelligentsia and the masses has remained very real in China up to the present day.

Meanwhile, in the countryside, *yangge* no doubt continued to be performed by peasants, with or without Party guidance, in the new circum-

[65] Zhang Geng, *Yangge yu xin geju*, pp. 34–35.

stances of the late 1940s and early 1950s. With the Party's attention relaxed and policy changed, what happened to *yangge* and to the reforms introduced by Luyi? One 1953 field survey from Jiaxian in North Shaanxi showed that, in by far the majority of troupes, the open umbrella of the old *yangge* was still at the front of the procession, and that in only a very small number of cases had the new form, the hatchet and sickle, replaced the old. The report indicates that peasants did not mind using the new political symbols, but were opposed to the elimination of elements the Party thought were feudal.[66] In effect an uneasy truce seems to have been declared, giving rise to a new form of syncretism in Chinese popular culture.

The Party's attitude, however, has not been the same in all places or equally tolerant of all forms of performance. On occasion the Party suppressed forms of art current among the people, as for instance when it first moved into the area of Hequ *xian* in Northwest Shanxi and banned the performance of *errentai* ("two-person stage").[67] In general, though, there seems to have been more tolerance than intolerance in the years before the Cultural Revolution. After 1966, performance of *yangge* in the countryside must have come under considerable pressure, owing to the campaign against religious practices. Very little was seen of *yangge* during the Cultural Revolution years (1966–1976), and it was seldom mentioned in the media. Jiang Qing's dislike of folksong was well known, and *yangge* was much too closely associated with the disgraced Yan'an generation to escape the general blight on forms other than Peking opera.

Since the death of Mao and the fall from power of the radical faction under Jiang Qing, *yangge* has been revived. During 1977 large-scale celebrations were held in the cities to herald what was seen as a return to correct government and the renewal of the Party's mandate under Chairman Hua Guofeng.[68] Thus even in 1977, after nearly thirty years of revolutionary transformation under the Party's leadership, we can still see *yangge* being used in a traditional way, to mark an important transition in public life and to symbolize the beginning of an era of "Great Peace."

[66] (Sun) Jingshen, "Shanbei Jiaxian," p. 83.

[67] Zhongyang yinyue yanjiuyuan Zhongguo yinyue yanjiusuo, ed., *Hequ minjian gequ* [Folksongs from Hequ] (Peking: Yinyue chubanshe, 1956), pp. 205–206. *Errentai* was a very simple form of drama, similar in both structure and function to the *yanggeju* of the Yan'an region.

[68] See the centerpiece in *Wudao* 4 (1977) and photographs in *Wudao* 5 (1977): 2–3, which show whole fleets of boats on dry land, waist-drum (*yaogu*) dancers, lions, and massed troupes of *yangge* dancers waving colored scarves.

TWO

Shanghai's "Orphan Island" and the Development of Modern Drama

Edward Gunn

In the summer of 1979, the plays *Ye dian* [The night inn, 1944] by Shi Tuo and Ke Ling and *Ye Shanghai* [Shanghai night, 1939] by Yu Ling were restaged in Shanghai. The events were part of a general, country-wide revival of pre-1949 works that had been revised in the 1950s and then banned during the Cultural Revolution. Yet these two works had a particular significance. They recalled an even earlier period of modern Chinese drama: its unique flowering in Shanghai during the War of Resistance to Japan (1937–1945). Although the city was under Japanese domination, the foreign concessions remained for several years free of direct Japanese authority—hence their designation as the "Orphan Island." It was within these enclaves that, despite the departure of many Chinese intellectuals and artists to the interior (which was not under Japanese authority), modern drama in Shanghai reached an unprecedented peak of popularity as a professional, commercial enterprise. The significance of this wartime theater boom for the development of modern drama in China is the subject of this study.

BACKGROUND

The form that modern drama took in China at that time was known as *huaju,* or "spoken drama," a term that indicates the form's identification with Western drama as opposed to traditional Chinese operatic forms. During the early years of the Republic period, appreciation of this modern drama lagged behind that granted to other modern, Western-influenced genres, and the most notable stage productions were those of foreign plays in Chinese. 1935 saw the beginning of a growing critical acceptance of Chinese productions of foreign plays in translation. This important development was the reward of years of patient effort to improve staging techniques. In June of that year a production of Ibsen's *A Doll's House* (*Nala*) starring Lan Ping (Jiang Qing) and Zhao Dan, in November Gogol's *Inspector General* (*Xun'an*) directed by Ouyang Yuqian, and in December an adaptation of Molière's *L'Avare* (*Caikuang*) starring Wan Jiabao (Cao Yu) were all given an unusually appreciative reception.

The plays themselves, intellectually serious in theme, had a certain topicality for Chinese society: Gogol's and Molière's works could be taken as expressions of the desire to *épater la bourgeoisie,* while Ibsen's play spoke to women's liberation and also to the rapid increase—assisted by a new marriage law—in the divorce rate among China's middle classes. Yet nothing in these comedies of Molière and Gogol is so insistent or obtrusive that they cannot be enjoyed for the sheer ludicrousness of the situations and the characters, given a degree of cosmopolitanism in the audience. Nor should the remark of Eileen Chang on the popularity of *A Doll's House* be discounted:

> A glance at the personal columns in Chinese newspapers ("Since you departed, mother refuses to eat or leave her bed. Grandmother had her heart attacks. Whole family daily washes face with tears. Return at once.") shows us that Chinese under thirty are prone to walk out of their homes because of abstract principles, domestic disputes, failure to pass examinations, the incompatibility of cultural atmosphere, etc. Perhaps no other work has influenced the average educated Chinese of this century so much as Ibsen's *A Doll's House,* and in this, as in everything else learned from the West, the Chinese are more impressed by the bleak beauty of Nora's gesture than by the underlying thought.[1]

Granted that audiences were ready for the presentation of problems they saw as pertinent to them, the theory of "the bleak gesture" offers some insight into the popular success of certain plays in the years yet to come. In 1935 the productions of these plays evidenced both new developments in the quality of acting and production and the limitation of these achievements: productions ran for a few days at most, and modern drama still remained the preserve of amateur and semiprofessional enthusiasts, its audience confined for the most part to a relatively small number of students and intellectuals.[2]

Another significant change was the renewed emphasis in 1936 and 1937 on popularizing the modern drama, especially among those committed to

[1] Eileen Chang, "On the Screen," *The Twentieth Century* 5.6 (October 1943): 432.

[2] Reviews of these productions include Xiao Qian on *Caikuang* in *Dagong bao* [L'Impartial], 9 December 1935, p. 9; Zhang Geng on *Xun'an* in *Wenxue* 5.6 (December 1935): 1053f.; and Zhang Geng on *Nala* in "Muqian juyunde jige dangmian wenti" [Some questions we face in the theater movement at present], *Guangming zazhi* 2.12 (May 1937): 1492–1495.

theater as a vehicle to propagandize anti-imperialism and resistance to Japanese aggression among the widest audience possible. Since the Manchurian Incident of 1931–1932, the Japanese had by steps penetrated deep into North China and had tightened their hold both politically and economically. Chinese dramatists responded, as part of the program for a "literature of National Defense," with such works as *Zousi* [Smuggling], exposing large-scale Japanese smuggling activities in North China; Xia Yan's *Sai Jinhua,* portraying the humiliation of China after the Boxer Revolt and satirizing by implication the ineffectualness of the Nationalist government in dealing with the Japanese; and Cui Wei's *Fangxia nide bianzi* [Lay down your whip], street theater revealing the misery of the Chinese under Japanese rule in Northeast China and implying the impending threat for all Chinese.

In Shanghai, *Smuggling* was banned by the Shanghai Municipal Council at the insistence of the Japanese, while the Nationalists cut short the production of *Sai Jinhua.*[3] These actions helped make the plays rallying points for popular frustration and indignation, which kept attention focused on them. But as agitation propaganda they were part of an organized political machine which, once subdued by Japanese force of arms, could ill afford to continue expressing itself so openly. Moreover, these plays drew attention to theater through a topical issue of widespread social concern, rather than relying on a permanently established taste for modern drama itself to attract an audience. Productions at the time of the Republican Revolution of 1911 and the Manchurian Incident of 1931 had aroused similar interest, but not enough to sustain a regular patronage once the issue had passed. Instead, the agitation-propaganda plays of this period have largely been ignored since, though their cause has never been forgotten. What did emerge from this period of 1936–1937 was a renewed interest in costume drama (*guzhuang xiju*) in plays, such as *Sai Jinhua,* that recalled the historical past, revised old operas, or revivified old legends and stories. The costume drama and its relation to traditional culture would become a major concern to writers.

CAO YU AND THE FIRST PROFESSIONAL COMPANY

Another important development in drama also occurred prior to the war. In certain significant ways it overshadowed the contributions of the

[3] A discussion of the ban on *Smuggling* appears in Yao Hsin-nung, "Drama Chronicle," *T'ien Hsia Monthly* 3.1 (August 1936): 45–52. For the problems of *Sai Jinhua,* one contemporary source is A Jizhe (pseud.), "Zhongxuanbuzhang he Xiong Foxishi tan jinyan *Sai Jinhua* zhi bianshuo yiji" [The chief of the Central Propaganda Bureau and Xiong Foxi discuss the justification for banning the performance of *Sai Jinhua*], *Guangming zazhi* 2.12 (May 1937): 1546–1550.

largely amateur movements in foreign drama and national defense literature. This development was the simultaneous and ultimately related rise of the playwright Cao Yu (Wan Jiabao) and the Zhongguo lüxing jutuan (the Chinese Traveling Dramatic Company, or CTDC). Tang Huaiqiu, a seasoned performer in amateur and semiprofessional modern drama companies, organized the CTDC in November 1933. He was determined to put spoken drama performances on a professional footing and to support the livelihood of his company solely through producing modern drama. From what little we know of CTDC's repertoire during the early years, it was not impressive. Short plays like Xiong Foxi's *Zuile* [The drunkard] and ordinary Western melodramas such as A. Walters' *The Easiest Way* (under the Chinese title *Mei Luoxiang*) appear to have been unpoliticized entertainment and edification addressed to students and the middle class. Given that its repertoire was unexceptional, CTDC's survival seems due mainly to the company's sheer acting skill and technique, which impressed audiences in cities outside Shanghai with productions markedly superior to those of the perennially failing local amateur groups.

It was also in late 1933 that Cao Yu finished the magnum opus of his undergraduate days at Qinghua University, *Leiyu* [Thunderstorm]; it was published in *Wenxue jikan* [Literary quarterly] in July 1934. Cao Yu was an unknown figure, hardly a part of the mainstream of the drama movement, and later even wrote, "At the time of writing *Thunderstorm,* I did not imagine that anyone would stage it."[4] Indeed, a little-publicized attempt by students in Peking to stage the play was banned by local authorities on the grounds that it portrayed incest. The first production, ironically, was by overseas students in Tokyo in April 1935.[5] But even there it was reported that the fourth act of the play was censored owing to the incest theme.[6] Among high-brow critics the only spokesman for the play was Li Jianwu, himself a well-known playwright, who wondered why the film industry, highly criticized for its lack of decent scripts, did not seize upon this work.[7]

[4] Cao Yu, "Wo zenma xie *Leiyu*" [How I wrote *Thunderstorm*], *Dagong bao,* 19 January 1936, p. 9. A translation of the preface appears in Yao Hsin-nung (trans.), "Thunder and Lightning," *T'ien Hsia Monthly* 3.3 (October 1936): 279. Yao Hsin-nung is better known by his pen name, Yao Ke.

[5] See Liang Menghui, "Chūgoku no hanageki to Nihon to no kankei" [The relationship between Chinese *huaju* and Japan], *Shingeki* [New drama] 155 (December 1962): 46–49. For a contemporary account of the performance, see Kageyama Saburo in the *Teikoku daigaku shimbun* [Imperial University news], no. 576 (May–June 1935).

[6] According to Wu Lifu, "Yinianlai Zhongguo wenxuejie" [The Chinese literary world during the past year], in *Zhongguo wenyi nianjian: 1935* [The yearbook of Chinese literature: 1935] (Shanghai: Beixin shuju, 1936), pp. 93–94.

[7] See Liu Xiwei (pseud. of Li Jianwu), *Juhua ji* [Ruminations] (Shanghai: Wenhua shenghuo chubanshe, 1936), pp. 115–125.

Word of the play spread slowly, and finally, in late December 1935, students at Fudan University (under the direction of Ouyang Yuqian) staged *Thunderstorm* for three days. Audiences were impressed, especially by the young actress Fengzi who threw herself weeping into her role.[8] But they were not impressed enough that the run had to be extended. In early 1936 the script appeared in book form, still without a major production. This it received only after the Chinese Traveling Dramatic Company returned to Shanghai in April 1936, discovered the play, and again offered it to Shanghai—this time, to everyone's surprise, for the unprecedented run of nineteen days.[9] As one critic has noted of the CTDC:

> Their performances at the Carlton Theater were so immensely superior to those of the amateur groups that the audience was thrilled. Again, *Thunderstorm* was the greatest favorite. The Shanghai theater-goers had never seen a play so well written or a performance so well done. Previously, the spoken drama audiences were confined to students and a small number of intellectuals, but now the house was packed with people who had never seen a modern play before. It was a tremendous success, both for the play and for the players.[10]

Even newspapers not noted for their sympathetic attention to the drama movement were moved to recognize the success of CTDC and *Thunderstorm*—at the bottom of the movie gossip columns.

The fact that the middle classes had joined students and intellectuals in an enthusiastic reception of a spoken drama was of crucial importance to those interested in building a permanent, publicly supported theater movement. There was in the content of Cao Yu's *Thunderstorm* much that must have appealed to its audience: a focus on the family, particularly on the older and younger generations in conflict and on tension between husband and wife; love and death, particularly as illicit sex and self-destructive acts, which might be considered "bleak gestures"; and revenge. Yet these elements were not new to the stage, and the cause for their successful combination lay in Cao Yu's tireless concern with technique, with a degree of manipulation of passions theretofore unwitnessed in a modern Chinese playwright, and with an embodiment of dramatic theory more often found before in handbooks and monographs than in actual playscripts. Linked with this breakthrough was the timely development of the CTDC, which, relative to other groups, deserved the title of "professional" for its mastery of staging technique. Cao Yu admired its work and confided to its members his criticisms of the failings of other companies that performed his

[8] According to Zhao Jingshen, *Wentan yiju* [Recollections of the literary scene] (Shanghai: Beixin shuju, 1948), pp. 60–61.

[9] Yao Hsin-nung, "Drama Chronicle," *T'ien Hsia Monthly* 3.1 (August 1936): 49.

[10] Yao Hsin-nung, letter to the author dated 16 July 1975.

plays.[11] Entrusted with *Thunderstorm,* and then with Cao Yu's second work, *Richu* [Sunrise], the CTDC set out again in 1936 on a successful tour of Chinese cities. They were still on tour when the war broke out in July 1937.[12]

Cao Yu and the CTDC aroused a mixed response among the literary left heading the theatrical movement for national defense literature. Cao Yu had no connections with the Communist Party, and his plays *Thunderstorm* and *Sunrise* did not tackle the themes of anti-imperialism and resistance to Japan considered appropriate for the times. Cao was to make up for such shortcomings in the years to come. But at the time his work seemed to be in competition with Party works, and Party critics such as Zhang Geng criticized Cao for attention to technique (*jiqiao*) over life (*shenghuo*).[13] These two terms were frequently and flexibly used by critics of the period. "Technique" sometimes referred to the nonrealistic style of traditional opera, sometimes to the unrealistic style of Hollywood acting (particularly unrealistic when transplanted to Chinese society); "life" was associated with contemporary realism. This view was not universally shared. Even when offered as a supreme compliment, it was not accepted by Li Jianwu for one of his works:

> Mr. Ba Ren [Wang Renshu] rendered the greatest assistance in the production of this modest work. He stated: "This is not a play, but life: no more, no less, it is human life. Is not life the highest level of art?" Mr. Ba Ren tends to get intoxicated and talk in his sleep.[14]

Zhang Geng, in criticizing Cao Yu, argued that his technique was realistic but his characters were implausible. This display of technique at the expense of real life Zhang contrasted with a play by and for workers he had seen, in which "immature" technique and dialogue still evoked a genuine response from the workers and evinced true life. Given that Cao Yu's characters are not altogether plausible, it might seem that Zhang was arguing that, while the middle class might be moved by implausible characters, a working-class audience could be moved only by plausible characters. However, the heart of Zhang's argument was not this shaky proposition, but rather his vision of Cao Yu's work as irrelevant to a theater by

[11] See Zhao Huishen, "Zai Zhongguo lüxing jutuan" [In the Chinese Traveling Dramatic Company], *Juchang yishu* [Theater arts] 6 (20 April 1939): 20–25.

[12] CTDC eventually settled in Hong Kong, and then returned to Shanghai in 1940 or 1941. Part of their audience in Hong Kong was composed of refugees who had fled Shanghai following the battle in 1937; they returned to Shanghai as the city was restored to normalcy.

[13] See Zhang Geng, "Yijiusanliuniande xiju" [Drama in 1936], in *Zhongguo wenyi nianjian: 1936* [The yearbook of Chinese literature: 1936] (Shanghai: Beixin shuju, 1937), pp. 95–96.

[14] Li Jianwu, *Zhe buguo shi chuntian* [This is only spring] (Shanghai: Wenhua shenghuo chubanshe, 1940), p. vi.

and for workers and peasants, which was a focus of concern among many Party cultural workers.

Similarly, the Party was not altogether pleased with the CTDC. The company was slow to respond to the call for plays dealing with anti-imperialism, and only grudging approval was given when the company produced *Zuguo* (a translation of Sardou's *Patrie,* done in foreign dress).[15] Moreover, as commercial theater, CTDC supposedly catered to the bourgeoisie, charging admission rates that only they could afford, to the neglect of the mass of the population.[16] And yet this vision of two different theaters with divergent ends does not adequately describe the situation or the attitude of those involved. For the contributions of CTDC were to the means of the theater in general as well as to a particular end. The endurance of the company and the growing recognition accorded it offered a promise of careers in modern drama, a chance, however challenging, that a performer might be able to devote his or her life to the stage. Further, the CTDC had provided an education in theatrical technique, an area that had lacked sufficient appreciation. And through this, CTDC had aroused broader enthusiasm for spoken drama among the public. All this encouraged writers to take up playwriting with greater hopes for the successful realization of better and more demanding works. As the war approached, more and more amateur and semiprofessional troupes followed the lead of CTDC and attempted to go onto a professional basis.

EXPERIMENTATION DURING THE JAPANESE OCCUPATION

The Battle for Shanghai that opened on August 13, 1937, was also a form of theater. The Chinese who planned the strike on the Japanese garrison there hoped to make the largest foreign community in China—and through them, the rest of the world—spectators to Japanese aggression. But no influence emanated from the International Settlement or the French Concession to their home governments in the West, which were preparing for war in Europe. While Greater Shanghai was laid waste, the Japanese increased their influence in the foreign concessions, and their armies pushed on at great cost to savage the city of Nanking, forcing the Chinese armies into the great interior of China. In December 1937 the foreign enclaves in Shanghai were an "orphan island," "neutral" outposts of Western commerce surrounded by the Japanese "New Order."

In Shanghai, the period from late 1937 through the spring of 1939 saw a setback in the ability of modern drama to attract audiences and the collapse of the trend toward professional companies. The city lost part of

[15] Zhang Geng, "Yijiusanliuniande xiju," p. 91.

[16] See Zhang Yangxin, "Changshade juyun" [The drama movement in Changsha], *Guangming zazhi* 2.12 (May 1937): 1543.

its audience and many of its writers and artists to Hong Kong and the interior, due to the battle and the retreat of Chinese forces. The theater artists and writers who remained sought the patronage of the French, who temporarily maintained the greatest degree of autonomy but who insisted that the Chinese should use their stage facilities for the promotion of French drama. By staging French plays in translation together with current patriotic Chinese plays (with the titles of the well-known ones altered to avoid confrontation with censors), semiprofessional theater was gradually restored, and the Shanghai juyi she (Shanghai Theater Arts Society, or STAS) was formed.

In the summer of 1939 STAS attempted to stage its first extended run of a production, *Ye Shanghai* [Shanghai night], by the local playwright Yu Ling. But the production fell far short of its scheduled engagement. *Shanghai Night* is in fact one of the best plays by Yu Ling, a veteran of Shanghai agit-prop theater. It is interesting for its literal portrayal of the problems of refugees in the International Settlement and the moral dilemmas of life under enemy occupation. But it is also, in conventional terms, too loose and melodramatic a concoction of crises surrounding too many uninteresting characters. Yet the causes for its failure to achieve popularity outside the Party probably lay elsewhere. *Shanghai Night* was seen by its apologists as a demanding play about the reality of ordinary life in Shanghai, in contrast to the theater of technique that offered skillful manipulations and sensuous spectacle.[17] In sum, *Shanghai Night* embodied the virtue of truth, while audiences were accused of preferring artificiality.

Essentially, the definition of the woes of *huaju* theater had shifted. Following the success of CTDC in 1936, and prior to the failure of *Shanghai Night,* there had been common agreement that the main need was to upgrade the quality of acting and production in *huaju.* No less a figure than Xia Yan, the author of *Sai Jinhua,* wrote that, so long as acting technique was not improved, there would be a dearth of demanding plays and the theater movement would not get beyond skits like *Lay Down Your Whip.*[18] But the left-leaning theater circle of Shanghai would find fault with neither Yu Ling's play nor its staging.[19] Given the box-office failure, then, the discussion shifted to the appeal of spectacle.

Nowhere was spectacle more evident on the stage than in the various

[17] See Shen Yi, "Wo zenyang kan *Ye Shanghai*" [How I view *Shanghai Night*], *Juchang yishu* 1.10 (August 1939): 4–5.

[18] See Xia Yan, "Lun cishi cidide juyun" [On the drama movement here and now], *Juchang yishu* 1.7 (May 1939): 1–2.

[19] Indeed, it was listed as one of the ten most representative plays of the war period by Hong Shen in *Kangzhan shinianlai Zhongguo huaju yundong yu jiaoyu* [The Chinese drama movement and education over the past ten years during the War of Resistance] (n.p., n.d.), p. 134.

traditional forms of opera, dominated at the time by Peking opera. In the view of a noted Shanghai critic and historian of Chinese theater, Zhou Yibai, Peking opera had become primarily a theater of music and movement, a vehicle for singers and acrobats, and no longer fulfilled its function of storytelling or of presenting characters and themes relevant to the present.[20] For instance, in the standard traditional theme of *zhong jun ai guo* (loyalty to one's ruler and love for one's country) only the latter half, patriotism, was relevant, whereas loyalty to any particular ruler was outdated.

Zhou's comments could in fact have served as a fitting introduction to the second play billed for an extended run by STAS in the autumn of 1939, *Mingmo yihen* or *Bixue hua* [Sorrow for the fall of the Ming, or Jade blood flower] by A Ying (Qian Xingcun). Part of a cycle of plays by A Ying on the fall of the Ming dynasty due to foreign (Manchu) invasion, this play succeeded in at least putting STAS financially in the black. While it reads as a very loose-knit set of scenes designed only to offer the rhetoric and gestures of patriotic defiance toward invaders and contempt toward collaborators, onstage *Sorrow for the Fall of the Ming* included singing and dancing and all the costumes, properties, and even the chanted dialogue (*daobai*) of traditional operatic spectacle. The characters, too, were easily recognizable stereotypes (as in traditional opera), led by a courtesan-turned-woman-warrior, another favorite opera type. Yet, as a commoner, she is made to represent patriotism apart from and in defiance of the established Ming aristocracy and civil service, who consort with the enemy and abandon the common people's struggle to save their country. Hence a modern interpretation of an old tale was delivered, and one that implied criticism of the Nationalists. It is worth noting, too, that the play offers scenes of domestic strife between older and younger generations and concludes with the heroine's gesture of martyrdom. The play thus capitalized on the techniques of traditional opera and restored its storytelling function in terms at least believed to be popular with audiences.

It would be wrong, in discussing this breakthrough, to overrate the automatic success of any part of its formula. Several other patriotic costume dramas by other local writers that followed were not as successful with audiences. Moreover, fellow playwrights and critics devoted to realism were critical of A Ying's work, from its stereotyped characters to its use of the artificial *daobai* in dialogue. Xia Yan, after his prewar costume dramas, had turned to contemporary realism in the belief that, since history is progressive, recreation of the past could not serve to illuminate the truth of the present. On this ground he dismissed A Ying's costume

[20] Zhou Yibai, "Pihuangxi weishenma yao gailiang" [Why revise Peking opera?], *Juchang yishu* 1.8 (June 1939): 4–5.

dramas.[21] There was, then, a reluctance on the part of many in modern drama to don ancestral garb and compromise with traditional opera.

In the following year, 1940, Shanghai theater's most successful production was an adaptation by Wu Tian of Ba Jin's *Jia* [Family]. Credit for its popularity must go primarily to the artists who staged it with as much color and innovation as the script permitted, and to Ba Jin as the most popular portrayer of the generation gap and the bleak gesture. The popularity of this production of *Family,* which did not deal even indirectly with the war, far outstripped that of *Sorrow for the Fall of the Ming*; it ran for some four months. This success reawakened the arguments that the role of theater was to support the resistance as well as the artists. *Family* might be taken as another turning point in theater, but not one that signaled any true failure of faith in or sympathy for the resistance. The play, while not focusing on the issue of national autonomy, does describe other social goals for which China was fighting.

The second great popular success, in the summer of 1941 a few months prior to the Japanese military occupation of the International Settlement, was Yao Ke's *Qing gong yuan* [Malice in the Qing court] (translated by Jeremy Ingalls under the title *The Malice of Empire*). This play, too, presented foreign invasion by the Western-Japanese expedition in retaliation for the Boxer Uprising, but the focus of the play was a study of tyranny centered on the Manchu court and on the patterns of mutual betrayal and the breakdown of trust experienced by those who lived in it. *The Malice of Empire* made much use of costumes and spectacle, while its structure followed from that of traditional opera. But it was far more conservative in its borrowing from opera and was realistic in style. In addition to providing spectacle, the play focused on the familylike feud between the Empress Cixi and her chosen heir, the young Guangxu emperor. Cixi's hatred is directed principally at the emperor's favorite consort, the Pearl Concubine, who drowns herself at the conclusion of the play.

DRAMA IN THE UNOCCUPIED INTERIOR

What distinguished the modern drama of occupied Shanghai from that in the Chinese-held interior (exclusive of the radical changes that emerged in Yan'an) is not entirely clear, in part due to the lack of a thorough-going critical history of wartime drama in the interior. Certainly up to 1942 the two areas had more in common than in contrast. For example, Yao Ke was himself engaged in a production of the patriotic play *Tuibian* [Metamorphosis] by Cao Yu (who was in the interior) when the Japanese took

[21] Liu Xiwei, *Juhua erji* [Ruminations II] (Shanghai: Wenhua shenghuo chubanshe, 1947), p. 82.

the International Settlement on December 8, 1941. Certainly such topical, patriotic plays dealing directly with the war disappeared from Shanghai stages by force of censorship. Yet in the interior, while such plays continued to appear (from such writers as Song Zhidi and Lao She), there was a decline in their numbers by force of popular taste. More dramas took up life in the interior as opposed to life at the battlefront. A flock of plays on the Taiping Rebellion, as well as other costume dramas by Guo Moruo, criticized the Nationalists for hardening their policy toward the Communist Party. These plays, however, made little impression on Shanghai theater, although they were discussed in the local magazines. In the interior there were delicious fantasies about the life to come at war's end, vapid comedies, and adaptations of foreign plays more or less concerned with patriotic themes. The Xin Zhongguo jushe (New China Dramatic Company), a professional Communist group touring the interior, relied mainly on Gogol's *Inspector General* (*Qincha dachen*), Ostrowski's *The Storm* (*Da leiyu*), and Cao Yu's *Sunrise.*[22] Even Xia Yan turned away from patriotic propaganda to dwell more on quotidian individual experience not limited to wartime existence. Perhaps what Shanghai missed from what the interior had to offer was satire as strong and outrageous as that of Chen Baichen. Chen did not originate social satire on the modern stage, but he did bring it to the point of liberation from formal realism, to public controversy, and finally to Shanghai after the victory over Japan.

Those who worked at theater in the interior have complained a good deal about the conditions there. Some of these conditions were more self-imposed than they were necessary, or so it would seem. Many writers justified their works entirely on the grounds that they contributed to national mobilization and education and adhered to a style of such overt didacticism that entertainment or delight became embarrassingly suspect concepts. Attitudes could become so contradictory that a play by Tian Han that pleased a certain Nationalist official was reportedly later hushed up and ignored by its author and a school of Party critics.[23] Even harder for many writers to accept was the fact that few artists working in theater had the stamina to remain in rural areas or near the front lines, but flooded back to the cities. There the goal of reaching the masses fell behind that of acceptance by the educated and the elite audiences.[24] In theory,

[22] See Wang Fan, "Xin Zhongguo jushede qinian jingli" [The seven-year experience of the New China Dramatic Company], in Tian Han et al., eds. *Zhongguo huaju yundong wushinian shiliao ji* [Historical materials on fifty years of the Chinese drama movement] (Peking: Zhongguo xiju chubanshe, 1958), pp. 277–304.

[23] Cao Juren, *Wentan wushinian (xuji)* [Fifty years of the literary scene (continued)] (Hong Kong: Xin wenhua chubanshe, 1973), p. 148.

[24] The phenomenon was generally noted. See in particular Hong Shen's chapter "Kangzhan xijude ziwo pipan" [Self-criticism on drama during the War of Resistance], in *Kangzhan shinianlai,* pp. 124–141.

drama originated historically among the common people but was monopolized by the elite to subdue the people.[25] But for the most part spoken drama was for the cities and the educated.

THE ECLIPSE OF THE FILM INDUSTRY IN SHANGHAI

One critical problem with which the modern dramatic artists in the interior were saddled from the start of the war was the scarcity of theaters and the competition with films and opera companies for what theaters there were.[26] By contrast, Shanghai hardly lacked theaters: the Carlton, the Lyceum, the Lafayette Garden, the Paris, the Crown, and other foreign-built theaters were designed for stage productions, and once the film industry in Shanghai was taken over by the Japanese and foreign films were embargoed, managers of several cinema houses had them converted to accommodate spoken drama productions.

Certainly the cinema had long dominated spoken drama in the public eye. In general this dominance probably had less to do with artistic reasons than with the cheapness and convenience of seeing films and the greater publicity and wider distribution that film companies could arrange. Rather than compete with film companies, many artists and writers of stage productions readily sought employment with them. Films also went through periodic crazes for costume dramas and endured reams of criticism in newsprint. Yet in 1940 and 1941, when independent Shanghai studios were still producing films in quantity, they were outsold by stage productions of *Family* and *The Malice of Empire*. A large part of the credit for this phenomenon must go to sheer improvements in the dramatic and staging techniques of writers and artists. It is true that the Japanese rendered a service to the Chinese modern drama movement by taking over the film industry and banning American films, thus increasing the number of artists and theaters devoted to stage productions. But this action added to, rather than created, a movement that had already built up momentum. At its height, drama companies occupied thirteen theaters.[27]

JAPANESE CONTROL OF THE ARTS

By turning their attention largely to films as the medium of mass entertainment and propaganda, the Japanese left the Shanghai theater establish-

[25] Tian Qin, *Zhongguo xiju yundong* [The Chinese drama movement] (Chungking: Shangwu yinshuguan, 1944, reprint ed., Shanghai, 1946), pp. 89–90.

[26] Ibid., p. 101.

[27] According to Gu Zhongyi, *Shinianlaide Shanghai huaju yundong, 1937–1945* [The drama movement in Shanghai over the past ten years, 1937–1945] (originally published in Hong Shen, *Kangzhan shinianlai* [n.p., n.d.]; reprint ed., Hong Kong, 1976), p. 22.

ment to the control of censors, to proscriptive rather than prescriptive measures. The tenuous margin of independence this allowed the theater and its audience was real and substantial enough to distinguish the stage from the motion picture industry. Authorities did intrude upon this arrangement on occasion. Writers and artists were lectured and encouraged to eulogize the new regime, and police arbitrarily visited intellectuals to question them on their political views. Finally, in 1943, the theater establishment was ordered to provide a performance at a celebration for the return of the Shanghai foreign concessions to Chinese administration (under the Wang Jingwei regime). After much threatening and procrastination, it agreed to revive an adaptation of Ba Jin's *Family*.[28]

At the other end of the spectrum of goverment control was one of the major hits of the war period, *Wen Tianxiang,* a popular resistance drama in costume written early in the war by Wu Zuguang and originally titled *Zhengqi ge* [Song of righteousness]. With the title discreetly changed to the name of the hero of the play (who was martyred while resisting the Mongol invasion of China) and the author's name left unpublicized (he was in the interior), censors allowed the play to run for several months in 1943. It did not, after all, directly insult the Japanese or the Nanking regime, and its performance happened to follow the decisive defeat of the Nazi German armies at the Battle of Stalingrad in February 1943—a clear signal to any who did not already believe it that the Axis powers were crumbling. Japan was concerned with maintaining a neutrality pact with the Soviet Union, and in Shanghai the Soviet cultural presence was never really excluded but was well propagandized in such locally published, Soviet-sponsored periodicals as *Liu yi* [Six arts] and *Shidai* [The epoch]. Politically as well as artistically, the Shanghai cultural world developed in ways no one could have predicted.

MODERN DRAMA'S RAPPROCHEMENT WITH OPERA

In theatrical terms the real challenge faced by modern drama in Shanghai seems to have been the traditional opera. This is by no means to belittle the real influence of censorship, self-imposed restraints, or competition with film so hastily reviewed above. But, in terms of its relationship to an audience that would support it, the theater of modern drama had most of all to contend with the popularity of traditional opera. The most striking response to this situation was also the most popular play of the war period. It was reviewed by Eileen Chang in May 1943, toward the end of its initial and unprecedented five-month run:

[28] Ibid., pp. 27–28.

> Never before has the hardened city of Shanghai been moved so much by a play as by *Autumn Quince* (Qiu Haitang), a sentimental melodrama which has been running at the Carlton Theater since December 1942. . . . The success of the play has given rise to a host of imitators. At one time there were no less than six plays showing simultaneously in Shanghai which dealt with the private lives of Peking Opera stars and backstage intrigues. . . . The color and atmosphere of Peking Opera strongly prevails in these plays, with here and there a brief interlude of actual Peking Opera. It astounds us to reflect that, although the new theater of China has taken a firmly antagonistic stand against Peking Opera from its very conception the first real triumph of the new theater is a compromise—a humiliating fact.[29]

Chang's remarks form part of a discussion on the endurance of Peking opera and other forms of traditional opera. One need not agree with all of her observations to join her in recognizing the centrality of the opera forms to the performing arts in China and the breadth and depth of this phenomenon.[30]

Here we may consider opera from three perspectives: as a form, as a social ritual, and as a psychological entity. It was widely recognized that as an art form, opera was replete with spectacle, with music, and with highly developed movement. This transparent devotion to technique was too often set in supposed contrast to the spoken drama, where the need for highly developed technique, albeit of a different kind, was frequently ignored or regarded as a bogy until the mid-1930s. Opera was also a mandatory social ritual in many public festivals and private entertainments, helping to define them and to lend social cohesiveness to leisure activities. As a professional activity, it attracted talented people who knew that it offered a potential livelihood and all the rewards of popular entertainment. By contrast, modern dramatists had set their genre up as predominantly a vehicle of radical social vision, deliberately at odds with established ritual and custom; they were often disdainful of the idea of "selling entertainment" as a means to make a living. Finally, the opera was psychologically an ideal reference point: as part of the "cultural identity" of the audience, as a response to the audience's preference to see itself in relation to the past. Be it an idealized

[29] "Still Alive," *The Twentieth Century* 4.6 (June 1943): 432. A Chinese version of this essay appears as "Yangren kan jingxi ji qita," in Zhang Ailing, *Liuyan* [Gossip] (reprint ed., Taibei: Huangguan zazhishe, 1969), pp. 100–109.

[30] A few dramatists decided before the war that traditional opera should be the central reference point for the modern drama. The most notable was Ouyang Yuqian, one of whose experiments (*Liang Hongyu*) was staged without much success in Shanghai in 1937, prior to his departure for the interior. Ouyang sought a combination of *huaju,* traditional opera, and Russian opera (such as he had seen in the Soviet Union), including the use of symphonic orchestration that would become a mark of "model revolutionary opera" in China in the 1960s. See "Houtai renyu" [Backstage talk], *Wenxue chuangzao* [Literary creation] (Guilin) 1.4 (15 January 1943): 42–47.

past, an idealized moment from the past, or simply an ideal moment in the past, idealization and the culture of the past seem to be, or to have been, intimately linked. The title role of *Qiu Haitang* is that of a female impersonator, an ideal cultural figure in Peking opera.

The presentation of such an ideal cultural figure was no doubt aided in its success by the timing of its appearance before a war-weary audience, and the burden of Qiu Haitang as a character whose true worth as a man is never recognized was no doubt a temporary relief from patriotic themes. *Qiu Haitang* also triumphed over its imitators because, it would seem, of the superior skill and technique of its writers and performers. The playscript as performed was the product of three prominent and versatile writer-artists (Fei Mu, Huang Zuolin, and Gu Zhongyi), who had reluctantly accepted the task of adapting the original work by Qin Shouou at the urging of their theater manager. The demanding role of Qiu Haitang himself—which required ability as an operatic female impersonator, an acrobat, and a realistic actor—was a vehicle for the actor-director Shi Hui to emerge as a principal artist of his time. All the writers and artists involved thought they had their esthetic and social vision set higher than *Qiu Haitang,* and fortunately writers in Shanghai made other contributions to the development of modern drama. Yet what made many of their various experiments possible was the commercial success of plays like *Qiu Haitang*.

WESTERN INFLUENCES

If Shanghai offered the maturing of theatrical technique, then some mention should be made of the appearance of the well-made play as a standard feature of commercial theater. While nothing might be considered more foreign to China than the plays of the nineteenth-century French masters of well-made drama, Scribe and Sardou, one of the best-known playwrights in Shanghai, Li Jianwu, adapted several of their works to the modern warlord era of China. While Li was criticized by fellow playwrights for turning his back on the reality of contemporary life, his plays, with all their undeniable artificiality, were not box-office failures. Zhou Yibai, writing to supply the CTDC with original plays, also made heavy use of the formulas of well-made plays for his dramas, and while he wanted his stories of young women falling prey to the seamier side of the entertainment world to be seen as serious social commentary, it is his ability to handle plot that is most noteworthy. Nevertheless, despite the moderate success of their well-made plays, both Li Jianwu and Zhou Yibai turned away from them toward the end of the war. While Zhou took up costume dramas of palace intrigues, Li Jianwu wrote one of his most accomplished original works, *Qingchun* [Youth], a comedy of love and courtship set in rural China on the eve of the Republican Revolution. Li was still no closer to the contemporary realities of Shanghai, but this nostalgic piece was evidence of a quickened sense of the potential of Chinese folk material as a source for modern drama. By the conclusion of the war Li had gone so far as to write a costume drama himself: *Ashina,* set in the Tang dynasty.

Next to costume drama the largest trend was to adaptations of Western works, from *Gone with the Wind* to Shaw's *Pygmalion.* There were some that received less recognition than they should have, such as Huang Zuolin's *Liangshang junzi* (from Molnar's *Doctor Ur*), and others that succeeded more than one might have expected, such as Huang's *Huangdao yingxiong* (from Barrie's *Admirable Crichton*) and Gu Zhongyi's simplified and sinified *King Lear,* titled *San qianjin* [Three daughters]. Perhaps it was the focus on domestic conflict that helped these plays impress their audience. Yet an important historical point about all such works is that they were adaptations, not translations; the latter form had virtually disappeared. Translations had never really captured more than a very limited audience. When one turns to the major adaptations produced during the war—*Da maxituan* [The big circus] by Shi Tuo (from Andreyev's *He Who Gets Slapped*) and *Ye dian* [The night inn] by Shi Tuo and Ke Ling (from Gorky's *The Lower Depths*)—one is struck by their degree of both sinification and intellectual simplification compared with their sources. Certainly this treatment was a response to lessons learned in the past, when productions of plays in translation had bored and confused audiences with their foreign names and difficult lines.[31]

Yet, whatever the limitations of *The Night Inn,* it was regarded as a breakthrough for commercial theater since it focused attention on the lower classes. An exposé of the misery of the poor, it stood on its own as professional, commercial theater among the costume dramas and well-made plays. Despite attempts in the 1920s and 1930s to stage proletarian drama, the literary left had had better luck with women as figures of oppression—hence the Noras and the sword-wielding heroines of tradition. The success of *The Night Inn* was a moment of proud achievement that fulfilled the vision of life and technique shared by so many artists.[32]

COMEDY IN MODERN DRAMA

Published in 1944 in a Shanghai magazine but not performed until 1945, *The Night Inn* is really very similar in structure and theme to Shi

[31] Wang Ying, "Jici yanbuchude xi" [Several unstageable plays], *Guangming zazhi* 2.12 (May 1937): 1541–1542.

[32] Wang Ying notes the failure to stage a translation of *The Lower Depths* in the 1930s (ibid.).

Tuo's other adaptation, *The Big Circus,* which had been staged with considerable success in 1942 and 1943. Yet a large part of the allure of *The Big Circus* (unlike that of *The Night Inn*) lay in the spectacle and ebullient comedy brought to it by its director, Huang Zuolin. Comedy was at least as much a part of wartime Shanghai theater as the strong satire of Chen Baichen was a part of the theater of the interior. Well adapted and staged, comedies based on foreign plays often sustained companies when more sober offerings failed, as witnessed by the attraction of *Tian jieer* (from Paul Gavault's *La Petite Chocolatière*), which brought fame to the noted film actress Huang Zongying.

The development of comedy in Shanghai was an unexpected gain for modern Chinese drama. It not only lured adaptors and weaned Li Jianwu away from French melodrama to an original work as good as *Youth,* but also provided the arena for an increasingly sophisticated drama, notably by the writer Yang Jiang. A smile of irony shrouds the heart of her comedies, which took the material of social exposé and reworked it into comments on human nature and sallies at literary stereotypes. The innocent orphan girl of *Chenxin ruyi* [As you desire], instead of being victimized, is united with her admirer and sent to university by the very forces than should have ruined her. The play *Nongzhen chengjia* [Swindle] opens with a classic argument between father and daughter over free love and concludes with a genuinely hilarious scene of forced marriage—offered hardly as an argument against free love but as an exercise in how people form assumptions and act on them. Audiences did not need to follow an intellectual line of development in her comedies in order to enjoy them.

Yet, when Yang turned to tragedy at the end of the war, her concern with irony and the centrality of psychological insight in her one achievement, *Fengxu* [Windswept blossoms], proved too demanding for the audience. Her central character was a sarcastic, assertive young woman, driven by a craving for freedom from the society she holds in contempt and unable to win it either with or without her egoistical husband or the self-effacing lawyer who has freed him from a prison sentence unjustly imposed for his attempts at agrarian reform. This was not the sort of drama Shanghai would support. But that this play was ever written is evidence of how far the Shanghai theater movement had gone and how far some would try to take it.

THE LEGACY OF SHANGHAI'S DRAMA MOVEMENT

Within a year after the victory over Japan, the drama movement in Shanghai was demonstrably in decline. Some theaters returned to showing the long-banned American films, while others were confiscated by the Nationalists over questions of ownership. The Chinese film industry was also experiencing a strong revival and absorbed many of those who had been active on the stage during the war. In fact, a number of wartime plays were turned into films. In theater itself a resurgence of regional operas and the rise of politicized *yangge* performances began to capture the attention of many on the left.

Yet during the war, modern drama in Shanghai had contributed in its own way to the sinification of theater. That Western drama was the source for the modern Chinese drama should not conceal the fact that very few foreign plays were presented in translation, as in the 1930s; most were adapted and sinified. This step back from cosmopolitanism was even more strikingly evident in the dominant role played by the costume drama and by the variety of hybrid forms explored by writers to lend to spoken drama some of the appeal of opera. These were signs of the times, as well as distant precursors of later theatrical developments in China. There were other, more apparent and lasting contributions. In particular, advances were made in directing, acting, and staging technique, and the quality of the whole was generally raised by unified and imaginative productions. Many of those who built their reputations in wartime Shanghai continued fruitful careers in China before and after the Cultural Revolution period. Finally, the period left behind it dramatic works that more than one generation of audiences and varying tastes could find appealing, from Li Jianwu's *Youth* to Yang Jiang's comedy and tragedy, from Yao Ke's costume drama to Shi Tuo's and Ke Ling's *The Night Inn*. Building on the hard-won prewar development, the modern Chinese drama of wartime Shanghai served the needs of its time and passed on more than it had inherited.

THREE

Critical Ground: The Transformation of the May Fourth Era

T. D. Huters

By 1936 the May Fourth tradition of literary reform had fallen on hard times. The sense of common purpose that had prevailed during the early 1920s had long since vanished; even the unity of the movement's left wing—a unity that had seemed so impressive at the time of the formation of the League of Left-Wing Writers in 1930—had disintegrated under the pressure of constant factional bickering. The Two Slogans debate of 1936, which presented the unedifying spectacle of a dying Lu Xun lashing out at younger League allies, indicates the depth to which spirits had sunk.

With the increasing encroachment of the Japanese, however, and the eventual invasion in 1937, the dispersed energies of the literary revolution began to reassemble. After July 1937, the various alienated heirs of May Fourth put aside their differences of personality and of literary philosophy to join the common war effort. In a sense, this revival in the early war years represented one more in a series of waves of politicization of the literary scene, much like those occasioned by the revolution of 1925–1927 and by the formation of the League in 1930. Those earlier occasions, however, had never been marked by the near-unanimity of response that greeted the mobilization of 1937. Nor had any earlier politicization proved very enduring, as the dismal events of 1936 demonstrated so well.

For a variety of reasons, the politicization of 1937 was to be both profound and long-lasting. For one, the war against Japan was to last for eight years. A more important factor, however, was the wartime growth of the Communist-held regions of North China. These provided a location where the cultural authorities of the Communist capital, Yan'an, could put into practice theories about mass literature and national forms that had been the focus of attention among literary theorists in the decade before the war. By the 1940s the results of this experimentation had been formulated into a comprehensive theory that stood in sharp contrast to the principal tenets of May Fourth writing. Whereas the new literature after 1919 had been urban, produced by the educated largely for the educated and highly influenced by Western forms, the revolutionary literature prescribed by Yan'an was predominantly rural, aimed at a mass audience and modeled on indigenous literary techniques.

During the war, writers outside the Communist zones were divided into two distinct groups: those who had remained in the occupied coastal cities and those who had migrated with the government to China's Southwest. While nearly all these authors shared a sense of political engagement with the writers in Yan'an, literary developments in the two regions proceeded along different lines. In the occupied cities a sense of virtuous resistance to an absolute wrong contributed to an abiding concern with politics, while the increasing venality of the Nationalist government generated a combination of heightened political awareness and cynical despair in the Southwest. Although the three regions were largely isolated from one another, each had a rough idea of cultural events in the other two. Given the plain frustrations of life (and art) in the non-Communist areas, authors there came to regard Yan'an as the seat of the political and cultural future. Thus, for the first time, the literary fruits of the May Fourth movement were held up to invidious comparison with works that existed in fact, not merely in theory. This was a powerful additional stimulus for the continuing political concern of the May Fourth writers.

With the end of the war against Japan in 1945, however, much of the motivation for continued politicization of literature in the newly reunified "White," or Nationalist-controlled, areas seems to have disappeared. At this time, in fact, most urban Chinese allowed themselves a moment of optimism about the future of their country. The simple fact that the debilitating struggle against Japan had ended combined with awareness of China's radically elevated status in world politics to foster this hope. These factors were further linked with popular confidence that, with the expected lowering of the barriers that had divided the three great areas of wartime China, public opinion would force formation of a liberal, democratic government. For its part, the urban literary establishment hoped that this new freedom and democracy would foster a burgeoning of arts and literature worthy of the nation's new prestige. Thus the respected critic Zheng Zhenduo declared, in the "Inaugural Words" to the new journal *Wenyi fuxing* [Literary renaissance], that the postwar period would at last witness the culmination of the "unfinished work of the May Fourth movement." What Zheng apparently had in mind was a fruition of the hope for a literary renaissance that had so inspired early May Fourth authors.[1] And in the 1920s, at least, this hope had clearly implied a literature written to international rather than to national standards.

Along with this optimism, however, Zheng also expressed the equally common feeling that this cultural development could not "be separated from society," that the humanitarianism of the new literature could not be divorced from a similar humanitarianism in the realm of public policy: "We do not write just for the sake of writing, but we also consider that we should accord with the overall direction of the new China and write for the sake of democracy and for the vast majority of the people."[2] Within this short statement, then, rest the two ideas—of a literary renaissance and of the ultimate dependence of literature upon politics—that had been the lodestones around which literary debate had polarized itself since the early days of the May Fourth era. While Zheng could maintain the two ideas harmoniously in early 1946, the central fact about the urban literary arena in the postwar years was that it progressively abandoned the former conception in favor of the latter. Events of the civil war were to immediately rekindle the political fervor that had characterized the period of the War of Resistance and to make impossible any return to the sort of exclusive concern with esthetics that had in the mid-1930s been such a strong element of the May Fourth heritage.

Factors both external to and within the urban literary arena precipitated the rapid turning away from the notion of literary autonomy, which many prewar academic authors had seen as implicit in the idea of renaissance, to the idea of literature as a vehicle of social concern. The bitter experiences both of writers and of the publishing trade in general provided powerful external compulsion for this transformation. Equally important was the fact that a long-unresolved theoretical debate, ongoing within Chinese literary circles even before the May Fourth movement began, came to a head during this period and pushed cultural opinion decisively in one direction. These parallel extrinsic and intrinsic trends combined by 1949 to put literature and writers into a position of almost total dependence upon politics. With the Communist victory in 1949, the ascendance of the literary line first promulgated in Yan'an in 1942 was to be expected, but the continuing acquiescence of the writers of the May Fourth tradition to this line comes as something of a surprise. However, a detailed look at

[1] Zheng Zhenduo, "Fakan ci" [Inaugural words], *Wenyi fuxing* [Literary renaissance], 1,1 (10 January 1946), p. 6. For similar hopeful statements, see C. S. Ch'ien (Qian Zhongshu), "Chinese Literature," in Cao Wenyan, ed., *The Chinese Year Book* (1944–1945) (Shanghai: Shanghai Daily Tribune, 1946), pp. 127–128.

[2] Zheng, "Fakan ci," p. 6. For other expressions of the sense that culture was dependent upon society, see, among others, Shi Ren, "Wenhua yu zhengzhi" [Culture and politics], in *Wen xun* [Literary inquiry] 8,1 (15 January 1948): 369.

events on the urban literary scene during the years after 1945 will demonstrate how this acquiescence came to be inevitable.

THE PRESSURE OF EXTERNAL EVENTS

In Shanghai during 1945 it would have been difficult to predict the denouement of this contest for the ultimate disposition of literature. At a meeting held on December 17, 1945, the Shanghai branch of the Chinese National Association for Literature and the Arts (Zhonghua quanguo wenyi xiehui) was founded. The chairman of the newly constituted group, Zheng Zhenduo, noted that the organization was the successor to the Chinese National Anti-Aggression Association for Literature and the Arts (Zhonghua quanguo kangdi wenyi xiehui), which had been formed at Hankou in 1938 and had managed through the entire war both to maintain itself and to retain the membership of writers from all shades of the political, if not the social, spectrum. Zheng remarked that nonpartisanship had been the strong point of the earlier group, that it had not had internal factions, and that it had had branches throughout the country, including Yan'an and occupied Shanghai.[3] Zheng also stressed that the new organization was meant to benefit authors by protecting copyrights and aiding the down-and-out. The writer Yao Pengzi (now best known as the father of Yao Wenyuan) followed with a more detailed report of the earlier association's activities in the Southwest, while the dramatist and critic Li Jianwu told of life in Shanghai under the Japanese.[4] The authors in attendance ranged from political activists such as Lu Xun's widow, Xu Guangping, to the dour Shi Tuo, who had been a member of the esthetically minded Capital clique (Jingpai) in 1930s Peking (then Beiping). At the end of the meeting three resolutions were passed. The first called for the removal of censorship, the second for the guarantee of copyright, and the third for a special committee to investigate traitors.[5]

The unity manifest in the collection of writers present at this meeting and in their various pronouncements stands in impressive contrast to the contentious groupings and verbal battling in the literary circles of prewar Shanghai.[6] More than this, much of Zheng's speech was devoted to the first two resolutions, which evince a determination to make writing a

[3] Zhao Jingshen, "Ji Shanghai wenxie chengli dahui" [Notes on the founding meeting of the Shanghai Association for Literature and the Arts], *Wenyi fuxing* 1,1 (10 January 1946): 125. For a chattier account of this meeting by the same author, see the chapter, "Shanghai wenyijie de yige shenghui" [A great meeting in Shanghai literary circles], in *Wentan yijiu* [Memories of the literary stage] (Shanghai: Beixin shuju, 1948), pp. 152–163.

[4] Zhao Jingshen, "Ji Shanghai wenxie," p. 126.

[5] Appended to Zhao Jingshen, "Ji Shanghai wenxie," p. 127.

[6] This unity is noted by Yao Sufeng in "Ai Shanghui wenhua" [Mourn for Shanghai culture], *Shanghai wenhua* [Shanghai culture] 8 (September 1946): 25.

viable profession. Along with this almost trade-union flavor, however, there was a political coloration not far below the surface. The declaration made by the meeting and appended to Zhao Jingshen's account of the gathering is full of references to the sense of wartime mission that had been the raison d'être of the parent Anti-Aggression Association. Its stress upon the responsibilities of literature to society clearly echoes Zheng Zhenduo's "Inaugural Words." Like Zheng's remarks, the declaration displays the ambiguity inherent in regarding literature both as autonomous and as part of the political process.

The wartime unity, however, had come about through the quintessentially political desire to resist aggression. Purely professional issues, such as defense of copyright, had yet to prove they could sustain this unity in postwar times. For professional issues ever to replace the resonant political themes of the war, the economy of the nation would have had to change from a wartime to a peacetime footing. Only this would have allowed professional writers to support themselves at their trade. That no such change took place must be counted as the major reason that professional considerations as such would ultimately be of minor concern to authors: given the economic situation of China in the late 1940s, no profession could arise about which to be concerned.[7]

The damage that inflation visited upon the urban middle class in this period is well known. Publishing, however, was hit doubly hard: it suffered both from the inflation of its basic costs as well as from its dependence—for its very existence—upon the ever-diminishing purchasing power of the petite bourgeoisie. It was thus caught in a squeeze between rising costs and its inability to raise prices fast enough to keep pace. Since wages were subject after April 1946 to automatic escalation according to a government-enforced cost-of-living index,[8] the only elastic cost was the manuscript fee. This fell to miserably low levels.[9] The modern Chinese

[7] Tian Han was astute enough to see that professionalization was a moot point as long as the civil war ravaged the economy. See "Zhao hun" [Calling back the soul], *Shanghai wenhua* 9 (October 1946): 18.

[8] See Suzanne Pepper, *Civil War in China: The Political Struggle, 1945–1949* (Berkeley: University of California Press, 1978), pp. 100–101.

[9] See also "Shanghai wenhua" [Shanghai culture] section of *Shanghai wenhua* 4 (May 1946): 6. Some of the more flagrant examples include the fact that newspapers could not afford to pay authors as much per word as it cost to set the type. The figures for early 1946 were 5000 *yuan* for each 1000 characters for manuscript fees, as against 6400 *yuan* per 1000 words in typesetting costs. See "Shanghai wenhuajie jiantao zuotanhui" [Panel discussion on the cultural situation in Shanghai], *Shanghai wenhua* 4 (May 1946): 14. The discussion group included Zheng Zhenduo, Tang Tao, and Ke Ling. To give some idea of prices at the time, the issue of *Shanghai wenhua* in which the panel discussion appeared cost 400 *yuan*.

Probably the most extreme example is the fee that Shen Congwen collected for royalties from the Kaiming Book Company. For an eighteen-year period, ending in the summer of 1946, Shen received a grand total of 360 *yuan*. See "Zhongguo wenhua" [Chinese culture]

writer's dream of supporting himself at his trade thus receded even further during the postwar years.[10] Even when also working as an editor, a writer had difficulty making ends meet. It was not unusual to find "literary workers" holding two or more jobs, one of which was invariably teaching, unpleasant as that pursuit was to many writers.[11] The cost to literary creativity of such scrambling to stay solvent should be evident.

This uncertainty of livelihood for individuals was matched by similar uncertainty among publishers of books, journals, and newspapers. All contemporary discussions of the state of the trade at this time mention its fragility as its most pertinent characteristic. That the first editions of most books ran between one and two thousand copies, that a book was regarded as a runaway bestseller if it sold over ten thousand copies, and that even a newspaper was regarded as doing well if its circulation reached twenty thousand—all give some substance to the constant reiteration of this tale of woe. Furthermore, purchases of advertisements were regarded by advertisers as little more than acts of charity, not as a vital part of a marketing procedure.[12]

---

section of *Shanghai wenhua* 9 (October 1946): 9–10. In this interview Shen shows that his relatively low rate of literary productivity made it impossible for him to live off his writing. He claims that Ba Jin was the only living Chinese writer to have been able to do so.

[10] This dream was given expression in an untitled 1945 article by Lao She, recently translated in *Chinese Literature* 11 (1978) (see especially pp. 59–60). Lao She says that he attempted to become a professional writer through the writing of *Luotuo Xiangzi* [Camel Xiangzi]. He did, in fact, succeed, but only through the "royalties" (actually a substantial honorarium) from the American edition of the English translation of the work.

[11] Lao She is very clear about this in the article cited above: "I do not like teaching. For one thing, I'm not a very learned person, and so I sometimes feel uneasy. Even if I had been able to teach well, it did not afford me the same pleasure as writing" (p. 60). Xu Xu, just as his bestseller *Feng xiaoxiao* [The soughing wind] was being published in 1940, gave voice to the feeling that teaching "harmed his creativity." See "Shanghai wenhua" section of *Shanghai wenhua* 9 (October 1946): 4.

As for moonlighting, Zheng Zhenduo (as of 1946), in addition to serving on official commissions in charge of recovering Chinese books that the Japanese and puppet rulers had collected, was editor of the "general interest" magazine *Minzhu* [Democracy], coeditor of *Wenyi fuxing,* and editor of the literary supplement (*Fukan*) of the newspaper *Lianhe ribao,* as well as being a sought-after contributor to other journals.

[12] Ba Jin indicates the precariousness of publishing in the afterword to his bestseller *Disi bingshi* [The fourth ward]. He notes that the original publisher folded before the book was released; see *The Fourth Ward,* "Houji" (Shanghai: Chenguang, 1948), p. 210.

For figures on the printing of books, see Lou Feng, "*Shanghai wenhua:* dushurende banlü" [*Shanghai Culture:* the reader's companion], *Shanghai wenhua* 7 (August 1946): 62. The author notes ominously that, of the 2000 copies printed, it was common to sell only 200 or 300. See also Lee-hsia Hsu Ting, *Government Control of the Press in Modern China, 1900–1949* (Cambridge, Mass.: Harvard University Press, 1974), p. 256, n. 15. For figures on newspapers and journals, see Zhuang Darong, "Zhongguo ye you 'zuixiaoshu' ma?" [Does China also have 'bestsellers'?], *Shanghai wenhua* 2 (10 February 1946): 6–7. The editors of *Shanghai wenhua* noted in their sixth issue (July 1946), p. 7, that they would like

The existence of a flourishing sensationalized popular press made these difficulties even harder to bear for the heirs of May Fourth, who worked in what they regarded as the mainstream of publishing. One commentator noted that, whereas the literary stage in prewar Shanghai had been dominated by the two mutually exclusive camps of "progressives" and "conservatives," that breach had been healed only to be replaced by one between the consolidated "orthodox" camp and a newly ascendant "pornographic" camp.[13] The split between leftist and "nonpolitical" writers had resolved itself into a more traditional opposition between what the urban literary establishment regarded as "high" and "low" culture. The principal medium for this sort of new popular literature was the "tabloid magazine" (*xiaobaohua zhoukan*), so called because it was the successor to the prewar tabloid "mosquito press." Such organs had become periodicals after 1945, when it proved easier to secure governmental licensing as weeklies than as dailies.[14] The healthy circulation of these tabloids gave evidence that, even were the publishing world to become financially viable, it would not necessarily redound to the benefit of serious writers. Awareness of this fact threw a long shadow over the literary arena: not only was doubt cast on the possibility of a literary renaissance, but the situation also conflicted with the humanitarian notion of literature in the service of the popular will. The only way out of the resulting impasse, and the one that the critic Yao Sufeng took, was to posit that contemporary culture had been poisoned at the source by some powerful force. Speculation about the nature of that force was not long in coming.

When one considers what was widely regarded as the general lowering of taste in the mid-1940s, the contrast with the courageous theater scene in occupied Shanghai immediately crops up. Not only had the luminaries of the Shanghai intelligentsia been attracted to playwriting, but the theater in

20,000 subscribers, which would be a "firm basis" on which to continue their venture. They also admitted that at the time they were quite far from that figure.

According to Cao Juren, the largest-selling periodical of the time was *Guancha* [Observer], a liberal Shanghai publication that had a circulation over 57,000. Cao notes, however, that had it not been for obvious government restrictions, its circulation would most likely have gone over 100,000. See *Caifang erji* [News coverage: the second collection] (Hong Kong: Chuangkan chubanshe, 1954), p. 95.

[13] See Yao Sufeng, "Ai Shanghai wenhua," p. 25. See also Zhuang Darong, "Zhongguo ye you," p. 6. The lack of a functioning writer's market is perhaps best illustrated by the fact that, even though manuscript fees in the popular press were between 7500 *yuan* and 10,000 *yuan* for each 1000 characters (i.e., almost twice the rate for the mainstream press [see note 9]), there was said to be a shortage of manuscripts. This is probably a good indication of the impossibility of earning a living wage via creative writing. See also note 14 below.

[14] For information on the tabloids, see "Xiaobaohua zhoukan wenti zuotanhui" [Panel discussion on the question of tabloid weeklies], *Shanghai wenhua* 4 (May 1946): 115–117. An interesting facet of the difficulty with licensing is that much of it sprang from the suspicion of the authorities about the tabloid publishers' complicity with the Japanese (ibid., p. 15).

those years had actually been commercially viable (a fact that caused some of the playwrights to grow defensive in the face of a certain amount of scorn from the left).[15] While reliance on the market—not to mention the fear of Japanese and "puppet" censorship—had precluded the sort of obvious political message apparently favored by the playwright Tian Han, the fact remained that the very act of participation in theatrical activities was highly political.[16] Thus, while plays produced at this time most often contained no explicit political content, authors such as Li Jianwu were *personally* politicized by their experiences. In other words, the Shanghai "theater boom" was interpreted in the years immediately following as evidence that the sort of highly charged political atmosphere that demanded personal commitment was of maximum benefit to the arts.[17] At the same time, there was a corollary tendency to regard the writers who had produced the unsocially conscious literature so common in wartime Shanghai as having been particularly predisposed to succumb to the blandishments of the Japanese and puppet governments.[18]

While there was an initial willingness to regard the "soft" (i.e., frivolous) literature that continued to appear after the war as the result of the reading public's natural desire to relax after eight years of enforced bad news,[19] this notion soon gave way to another interpretation. As sensation-

[15] For a capsule description of drama in occupied Shanghai that displays a certain defensiveness of tone, see Li Jianwu's statement in "Zhanshi zhanhou wenyi jiantao zuotanhui" [Panel discussion on literature and the arts during wartime and after], *Shanghai wenhua* 6 (July 1946): 14. For a left-wing criticism of the commercialization of the Shanghai theater, see Tian Han, "Zhao hun," p. 18. See also Edward Gunn's article in this volume.

[16] Li Jianwu, for instance, was eventually jailed during the final years of the war. See Zhao Jingshen, "Ji Shanghai wenxie," p. 126.

[17] The fact that so many writers produced either their best or their only works of fiction or drama during the war consituted an empirical basis for such a belief; this phenomenon is discussed at greater length below. The contrast between wartime progress in the literary movement and the stagnation thereafter is duly noted by Hu Feng in "Xian cong chongpo qifen he duoxing kaishi" [Begin with breaking up the atmosphere and the inertia], *Zhongguo zuojia* [The Chinese writer], inaugural issue (March 1948): 8–11. This journal was the official organ of the Literature and the Arts Association and was heir to *Kangzhan wenyi* [Literature and the arts of the resistance]. The latter magazine, as noted by Yao Pengzi (in Zhao Jingshen, "Ji Shanghai wenxie") managed to publish throughout the war in the face of great difficulties. The greater difficulties of writers in the late 1940s is shown by the fact that the successor magazine, originally scheduled to appear in August 1946 (see "Shanghai wenhua" section of *Shanghai wenhua* 7 [August 1946]), did not actually appear until March 1948 and then published only three issues.

[18] See, for example, Guo Shaoyu, "Cong wenrende xingqing sixiang lundao juanxingde wenren" [Literary people: from sensibility to timidity], *Wenyi fuxing* 1,1: 8.

[19] Ibid. In this article Guo gives this account of the genesis of "soft" literature while showing the dangers to which it was subject. Lou Feng ("Dushurende banlü," p. 62) also blamed the flood of pornographic materials on war-induced hedonism. Ke Ling seems to be one of the few people who regarded the phenomenon of bad taste more or less simply as an insoluble problem of human nature. See "Shanghai wenhuajie jiantao," p. 13.

alistic writing came increasingly to dominate the market and as the political situation continued to deteriorate, many critics felt that the Nationalist government was deliberately fostering frivolous literature to distract the mass mind from serious concerns of state.[20] That escapist literature had been a prominent feature of the literary scene in the Southwest in the dreary years after 1938[21] could only have increased this suspicion. Thus, by 1947, when the literary left was being progressively forced by strong governmental action to move from Shanghai to Hong Kong, the left-wing critic Lin Mohan could accuse this sensationalist stream of writing of being nothing other than the cultural expression of the right-wing government: "In these pornographic publications they are in fact depicting their own lives."[22] The cultural desert in which hopes for a literary renaissance had come to languish was thus to be increasingly characterized in political terms.

The presence of American culture in postwar China also contributed to this politicization. If American predominance in the postwar world had a secure foundation in realpolitik fact, China's new leadership position in world councils threw an even sharper light on its actual material weakness. This was as true in the arts as it was in politics. Furthermore, because of China's physical size and population, it was inevitably compared with the United States and the U.S.S.R.[23] The close contacts between the Chinese and American governments, as well as the traditional Western dominance in the treaty ports, made the United States' position in China definitely pre-eminent over that of the Soviet Union. While America's steadfast support for the Nationalist regime was, after 1947, to cause an already politicized intelligentsia to regard that country and all its works as evil on simple political grounds, in 1945 there were already several cultural reasons for Chinese literary figures to be alarmed about the American presence. The general attribution of the wartime "drama boom" to the Japanese-imposed ban on Hollywood films illustrates the substance of the concern. The end of the war and the resumption of the supply of American films saw the abrupt end of this vibrant theater.[24] But, as Ke Ling also

[20] See Shen Congwen, "Zenyang ban yifen hao baozhi" [How to run a good newspaper], *Shanghai wenhua,* 8 (September 1946): 23. Shen notes the prevalence of this theory while denying its plausibility. Guo Shaoyu, in "Cong wenrende xingqing," discusses hedonistic literature and the cult of estheticism as arising from the same *shi yan zhi* ("poetry as [personal] expression") sources.

[21] Lee-hsia Hsu Ting, *Government Control,* p. 148.

[22] Lin Mohan, "Chuiside 'liumang wenhua' " [On the dying "hoodlum culture"], in *Shi he long* [Lions and dragons] (Hong Kong: Renjian shuwu, 1949), pp. 30–31. The article was originally published in the 10 January 1947 issue of the Hong Kong newspaper *Hua shang bao.*

[23] See Zhuang Darong, "Zhongguo ye you," p. 6.

[24] See Ke Ling's comments in "Shanghai wenhuajie jiantao," p. 14. It is important to note, however, that Ke Ling also saw increased fear of censorship as contributing to this demise of live theater.

notes, the flood of American movies was only the most conspicuous part of a general trend.

Throughout 1946, the magazine *Shanghai wenhua* [Shanghai culture] discussed the enormous quantity of American cultural imports of all kinds as probably the most serious long-range problem facing a nation seeking to establish a new culture of its own.[25] The magazine, for its part, did its best to balance each article it published about the cultural scene in the U.S. with one about the Soviet Union, but this effort could not overcome the tremendous commercial advantage that American publications had in the coastal cities.[26] Most cultural figures felt both envious of the American success (while wishing somehow to emulate it) and resentful of the consequences of this success for the future of Chinese culture.[27] Such a mixture of feelings led inevitably to very strongly held convictions. The tremendous hostility toward the United States that came into existence among left-wing intellectuals by 1949 thus, plainly, had other than strictly political roots. To the extent that American culture had by then pre-empted the local market, Chinese authors regarded the U.S. as a primary obstacle to creation of an indigenous cultural milieu; and to the extent that American cultural artifacts appealed to their audience's escapist tendencies, rather than to the high seriousness that wartime experiences had imbued in "orthodox" Chinese writers, the United States was regarded as a force for cultural reaction regardless of its activities in the civil war.[28]

While economic issues were central to the eventual disaffection of the great majority of writers, it is unlikely that the turn away from the government would have been so complete without the intermittent despotism of the Nationalist Party's policy toward publishing and the world of letters. Virtually every policy the Party pursued politicized authors against it. The most obvious example was government control of the press. The variety of

[25] See, for example, "Shanghai wenhuajie jiantao," p. 14, and especially "Weixiande 'dancheng jiaotong' " [A dangerous "one-way traffic"], *Shanghai wenhua* 8 (September 1946): 13.

[26] The "Shanghai wenhua" section of *Shanghai wenhua* 9 (October 1946), for instance, notes (p. 5) that *Time* and *Life* had a combined circulation of 9000 in China in 1946. It is unlikely that many magazines published in China achieved that figure. The problem of the American presence in periodical sales is also discussed in "Shanghai wenhuajie jiantao," p. 14.

[27] This combination of envy and resentment is apparent in the article of Zhuang Darong, "Zhongguo ye you." It is also a feature of Sun Dezhen's piece, "Guanyu wenhua jiaoliu" [On cultural exchange], *Shanghai wenhua* 3 (March 1946): 12.

[28] The notion that the United States was a force for cultural reaction can be found in many articles of this period. One of the most conspicuous is Mao Dun's "Hai xu zhunbei changqi er jianjuede douzheng" [We must still prepare for a long and arduous struggle], in *"Wusi" sazhounian jinian zhuanji* [Collection commemorating the thirtieth anniversary of the May Fourth movement] (n.p.: Xinhua shudian, 1949), especially pp. 40–41.

As another example, Cao Yu, on his American tour—as reported in the "Shanghai wenhua" section of *Shanghai wenhua* 8 (September 1946): 6—wrote back that the United States was a place wholly devoted to the material and thus devoid of any inspiration to the writer.

direct and indirect actions the authorities took against dissenting publications was remarkable,[29] if eventually counterproductive. While the government had pursued essentially the same methods before the war, the intellectual environment in the intervening years had changed significantly. In the 1930s the split between leftist and "nonpolitical" writers had tended to isolate grievances against governmental suppression within what had been after all only a faction, influential though it may have been, in the publishing world. However, the postwar unity of the intelligentsia—a unity forged originally in opposition to the Japanese and maintained afterward by determined resistance to the government's prosecution of the civil war—caused governmental action against any segment of the print media to be construed as an attack on the whole estate. Hostility between the Nationalist Party and the intellectuals became aggravated as each attack on official policy invited a reprisal, which in turn resulted in more dissidence. Ironically, the effect of the rhetoric of unity and freedom that the government had encouraged in the early years of the war proved impossible to contain when the ruling party changed its tack.

The politicization of the intelligentsia was a long process that had proceeded variously in the three great regions of wartime China. By the time that the Southwest and the occupied zone were reunited at the end of the war, the cultural figures in each region had evolved different perspectives on the situation of China. One can gain a clear picture of the demoralization and consequent search for political solutions that occurred in the Southwest by reading the wartime polemical writings of such prewar pillars of the Capital clique as Li Guangtian and the very influential poet Wen Yiduo. It seems that the more naive about politics these men had been in 1937, the more they were affected by the dismal realities of Nationalist rule after 1938.[30] While physical privation was something for which they were prepared, the spiritual oppression that afflicted them increasingly as the war dragged on came as a real shock to the free-China intellectuals. On the other hand, the cultural figures who had remained in Shanghai had expected little but oppression from the Japanese occupiers; there was no disillusionment when it proved to be forthcoming.[31] The simplicity of the Shanghai situation of "us" and "them" was, in fact, decisive in increasing the sense of personal involvement that characterized the drama movement.

[29] For a partial listing, see Lee-hsia Hsu Ting, *Government Control,* p. 167f.

[30] The best account of this disillusionment is to be found in Wen Yiduo, "Baniande huiyi yu ganxiang" [Thoughts and memories of the past eight years], in *Wen Yiduo quanji* [Complete works of Wen Yiduo], (Shanghai: Kaiming, 1948), Jiji [Section F], "Yanjiang lu" [Record of speeches], pp. 17–22.

[31] Probably the best account of a Shanghai intellectual's impressions of the war is Zheng Zhenduo's *Zhiju sanji* [Hermit's miscellany] (Shanghai: Shanghai chuban gongsi, 1951).

The shock for those who stayed behind came, rather, in 1945. Instead of a sympathetic government of compatriots, the Shanghai writers encountered a ruthless and self-seeking group of bureaucrats, from whom the most prominent intellectuals in the interior had long been alienated. When cultural notes were compared, for instance, it soon became apparent that theater had been freer in occupied Shanghai than it had been in "free" Chungking.[32] At first, those who had gone inland hectored those who had stayed behind: writers who had not lived under the wartime Nationalist government were told of the serious political lessons they had yet to learn.[33] But those who had stayed behind, if they had made any attempt to resist the blandishments of the enemy, had undergone a very hard time of it themselves.

Moreover, it was also true that communications between Shanghai and the Southwest had never been completely severed. A number of plays written in the interior, for instance, had been produced in Shanghai in the early 1940s. It is thus fairly certain that the Shanghai writers had more knowledge of conditions under the wartime Nationalists than Li Guangtian gave them credit for. Zheng Zhenduo's address at the inaugural meeting of the Association for Literature and the Arts (discussed above) can, in fact, be read as an implicit warning to the returning authorities against trying to impose in Shanghai the repression that had bred so much discontent in Kunming and Chungking. If it is true that Zheng and other writers were willing to let bygones be bygones if the government was intent upon real liberalization, it is equally true that advance knowledge of the dismal record of Chiang Kai-shek's government had primed the Shanghai writers to be particularly sensitive when as early as 1945 official interference began to make itself felt.[34] For those unaware of the Nationalist Party's wartime behavior, comparisons between the Japanese and the newly returned government rapidly increased their political awareness, already raised by wartime experiences. In any event, any initial differences between the two groups were soon effaced by the realization that the situation confronting them both after 1945 was as demanding as anything they had had to deal with in the years of the resistance struggle.

When writers eventually sought to express their concern over the realities of postwar China, however, they were confronted with more than just

[32] Zheng Zhenduo makes this observation as part of the "Zhanshi zhanhou wenyi jiantao," p. 14.

[33] Li Guangtian was among those admonishing the writers who stayed in Shanghai; see his 1946 essay, "Rende gaizao yu wenyi fangxiang" [Personal reform and the direction of literature and the arts], in *Lun wenxue jiaoyu* [On literary education] (Shanghai: Wenhua gongzuoshe, 1950), pp. 1–10, especially pp. 8–9. The article is significantly subtitled "Gei kangzhan qijian liuzai lunxianqulide pengyoumen" [For our friends who remained in the occupied areas during the War of Resistance].

[34] Lee-hsia Hsu Ting, *Government Control*, p. 167.

censorship. Because of both the feeble economic base of publishing and the proliferation of bureaucratic racketeering, much publishing (and nearly all newspaper publishing) came under direct governmental control.[35] Even the highly praised and editorially liberal newspaper *Dagong bao* [L'Impartial] was backed by a faction within the Nationalist Party.[36] Domination of the market by such semi-official agencies made it that much easier to silence the opposition by first isolating it and then shutting it down.[37] As a result, cultural figures increasingly came to feel that they could only counter this heavy official hand through political participation of their own. The initial sense among writers and journalists that they formed an estate eventually developed into a consciousness of something like a class distinction between working writers and well-connected publishers. And since, by 1947, writers had learned by hard experience that politics had come to mean nothing more than armed struggle, the only place they could turn was to the Communist Party. The Party, for its part, was willing to hold out the promise of complete freedom of the press, something the beleaguered Nationalists could not bring themselves to support, even in theory.[38] While it is unlikely that many writers took the Communists' promises at face value, one may presume that, by a certain point in the late 1940s, it no longer mattered. Writers had become so inured to political control, whether imposed by the censor or by their own employers, that it had come to seem inevitable. Objections came to center on the way it was exercised, rather than on the fact of political control itself.

In such circumstances, it was impossible for anyone to adhere long to the notion of a free and autonomous cultural realm. Thus Derk Bodde could report from Peking in early 1949: "Most Chinese newspapermen sincerely favor what the new government is doing and therefore accept the new regulations without hesitation. This explains the ease with which their publications have changed since liberation, despite the fact that in many cases the staff of these publications has remained relatively intact save for

[35] See Cao Juren, *Caifang,* p. 148, and Lee-hsia Hsu Ting, *Government Control,* pp. 165–166. On pp. 148 and 168 Hsu Ting also notes the dependence of publishers upon government contracts for textbooks.

[36] Pepper, *Civil War in China,* pp. 436–439, details the extent of the relationship between the government and *Dagong bao.* Cao Juren (in *Caifang,* pp. 149–150) explains the peculiar independence of the newspaper, in spite (or, indeed, because) of this relationship.

[37] The government's preferred mechanism here was to wait for the independent newspapers, such as *Wenhui bao,* to publish accounts of events that could be construed as being unfavorable to the government. Since these events were not reported in the controlled portions of the press they were, in the eyes of the government, "opinions" and "rumors" that were deliberately provocative, rather than news and thus grounds for action against the newspapers that had published them. See Lee-hsia Hsu Ting, *Government Control,* pp. 168–169, 177.

[38] The policies of the government and of the Communist Party are set forth by Pan Gongzhan and Chen Jiakang, respectively, in "Xinwen ziyou wenti zuotanhui" [Panel discussion on the question of freedom of the press], *Shanghai wenhua* 9 (October 1946): 12–13.

a few shifts in the higher echelons."[39] Although its full consequences cannot be explored here, a devastating sequence of external factors had in these years pushed the literary establishment into a position of political dependence from which it would prove impossible for it to extricate itself after Liberation, even during those times when the Party momentarily loosened its grip.

INTERNAL MOMENTUM

Like the external situation, the internal disposition of the urban literary world influenced its evolution. Some changes were merely responses to the external pressures, others the culmination of trends long extant in writing and criticism. The hopes for a literary renaissance seemed to find justification immediately after the war in the publication of a spate of works written during it that expressed either their authors' experiences of the war or a sophisticated view of the problems of modern China. Such works included Qian Zhongshu's *Weicheng* [Besieged city], Shi Tuo's *Guoyuancheng ji* [Records of Orchard City], and Li Guangtian's *Yinli* [Gravitation]. The news that Bian Zhilin, Feng Zhi, and Zang Kejia were all writing fiction provided hope that such work would continue to flourish. In the realm of the theater, the publication of such fruits of the Shanghai wartime drama movement as Shi Tuo and Ke Ling's *Ye dian* [The night inn] and the work of Li Jianwu was similarly auspicious.

It is interesting, however, that none of these writers—with the exception of Shi Tuo and Li Jianwu—had previously been associated with fiction or drama: they had all been poets and essayists before the war, and most were literary scholars as well. This outstanding group of works obviously reflected a new literary proficiency in China, but it pointed in several other directions as well. For one thing, it was emblematic of the new unity in the literary arena that these prewar "esthetes" wrote in the genres favored by the leftist realist writers of the 1920s and 1930s, instead of the traditional—and conservative—genres of poetry and the essay. This new turn to fiction and drama was also symptomatic of the authors' need for new means of expression that were both more "faithful to reality" and not bound up by tradition—a tradition that the war had convinced some was most undesirable.[40]

[39] Derk Bodde, *Peking Diary* (Greenwich, Conn.: Fawcett, 1967), pp. 142–143.

[40] On the unsuitability of traditional ways of writing, see Wen Yiduo, "Xin wenyi he wenxue yichan" [The new literature and arts and the literary heritage], in *Quanji*, Jiji, pp. 29–30. For an account of the turn to drama as a means of seeking realism, see Guo Tianwen, "Li Jianwu lun" [An account of Li Jianwu], *Shanghai wenhua* 6 (July 1946): 30–31. For a theoretical account of the lowering of literary mode to express feelings believed to be inexpressible in established modes, see Qian Zhongshu, *Tan yi lu* [Discussions on arts] (Shanghai: Kaiming, 1948), pp. 42–43.

The writers who moved into these new genres, however, did not do so with the zeal one expects of converts—a hint that, external impediments to literary expression aside, there were factors inhering in the literary situation that militated against a sense of an imminent explosion of creativity. The actual attitude of these new novelists is revealed in their comments about their new work, which are invariably more than ordinarily self-effacing. Even as critics were proclaiming the new age of literature, some of the more successful practitioners were oddly lacking in enthusiasm. Li Guangtian, for instance, wrote in an afterword to *Gravitation* that, after reading *Madame Bovary,* he

> realized that all I can do is follow a narrow path and edge straight ahead; it really is quite pitiful. Ba Jin's *Qiyuan* [Leisure garden] is a good book, the best among those of his works that I've read. . . . In the afterword he says that "this novel is my creation." This sentence moved me because most of my sense of disillusionment [with myself] comes from my realization that my own novel cannot be considered "a creation"; all it does is to profile history and, at that, it only draws a simple outline. I almost believe that I have a limitation that cannot be overcome, that I am only fit at best to scribble a few short essays. When I thought of this, I could not help but sense a hopeless sort of sadness.[41]

Qian Zhongshu wrote in a similar vein in the preface to *Besieged City*: "I conceived how this book should be written, but my abilities were not up to it; as it is actually written it does not accord with my ideal. The ideal is nothing but an enticement, or even a jibe. Before the writing it is a beautiful objective; after the writing is finished, it becomes a cruel contrast."[42] The tone of these comments suggests Cao Xueqin's famous indictment of his own *Shitou ji* [The story of the stone] as nothing but "pages full of idle words"[43] and carries with it the same ambiguity about the legitimacy of the undertaking.

Li Jianwu, in a published "letter," made explicit some of the reasons for this reticence. Remarking on how he came to write plays for a living, he says: "I jumped from the ivory tower, discarded my high-mindedness, removed myself from the temptation [of being used by the enemy during the war] and from that point on took the theater as my livelihood. I became what the gentry regard as an unspeakable thespian [*xizi*]."[44] Li goes on to comment, almost offhandedly, that although he is now considered to be a dramatist, he has no plans to write more plays.

These statements have several facets. The need to express the trauma of

[41] Li Guangtian, "Houji" [Afterword] to *Yinli* (Shanghai: Chenguang, 1948), p. v.

[42] Qian Zhongshu, "Xu" [Preface] to *Weicheng* (Shanghai: Chenguang, 1949), p. i.

[43] David Hawkes, trans., *The Story of the Stone* (Harmondsworth: Penguin, 1973), 1: 51.

[44] Li Jianwu, "Yu youren shu" [Letter to a friend], *Shanghai wenhua* 6 (July 1946): 28.

the war is clear, but other components are more problematic. One of these factors is the evident sense of shame and unfamiliarity in working in what had always been regarded as genres unworthy of the highly educated man. Another, more nebulous, is a sense of the futility of literature itself. That is to say, the feeling of not being able to reach the ideal was perhaps not so much one of personal failure as the manifestation of an awareness that, given the circumstances of the times, literature was a particularly frail institution.[45] In a sense, the time for a flourishing of modern Chinese literature had passed before it had really arrived: the great works of European fictional and dramatic realism held out a promise that was, at the same time, a reminder that the conditions that made them possible were not to obtain in China. Highly educated and cosmopolitan Chinese authors were condemned, if not to live in the past, then at least to be unable to find a place for their talents in the present. From their standpoint the literary future was bleak and uncertain.[46] Seen in this light, the fact that Li Jianwu should cease to write plays, or that *Gravitation* was its author's only novel, becomes less surprising. Rather than marking the beginning of careers in creative writing, these wartime works were unique responses to the times in which their highly educated authors lived. The literary tradition in which these men worked seems to have prevented them from assuming a more affirmative posture toward the creation of a new literature, at least by them.[47]

If fiction and drama were marked by an initial efflorescence followed by progressive stagnation, literary criticism enjoyed a vogue during the entire period. Paradoxically, the enthusiasm lacking in an author's comments upon his own work is often found instead in his comments as a critic.[48] The high esteem accorded criticism is indicated by the prevalent opinion that the failure of modern China to produce a successful body of creative

[45] Leo Lee's comment that he detects in Lu Xun's writings after 1926 "the hollow echo of a despairing note: that the written word is ultimately futile against the onslaught of the inhuman" almost certainly applies to the group of writers under discussion here as well. See Leo Lee, "Literature on the Eve of Revolution: Reflections on Lu Xun's Leftist Years, 1927–1936," *Modern China* 2, 3 (July 1976): 290.

[46] See Li Jianwu's "Yu youren shu," p. 29, which he ends with just such an expression of pessimism.

[47] Writing in 1979, Bian Zhilin painted a melancholy picture of his attempts at fiction writing in the 1940s. His sense of being driven by the nature and pace of events to work in a genre in which he did not feel quite comfortable emerges clearly from the account. See Bian Zhilin, "Wancheng yu kaiduan: jinian shiren Wen Yiduo bashi shengchen" [Completion and beginnings: commemorating the eightieth birthday of the poet Wen Yiduo], in *Wenxue pinglun* [Literary review] 3 (1979): 70–71.

[48] See, for instance, Li Guangtian's defense of literature in "Wenxue yundong yu wenxue chuangzuo" [The literary movement and literary creation], in *Lun wenxue jiaoyu*, especially p. 21. See also C. S. Ch'ien, "Chinese Literature."

literature was largely attributable to the lack of objective and conscientious criticism. Concern focused on two areas of critical inquiry: criticism as a necessary prerequisite to an autonomous profession of literature and criticism as the mediator between contending theories of literature. As Zhu Ziqing (himself an influential critic) noted, the fact that there appeared at this time more histories of Chinese literary criticism than of literature per se reflected, among other things, an attempt to raise the status of criticism.[49]

Criticism considered as a prerequisite, the first area of concern, was essentially a catch-all. It reflected a mistaking of cause for effect: failing to see the deep structural reasons, both external and internal, for the inability of postwar Chinese literature to establish itself, writers placed the blame on various technical features of the literary establishment itself. Shen Congwen gave voice to this idea in an article entitled "On the Movement to Liberate Book Reviews," originally published in the Tianjin *Dagong bao*. The failure of modern China to produce any great works of literature should not be considered remarkable, he avers, in light of the fact that literary circles are organized in self-protecting old-boy networks in which critics occupy a beggarly position. Authors are thin-skinned and do not admit the right of critics to take them to task. Accordingly, few serious reviews are published, and there is no pressure on authors to raise the level of their work.[50] Li Changzhi, in an article published in May 1946, makes very similar points, adding that whenever he asks friends to write reviews they smile, sigh, and beg off for fear of becoming involved in personal vendettas. (Earlier, while the war was on, they had declined for fear of harming the community effort against the enemy.)[51] Both men advocated the creation of a journal devoted exclusively to serious, impartial book reviews.

The full extent to which the lack of good criticism was seen as an impediment to the professionalization of writing, however, is outlined by Mao Dun in an article he wrote for *Shanghai wenhua*. In condemning what he calls the "star system" (*mingxing zhuyi*) of modern Chinese letters, he bemoans the difficulties of publishing the works of young writers. Since there are no authoritative book reviews, reader and publisher alike can only trust to past experience in selecting authors. This has led to a sort of feudal system in which, even if a publisher takes a chance on a new

[49] Zhu Ziqing, " 'Shiwenping' de fazhan" [The development of the "critical note"], *Wenyi fuxing* 1,6 (July 1946): 759–760.

[50] Shen Congwen, "Shupingde ziyou jiefang yundong" [The movement to liberate book reviews], *Shanghai wenhua* 4 (May 1946): 18.

[51] Li Changzhi, "Wenyi piping zai jintian" [Literary criticism today], *Wenchao yuekan* [Literary tide monthly] 1,1 (May 1946): 9–10.

author, he will only do so under the sponsorship of, and with a preface written by, an already established writer.[52]

While each of these points was valid, the assumption that remedying them would solve writers' problems represents an optimistic—even characteristic—unwillingness to grasp the more nettling underlying problems. Hu Feng, for instance, goes so far in discounting purely economic factors as to say that, in the past, material difficulties (combined with political pressure) had even provided the impetus for the development of the movement for a new literature.[53] The almost willful confusion of cause and effect involved in assigning such a large portion of the blame for the literary stalemate to deficiencies in criticism was not, however, something new in the history of modern Chinese literature. Liang Qichao's assessment of the novel as key to the "renewal" of the Chinese nation is an earlier and even clearer example of such confusion.[54] The enormous influence granted to criticism reflected not only a sense that good literature could be legislated into existence, but also a deep ambivalence about the nature of literature itself. On one hand, the very fact that so much attention was focused on the revival of literature bespoke a feeling that it was one of the dominant categories of thought and a determining constituent of the culture as a whole. On the other hand, the heavy emphasis on criticism implies that literature was considered profoundly tractable, a mere handmaiden to the more primary intellectual endeavors, important as it may have been as esthetic packaging for them.

These two perspectives can in fact be related directly to the debate over literature's status that constituted the second area of critical concern. This debate had long been at the center of modern Chinese literary theory. The generation of writers and critics who had been through the war included a fairly specific notion of social accountability in their definition of "good" literature. As had been the case throughout the period after the May Fourth movement, however, critics sought—not always very successfully—to differentiate their ideas of literature's social role from the discredited Neo-Confucian doctrine of "literature as the conveyance of the Tao" (*wen yi zai dao*). The problem in denying this didactic theory was that its

[52] Mao Dun, "Jiuzheng yizhong fengqi" [Correct a certain trend], *Shanghai wenhua* 8 (September 1946): 20–21. Although Mao Dun is critical of trends in Chinese publishing, he maintains that the situation in China for young authors is better than it is in New York. At least Chinese newspapers have their *fukan* ("feuilleton") section, where new books can be published serially and audience response measured. Shen Congwen, in his article "Zenyang ban yifen hao baozhi," (p. 23) also stresses the importance of the *fukan* to Chinese literature.

[53] Hu Feng, "Xian cong chongpo qifen," p. 9.

[54] Liang Qichao, "Lun xiaoshuo yu qunzhizhi guanxi" [On the relationship between fiction and civil government], in *Yinbingshi wenji leibian* [Collected writings from the Ice-Drinker's Studio arranged by category] (Taibei: Huazheng shuju, 1974), pp. 382–386.

traditional alternative, tagged with the name *shi yan zhi*—"poetry as [personal] expression"—by Zhou Zuoren in 1931, struck the more politically conscious writers of the May Fourth generation as offering merely a license for indulgence in esthetic trivia.[55] As early as 1919 certain writers (soon to be founding members of the Literary Research Association) had begun to search for elements from the tradition that could serve as foundation for a new Chinese literary esthetic.[56]

That these efforts to create a theory of literature that combined a sense of social responsibility with freedom of expression were largely unsuccessful is indicated by the continuing debate over how the fusion was to be effected. Wen Yiduo, whose education and position as one of the first poets to create satisfactory new verse after 1919 lent him enormous prestige in the literary community, added his voice to this search for a fusion of the two theories in a 1944 article entitled "Poetry and Criticism" (*Shi yu piping*). Wen set "poetry as irresponsible propaganda" against "poetry as beautiful language."[57] What was new in this essay was the idea that, although literature is "propaganda," it is "irresponsible"; in other words, literature's effects are not necessarily commensurate with the intentions of the author. Wen does not, however, abandon the idea that such effects are real and important to society or that literature might even ultimately need some sort of external control. Since any notion of external control comes close to censorship, which he rejects out of hand, Wen would appear to be in a dilemma at this point.

Again, his reasoning in rejecting censorship is innovative: while censorship could influence contemporary literature, he claims, it could have no control over the reception of works produced in the past. A more active governmental policy, such as that employed in the Soviet Union, of compelling the creation of specific types of literature—what Wen calls "leading writers by the nose"—is even less desirable. His reasoning goes as follows:

> If, like leading oxen by the nose, the government forces poets to create responsible poems—to commemorate each event and the completion of each building—then a lot of poetry will be produced, but the result will be that the works so produced will be only propaganda and not poetry. And since it

[55] Zhou's theory about these two opposing modes of literature is most fully set forth in *Zhongguo xin wenxue de yuanliu* [The source of the new Chinese literature] (Beiping: Renwen shudian, 1934).

[56] Some of the essays that treat this question include: Shen Yanbing (Mao Dun), "Shenma shi wenxue?" [What is literature?], in Zhao Jiabi, ed., *Zhongguo xin wenxue daxi* [Comprehensive anthology of the new Chinese literature], cited hereafter as *Daxi* (Shanghai: Liangyou, 1935–1936; reprint ed., Hong Kong: Wenxue yanjiu she, 1972), 2: 167–173; Zheng Zhenduo, "Xin wenxueguande jianshe" [The establishment of a new view of literature], *Daxi* 2: 173–175; and Zhou Zuoren's "Rende wenxue" [Human literature], *Daxi* 1: 219–225.

[57] Wen Yiduo, "Shi yu piping," in *Quanji,* Jiji, p. 43.

> will not be poetry, then its force as propaganda will be diminished or will vanish altogether. What will remain will be neither poetry nor propaganda, but nothing at all.[58]

The subtlety of Wen's thinking can be seen here: although he asserts that all literature is propaganda, he simultaneously points out that literature stripped of its esthetic features is not only not literature, but cannot even serve usefully as propaganda.

Having seemingly eliminated most sources of control over literature that could bring about his desired synthesis, Wen works his way out of his dilemma by turning to the one remaining source. After summarizing his arguments, he suggests at the conclusion of the essay:

> Poets cannot be held responsible [for the consequences of their work]. I have said above that external pressure is necessary, but this external pressure [should] not come from the government, but from society. And I think that the gentlemen from the Bureau of Investigation are not up to the task of determining whether or not poetry is "responsible propaganda." *This task should be entrusted to the critics.* (p. 45, emphasis added)

Wen's position, then, was to hand the major theoretical problems of modern Chinese literature over to the critics. To his credit, he recognized the difficulties this idea presented. In the summary to the essay he writes: "Thus we need critics who understand life, understand poetry, understand [literary] effects, and understand what values are to make [literary] tools and anthologies. But then, who are these critics to be? I do not know" (p. 49).

Wen's essay makes explicit the unspoken premises about the potential authority of the critic that lay behind the various formulations of criticism's role in creating good literature. This responsibility entailed a number of difficult tasks: to show how harmful literature was also bad literature; to praise and point out the key features of good literature and thus to serve as the arbiter of what should survive; to educate public taste through this process; and to illustrate to the public which works of traditional literature should continue to be appreciated and why.

Behind all these tasks, however, lay the more basic one of uniting theories of the esthetic and pragmatic functions of literature. Any unity proposed would have to be tenuous, especially if authorial intention was not to be accountable for the work's effect. The whole question of literature's pragmatic function, moreover, raised the specter of external control; the authoritative position assigned to critics by Wen only intensified this potential danger. The agreement among most literary people that there should be such a linkage, combined with the clear impossibility of any purely literary solution to the problem, left a void in urban literary

[58] Ibid.

thought that demanded some sort of general theory. Because such a theory was so difficult to conceive, it came to be considered the primary task of the critic to provide the solution. Yet while Wen sought—through the institution of the critic—to have both freedom and control, even his subtle mind ultimately had to beg the question of where this critical authority was to come from. This failure, in turn, left open the possibility that, as the demand for social responsibility became ever more insistent, it would be met in the cruder form of legislation.

In fact, the polarities that this supercritic was meant to resolve had begun to reassert themselves even as Wen was writing. The patriotic, enthusiastic style of writing of the early war years, which had commanded near-universal allegiance, had long since broken down into a uniformly optimistic and sloganeering literature known to all as *kangzhan bagu* ("resistance formula"). The dominance of this style had caused a reaction, which saw a number of writers abandon the official line in search of more individual means of expression.[59] Given the contemporary intellectual climate, however, it was impossible for these writers to be very positive about what they were doing. One such figure was the linguist Wang Li, who wrote under the pen name Wang Liaoyi. In the preface to his collected essays, he defends his "light" and "soft" style, maintaining that it is accompanied by a certain seriousness of feeling that the sensitive reader will be able to discern.

After referring explicitly to Cao Xueqin's prefatory remarks to *The Story of the Stone,* Wang goes on to admit that

> there are some essays that talk only of the moon and wind and that are truly foolish. We should also recall, however, just what sort of circumstances force [writers] to talk only of wind and moon. [The writers] are like a naughty boy who does not wish to trace characters; the teacher will not allow him to write on the wall, so all he can do is draw a picture of a crow on his text.[60]

While Wang qualifies the apparent detachment of this image with the remark that "a clever teacher, however, will perhaps be able to divine a good deal from this crow," his desire to escape from literary dictation is plain. But more than that, Wang's attitude reflects the continued influence of the *shi yan zhi* idea narrowly defined, with its severe restriction on the scope of literature's relevance. While Wang does argue for a residual and subtle significance to his essays, the fusion of esthetic and social function that is the task of Wen's critic is not made easier by the rather passive conception of literature that Wang's apology represents.

[59] Cao Juren, *Wentan wushinian* (*xuji*) [Fifty years in the literary arena, II] (Hong Kong: Xin wenhua chubanshe, 1971), pp. 156–157.

[60] Wang Liaoyi (Wang Li), *Longchong bing diao zhai suoyu* [Miscellany from the Dragon-and-Insect Carving Studio] (Shanghai: Guancha she, 1949), p. 4.

Given his disposition to see criticism as the salvation of literature, the temptation to legislate the role of the author was something that Wen could not wholly resist. In a speech entitled "The Path of Postwar Literature and the Arts" (*Zhanhou wenyide daolu*), Wen withdrew the theoretical freedom that he had allowed authors in "Poetry and Criticism." The speech begins with Wen outlining a three-stage evolution of humankind, beginning with slave society, moving on to "free men," and ending with "the stage of masters." Literature in each stage is bound by the spirit of the age in which it is produced. Wen also stipulates, however, that these stages are metaphysical rather than historical. The age of slavery, for instance—for intellectuals, at least—can exist independently of specific historical conditions: it is dependent, rather, upon the mentality of any given writer.

In outlining the characteristics of each age, Wen first set forth the notion that the literature and arts of the era of slavery are the "flowers of physical or psychological wounds." Beyond this, in such a society, "all literature and arts are pitiful: talented slaves are appreciated by their master, and the master thus releases them from work and patronizes them; [the slaves], in turn, sing the praises of the master and propagate his thought. In exchange for their keep they assist the master in oppressing their own kind."[61] Even the "freedom" characteristic of free society is nothing but the liberty to choose whether to continue as a slave (as with the Confucians) or (as with the Taoists) to seek a passive freedom *from* commitment rather than choosing affirmatively how to live. The Taoists are thus only freed slaves rather than truly free men. The final stage, Wen implies, when men seek mastery over their own destinies, will come about only when the authorities revoke even the illusory freedom of the second stage and the "freemen join the struggle of the slaves for mastery of their own lives" (p. 36).

In contrast to the crucial role assigned to the critic in "Poetry and Criticism," "The Path of Postwar Literature and the Arts" dwells almost exclusively upon the role of the writer. Whereas in the former this role was not specified, and authors were allowed "irresponsible" (i.e., disinterested) esthetic contemplation, the clear import of the latter is that esthetic feelings result from resistance—whether active or passive—to political oppression. This point is made more explicitly in an article on Qu Yuan written by one "Fan Shi" and published as the first of a series on Chinese writers in *Shanghai wenhua*. Taking Qu Yuan as the originator of "pure" literary writing in China, the article goes on to speculate that "Qu Yuan's achievement in literature is, of course, due to his personal cultivation. But his

[61] Wen Yiduo, "Zhanhou wenyide daolu" [The postwar path of literature], in *Quanji*, Jiji, p. 33.

circumstances also contribute to his success. Had he not had an adverse fate, then he would have had no basis for writing his dolorous works."[62] The popularity of Qu Yuan as a symbol of literary resistance to oppression in the 1940s[63] illustrates the extent to which resistance to a wretched political environment came to be seen as essential to the creation of literature. Government sponsorship of the formulistic *kangzhan bagu,* which had become to all intents and purposes completely apolitical by the end of the war,[64] helped to popularize the notion that, in some fundamental way, all real literature was a refined sort of political protest: if the Nationalists advocated anything, it was up to all people of conscience to hold to the opposite. Thus even the minimalist Wang Liaoyi did not deny that his work had a deeper and, by implication, political coloration.

This rush to identify literature so closely with the political high tide of the day easily swept aside alternative explanations of the origins and functions of literature. As the political situation had forced the publishing industry into a dependent position, so did conceptual developments in the cultural sphere force literary thought into a similar posture: there were calls from every quarter for writing to deal exclusively with the "current situation."[65] The problem of didacticism in the arts that had been so obtrusive in the early May Fourth period thus regained complete pre-eminence, coming in, as it were, through the back door. Literary theory had marched off in a united front to resist first Japan and then the Nationalists. With the final defeat of the forces of reaction in 1949, literature was left with no resources of its own on which to build: little or no literary theory developed after 1937 to offer either justifications or methods for writing independently of political fluctuations.

The turn that many writers by the 1940s had made toward traditionalism perhaps best indicates their frustrations with the literary vocation. The revival of the "literary heritage" offered them a safe haven from the exigencies of continuing to push for a genuine realignment of cultural ideas. That the traditional modes of writing were sanctioned by the entire political spectrum from Mao Zedong on the left to the Nationalists on the right

[62] Fan Shi, "Meiwende kaishanzhi zu—Qu Yuan" [Qu Yuan—the originator of esthetic writing], *Shanghai wenhua* 2 (March 1946): 24.

[63] See, for example, Wen Yiduo, "Renminde shiren—Qu Yuan" [Qu Yuan—the people's poet], in *Quanji,* Jiaji [Section A], pp. 259–262.

[64] See the interesting comments by the actress Huang Zongying in the "Zhongguo wenhua" section of *Shanghai wenhua* 7 (August 1946): 9. She complains about the lack of response the officially sponsored play *Wanshi shibiao* [Model teacher] received in Peking in 1946. When she maintained to a friend that the play was a worthwhile expression of the feelings of the people in the wartime Southwest, the friend replied caustically that people in the occupied areas were sick of seeing government propaganda and wished to see instead plays that gave expression to their feelings of discontent with the postwar situation.

[65] Guo Moruo's remarks in "Zhanshi zhanhou wenyi jiantao," p. 15, are typical.

made the journey to the past that much easier. Even within the broad agreement on this point, however, certain fissures indicated a lack of consensus about what literature was. Chang Fengzhuan, for instance, stressed the inevitable continuity between new and old, since both were the records of one nation.[66] The goal of all literary study, he said, should be to locate the "literary mind":

> The process of creation and the psychology of authors, ancient or modern, Chinese or foreign, in creating a successful work probably do not differ very much. When we study ancient authors we should seek in their works for this psychology and this process of creation. In discussing literary theory we should not seek any "ism" or any faction, nor should we seek after intellectual trends; what we should pay attention to are the esthetic features of literature, to unearth the "literary mind." . . . We wish to connect the new and the old, to build a bridge between them. . . . [If we do this,] we shall know what treasures are in our literature and we will, as a matter of course, eliminate the arbitrary barriers between the new and the old that are the result of our ignorance and lack of wisdom. (pp. 35–36)

Thus, while both Chang and the leftist heirs to the debate over national forms[67] and to Mao's admonitions at the Yan'an "Talks" advocated the study of the past, the similarities end there. Chang's faith in esthetic universals seems vastly removed from the utilitarian attitude toward tradition that Guo Moruo exemplified in 1946 when he announced the need for scholars "to use a new point of view [i.e., Marxism] to put our national heritage straight."[68]

It was perhaps the great distance between these two views that caused Wen Yiduo, in two of his last speeches, to question iconoclastically the left's wisdom in adopting old forms at all. For, as he says, "old forms are a type of old habit. If we consider that we must use old forms, then this is tantamount to admitting that old habits cannot be changed. I am, however, by nature a radical and am thus opposed to all old things and hope that even the best of them will be eliminated."[69] The other talk is just as

[66] Chang Feng (pseud. of Chang Fengzhuan), "Xin wenxue yu gu wenxue" [New literature and old], *Wenxue zazhi* [Literature magazine] 2,3 (August 1947): 28.

[67] For the background of the national forms debate of the late 1930s, see Marian Gálik, "Main Issues in the Discussion on 'National Forms' in Modern Chinese Literature," *Asian and African Studies* (Bratislava) 10 (1974): 97–111.

[68] See his statement in "Zhanshi zhanhou wenyi jiantao," p. 15. For an excellent discussion of the traditionalism in Mao's view of literature, see Bonnie S. McDougall's "Introduction: The Yan'an 'Talks' as Literary Theory," in Bonnie S. McDougall, ed., *Mao Zedong's "Talks at the Yan'an Conference on Literature and Art": A Translation of the 1943 Text with Commentary* (Ann Arbor: University of Michigan Center for Chinese Studies, 1980), pp. 3–41.

[69] Wen Yiduo, "Lun wenyide minzhu wenti" [On the question of democracy in literature and the arts], in *Quanji*, Jiji, p. 42.

extreme; Wen compares the idea of literary heritage (*wenxue yichan*) to the late Qing notion of national essence (*guocui*) and to earlier ideas of hermit literature (*shanlin wenxue*).[70] The same Wen Yiduo who had spent so much time researching early Chinese literature, and who had earlier expressed such strict ideas about the responsibilities of literature, here retreats from what would appear to be the logical culmination of his various pursuits. The explanation would seem to be that, while he had long since abandoned purely esthetic theories of literature, he also perceived that the later notion of literature as a critical vantage point on reality would be endangered by a too-rapid assimilation of a tradition shot through with elements of the Confucian *wen yi zai dao* convention.

Finally, the didacticism that was coming to the fore in the 1940s was augmented by the nature of the literary audience and by the social position of writers in Nationalist-held areas. For all the talk about writing for the masses that had gone on before the war and at Yan'an, in 1946 even such a staunch progressive as Guo Moruo could still announce that the target of urban literature was "educated youth," which essentially meant secondary-school students and, to a lesser extent, university students.[71] That, as I have already mentioned, most writers were at the same time teachers surely lent a pedagogical cast to the relationship between writer and reader. A rather poignant example is Mao Dun's admission that he changed the original plan for his serialized novel *Fushi* [Putrefaction, 1941] in response to audience reaction. The first part of the novel depicts the main character, Zhao Huiming, working in unwilling complicity with the political police of the wartime Nationalists. Having been a left-wing activist who was abandoned, pregnant and destitute, by her equally militant lover, she had had no recourse but to go to work as a government agent. For a time she is able to convince herself that by deliberately doing poor work she is doing no real damage to her old cause. When her former lover is captured, however, and she is made his interrogator, the situation changes. The novel, written in diary form, then becomes a tortuous narrative of her subjective mental anguish over the question of just what her objective contribution has been to the inquisition and eventual execution of the captured man. The work to this point is thus a portrayal of a uniquely ambiguous character; her subjective innocence and objective guilt are contrasted in a highly sophisticated manner.

[70] Wen Yiduo, "Xin wenyi he wenxue yichan," p. 30.

[71] "Zhanshi zhanhou wenyi jiantao," p. 15. A poll of reader preference taken by this magazine in early 1946 seems to establish that there were significant differences in literary taste between those "educated youth" that were in school and young literate people already in the work force. According to the magazine's statistics, those in the work force had a preference for the "sensational" sort of book discussed above. See Sun Dezhen, "Ni zui ai . . ." [You most prefer . . .] *Shanghai wenhua* 2 (February 1946): 22–23.

In an afterword to the 1954 edition, Mao Dun admits that his original intention had been to end the work with the lover's execution, thereby maintaining this disturbing ambiguity of character. Because, however, of "readers' requests to give her a way to reform herself,"[72] he added a few sections in which Zhao Huiming regains her political equilibrium and begins to act again resolutely in the right cause. The author is at some pains to point out that the execution's reradicalization of Huiming had "actually not been the original plan; pressed by these demands, however, I managed to find a way to 'pull' her out." He goes on to explain how he had meant the novel to be read:

> The self-blame, self-mockery, and rationalizations of Zhao Huiming in her diary, if taken too literally, will cause one to develop an unqualified sympathy for her. On the other hand, if one considers the particular nature of novels in diary form and does not take literally Zhao Huiming's self-blame, self-mockery, and rationalizations, one can see how [these] are meant to expose [her] contradictions. (p. 307)

Dependence upon a school-age group of readers, rather than upon an older, more sophisticated audience capable of accepting ambiguity, constituted a definite limitation to the space in which literature had to grow. In addition to a sense of social obligation and to internal critical momentum, then, audience expectation was another strong factor in the push toward the total politicization of literature.

ON TO LIBERATION

The concatenation of external and internal elements that moved literature into a dependence upon politics has had great consequences for post-Liberation Chinese culture. One such consequence has been the apparent (and, to Westerners, somewhat surprising) acquiescence of most of the principal literary figures of late Republican China to the new regime's strict enforcement of the "politics takes command" line in cultural policy. While this acquiescence is often attributed to the severity of government policy, the contrast between the Chinese situation and that of the early Soviet Union suggests that other factors were at work. The rapid fall in the fortunes of literature and of the literary establishment during the last years of Nationalist rule must surely be among the most significant of these elements. The miserable position of writers in the 1940s must also figure in the continuing loyalty of the leading writers of that period to the new regime. Like the proletariat, they owed their new-found job security and more than adequate wages to the new government. Professional writers as

[72] Mao Dun, "Houji" [Afterword] to *Fushi,* in *Mao Dun wenji* (reprint ed., Hong Kong: Jindai, 1966), 5: 305.

an estate would not have come into existence but for the victory of the Communist Party.

However, I would like to suggest tentatively, after Liberation the apparent similarity between the positions of the writers and the proletariat became the source of new problems. Claiming that they had been as oppressed in the old society as any other group, the urban writers, with livelihood at last secure, could theoretically justify filling the top jobs in the newly established literary hierarchy. But, at the same time, these veteran writers were inevitably imbued with elitist and cosmopolitan literary assumptions that ran counter to the Yan'an line. The Communist Party's campaigns to promote amateur and proletarian writing after 1949 were thus to be presided over by people whose training and background hardly suited them to the role.[73] It is a great historical irony that, simultaneously with their attainment of secure incomes and social status, the writers of the May Fourth generation found themselves in a position where their creative training and experience became, at best, irrelevant. The uncertainty resulting from the differing assumptions of May Fourth and Yan'an has clearly been a major factor in the notably unstable literary situation of post-1949 China. That the clashes have not been more open or clear-cut, however, is due to the experiences of the urban writers in the late 1940s.

The period since Liberation has witnessed a parting of the ways, even in areas where the Party and the writers were in complete agreement during the Republican years. The assumption, for instance, that literature is the highest and most legitimate forum for the working out of policy persisted in literary circles long after it had become obsolete in terms of Party needs. Hu Feng's behavior in the years immediately after Liberation plainly reflects the idea of the literary critic as the purest sort of legislator that was so prevalent in the Manichean days of the late 1940s. For all the working at cross-purposes and the false assumptions of unity between writers and the Party in this period, however, it is remarkable how, even in times when controls were loose, very few Chinese writers espoused purely esthetic views of the function of literature. The legacy of the Capital clique seems to have vanished without a trace from public view for years to come. Examination of the critical ground of the 1940s indicates that writers had begun to take a political view of the role of literature long before the Party exercised its control.

[73] For an illuminating discussion on this subject, see Lars Ragvald, "Professionalism and Amateur Tendencies in Post-revolutionary Chinese Literature," Göran Malmqvist, ed., *Modern Chinese Literature and Its Social Context,* in Nobel Symposium 32 [Stockholm, 1977], pp. 152–179.

Part II

The Push to Popularize, 1949–1979

FOUR

The Genie and the Lamp: Revolutionary *Xiangsheng*

Perry Link

There is wide agreement that since the revolution, a chief function of Chinese literature and performing arts has been to influence the attitudes, and hence the behavior, of its audience in socially beneficial ways. Many examples are available, and the devices through which correct attitudes are meant to be imparted are apparent enough. But there is, at least outside China, very little evidence for what actually *is* imparted and for how the messages thus received fit in with everything else in the audience's minds. Who actually reads or sees what? Why? With what attitude? Is "model" behavior genuinely imitated? Used only in outward presentations? Boring, perhaps?

Ironically, Western scholars have until recently been in a better position to understand audience response to the popular Chinese literature of fifty years ago than of current times. In 1929–1930 Zhang Henshui's *Tixiao yinyuan* [Fate in tears and laughter] became a top best-seller because of its wide appeal to urban readers. Today we can pick up this novel and get a good feeling for why it was popular. The reasons are complex, to be sure, but at least they are laid before us, in rich detail, by the text itself. Since the revolution, works have become best-sellers mainly because they are available and have official approval, and far less because of any close congruence with actual (as opposed to ideal) reader psychology. The distance between text and reader cannot, except in rare cases, be bridged by examining the texts themselves. For that one needs other, more direct, access to Chinese society.

The rare cases where a text can itself provide clues to its audience's response include comedians' "face and voice" routines, or *xiangsheng*.[1]

[1] The term *xiangsheng* has a complex and largely obscure history. The characters used in the modern term refer to "face" and "voice," which are two chief modes of the comedians' expression, although gesture is also important. The first character, *xiang*, has been widely

Modern *xiangsheng* is usually performed by two comedians, who stand side by side onstage before an audience. They tell stories, crack jokes, do imitations, sing songs, and generally attempt to induce laughter and lightheartedness. Satire is the essence of the show, and their topics often include contemporary social problems such as bureaucratism, consumer shortages, abuse of special privileges, and the overpoliticization of art. The audience laughs freely at the performances (there are no laugh cues), and when tapes are made they include clearly audible audience response. Tapes of successful pieces are sometimes broadcast across China over radio or television. A few tapes are exported. To see *xiangsheng,* or to listen to tapes of it, gives us access to at least one type of immediate, unconditioned audience response in China. Interpretation of the laughter can of course be difficult; but its hard kernel of authenticity is unquestionable.

The relation between *xiangsheng* and its audience is distinctive among contemporary Chinese art forms in several ways. For one, it may have the largest audience. People of every description—cadres, intellectuals, workers, and peasants, of all ages and both sexes—all listen to *xiangsheng.* Though it was originally centered in the cities of Peking and Tianjin, radio and loudspeakers have now brought it everywhere. Four-fifths of the provinces have performing troupes of their own, and over a thousand pieces are officially in circulation. In addition, amateurs in work units perform in-house shows about local issues. How many private, informal performances there are below this level is impossible to estimate. *Xiangsheng*'s simple, oral medium avoids problems such as illiteracy and the cost and availability of books or theater productions.

Xiangsheng enjoys, moreover, a generally wider scope for political and social satire than is officially allowed to other contemporary forms. The reasons for this are unclear but seem to stem partly from the assumption that jokes are essentially unserious and that an oral form is by nature less subversive than a written one. In any case, it is *xiangsheng* above everything else that people say "vents one's gall" (*jiehen*). Audience members often cry out, "Exactly!", "Couldn't have said it better myself!", and so on. It seems clear that one reason people listened to *xiangsheng* during the thaw after 1976 was to get the latest word on what social problems could be openly discussed and how frank one could be about them. Plays and short stories have also served these purposes, but *xiangsheng* has been not only bolder than these but also quicker to reflect popular concerns. To produce a play or publish a story can take many months, whereas *xiangsheng* pops up in a matter of weeks or even days. After the fall of the Gang

misinterpreted to mean "facing" or "mutual," so that one often sees *xiangsheng* translated as "crosstalk" or "comedians' dialogue." It is true that most performances are dialogues, but monologues are also common, and three-, four- and even five-cornered performances also occur.

of Four, *xiangsheng* was second only to wall posters in the speed of its attack. Such speed is possible not only because of the simplicity of producing *xiangsheng* but also because of its closeness to popular oral culture, including the rumor mill. Unflattering anecdotes about famous figures abound at this level, and in October 1976, when it suddenly became permissible to relate these about four such figures, *xiangsheng* had a ready stock to draw from.

The semi-underground cabaret humor of the Eastern European countries cracks its jokes at the expense of the Communist Party. Chinese *xiangsheng,* at least the aboveground performances, does the opposite; it satirizes enemies of the Party both at home and abroad. Yet in terms of audience appeal—i.e., of what is actually making people laugh—cabaret and *xiangsheng* may not be poles apart. The point of a *xiangsheng* joke is often ambiguous, and the reason for laughing is perhaps sometimes different from that which won the joke official approval. Consider a 1977 piece by Chang Baohua and Chang Guitian called "Maozi gongchang" [The hat factory].[2] It is ostensibly aimed at the Gang of Four—especially at the way they scattered unfair accusations (making people "wear hats")—but one must wonder how much of the spirited laughter it arouses has to do with more general conditions in Chinese society. The piece begins:

A: Recently . . .
B: Yeah?
A: . . . the goods of a certain factory have not been able to sell.
B: There actually exist factory goods that can't be sold?
A: Nobody wants them!
B: What kind of product?
A: Hats.
B: I'll take one! (audience laughs) It just so happens I don't have a hat. (B chuckles)
A: But these hats are *big* . . .
B: O.K.! An oversized hat makes you feel spiffy! (audience laughs)
A: But it's *heavy!*
B: Then it must be good and warm!
A: You can't stand wearing it. (laughter)
B: What's "standing it" got to do with wearing a hat? I can stand it.
A: Once it's on you can't get it off!
B: What kind of hat is this?
A: A counterrevolutionary hat.
B: (shouts) *I can't stand it!* (laughter) What factory sells this kind of hat?
A: The hat factory established by the Gang of Four.

The piece continues, a few moments later:

[2] Included in a tape called "Baigujing xianxingji" [White Bone Demon unmasked], Art Tune tapes, Hong Kong, no. BA-138.

A: And they [the hats] are divided into three sizes: large, medium, and small.
B: They even have sizes! (laughter)
A: She [Jiang Qing] sticks various people with various hats.
B: What are the large hats?
A: Things like "renegade," "spy," "big warlord," "anti-Party element," "careerist," "capitalist-roader," "capitulationist," "revisionist," "local tyrant."
B: Wow! And the medium size?
A: "Black-line personage," "unrevolutionary," "deceitful scholar," "backstage manipulator," "sinister gangster," "empiricist," "democrat," "middle-of-the-roader," "chameleon." (laughter)
B: The medium hats come in pretty good proportions, too, I see. (laughter) The small hats must . . . must be . . . a little smaller, right?
A: The small ones?—"stumbling block," "bender with the wind," "goodie-goodie," "revisionist sprout," "rumor company," "message tube," "countercurrent," "evil wind," "little reptile."[3] (laughter)
B: *All* these hats are pretty heavy!
A: Which size hat . . . do you think would fit you?
B: I couldn't stand any of them!
A: Well! Then how about one at reduced prices?
B: O.K. . . . No! (laughter) Not one of those either.
A: If they want you to wear one, then you have to wear it. Whether it fits or not, wear it!
B: Oh! Yeah? Then who . . . *doesn't* wear one?
A: Anyone who says "yes" well, . . .
B: Oh?
A: rats diligently, lies a lot, or toadies conspicuously (laughter) doesn't have to wear one.
B: Oh, you have to *toady!* (laughter)
A: Yeah! For example: if they say, "Charcoal briquettes are white" . . .
B: What?! Charcoal briquettes are white? Boloney! That's "turning the truth upside-down."
A: Hm . . . based on this skeptical attitude of yours . . .
B: (uneasy) . . . er . . . uh . . .
A: you get a small size hat!
B: What? (laughter) I've poured on lighter fluid!
A: You have to go along with them!
B: Have to go along?
A: Yup!
B: Charcoal briquettes? (ironically) They look just like New Year's dumplings [which are white]. (laughter)
A: But "rubber balls are square." (laughter)
B: All balls are covered with edges and corners! (laughter)
A: (imitating Jiang Qing) "The moon abroad . . .

[3] Here the second half of the name list is especially funny because of the rhythmic appeal of a 2-2-3 syllabic pattern.

B: uh huh . . .
A: is brighter than China's moon." (laughter)
B: Right! One moon per location. (laughter)
A: (still imitating Jiang) "How accurate he is!" (laughter)
B: (aside) Can you imagine how guilty I feel?
A: If they say, . . . "Even foreigners' farts are fragrant" . . .
B: I should voice my agreement . . . and express my appreciation! (laughter)
A: If you do you won't have to wear their hats!
B: Yeah, right, and I'm turned into a miserable wretch! (laughter)
A: Provided you speak up with words they want to hear, and do things they want done; whether it be making up a little song, or singing an aria, or dancing a dance, or handing in a school assignment—if you've said *anything* that praises them . . .
B: What happens?
A: then you can leap to heaven at a single bound, go straight to the top—live in a little mansion, eat special food, ride in a sedan.
B: Then—I've become a little crab! (laughter) Hey! So I have to obey orders and work for them?
A: But Boss Jiang . . .
B: Yeah?
A: can get you into the Party!
B: Me?
A: One word will do it!
B: (pretending to address Jiang Qing) "My grandfather is a . . . ha ha . . . old Trotskyite!" (laughter)
A: (imitating Jiang) "Nothing of the sort!"
B: "My father's a renegade."
A: "Doesn't count!" (laughter)
B: "And my history is . . ."
A: "pure!" (laughter)
B: "On examinations I could never answer anything!"
A: "That shows you have the spirit to go against the tide!" (laughter)
B: "You're really a guardian of standards."
A: "And *you* can be deputy minister!"
B: "Thank you." (suddenly dropping his irony) Oh, mother! (laughter) This is pure factionalism and selfish interest!
A: What's that?
B: Their line is simply: "Those who cooperate flourish and those who oppose perish."
A: We must struggle resolutely against them.
B: Struggle?
A: Yeah! All who obstruct their power-grabbing, who oppose their evil deeds, who disobey them, who do not submit to their control, who are not in accord with their ideas, or whom they dislike for any reason, are all potential clientele of the hat factory.

The pronouns "they" and "their," which refer here to the Gang of Four, have for several years been used in common parlance to mean the leadership generally, at whatever level. Such ambiguities as this are fundamental to *xiangsheng's* vitality. A full account of why such passages are amusing would be extremely complex; probably no one who performs or listens to *xiangsheng* (much less anyone who administrates it) completely understands the complexities.

THE APPEAL OF *XIANGSHENG*

To the untutored observer the performance of *xiangsheng* appears natural, almost casual. In fact, all pieces are set and are carefully rehearsed. An elaborate classification system accords to every kind of joke and other device a place and a special name. In modern *xiangsheng,* four basic skills are recognized: speaking, imitating, joking, and singing. A performer must be competent in all four but usually specializes in one or two. Each skill has its subcategories. Joking, for example, includes more than a dozen precisely labeled ways of setting up a punch line. No one has adequately catalogued all these terms, although Hou Baolin, China's premier *xiangsheng* performer, does have plans to edit a dictionary of *xiangsheng.*[4] Such an effort is clearly beyond our scope here; instead, we may note some of the attractions that listeners find in *xiangsheng.*

As soon as *xiangsheng* performers walk onstage they begin to establish an atmosphere. One, frequently, is tall and thin, the other short and round. They speak in droll tones, using simple language to address some immediately interesting question. In the style of Hou Baolin, which is imitated by Ma Ji and others of the "Hou school," they often ease the approach to their audience by talking about the most immediate topic of all; *xiangsheng* performance itself: "I hear that *xiangsheng* performers are all rich in social experience,"[5] "*Xiangsheng* performers have to be scholarly, right?",[6] "It's really tough to be a *xiangsheng* performer . . . at the very least you have to know how to talk."[7] As the dialogue continues one of the performers, the "joke cracker" or *dougende* takes off from the comments of his "joke setter" or *penggende.* The success of the performance depends upon maintaining the audience's sense of familiarity with the characters, though each is familiar in a different way. The *penggende* often speaks common sense, articulating the audience's own responses to

[4] Hou Baolin, lecture at Peking University, 28 September 1979. Gu Yewen has done some preliminary cataloguing of *xiangsheng* terms in *Xiangsheng jieshao* [Introduction to *xiangsheng*] (Shanghai: Wenyu chubanshe, 1952), pp. 52–64, as has Luo Rongshou in *Xiangsheng biaoyan mantan* [A casual discussion of *xiangsheng* performance] (Shanghai: Wenyi chubanshe, 1979), pp. 35–46.

[5] Hou Baolin and Guo Qiru, "Xiangmian" [Physiognomy].

[6] Hou Baolin and Guo Qiru, "Waipi *Sanguo*" [A crazy annotation of *The Three Kingdoms*].

[7] Hou Baolin and Guo Qiru, "Xiju yu fangyan" [Plays and dialects].

the less predictable *dougende*. But the audience can also feel they know the *dougende* precisely because of the narrow and distinctive range of his behavior.

Like Archie Bunker, the *dougende* is a "character" in the sense of a well-known eccentric, someone whose general style is as consistent as his particular responses are outlandish.[8] For example, in a piece called "Xiju zatan" [Random talk on plays], Hou Baolin is explaining (in jest) how he learned to sing Peking opera as a child. He practiced in the classroom every day, he says, and the teacher liked him a lot:

A: He paid me immense "attention" [the word means both "solicitude" and "surveillance"]. Every day he helped me "develop" [meaning both "develop singing" and "develop better habits"].
B: He *had* to get you to "develop"! With you in the classroom there singing opera!
A: You think I was too naughty?
B: You bet you are! [the present tense implies that he still is].[9]

Here the mischievous irreverence of the *dougende* is projected onto a child. The *dougende*'s iconoclasm, like that of a child, or of Sun Wukong, is funny because it appears to be a threat to social proprieties but in reality is not. It offers the audience the psychic release of realizing that a threat is only illusory, and this induces laughter.[10]

The *dougende*'s extravagant boasting works on the same principle. Talk that would be repugnant in a normal social context is funny coming from the mouth of the *dougende*:

A: If I were to perform Peking opera, now *that* would be beautiful. (laughter)
B: Oh?
A: Only . . . right now . . . the way it looks . . . I would say . . . I'm not so completely *imposing* . . . (laughter)
B: Why's that?
A: Well I haven't got on my makeup or my Western suit, so I don't look so . . . 100 percent beautiful! (laughter)
B: Right.
A: But I'm already pretty darn good!
B: Huh? You think you are, huh?[11]

[8] According to J. R. Hoggart, the culture of the English working class places a high value on distinctive "characters," in life and in fiction, whom the average person can get to "know" and who can express vicariously certain things he or she would like to express (*The Uses of Literacy* [New York: Oxford University Press, 1970], pp. 154–155).

[9] Hou Baolin and Guo Qiru, "Xiju zatan" [Random talk on plays].

[10] Psychologists have found that similar bases underlie many kinds of laughter: people laugh when tickled, for example, because tickling is a mock attack. See Arthur Koestler, "Humour and Wit," *Encyclopedia Brittanica*, 15th ed., 9:9.

[11] Hou and Guo, "Xiju zatan."

One of the *dougende*'s endearing qualities, which makes us forgive all, is the sprightly cleverness that he both possesses himself and portrays in others. In a piece about the People's Liberation Army braving the snows of Everest, an avalanche suddenly roars down, leaving a great wall of snow in the camp. The *dougende* tells how the soldiers fashion it into a movie screen.[12] In another piece we are made to feel happy when a child is smart enough to sneak into an opera house—past intimidating guards—by pretending he is a waiter delivering soup to a singer.[13] Such cleverness is reminiscent of Zhuge Liang's, which has always been exhilarating to the Chinese mind. But to this cleverness the *dougende* sometimes adds the extra spice of paradoxical nonsense. He even wants, sometimes, to make sense of the absurdly irrational. He can relate things that seemingly have no relationship, as when Hou Baolin explains the close connection between opera and irrigation (singers need water),[14] or as when he says that *The Three Kingdoms* is called "three" because everything in the story comes in threes. When someone points out a higher number in the text, Hou counters, "But you have to pass through three to get there."[15]

Such cleverness can also explain away paradoxes, e.g., that of "tears that make you laugh."[16] Hou Baolin explains that some film and theater actors are so unnatural in their portrayals of weeping that one can only laugh at them. He provides some imitations, and the audience roars in admiration of both his wit and his performance. Later, impossibly cornered by one of his own boasts, he can still find a way out:

A: After I graduated from college I took up a career in drama.
B: Uh huh.
A: Right until the present day.
B: Oh.
A: I've been studying drama now for more than fifty years!
B: Huh? What's that? Hey . . .
A: So my grasp of drama . . .
B: Hey! Hey! You . . . Hey, excuse me, but . . . (gets A's attention) How many years have you studied drama?
A: Over fifty.
B: Oh. Over fifty.
A: So my grasp . . .
B: Na, na, na, na, na! (laughter) May I please know how old you are this year?
A: Thirty-eight.

[12] Wang Jinbao, "Gaoyuan caihong" [Rainbow hues on the plateau], performed by Ma Ji and Tang Jiezhong.

[13] Hou and Guo, "Xiju zatan."

[14] Ibid.

[15] Hou and Guo, "Waipi *Sanguo*."

[16] Hou and Guo, "Xiju zatan."

B: Thir— (laughter) I thought so!
A: So my . . .
B: Now hold on just a minute! (laughter)
A: Huh?
B: If you're thirty-eight this year, how can it be you've been studying drama for over fifty years?
A: What?
B: Yeah. How . . . how . . . can you explain this?
A: (embarrassing silence) Sure!
B: Hm?
A: It . . . well . . . it may be a bit short!
B: A *bit* short? (laughter) You're *way* short!
A: I see. You . . . you find something strange in what I said, is that it?
B: Of course!
A: Sure! Even I find it strange![17] (laughter)

The device whereby the *dougende* persists on his merry way ("So my grasp . . . "), ignoring the problems at hand, is also standard. It emphasizes his comical narrow-mindedness, but also suggests a deliberate ploy, a cowardly attempt to cover his mistakes, boasts, or whatever.

The careful planning that goes into *xiangsheng* routines is evident in the texture of the dialogues. One device that operates at this level is a kind of reprise, originally borrowed from opera, in which a phrase from one point in the dialogue reappears in a later and quite different context, usually in retaliation against the person who first used it. In the exchange directly above, for example, we have B saying, "A *bit* short? You're *way* short!"—presumably to the embarrassment of A. Later in the same piece, when it has moved on to an entirely different subject, B asks whether he looks sufficiently delicate to sing the *huadan* opera role. He's afraid he might fall a bit short in this department. "A *bit* short? You're *way* short!" snaps A. In addition to verbatim snatches, the reprise can involve words that are merely similar. In a piece called "Xiangmian" [Physiognomy], B observes that if A cannot distinguish B's right hand from his left, "I've become a duck (*yazi*)."[18] At another point, far too distant to be considered a parallelism, B says that, if A does not admit that all his [B's] facial features are on the front of his head, then "I've become a goblin (*yaozi*)." Such ringing of the same bell at various points in the same piece not only gives the piece unity but suggests to the listener the operation of a second-level intelligence, whimsically observing and remembering what goes by.

The audience is tantalized when jokes are set up but not sprung, at least not immediately. In "Xiju yu fangyan" [Plays and dialects], Hou Baolin tells how he learned in a Shanghai barbershop the Shanghainese expression

[17] Ibid.
[18] Hou and Guo, "Xiangmian."

for "to shampoo": *da tou* (homonymous with "beat head" in Mandarin). Quite purposefully, Hou refrains from immediately cracking the obvious joke. While the listener is left to anticipate the possibilities—privately, for the moment—the spoken dialogue proceeds with an innocuous review of how anything washed (*xi*) in Shanghainese is *da*. Handled poorly, such a delay might frustrate the listener. But Hou's fine sense of timing enhances the listener's pleasure by drawing him into fuller participation. For several moments one awaits the re-emergence of head-beating. Then:

A: There I was sitting in front!
B: Right!
A: And he [the barber] was standing behind, pointing at my brain and asking . . .
B: Asking what?
A: (imitating a Shanghainese accent) "This. Hit it?" (laughter)
B: Gonna *hit* you!
A: And I thought to myself: what's this? I just get a shave and he has to *hit* me?
B: You might have asked him about it!
A: I sure did! I pulled a long face and asked him . . .
B: Yeah?
A: Uh . . . are you . . . singling me out? (laughter) Or are you gonna hit everybody here? (laughter)
B: What'd he say?
A: He said, "Oh yeah, everybody gets hit!" (laughter)
B: Everybody?
A: So I thought, "Well, if everybody gets clobbered . . . "
B: Then how about you?
A: "then . . . well . . . I guess we shouldn't destroy the custom!" (laughter; then A, aloud to the barber) "mm . . . mm . . . O.K., clobber!" (laughter) So he washed my head, applied the blow dryer, held up a mirror to show me and said, "All set!"
B: All set?
A: "All set? How come you didn't hit me?" (laughter)
B: And what'd he say?
A: "I *did!*" (laughter)
B: He did?
A: "How'd you do it so painlessly?" (laughter)[19]

Hou's clever pacing elicits about eight good laughs from a single joke. In *xiangsheng* jargon this kind of teasing of the audience is called *wuhui fa* ("the misapprehension method"). As formally defined, it requires that the audience be privy to both sides of a misunderstanding that the principals (here, shampooer and shampooee) each see only one side of. The method is distinguished from the *cuojue shi* ("the misconception mode"), in which

[19] Hou and Guo, "Xiju yu fangyan."

the audience is kept in the dark until the punchline liberates them. For example, a thirty-eight-year-old can have researched the theater for over fifty years because he's done so at two different periods, one lasting seven and one eight years—and chooses to multiply rather than add to get the total.

Puns are perhaps *xiangsheng*'s best-established and oldest devices. In studying the origins of the form, the eminent modern linguist Luo Changpei found puns among the earliest examples of proto-*xiangsheng* in the Xiantong period of the Tang dynasty (A.D. 860–873).[20] These and most later puns are based on sound. But some modern examples are based on opposing the literal versus figurative meanings of interesting terms, such as the Japanese-invented words for new Western things. In "Plays and Dialects," Hou Baolin asks his partner to both stand up straight and play the part of Liang Shanbo, who is lying dead:

B: Huh? Stand up even though I'm dead?
A: Well, since we're doing three-dimensional art here . . . ["three-dimensional" = *liti* = "standing body"]

The humor of puns such as this is clearly based on the release of tension: one's thoughts are abruptly dropped from one plane ("three-dimensional" connotes new, stylish, foreign, challenging) to another, more mundane one ("standing body" is the simple meaning of the Chinese characters).

While puns are one of the oldest and crudest devices that use this principle, they are by no means the only one.[21] In fact, building the listener's expectations only to deflate them is an extremely common procedure in all *xiangsheng*. Consider the following piece by Ma Ji from the time of the Gang of Four, in which we are told in bright, rapid tones how a group of spirited young women set out to catch fish for the State:

A: When they got on board they were full of talk and laughter.
B: Sure! They were happy!
A: And in a moment were shouting and singing.
B: Happy!
A: Everyone together skipping and jumping!
B: Happy!
A: And in the end vomiting and groaning!
B: Happy! (suddenly realizing) Huh? Vomiting?[22]

[20] Luo cites an example of an entertainer named Li Keji, who is said to have performed before the Xiantong emperor. He "proved," by punning on the classics, that the founders of Confucianism, Buddhism, and Taoism were all women. Luo Changpei, *Xiangshengde laiyuan he jinhou nuli de fangxiang* [The origins of *xiangsheng* and the question of where we go from here], *Beijing xiangsheng gaijin xiaozu tekan* [Special publication of the Small Group for the Improvement of Peking *xiangsheng*] Peking, November 1950, p. 1.

[21] Indeed, some have argued that every joke is rooted in this principle. See Koestler, "Humour and Wit," pp. 5–6.

[22] Ma Ji and Tang Jiezhong, "Haiyan" [Stormy Petrel] (text by Ma Ji).

A then tries to save us from a starkly unrevolutionary conclusion by explaining that it is only natural that a "howling wind and three-foot waves" should make "a bunch of girls" nauseous. But his explanation is not as memorable as his joke, whose joy lies in satirizing excessive fervor for the State. At a less overt level, it also satirizes the very propaganda point which the whole piece is ostensibly making: that women can hold up half the sky.[23]

The listener is misled in the passage above partly by its rhythm. The pattern of two verbs in A's lines followed by "Happy!" in B's beguiles the listener into feeling that everything is correct and in place. The upset occasioned by A's last line is in even clearer relief because it is semantic only. It does not violate the prevailing rhythm. In the jargon this device, of which Ma Ji is particularly fond, is known as *sanfan sidou* ("three turns and a fourth jolt"). But it is only one of many ways in which rhythm is important in *xiangsheng.* Aside from setting up jokes, rhythmical patterns can also have a variety of purely esthetic functions. Four- and five-syllable descriptive phrases can use rhythm as well as rhyme and semantic parallelism. Seven-syllable lines have a lilt that borrows something from both poetic convention and tongue-twisters. The *xiangsheng* art called *guankou* ("talk-strings") involves a rapid-fire recitation of words, something like an American auctioneer's. The esthetic qualities of this and other devices, numerous though they are, are nearly impossible to translate. Hence we will pass over them with this unfortunately brief notice.

Hou Baolin has observed that a good *xiangsheng* performer must achieve four general standards: speed without confusion (*kuai er buluan*); slowness without lapse (*man er buduan*); doing new pieces without strain (*sheng er bujin*); and doing old pieces without unctuousness (*shou er buyou*).[24] "Speed without confusion" applies to rapid-fire talk such as *guankou.* "Slowness without lapse" refers to the sense of timing necessary to maintain the interest of the audience even during pauses. Hou Baolin's performances do indeed include pauses, sometimes surprisingly long ones. But they are fascinating. The last two standards refer to the dilemma that, with not enough practice, one lacks confidence, while with too much practice one can lose freshness.

Freshness is especially important in mimicry, one of *xiangsheng*'s basic skills. Contemporary artists imitate the sounds of birds, animals, natural events, machines, and musical instruments, in addition to people of every

[23] One might resist this conclusion at first, but can hardly deny it when a moment later the young female leader—brave, correct, and exemplary—stands up to save the situation. "Girls!" she cries, "The struggle has begun! I mean—comrades!—let's all not be afraid of vomiting, let's all concentrate on not vomiting, just look at me . . . I . . . " (The sound of vomiting follows.)

[24] Hou Baolin, "Wo he xiangsheng" [*Xiangsheng* and me], *Dagong bao,* 15 February 1979. The rhythm and parallelism of Hou's formula itself are worth noting.

description. Accuracy is obviously a desideratum, but so is range. The sheer novelty of one mouth making an immense variety of noises is an important part of the appeal. Variety in imitating people also implies a rich social experience, even a kind of deliberate social research, which is appealing in somewhat the same way that the panoramic "social novels" of Li Hanqiu (or of Dickens or Zola) are: one enjoys the versatility of a guide who can take one through several layers and into many crannies of society. Hou Baolin is famous for his imitations of all kinds of regional and local opera. These often draw laughter, but not always because they are burlesques. They are sometimes funny because they are in fact extremely accurate; the listener is delighted that a nonoperatic performer can suddenly produce such uncannily good imitations—let alone that he can switch among very different types within moments.

Not all *xiangsheng* humor is rhythmical, light, and fresh. Much of it, especially before 1949, has been extremely earthy. Jokes sometimes took the form of crude insults dealt by one performer to the other, or to some other unfortunate person. Country bumpkins were ridiculed, as were cripples and the mentally retarded. Speaking of Chinese humor in general, C. T. Hsia observed in the early 1950s that "the Chinese still retain a childish delight in taking notice of any physical and moral deviation from the norm; their fellow creatures, so unfortunate as to be physically deformed and disabled, are usually objects of ridicule."[25] Though considerably toned down since the revolution, such tendencies have persisted, at least in *xiangsheng*. In "Physiognomy" (Hou Baolin and Guo Qiru, 1962), A makes considerable fun of B's physical abnormalities, real and imagined. He is bald. Had he never grown hair? But his ears are O.K.—he has one on each side. And his nose, too—the holes face downward. Or consider the following satire of Jiang Qing in Ma Ji and Tang Jiezhong's "Baigujing xianxingji" [White Bone Demon unmasked, 1976]:

> When she gets out of the car she peers east and leers west; trumpeters up front lead the way; a dog-headed military man clasps her stale feet; a guard on each side, one male, one female; and she in the middle, three sways per step! (laughter)

The manner in which limits have been set on the cruder aspects of its humor has been only part of the complex effort to shape postrevolutionary *xiangsheng*.

XIANGSHENG AND THE REVOLUTION

Some historians have traced the roots of *xiangsheng* as far back as the *Shiji* [Historical records]; more agree that its precursors were the *canjun*

[25] "The Chinese Sense of Humor," *Renditions* 9 (Spring 1978):30–36.

plays of Tang and Song times.[26] Like *xiangsheng*, these plays used a dialogue structure and punned frequently. They also, it is interesting to note, were used to remonstrate with the emperor. There is no good evidence of a direct line to modern times, however, and intervening references in Qing poetry and fiction suggest, if anything, a different tradition.[27] The Tang and Song examples are all from a very elite level—i.e., the imperial court itself—whereas the *xiangsheng* of the twentieth century is clearly a more popular form.

The popular tradition includes various lines of masters and disciples, much as in other popular art forms. When the lines began is unknown, but they are often traced from the early reign of the Tongzhi emperor of the Qing (mid-1860s). During the national mourning for the preceding emperor, Xianfeng, entertainment was prohibited. Performers from the theaters, temple-fairs, and other organized amusements had to seek alternate employment. Hou Baolin's "Gaihang" [Changing jobs, recorded in 1963] is an imaginative burlesque of what it might have been like for various kinds of entertainers—drum singers, opera singers, and so on—suddenly to enter the marketplace hawking vegetables in their various performing styles. What actually happened, however, is that these artists took to the streets to supply in an informal way what officially was still proscribed.[28] Street-corner entertainers could thus evade suppression, but they also had to do without the accompaniment of their troupes. These conditions gave rise to *xiangsheng*: one or two people could perform it anywhere and could change location quickly if necessary.

In the first half of the twentieth century, *xiangsheng* was performed at what Hou Baolin playfully calls "bare-ground teahouses" (*pingdi chayuan*). Performers would stake out a patch of ground at a market or entertainment area by carefully sprinkling white sand, in a ritual style said to date from Song times, to form characters that announced their program. They then sat facing each other at some distance while their assistants arranged benches in an oval around the open space between them. Spectators who could not get a seat on the benches stood behind them, forming a larger oval at the back. When a piece was finished, the performers would

[26] See Gu Yewen, *Xiangsheng jieshao*, ch. 2; and Luo Changpei, *Xiangshengde laiyuan*. Luo and Gu both rely on Wang Guowei's *You yu lu* [Quotations on entertainers], in *Wang Jing'an xiansheng yishu* [The posthumously collected works of Mr. Wang Jing'an] (Shanghai: Shangwu yinshuguan, 1940) vol. 45.

[27] The term *xiangsheng* appears to have originated in Song times, although using the character *xiang* for "phenomena" and *sheng* for "life." The term seems, at least until mid-Qing, to have signified (1) sounds of things in nature or (2) sounds imitated in a lifelike way. Cf. Wu Zimu, *Mengliang lu* [Ephemeral visions], vol. 19, quoted in Gu Yewen, *Xiangsheng jieshao*, p. 15; Hou Baolin, "Wo he xiangsheng," *Dagong bao*, 13 February 1979; Cao Xueqin and Gao E, *Hong lou meng* [Dream of the red chamber] (Peking: Renmin wenxue chubanshe, 1964), chap. 35, p. 416.

[28] Hou Baolin, "Wo he xiangsheng," *Dagong bao*, 13 February 1979.

rise and the *penggende* ("joke setter") would take a pan from a table behind him to collect donations. Social pressure obliged the seated customers to toss in a few coppers, while the standees could contribute or slip away as they pleased. The crowd included no women because the jokes were considered too coarse for them. If a woman wandered within earshot, the performers would rise in silence and bow, inducing her to leave.[29]

Xiangsheng was learned within totalistic master-disciple relationships, which were bonded by sworn oaths and sometimes by written contracts as well. Training was strict. Disciples were expected to learn set pieces by rote. Every gesture, expression, and intonation of the master was copied; only after leaving one's master could one exercise creativity.

After the change of power in 1949 *xiangsheng* underwent a rapid and genuine revolution. The new regime set up a Small Group for the Improvement of *Xiangsheng* (Beijing xiangsheng gaijin xiaozu), whose objective was to rid *xiangsheng* of dirty jokes, bad class attitudes, and other ideological flaws. Cleansed examples of *xiangsheng* were immediately put to use to entertain Chinese troops in the Korean War; and in general the army played an important part in the rapid spread of *xiangsheng* across China. It was heard on stage, on the radio, and over loudspeakers, while texts circulated in literary magazines.

One reason for the special emphasis on *xiangsheng* was that it was an oral form and used plain language. It could communicate new ideology more efficiently than written forms, more so even than opera or other popular forms. Since it used the Peking dialect, it could also help spread standard pronunciation. Some argued, moreover, that *xiangsheng* represented the viewpoint of the masses. It was "rich in a history of struggle" and "already before 1949 had become a powerful weapon for satirizing the ruling class."[30] Hence, part of the effort expended on *xiangsheng* involved a search for more of this tradition. Young artists were sent out among the masses everywhere to collect jokes and other material.

The reform of *xiangsheng*'s content proceeded simultaneously. Certain technical improvements were easy, such as excising the linguistic localisms of the Peking-Tianjin area to make the dialogues more widely understandable. The jargon terms *dougende* and *penggende* were changed in many pieces to more descriptive labels: for example, "A the boaster, B the sprinkler of cold water"; or "A the eyeless, B the brainless."[31] But in more substantial matters the interaction of leadership from the top and local

[29] Interview with Hou Yaowen, 28 October 1979; Hou Baolin, " 'Pingdi chayuan' manyi" [Casual recollections of the "bare-ground teahouses"], *Beijing ribao* [Peking daily], 21 October 1979. Today women and children mingle easily in *xiangsheng* audiences, though it is worth noting that there are still no female performers.

[30] Gu Yewen, *Xiangsheng jieshao,* p. 1

[31] Ibid., p. 36.

expression from below created some interesting "dialectics," which included some contradictions and ambiguities.

One problem was that prerevolutionary *xiangsheng* had not, in fact, been primarily a weapon for satirizing the ruling class. It did so occasionally, to be sure, but far more often the humor had to do with country bumpkins and sex. In the 1930s and 1940s, as the division between the modern, Western-influenced cities and the still-Chinese hinterland became more obvious and more worrisome, country-bumpkin jokes had been a useful way to relieve psychological tension. A listener could bolster his own sense of security by laughing at someone who was doing even worse than he was at interpreting modernization. Jokes based on this principle abounded in popular fiction,[32] and *xiangsheng* offered the added attraction of lively down-country accents, sprinkled with foul language.

But country-bumpkin and sexually suggestive jokes were not, to say the least, considered appropriate after the revolution. In a 1951 piece that formed part of the Campaign to Resist America and Aid Korea, A grows angry at B for persistently misunderstanding the meaning of "Americaphobia." He says: "Clearing things up with a guy like you is like wiping your ass with a watermelon rind."[33] The line was immediately criticized as "an impure thing" by the *Xiangsheng* Group of the Nanking Folk Art Work Troupe.[34] After the early 1950s, the earthy language completely disappeared, although hints of it do resurface occasionally. The attack on the Gang of Four is allowed to include "Oh, mother!" (a mild form of a common Chinese oath).[35] And Hou Baolin points very gently to sexual implications when he insists, in a 1963 piece, that in order to tell his friend's fortune the friend must provide him with more than a birthdate—he must tell Hou when he was conceived. Hou gets a laugh from this impertinent question and two or three more from his suggestions about how to figure out the answer.[36] The old game of ridiculing someone for his country accent also reappears in one of the recent attacks on Jiang Qing's lieutenants.[37]

The disappearance and reappearance of features such as these are noticed by performers and audiences and accord to some extent with changes in conscious policy. Yet there are aspects of *xiangsheng* performance that are not subject to policy because they are too difficult to control. At the

[32] Perry Link, *Mandarin Ducks and Butterflies* (Berkeley: University of California Press, 1981), pp. 317–323.

[33] Li Qun, "Zhuanzhi kongmeibing" [A specialist in curing Americaphobia], *Wenhui bao,* Shanghai, 18 March 1951.

[34] Quoted in Gu Yewen, *Xiangsheng jieshao,* p. 85.

[35] Ma Ji and Tang Jiezhong, "Baigujing xianxingji" [White Bone Demon unmasked].

[36] Hou and Guo, "Xiangmian."

[37] Ma Ji and Xi Jun, "Wutai fenglei" [Tempest onstage].

simplest level there is the problem of a performer's slipping inadvertently into old habits. Too great a concentration on the technical aspects of performance can allow unauthorized "impurities" to slip by. In one recorded instance of Southern comic dialogue (*Jiangnan huaji*) in the early 1950s, a volley of rhythmical talk ends with "Long live the Republic of China."[38]

Much more difficult to resolve have been problems involving the rhetoric of *xiangsheng* and the subtle question of audience response. *Xiangsheng* is essentially satirical,[39] but the questions of whom to satirize, and how, have been difficult ideological problems. Other postrevolutionary arts have been asked to praise (*gesong*) the achievements of the new society. But could *xiangsheng* praise anything? From the Antirightist Campaign of 1957 until the fall of the Gang of Four in 1976, the matter had been decided from above by a firm policy that it must; the only question was how. Some performers tried to combine satire and praise in something called "benevolent admonition" (*shanyide guiquan*). This was satire "among the people," an expression in *xiangsheng* of Mao's notion of nonantagonistic contradictions. An example, according to Hou Baolin, would be to make fun of people who disobey traffic rules. But, he adds, the effort required to keep such jokes both nonantagonistic and funny is strenuous.[40] The method was not widely adopted.

Xiangsheng performers came up instead with a new, segmented form that alternated the "flesh and blood" (*rouzhongxue*) of a piece with "flowers inserted from outside" (*waichahua*). The flesh and blood was the main theme and did not have to be funny. The jokes were the inserted flowers, incidental to the main theme. For example, a piece in praise of women truck drivers would make fun of various people who doubted that women could drive trucks.

Yet this is a tricky business. How can one be sure that nobody will be amused for the wrong reasons? An experimental piece from the early 1950s tried to praise newspaper-reading by satirizing people who did not read enough. But when B says, "*Liberation Daily* always has the same old stuff; it gives me a headache just to look at it,"[41] why does the audience laugh? If some laugh *with* B rather than at him, who is responsible? Even when laughs are "correct," it is not always simple to say what ideas remain with the audience. Consider the following exchange, also from the early 1950s. A is telling B about his travels in America:

[38] Gu Yewen, *Xiangsheng jieshao*, p. 46. Since the People's Republic of China had already been founded, it was an obvious and serious error to wish long life for the Republic of China, which had been exiled to Taiwan.

[39] Hou Baolin, "Wo he xiangsheng," *Dagong bao*, Hong Kong, 15 February 1979.

[40] Hou Baolin, "Wo he xiangsheng," *Dagong bao*, Hong Kong, 16 February 1979.

[41] Li Qun, "Zhuanzhi kongmeibing."

B: Then why don't you tell me . . . how many stories tall is the tallest building in America?
A: That I can't even say. All I remember is that one time I was in an elevator for three hours without reaching the top.
B: If that's so, there must have been over two hundred stories!
A: Says who?—The elevator workers were on strike.[42]

The joke may be properly revolutionary, but B's original question is not answered. How high *are* American skyscrapers? Even today this is one of the most popular questions about America in China. Raising the question in a *xiangsheng* piece implicitly asserts that it is an important, or at least relevant, question. Though it is implied that skyscrapers fall short of two hundred stories, how high they actually are is left to the imagination.

Ambiguities inhere in a performer's role as well as in what he says. When Hou Baolin declares that fortunetellers, whether rich or poor, Chinese or Western, are all frauds, he is displaying correct revolutionary antisuperstitionism.[43] But who is "he"? Not Hou Baolin the man, but Hou Baolin the stage persona who has been saying ludicrous things for several minutes running. Where does Hou Baolin the man stand? (We can know this answer, but not from the piece itself.) Listeners' impressions might vary widely, depending on their individual predilections. In the last analysis, of course, there is no limit to the possible audience interpretations. Moreover, even if one postulates that all jokes are properly told and properly interpreted, it can be—and has been—argued that laughter is by its very nature ill adapted for extolling the revolution. In the words of one Party critic: "In this work, certain things that ought to be treated seriously are sullied by the casual throwing together of some slippery and pointless language . . . . the serious can seem unserious and bring counterproductive results."[44]

The difficulty of creating properly revolutionary *xiangsheng* did not become fully apparent until some initial attempts were made. An interesting example of the first workings of the critical process after 1949 concerns a piece called "Dui duilian" [Matching couplets] by Lao She. (The eminent novelist had not written *xiangsheng* before the revolution but, inspired by the idea of creating a new, healthy, humorous, popular art, contributed his talents enthusiastically in the early 1950s.) In "Matching Couplets" his hero, who is a virtuoso of verbal parallelism as well as a feisty critic of capitalism, travels to America.[45] As soon as he arrives he pastes up a couplet:

[42] Xi Xiangyuan and Sun Yukai, "Ruci Meiguo" [Such is America], quoted in Gu Yewen, *Xiangsheng jieshao*, p. 110.

[43] Hou and Guo, "Xiangmian."

[44] "Gei 'Dui duilian' ti de yijian" [Some opinions on "Matching Couplets"], in Gu Yewen, *Xiangsheng jieshao*, p. 109.

[45] Lao She, "Dui duilian," in Gu Yewen, *Xiangsheng jieshao*, pp. 88–89.

B: And on it I wrote: "I speculate, I get rich, I live it up, my life is good; pleasure's all I seek."
A: How come everything's "I . . . "?
B: Because the matching line is all "You . . . "
A: And how does that read?
B: The matching lines are: "You're honest, you're poor, you're hungry, your life is shot; death serves you right"!
A: (misinterpreting the "you" as referring to himself) Death would serve *you* right!
B: I don't mean you! This is about the gap between rich and poor in America!
A: I misunderstood. And so what did you write as the crosspiece?
B: The crosspiece was four big characters: "All men are equal."

B goes in succession to a dance hall, a hospital, a draft board, the Supreme Court, the FBI, Hollywood, and a few other places. At each he writes his satiric parallelisms, cleverly avoiding capture or punishment by the police. At first appearance, "Matching Couplets" seems a most successful piece.

But political critics in the early 1950s found some serious complications in it. First, is it correct to make light of serious topics like the FBI? Can a comic figure, like this couplet-writer, be a model hero? Might ironic statements be taken literally? While the critics were concerned almost exclusively with the piece's possible ideological effects on its audiences, the immensely complex question of how such effects actually happen was poorly understood, and Party policy left no time for careful investigation of such issues. The result, unfortunately for the artists, was that critics could only urge avoidance of certain hastily conceived "tendencies." On most questions the advice amounted to, "Don't go too far this way" but "Don't go too far the other way, either." Guidelines developed in contradictory pairs. For example:

> First of all, *xiangsheng* should be intensely satirical and its talk comical, full of raillery and banter, so that it makes people laugh.[46]

Yet in the case of "Matching Couplets":

> The audience of *xiangsheng* is, for the most part, the broad masses, and one must not assume that all of them are clear about the basic nature of American imperialism and its internal contradictions. There are bound to be misunderstandings if one uses the satiric mode exclusively. The ironic use of a string of phrases like "democracy," "freedom of speech," "due process," "scientific civilization," "full supply of soldiers," and "a million crack troops" is bound to create a certain amount of confusion in the realm of thought.[47]

[46] "Gei 'Zhuanzhi kongmeibing' ti de yijian" [Some opinions on "Curing Americaphobia"], in Gu Yewen, *Xiangsheng jieshao,* p. 78.
[47] "Gei 'Dui duilian' ti de yijian", p. 109.

One must, in other words, be satiric, and at the same time be responsible for the possibility that one's audience will misunderstand one's satire. Since the critics did not themselves write *xiangsheng*, one can only surmise what they would have taken to be a safely explicit joke. One clue might be that they criticized the passage quoted above because the couplet "I speculate, I get rich. . . . You're honest, you're poor" does not identify "I" and "you" in class terms. "I" should be "capitalists," according to the criticism.[48] But such a revision would kill the humor on grounds of rhythm and briskness alone, and would not really aid—in fact, through loss of effectiveness, would impair—the ideological goal of the piece.

Another pair of contradictory critical guidelines concerned form. "Matching Couplets" was criticized for being too old-fashioned:

> Because of its excessive emphasis on the pursuit of *xiangsheng* form, it shows itself to be insufficiently ideological as a work of art and insufficiently serious as a political statement.[49]

This critique seems to call for a de-emphasis of form. Yet shortly thereafter a writer of *xiangsheng* was told that:

> In this piece the author does not employ *xiangsheng* form very well.[50]

One of the more serious complaints about "Matching Couplets" was that the funny man running around delivering his barbs and evading the American police was basically a coward, an A Q:

> How incorrect this is! What unhealthy psychology! It gives readers evil and harmful influences. Today the Chinese people have stood up in the world. They should not and certainly will not ever bow before the enemy [even when tricking him]. In order to strengthen patriotic thought and education, all creative work should correctly describe the industrious and courageous character of our people.[51]

So one should portray strong model characters, proudly saying and doing correct things everywhere, without fear? Apparently not. Three pages later the same critic says:

> The most ridiculous thing is that B, in the status of a mere couplet writer, can actually run in and out of places like an American draft board, Department of Defense, Federal Bureau of Investigation, the Voice of America broadcasting station, and other such spy organizations without suffering the slightest difficulty or cruelty. The facts of present times have taught us that there is no limit whatever to the prejudice toward and mistreatment of

[48] Ibid., p. 113.

[49] Ibid., p. 108.

[50] "Gei 'Zhuanzhi kongmeibing' ti de yijian", pp. 77–78.

[51] "Gei 'Dui duilian' ti de yijian", p. 108.

> overseas Chinese by American imperialism. . . . So to let B freely and merrily shout and run about as he likes, right inside the tiger's mouth of American imperialism, obviously runs the risk of obstructing an understanding of the true facts on the part of readers or viewers.[52]

Criticisms such as these made it clear that the creators of *xiangsheng* (and of other art forms) would have to tread the middle ground of several dilemmas, never knowing upon which horn of a dilemma the critics would push them next.

At times, such as during the Cultural Revolution, the middle ground became so narrow as to resemble a trap: to move in either direction was wrong, but to stand still was also wrong. Some lively descriptions of this trap have appeared in *xiangsheng* themselves, especially in the year following the fall of the Gang of Four:

> A: If you try to go up you can't go up, go down you can't go down, live you can't live, die you can't die.
> B: What if I'm defiant toward her [Jiang Qing]?
> A: Defiant? She'll charge you as a dyed-in-the-wool Party hater.
> B: Then I'll keep my distance from her.
> A: And she'll charge you with lack of feeling for the Party.
> B: I'll be formally correct but stay noncommittal.
> A: She'll charge you with an unsteady class standpoint.
> B: Then I have to go over to her side!
> A: And she'll charge you with pressuring her—carrying out counterrevolution!
> B: Gee! How'm I supposed to live?[53]

In the matter of artistic creation in particular, Jiang Qing is said to have been ready with complaints like "this work has no depth, and is lacking in breadth, and is short on width, and needs more height and is insufficiently thick." The piece continues:

> A: Whatever you say [in a play] is inadequate.
> B: Then alter it as she wishes!
> A: That's called "perfunctory dabbling"!
> B: O.K., so use another play!
> A: "Changing the soup without changing the herbs."
> B: Then write a whole new one!
> A: "Old wine in new bottles."
> B: Then you might as well give up!
> A: "Wrecking the revolution in literature and art."[54]

[52] Ibid., p. 111.
[53] Ma and Tang, "Baigujing xianxingji."
[54] Ibid.

SOME UNDERTONES, CONSCIOUS AND UNCONSCIOUS, IN *XIANGSHENG* PERFORMANCE

Without doubt, much of the audience's enjoyment of *xiangsheng* in recent years has come from the satire aimed at authority figures. These figures are foils, often duly labeled as Gang of Four types, but are readily identifiable with whatever arrogant bureaucrat the individual listener may have in mind. The unspoken communion between performer and audience is reinforced by a respect for the performer's courage and even by an implicit concern for his welfare. How far will he dare to go? Like any forbidden fruit, satire of the leadership is all the more delicious precisely because it is prohibited. A famous piece called "Kong cheng ji" [Stratagem of the empty city] begins by titillating the audience with what appears at first to be a criticism of censorship:

A: I . . . I . . . I really like plays!
B: Do you go often?
A: Well, I used to. I used to go a lot. But after Liberation, I haven't very much.
B: Huh? What? You haven't got time?
A: No, it's not that. The kind of plays I like . . . don't exist now!
B: What?! Your kind of plays don't exist now? *All* kinds of plays are developing these days.
A: Oh? *My* kind of plays haven't developed.
B: I see. What you like is *gaoqiang.*
A: *I* can't understand *gaoqiang.*
B: *Kunqu?*
A: Same with *kunqu.* And anyway, look how good *Fifteen Strings of Cash* is these days! No, that's not the kind of play I mean. My kind of play—it's going nowhere these days!
B: What's going nowhere—this play of yours?
A: It's . . . loiterers' plays!
B: Oh, freeloading!
A: Right! Right![55]

"Loiterers' plays" means hanging around the stage close enough to listen and get some glimpses without buying a ticket. The humor of the punchline here, which can be analyzed as involving a relief of tension, is many-layered. The line reveals A as a mere cheapskate rather than the connoisseur of some obscure form of drama; it also solves the intellectual riddle of what kind of play has gone nowhere since Liberation; but, perhaps most importantly, it dispels the specter of open conflict with Party policy.

Another kind of joke, which plays upon the same tension, involves the "innocent" use of politically charged phrases. In "Random Talk on Plays"

[55] Hou Baolin and Guo Qiru, "Kong cheng ji" [Stratagem of the empty city].

the word "contradiction" appears this way, as does the term "reference material" (the name given to classified material derived from hostile or neutral sources). A is showing off his ability to act various parts:

A: Have a look at this gesture.
B: O.K.
A: Hm? Whoever brought a camera . . . might take a shot! (laughter) Keep it as reference material. . . . (laughter)
B: O.K.! Enough, enough!

Why such jokes have been allowed is a fascinating question. Are they not noticed? Not carefully interpreted? Thought unimportant? In times of political relaxation they may be considered harmless play. The surprising thing is that they appeared even during the Cultural Revolution, when controls forced other art forms into a frightenend uniformity on all political questions. In "Gaoyuan caihong" [Rainbow hues on the plateau, early 1970s], the courageous chief of a People's Liberation Army squad is said to "lead the way" in several senses:

A: Well, for starters, he leads the way in study. . . .
B: (Translating A's meaning into political jargon) He conscientiously reads Marxist-Leninist books and the works of Chairman Mao.
A: He leads the way in job performance.
B: He struggles arduously and bravely assumes great burdens!
A: He leads the way in upholding discipline.
B: He carries out the Three Rules of Discipline and Eight Points for Attention!
A: He leads the way in eating.
B: (pause) Huh? Leads the way in eating?
A: Yes, because many soldiers from the lowlands, when they first arrive at the roof of the world [the Himalayas], are unaccustomed to the rarefied air and must be trained in how to eat and sleep. . . .

Again we have an explanation that saves the situation without destroying enjoyment of the joke. At the end of the piece the "Great Leader" image is again punctured:

A: When our squad leader's two feet are planted in the earth, his head pierces the clouds in the sky.
B: How could he be that tall?
A: He was standing on top of the mountain!

Whether or not the implications of jokes like these evade the authorities, they are certainly not lost on the audience. Such implications are often precisely what the audience is looking for.

Yet there are many other jokes whose unrevolutionary implications seem usually to escape everyone—audience, authority, and performer alike. People know that they are laughing, of course, but may be unaware that the humor actually rests on some backward ideas. Attitudes about the place of women are a good example. The Cultural Revolution piece called "Haiyan" [Stormy Petrel] tells about a model young woman leader:

A: Stormy Petrel is one of the busiest people in our village. Outsiders who don't know what's going on find it hard to track her down.
B: That's all right, I'll go find her at home.
A: You won't find her there.
B: I'll look for her on the boat.
A: Won't find her.
B: I'll look for her at the brigade.
A: Won't find her.
B: Then where am I going to find her?
A: I'll tell you a place where you'll find her for sure.
B: Where?
A: On the power-line poles!
B: Hm? What does she do on power-line poles?
A: In order to work on the high seas you have to develop strong arms, so Stormy Petrel spends a lot of time climbing up and down power-line poles.

It is very likely that the audience follows the political satire here quite consciously. It is much less likely that they are aware of the antifeminist implications. The piece continues:

A: She's spirited! Stormy Petrel dares to think and dares to act! Her work style is ferocious! She's like a boy—exceptionally strong!
B: Oh!
A: She'll grab a hundred-pound load in her arms and take it away!
B: Wow!
A: . . . toss a two-hundred pound load on her shoulder and take it away!
B: Fantastic!
A: Raise up a one-ton load of steel and take it away!
B: Huh? Raise a one-ton load and take it away?
A: She runs the crane!
B: Hah! I thought so!

More blatant examples of antifeminism can be found in the attacks made on Jiang Qing since the fall of the Gang of Four. She is frail, hoarse, crotchety, and breaks every rule of personal morality: she drinks, gambles, sleeps late, and puts on airs. While these charges are not necessarily antifeminist—in fact are reminiscent in tone of the attacks on corrupt bureaucrats in the late-Qing "castigatory" novels (*qianze xiaoshuo*)—Jiang is also derogated as "an old biddy" (*lao pozi*); she is even made to call herself that. She is a "demon," but with the prefix *nü* gratuitously added to make it "woman demon." She is linked not merely with power-grabbers in China's past but with female power-grabbers in particular:

White Bone Demon
[Jiang Qing]: Comrades, I've been worried these days. Who do you think should take over the country? I really don't feel too comfortable going ahead with present plans. Don't you think women are really better than men?
B: (a righteous member of the masses): You grab position and snatch power even in your sleep!
WBD: I recall that history tells of great women who have been pre-eminent in their time, such as the Empress Lü.
B: Empress Lü was one of the great unscrupulous careerists in history!
WBD: Wasn't she a woman?
B: She was indeed.
WBD: Yeah, and then there was Empress Wu Zetian!
B: A woman indeed.
WBD: And Empress Dowager Cixi!
B: A woman indeed.
WBD: And Song Jiang!
B: A woman indeed . . . huh? . . . No! That capitulationist Song Jiang was a man!
WBD: Men are also born of us women, aren't they? (laughter)[56]

Other examples of jokes with unprogressive implications concern attitudes about peoples who are less civilized than the Han Chinese. Everyone in the audience may know that the official policy is to treat all peoples of the world with equal respect. But this does not prevent laughter at jokes based on condescension. Two pieces of Cultural Revolution vintage, both Ma Ji's, are called "Gaoyuan caihong" [Rainbow hues on the plateau] and "Youyi song" [In praise of friendship].[57] They share the theme of courageous young Chinese battling difficult physical environments in strange cultural contexts. "Rainbow Hues" is set in the snows of the Himalayas and "In Praise of Friendship" along the Tan-Zam Railway in East Africa. The Tibetans live in the most awkward places, such as lean-tos precariously poised over streams. One has to concentrate intensely to avoid falling into the water. In Africa the situation is even more surprising. Standard facilities are simply lacking, but because of "friendship" one cannot admit the fact:

B: Which government guesthouse did you stay in?
A: We weren't there as guests, so we didn't stay in a guesthouse.
B: Then what boardinghouse did you live in?
A: We supplied our own board, so we didn't live at a boardinghouse.

[56] All of the examples above are from Ma and Tang, "Baigujing xianxingji," and Ma and Xi, "Wutai fenglei."

[57] "Youyi song" was performed by Ma Ji together with Tang Jiezhong. It was written by the Amateur Literature and Arts Propaganda Team of the Third Railway Planning Institute of the Ministry of Communications.

B: Then where were you received?
A: We came to learn. We didn't need any reception.
B: You . . . well, anyway, you had to live *somewhere!*
A: Oh, of course! The place we lived in was great: tall mountains at our backs, the wide sea before our eyes, big high-ceilinged rooms, spongy carpets, a garden all around, variegated butterflies fluttering in the air, myriad flowers flaunting their beauty.
B: Oh, I see! You lived at a resort [*bieshu*]!
A: No, except for coconuts there are no other trees [*biede shu*] there.
B: What? I'm talking about the *resort* you lived in.
A: It was the residence of our survey team.
B: Tell me more about the high-ceilinged rooms.
A: They were tents, pointed at the top, wide at the bottom.
B: And what about the spongy carpets?
A: Grass.
B: And the surrounding flower garden?
A: The scenery was nice and the climate agreeable. It was *like* a big garden.
B: What about the variegated butterflies and the myriad flowers?
A: The four seasons are all like spring there, and vegetables grow all year around. When the cabbage wilts the turnip blooms; when the rape wilts the spinach blooms; when the cucumber wilts the hot peppers bloom; when the chives wilt the eggplant blooms. . . .
B: Huh? What were chives and eggplants doing there?
A: Our vegetable plot!

There are, to be sure, several ways in which the audience can find this passage funny. Those politically astute in the requisite way will smile at A's desire for bourgeois comforts or at his boasts that turn out to be shams. Perhaps the authorities during the Cultural Revolution counted on such responses; but they may also have neglected to analyze carefully what underlies certain parts of the humor. In any case, there is little question that the predominant attitude of the piece assumes Chinese superiority and finds "people's diplomacy" amusing. At one point the piece makes fun of the improbable sounds of the Swahili language; at another a Chinese crazily embraces a smokestack because African friends are so "warm."[58]

We may delight in *xiangsheng*'s relatively free satire and liberated thought. In China it is a remarkably democratic art. But if it is free to express democratic notions it also expresses some "feudal" ones, and for the same reason: they are popular. In the thirty years since the revolution the biggest "contradiction" in Chinese society has been not between variant modern ideologies but between traditional attitudes and modern ideologies generally.

[58] This last incident, of the man embracing the smokestack, appears in the "internal circulation" version of the piece but not on the tape prepared for export. Apparently its unfortunate implications were obvious enough that a censor finally noticed them.

THE GENIE AND THE LAMP

The Chinese Communist Party has attempted to weed out feudal ideas from *xiangsheng*. In the past, however, the more tightly that Party critics have applied controls the more they have inhibited everything—feudalism, progressivism, and creativity itself. During the Cultural Revolution, according to Hou Baolin, no one listened to *xiangsheng* more than did Chairman Mao; but in his private viewings every Wednesday and Saturday night, Mao chose to listen only to traditional pieces from before the revolution.[59] The ordinary people had no choice but to listen to contemporary pieces.

Of course, one reason for the low quality of many pieces is that artistic reform has been combined with the assertion of political power, which has intimidated artists. Sophisticated humor has been discouraged by the requirement that artists take responsibility for how their work is interpreted. During the Cultural Revolution, if the authorities determined that the social effects of one's work were counterrevolutionary, that was automatic evidence that one's motivation had been counterrevolutionary, too. And punishments were severe.

But even if fear could be removed as a factor, and the question were simply how best to combat feudalism, it is doubtful that anyone would know quite how to instill correct attitudes through a device as tricky as *xiangsheng* humor. Those who could come closest would be artists, not bureaucrats. The false assumption is often made (and not only in China) that, since humor is a "light" thing, the principles by which it works and its relation to thought and action are quite trivial. In fact, the extensive literature on the psychology of laughter has been unable to analyze its operations with confidence. But the authorities in China have acted basically on the theory that any laugh at a bad person is ipso facto a correct laugh, whatever the reasons for laughing, and that any joke cracked by a person with correct thoughts ipso facto supports correct thoughts in all its implications. Judging from the results of the Cultural Revolution years, one could even argue that, the more simplistic political criteria are made to be, the more likely it is that such criteria will tolerate jokes that more sophisticated analysis would easily show to be reactionary. So long as you poke fun at Jiang Qing, it is all right to belittle feminism. So long as you go to Africa in "friendship," it is all right to laugh at how primitive Africans are. So long as you explain how wonderful a Party leader is (overlooking the possibility of irony), it is all right to joke about pulling his pedestal from beneath him.

It is true that some *xiangsheng* jokes do genuinely support the Party and its values and that many others are essentially apolitical. But the creative

[59] Interview with Hou Baolin, 31 October 1979.

genius that goes into a good *xiangsheng* piece will not confine itself to any of these categories, any more than Aladdin's genie would retreat inside its lamp. Theoretically, I suppose, political confinement of *xiangsheng* could be achieved, after long and sophisticated research into how *xiangsheng* works and after giving writers long and arduous training in the results of such research. Yet, surely, one would then discover, with E. B. White, that "humor can be dissected, as a frog can, but the thing dies in the process."[60] Perhaps the only real alternative for those who "guide" *xiangsheng* in China is to give individual artists a freer rein and to expect that, if the environment is basically salubrious, their humor will be so too.

Aside from the deliberate attempts made after 1949 to purify *xiangsheng*'s content, another revolution—quieter but more durable—has taken place in the way the art is performed. Today the relations of the performer to his teacher, his materials, and his audience are radically different from what they were in the 1940s. The master-disciple chains are gone, and with them the strict and intensive training that used to forge a performer's basic skills and to give him a certain mystique before the outside world. Today thousands of amateurs learn by watching television and practicing on their own. A few are lucky enough to study with an old master, but the relationships are much more relaxed than before. In the past, artistic virtue lay in the perfection of set traditional pieces; today it is a virtue to present new material, drawn from the problems of the day. No serious performer today performs without creating, too. Whereas in 1949 there were only about a hundred *xiangsheng* pieces in circulation, all of them well known and well polished, today there are countless pieces at many levels of quality.

Yet the modern form has its own inflexibilities. Pieces for the radio must fit within the fifteen or twenty minutes allotted. More importantly, the rapport with the audience—an essential factor in traditional performance—has changed in nature and been severely curtailed. Instead of sitting at opposite ends of a "bare-ground teahouse" with the audience forming an oval around them, performers today are onstage, higher than the audience, and side by side. A microphone intervenes, bringing the performance to a basically anonymous audience, and sometimes to a vast, unseen radio or television audience. Since both performers are in plain view at the same time, there is a new problem of how to avoid looking awkward while one's partner is talking. In the past, performers would begin with short warm-up pieces, designed to attract an audience and to get to know them. What was their mood? What pieces would they respond to? If they responded well, there were more coppers to be had when the hat was passed. Today the audience pays a set admission charge and sits in

[60] E. B. White, "Some Remarks on Humor," in *The Second Tree from the Corner* (New York: Harper, 1935), p. 173.

rows. There are no warm-up pieces, but a new kind of short piece has been designed for use as a Western-style encore.

Although switches and even complete reversals have marked the political control of *xiangsheng,* these changes in its mode of performance have been unidirectional. It is improbable that they will ever reverse. The new *xiangsheng* medium does, of course, affect the nature of its messages, and it seems futile to expect a return of the old-style art with its finely wrought performance style. Hou Baolin has commented, for example, that modern tape recorders have often been more of a drawback than the aid they were supposed to be. The machine's ability to repeatedly play back any phrase has led young artists into thinking that they can always rely on their recorders for practice; hence they neglect the rigorous ear-training that was traditionally required of *xiangsheng* students.[61] Increasingly, people come to *xiangsheng* performances to appreciate what its authors have to say, rather than, as in the past, to appreciate the skill with which a familiar piece is rendered—a shift somewhat like that toward spoken drama (*huaju*) in the 1920s. As a more cognitive art, the new *xiangsheng* will continue to answer a need that has not, at least for most of the postrevolutionary years, been satisfied by China's more formal media. The scope within which it operates will, however, be subject to future changes.

[61] Hou Baolin, "Wo he xiangsheng," *Dagong bao,* Hong Kong, 17 February 1979.

FIVE

Geming Gequ: Songs for the Education of the Masses

Isabel K. F. Wong

Songs for the masses, sometimes called "revolutionary songs" *(geming gequ),* are simple, relatively short tunes with didactic or political texts. Most of these songs have moderate melodic ranges and have been influenced in style either by Western music or by traditional Chinese folk music. They are created to be sung at political rallies or other public assemblies and by individuals in their more relaxed moments. The texts are all written in an easily comprehensible vernacular, whether the language is terse, hortatory, and sloganlike or more personal and lyrical. The songs serve various political functions. Some are meant to arouse patriotism and to motivate a maximum collective effort to build a strong socialist state; others promote group solidarity or express partisan sentiments. In a large number of these songs the key words come straight from current party directives, as published in official newspapers such as the *Renmin ribao* [People's daily]. These songs, of course, are meant to familiarize the masses with government policies and to motivate them to support the realization of these policies.

Because mass songs are so important in China today, I propose to trace here their origin and development, to investigate their creation and dissemination, to consider the political messages of their texts, and, finally, to examine their musical characteristics.

ANTECEDENTS

The use of music as a social, political, and educational tool, as advocated by Chinese Marxists, is not alien to traditional Chinese thinking. It has been a serious governmental concern since the time of Confucius, who himself edited and wrote music for some three hundred poems intended as educational tools.[1]

Despite the opinion and example of Confucius, however, the Chinese have not traditionally used songs to help forge ideological bonds among different groups. In relatively recent times, Hong Xiuquan (1814–1868), leader of the Taiping Rebellion (1851–1864), rediscovered the idea in the congregational hymn singing that Protestant missionaries had brought to China in the nineteenth century.[2]

In 1847, having heard about Hong's self-assumed missionary activities in Guangxi, I. J. Roberts (1802–1871), a Baptist minister from Missouri, invited Hong to his mission in Canton to study Christian doctrine. During his three-month visit, Hong became acquainted with various features of the Protestant ritual, such as the recitation of psalms and prayers, the presentation of sermons, and congregational hymn singing. He later adopted all these elements in the Taiping Heavenly Kingdom.[3]

Among the hymns Hong learned was "Old Hundred," which he later used, with a new text, as the state hymn of the Heavenly Kingdom. Its new title was "Tianchao zanmei ge" [Ode praising the Heavenly Kingdom]. This ode was sung in all rituals and rallies, whose major ingredients Hong had also borrowed from Protestant rituals.[4] Many other hymns were also created specifically for these occasions; a few of their texts are still extant.[5] Although we know nothing about their music, except in the case of the state hymn, we may surmise that some of the hymns also used Protestant melodies.[6] Recently, some folksong texts about the Taiping Rebellion were collected from oral tradition in the areas once occupied by the rebels, and

[1] Sima Qian, "Kongzi Shijia" [Biography of Confucius], in *Shiji* [Historical records] *juan* 47 (Peking: Zhonghua shuju, 1973), vol. 6, pp. 1914, 1935–1938.

[2] Christianity's influence on Hong Xiuquan has been well documented in Eugene P. Boardman's *Christian Influence upon the Ideology of the Taiping Rebellion, 1851–1864* (Madison: University of Wisconsin Press, 1952). For the early life of Hong, see T. Hamberg's rare *The Visions of Hung-Siu-tshuen and the Origin of the Kwang-si Insurrection* (Hong Kong: n.p., 1854). Jen Yu-wen (Jian Youwen) has published a Chinese translation of Hamberg's book that also reprints the English version (*Taiping tianguo chiyiji* [Record of the Taiping Revolution] [Peking: Yenching University Library, 1935]). For further bibliographical information on the Taiping Rebellion, see Teng Ssu-yü, *Historiography on the Taiping Rebellion* (Cambridge, Mass.: Harvard University Press, 1962).

[3] For a biographical sketch of I. J. Roberts, see Jen Yu-wen, *Taiping tianguo dianzhi tongkao* [Study of the rituals and ceremonies of the Heavenly Kingdom] (Hong Kong: Mengjiu shuwu, 1958), 3:1588–1590.

[4] Ibid., pp. 1716–1720, 1761–1766, 1832–1854.

[5] Some of the song texts are printed in Jen Yu-wen, *Taiping tianguo*. Most of the manuscripts of the Taiping song texts are in the British Museum and the Bibliothèque Nationale, Paris.

[6] According to Jen Yu-wen, four Taiping hymns are still included in a modern Hong Kong hymnal. However, Jen does not make clear whether it is the tunes of these hymns or their texts (or both) that derive from the Rebellion. See Jen Yu-wen, *Taiping tianguo*, p. 1733.

these have been published in China.[7] A comparison of the Taiping song texts with those of the songs for the masses of the PRC reveals that there are many similarities between the content, style of language, titles, and use of metaphors of these two bodies of texts. For example, a short text by Hong Tianguaifu praising his father Hong Xiuquan goes as follows: "The Sun King, illuminating all corners of the world."[8] Here the employment of the metaphor "Sun King," which Hong Xiuquan liked to apply to himself,[9] brings to mind numerous songs in which "the sun" is also used as a metaphor for Mao Zedong, as in the famous "Dongfang hong" [The east is red]: "The east is red, the sun arises, in China there appears a Mao Zedong . . ."[10] Further similarities are suggested by a comparison of the following pairs of song titles:

Titles of Taiping Songs	*Titles of Songs for the Masses*
"Xiao bei qing cha jing Zun Huang" [Boiling a cup of tea for Duke Zun][11]	"Tiao dan cha ye shang Beijing" [Carrying a basket of tea to Peking (for Chairman Mao)][12]
"Yi Huang pai guang dao wo jia" [Duke Yi is sending officials to my home][13]	"Jie fang jun ye ying dao shan zhuang" [The Liberation Army is camping in our village][14]

Given such similarities as these and the fact that the Taiping introduced the practice of congregational hymn singing, it is not unreasonable to view the Taiping hymns and their use as precedents for the use of mass songs as a modern political and didactic tool, whether or not a conscious imitation can be documented.

The Taiping Rebellion, coupled with increasing Western intervention in China during the 1860s, forced the Qing government to change its foreign

[7] Luo Ergang, *Taiping tianguo shiwenxuan* [Selections of poems and song texts of the Taiping Kingdom] (Shanghai: Zhonghua shuju, 1960); Zhongguo kexueyuan Jiangsu fengyuan wenxue yanjiusuo, ed., *Taiping tianguo geyao quansuoji* [Collections of folksong texts and legends of the Taiping Kingdom] (Jiangsu: Wenyi chubanshe, 1960).

[8] See Luo Ergang, *Taiping tianguo shiwenxuan,* p. 203.

[9] Ibid., pp. 203–204.

[10] A recording of "The East is Red" is included on China Record M861, sd. 1, bd. 1, and also on China Record XM1031, sd. 1, bd. 1, and sd. 2, bd. 1 (played by a band).

[11] See Luo Ergang, *Taiping tianguo shiwenxuan,* p. 225. Duke Zun, whose name was Li Wenguang, was one of the commanders-in-chief of the Taiping army. For reference to Duke Zun and the background of this song text, see *Taiping tianguo shiwenxuan.* The same song text is also included in *Taiping tianguo geyao quansuoji,* p. 35.

[12] A recording of this song is included on China Record XM1041, sd. 1, bd. 3.

[13] Duke Yi, whose name was Shi Dakai, was one of the commanders-in-chief of the Taiping army. For the text of this song, and for references to Duke Yi and the circumstances under which this song was created, see Luo Ergang, *Taiping tianguo shiwenxuan,* p. 211.

[14] A recording of this song is included in China Record M957, sd. 2, bd. 3.

policy in 1861 and to reform some of its institutions. Both of these measures contributed to the spread of congregational singing. The new foreign policy, among other things, allowed missionaries to move freely in the interior of China and thus to introduce congregational hymn singing to more and more Chinese.[15] At the same time, the German military instructors hired to help reform the army introduced singing as an instructional tool. Since then it has been a common army practice to sing songs while drilling.[16]

The first large-scale didactic use of group song singing came in the modern Chinese school system, established after the 1911 revolution.[17] The first Minister of Education of the Chinese Republic, Cai Yuanpei, held that a complete modern education must include esthetics; hence, under his direction, classroom music was formally incorporated into the Chinese school curriculum.[18] Cai, a scholar thoroughly trained in the traditional Chinese classics, had also studied in Germany. There he acquired a taste for Western music and came to regard Chinese musico-theatricals and other popular forms of musical entertainment as vulgar and simple-minded. Obviously they were not appropriate for classroom use.[19] Cai and other authorities encouraged the development of a modern style of Chinese

[15] In 1877, at the Shanghai Christian Conference, it was reported that sixty-three categories of hymn books had been published in Chinese; among these hymns were several of the first to be composed by a Chinese, pastor Xi. Another report shows that a hymnal, compiled by Jonathan Lees under the aegis of the Church of England, had a circulation of twenty-three thousand. See Kenneth S. Latourette, *A History of Christian Missions in China* (New York: Macmillan, 1929), pp. 416–434, 495–641.

[16] For the texts of some early army songs, see Yuan Shikai, *Xinjian lujun binglüe lucun* [Records of curriculum for the newly established army] (facsimile reproduction of the 1898 ed., Yonghezhen: Wenhai chubanshe, 1966), pp. 310–318. There is little documentation available about the singing of marching songs. The practice seems to have been well established by the 1910s. In the city of Canton, where my father was living at that period, it was common for soldiers to march around town singing "new style" songs. "New style" here describes songs similar to those sung in the new-style schools established by foreigners.

[17] An imperial decree issued in 1904 tentatively proposed the inclusion of singing sessions in the curriculum of the national primary and middle schools. The decree praised the foreign use of music in classrooms for its recreational and didactic value. However, the edict continues, given the lack of suitable songs, Chinese schools should teach their students to chant simple didactic poems or nursery rhymes. See Toga Akigoro, ed., *Jindai Zhongguo jiaoyushi ziliao* [Materials on the history of education in modern China] (Taiwan: Wenhai chubanshe, 1972), 1:284, 312.

[18] For an English translation of Cai's writings on his philosophy of education, see Teng Ssu-yü and John K. Fairbank, *China's Response to the West: A Documentary Survey, 1839–1923* (Cambridge, Mass.: Harvard University Press, 1954), pp. 234–239. For the contents of Cai's new educational policy for the Chinese republic, see Toga, *Jindai Zhongguo,* 2:571–574.

[19] Cai Yuanpei, "Wenhua jiaoyu buyao wangliao meiyu" [Esthetic education should not be forgotten in cultural education], in Lou Zikuang, ed., *Minsu congshu* [Folklore series] (Taiwan: 1969), 101:43–44.

school songs, based upon the music that foreign missionaries and educators had introduced to China.

The melodies of this new type of tune were usually simple and short. At first they were based on the Western diatonic scale, but soon pentatonic melodies became predominant.[20] For several generations, this type of westernized song has been the major ingredient in the musical diet of Chinese students.

Since these songs were intended to promote social and political change, their texts naturally reflect the general national concerns of the time, such as patriotism, self-discipline, self-reliance, morality, social reform based on Western liberal ideals, and civic-mindedness. Soon these songs were sung not only in schools but also at other civic gatherings. Before long they had become a genuine form of Chinese music suitable for the expression of modern China's national aspirations.

Around the 1920s, Chinese composers who had received Western-style music training either at home or abroad began to make their presence felt in educated circles. Three of the most influential new-style composers were Y. R. Chao (Zhao Yuanren, 1892–1982), Huang Zi (1904–1938), and Sitson Ma (Ma Sicong, b. 1913). All three were trained in the West and all wrote a quantity of songs carrying didactic messages. Ma pioneered the idea of incorporating the style of folksong into that of didactic songs, while Chao, a linguist as well as a composer, sought to continue the traditional Chinese approach to song writing by composing melodies that reflected the contours of the linguistic tones of the song-texts. Chao's approach, however, was not widely followed.[21]

THE DEVELOPMENT OF SONGS FOR THE MASSES

No sooner had the republican government been established than warlords began fighting each other in much of China. Japanese aggression also

[20] For a discussion of some of the music in this period and for transcriptions of some of the songs, see Yang Schuman Chao, "Twentieth Century Chinese Solo Songs: A Historical and Analytic Study of Selected Chinese Solo Songs Composed or Arranged by Chinese Composers of the 1920s to the Present," 2 vols. (unpublished Ph.D. dissertation, George Peabody College of Teachers, 1973).

[21] For a discussion of the relationship between the contours of linguistic tones and melodies in several traditional Chinese genres, see Y. R. Chao, "Tone, Intonation, Singing, Chanting, Recitation, Tonal Composition, and Atonal Composition in Chinese," in Morris Halle, ed., *For Roman Jakobson* (The Hague: Mouton, 1956), pp. 52–59. Chao admitted that he was an exception among contemporary Chinese composers in allowing the contours of linguistic tones to influence his melodies (see *For Roman Jakobson*, pp. 58–59). For further discussion on song writing by Chao, see his introduction to his *Xinshi geji* [Tunes for new poems] (Shanghai: Shangwu, 1928; reprint ed., Taibei: Shangwu, 1960), pp. 1–16. For the most recent re-evaluation of Chao's contribution to modern Chinese music, see Wang Yuru, "Tantan Zhao Yuanren zuopinzhongde jige wenti" [A discussion of some questions in Y. R. Chao's works], *Renmin yinyue* [People's music], 1979, 5:12–16.

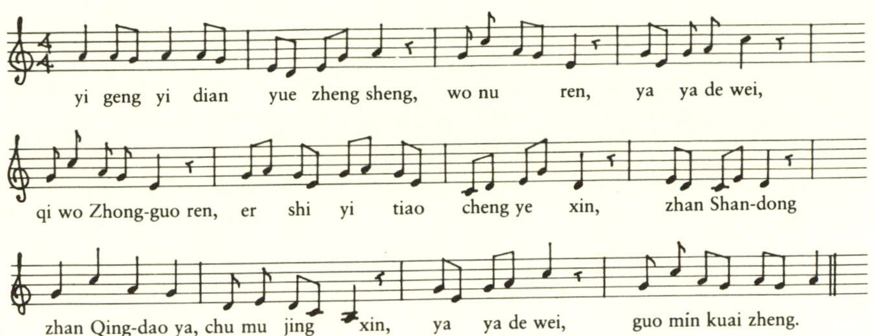

EXAMPLE 1. Wu geng diao [Five watches]
Translation: The first watch strikes one, / the moon has just risen. / The dwarf slaves / ya-ya-de-wei / have insulted us Chinese, / presented the Twenty-one Demands, / revealed naked aggression, / have taken Shandong and occupied Qingdao. / How frightening and worrisome. / ya-ya-de-wei / Countrymen, hurry to combat them.

increased. In 1914 Japan seized Qingdao from German control. In the following year, Japan forced China to accept the Twenty-one Demands, which severely infringed upon Chinese sovereignty. The Chinese expressed their outrage in many songs of protest; these songs, which circulated widely, may be regarded as the immediate predecessors of contemporary songs for the masses.

While some of the protest songs were set to indigenous folk tunes, possibly out of nationalism, on the whole their style of music resembled that of the contemporary didactic songs. What made the protest songs different was their message. While the didactic songs usually stressed general principles of good citizenship, the protest songs focused on current political issues and events. Present-day songs for the masses have preserved this focus. Example 1 is one of the earliest extant protest songs; it is set to a folk tune called "Wu geng diao" [Five watches]. The text, written anonymously, expresses frustration and anger over the Twenty-one Demands.[22]

On May 4, 1919, the intellectual and political ferment that had been brewing for some time culminated in a nationwide series of student demonstrations. The immediate provocation was the decision of the Versailles Peace Conference to award the German-leased territory in Shandong province to Japan. Immediately, songs attacking the Versailles decision or

[22] The musical transcription in example one is based on the transcription in number notation in Liang Mao, "Wusi shiqi de gongnong geming gequ" [Workers' and peasants' revolutionary songs in the May Fourth period], *Renmin yinyue*, 1979, 4:7–9.

calling for a boycott on Japanese goods began to circulate orally and in the pages of some newspapers.[23]

By this time, many intellectuals, disillusioned by both national and international events and inspired by the success of the Russian Revolution, had turned toward Russia and Marxism-Leninism for a solution to China's problems. Some activists began to organize Marxist study groups; one of the earliest was formed around 1919 by teachers and students of Peking University. In January 1921, members of this group went to the Northern Terminal (the Chang Xin Dian) of the Peking-Shanghai Railroad in Peking to introduce the railroad workers to Marxist politics. They established an adult school and a recreational center for the workers. The activists had learned from Lenin's writings that the arts could serve a political function in a socialist state and from their own participation in demonstrations that songs could effectively unite a body of people. Thus they made a practice of teaching the workers some of the protest songs and also created new political songs for them to sing. With these early efforts, the modern Chinese song for the masses was born.[24]

One of the earliest extant songs from the Northern Terminal is the "Wuyi jinian ge" [May First memorial song]. Set to a classical *qin*[25] tune called "Meihua sannong" [Three variations on the theme of plum blossoms], the text calls for the workers to unite and to eliminate their oppressors. The railroad workers sang this song in their May Day demonstration—the first ever held in China.[26]

In 1922, a year after the establishment of the Chinese Communist Party, Liu Shaoqi and his colleagues began their organizational work among the mine and railroad workers in Jiangxi province, in an area known as Anyuan Lukuang [Anyuan Road Mine]. These activists also used songs; Liu himself is said to have written the text of a song for the workers' recreational center (Example 2).[27]

This song was sung during the Anyuan strike, which was organized by Liu in September 1922 and which was the first workers' strike in China.

[23] Ibid., pp. 8–9.

[24] Ibid., pp. 11–12; see also Shanghai yinyue xueyuan xiandai Zhongguo yinyue shiliao zhengli yanjiuzu (Shanghai Conservatory Contemporary Chinese Music History Editorial Board; hereafter, Shanghai yinyue xueyuan), "Wusi dao diyici guonei geming . . . gongnong geming gequ" [Revolutionary songs for peasants and workers from May Fourth to the first civil revolution], *Renmin yinyue*, 1961, 7–8:3.

[25] A *qin* is a seven-stringed zither traditionally associated with the literati. R. H. van Gulik translates the word as "lute" in his *The Lore of the Chinese Lute* (Tokyo: Sophia University, 1940).

[26] Liang Mao, "Wusi shiqi," pp. 11–12.

[27] Shanghai yinyue xueyuan, "Wusi dao," p. 3. The musical transcription is based on the transcription in number notation found in Liang Mao, "Wusi shiqi," pp. 11–12.

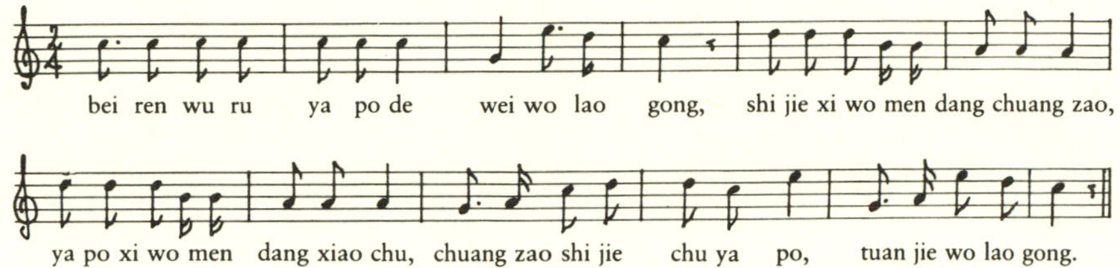

EXAMPLE 2. Anyuan Lukuang gongren julebu buge [Anyuan Road Mine Workers' Recreational Club Song]

Translation: We workers are the oppressed people. / We will create a new world, / eliminate oppression, / create a new world . . . / Workers unite.

The song later became the strike anthem for other worker groups.[28] No fewer than three versions of the song exist today.[29]

In early February 1923, a Peking-Shanghai Railroad strike was brutally suppressed by the authorities; hundreds of participants were killed. Shortly after, an anonymous song called "Fendou ge" [Song of struggle] appeared (Example 3). Its rousing text, focused on the most sensitive political issue of the day, made it immediately popular, and it was sung in all the subsequent strikes in support of the Peking-Shanghai Railroad workers.[30]

Meanwhile, in 1921 Peng Pai had begun a concerted effort to organize the peasants in the Hailufeng district of Guangdong province. Peng, himself a music lover, left behind a large number of songs, in which he had set texts about land reform to tunes from Hailufeng's rich folksong tradition.[31]

In 1923 the "Internationale" was introduced to China by Qu Qiubai, who published his translation in the progressive journal *Xin qingnian* [New youth], which he edited. The words of the "Internationale" were written in 1871 by Eugène Pottier, who had participated in the Paris Commune of that year. In 1888 Pierre Degeyter set the text to music.[32] The song became closely identified with the European labor movement of the 1890s and was sung by the workers in their demonstrations and strikes. Recommended by Lenin, the song was introduced to Russia, where it became the battle hymn of the Bolshevik revolution. In 1920 the newly

[28] Liang Mao, "Wusi shiqi," pp. 11–12.

[29] The second version of this song can be found in Liang Mao, "Wusi shiqi," pp. 12–13; for the third version, see *Geming gequ dajia chang* [Everybody sing revolutionary songs] (Peking: Yinyue chubanshe, 1965) 2:190--191. Here the music is attributed to Shi Lemeng.

[30] Liang Mao, "Wusi shiqi," pp. 13–14.

[31] Reportedly, many of the songs arranged by Peng Pai are still sung in the Hailufeng district. See ibid., p. 15.

[32] Nikolai Lenin, "Eugène Pottier," *Renmin yinyue,* 1962, 12:7 (translated into Chinese from Lenin's Russian text, which first appeared in *Pravda,* 3 January 1913).

jun fa shou zhong tie, gong ren jing shang xue,
tou ke duan, zhi ke lie, fen dou jing shen, bu xiao mie,
lao ku de qun zhong men, kuai kuai qi lai tuan jie.

EXAMPLE 3. Fendou ge [Song of struggle]
Translation: Iron rods held in the warlords' hands, / blood flows from the workers' necks. / Heads may roll, / bodies may break, / the spirit of struggle never ceases. / People oppressed by hardship, / rise up and unite.

established French Communist Party chose it as its official song.[33] Because of the historical and political significance of the "Internationale," its introduction to China in 1923 has come to be regarded as the signal of China's entrance into the world Communist movement.[34]

Many Russian songs were introduced to China in the 1920s and quickly gained currency in Marxist circles; some remained popular into the 1950s. One of these tunes, called in Chinese "Zuguo jinxing qu" [March of the motherland] (Example 4), inspired a host of Chinese songs for the masses. Like their model, these all begin with an upbeat from the fifth degree to the first degree of the scale and then proceed in a stately, moderate $\frac{4}{4}$ meter.[35] The style of the Russian tune itself shows a marked similarity to the "Internationale."

Another wave of protest songs was inspired by the May Thirtieth Incident of 1925, when police in Shanghai's International Settlement opened fire on students and workers who were demonstrating against the occupation of Chinese territory by imperialist powers. The police's killing of several demonstrators touched off a series of workers' strikes in Shanghai, Canton, and Hong Kong, in all of which protest songs were sung about the incident to rally public outrage.[36]

By this time propagandists had firmly grasped the power of songs performed en masse. In 1926 the Chinese Communist Party published a song

[33] Ibid. [34] Liang Mao, "Wusi shiqi," pp. 13–14.

[35] The notation is based on my own memory of the song. For a summary review of Russian influence on Chinese mass songs, see Xiang Yu, "Sulian geming gequ dui woguo geming gequde yingxiang" [The influence of Soviet revolutionary songs on our revolutionary songs], *Renmin yinyue,* 1957, 11:2–3, 6.

[36] Shanghai yinyue xueyuan, "Wusi dao," p. 5.

EXAMPLE 4. Zuguo jinxing qu [March of the motherland]
Translation: My motherland, how great and spacious. / She has enormous fields and countless forests. / I have not seen any other country of the world in which the people can breathe so freely.

handbook called *Geming ge ji* [Collection of songs for the revolution], edited by Li Qiushi. Included in the handbook were all the then-current protest songs, scores of Russian songs with Chinese texts, and the "Internationale." In his preface the editor stressed the songs' importance as historical documents of modern Chinese nationalism and as expressions of the spirit of revolution. Li called for a systematic promotion of songs to foment revolution. To facilitate circulation of these songs, the editor provided musical notation in addition to the song texts. The Western staff is used, with a simplified form of notation that uses Arabic numerals to represent the pitches of the diatonic scale, a system that was and still is popularly used in handbooks of Chinese music.[37]

The value of songs as propaganda was also recognized by Mao Zedong himself. In July 1924 he included singing sessions in his thirteen-week seminar on the organization of a peasant movement in Canton. Reportedly, among the songs sung there were some of those arranged by Peng Pai, who had used the folk tunes of Guangdong province. After Mao established a revolutionary base in the Jinggang Mountains in Jiangxi, in 1927, he instituted the use of songs to win the goodwill and cooperation of the local people. Songs also served to help train the cadres of the Fourth Army of the Chinese Workers' and Peasants' Red Army, which he formed with Zhu De in 1928.[38]

Mao demonstrated his belief that song is part of the political didactic machine in 1929 in his draft for the resolution of the Gutian Conference. He called for the formal inclusion of song teaching in the training program for cadres and soldiers and for the establishment of a committee to pro-

[37] Ibid. [38] Ibid.

duce appropriate songs.[39] However, due to the lack of personnel trained in music, very few original songs were composed during the Jiangxi period; instead, suitable new texts were written for folk tunes from the Jiangxi region, tunes from old protest songs, and Russian tunes brought back to China by returning cadres. Few of the songs produced in this period are accessible to this author, but one may gain some idea about their political themes from their titles. In the following list of some of these titles one may detect the beginning of a tendency, reinforced later, to use westernized tunes for texts dealing with general dogma and folk tunes for texts dealing with rural life.[40]

Song titles of the Jiangxi Period

a. Titles of songs whose tunes were adapted from Russian sources
   "Wuyi douzheng ge" [May First struggle song]
   "Zhongguo gongnong hongjun ge" [Songs of the Chinese Workers' and Peasants' Red Army]
   "Gongchanzhuyi jinxing qu" [March of Chinese Communism]

b. Titles of songs whose tunes were adapted from folk tunes
   "Gongnong baodong ge" [Songs of workers' and peasants' revolt]
   "Shi song lang dang hongjun ge" [Song in ten stanzas: on sending my lover to join the Red Army]
   "Chun geng yundong ge" [Spring ploughing song]

The 1930s saw the beginning of a new development in song writing, led by a group of young composers associated with the National Shanghai Conservatory of Music and by composers working for Shanghai's newly developed popular musical stage and film industry. The movement was initially an artistic experiment that aspired to unite Western and Chinese elements in a new form of Chinese song. As Sino-Japanese relations continued to deteriorate and Chinese nationalistic feeling became more intense, composers quickly exploited this newly developed medium to expess their patriotism. One of the young composers most active in this development was Nie Er (1912–1935).

Originally self-taught, Nie Er had later studied violin and composition with Russian instructors at the Shanghai Conservatory. He had left his native Yunnan province for Shanghai in the early 1930s and there he eked out a precarious living by writing music for films and the stage. Some of his songs for films became widely known. In 1932 he was befriended by the leftist writer Tian Han, at whose instigation he and two other young musicians, Ren Guang and Zhang Shu, formed the Sulian zhi youshe (Society of Friends of the Soviet Union) to study contemporary Russian

[39] *Renmin yinyue,* 1961, 1:12.
[40] Xiang Yu, "Sulian geming," p. 6.

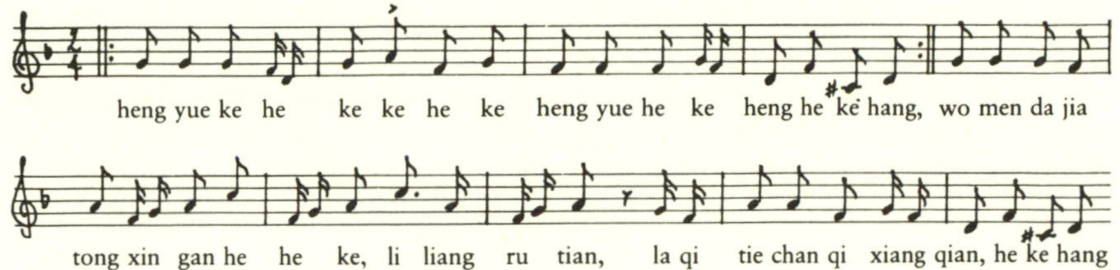

EXAMPLE 5. Dalu ge [The great road]
Translation: Heng yue ke he ke ke he ke, / heng yue he ke heng he ke hang. / Let us unite and work together, / he he ke, / use our great strength. / Push the shovel, forward march / he ke hang. /

music and the Marxist esthetic principle of social realism. Through this connection Nie was introduced to the Russian propaganda films of the 1930s, which were occasionally shown among leftist circles in Shanghai. Nie was particularly impressed by how the Russians used music to enhance the film's narrative and later endeavored to emulate the technique. Russian influence is plainly discernible in the songs Nie composed after 1932. "Dalu ge" [The great road] (Example 5), which Nie composed for a film of the same name, plainly echoes "The Song of the Volga Boatmen."[41]

In 1933 Nie joined the Communist Party and began to dedicate a large amount of his time to composing patriotic songs aimed against the Japanese, a campaign initiated by composers based in Shanghai. In 1934 Nie wrote nearly forty such songs to texts by Tian Han, who excelled in writing rousing texts laden with political slogans. As Nie's tunes allowed the lyrics to be clearly enunciated, they were particularly suitable for use in mass movements. In 1935 Nie wrote "Yiyongjun jinxing qu" [March of the volunteers] (Example 6) for a patriotic film called *Fengyun ernü* [Children of the storm].

The short declamatory phrases of the song and its marchlike rhythm fitted the rousing and defiant text perfectly, and the song so captured the national anti-Japanese sentiment that it was soon sung all over China. In 1937 it was chosen as the official song of the Communist New Fourth Army, an association that prompted Chiang Kai-shek's government to censor the song severely. When the People's Republic was established in 1949 "March of the Volunteers" was chosen as the national anthem.[42]

Another well-known composer who also joined the Communist Party and also wrote songs attacking Japan was Xian Xinghai (1905–1945).

[41] Hong Qiu, "Nie Er nianbiao chugao" [First draft of a Nie Er chronology], *Renmin yinyue,* 1955, 8:5–9. For the music of "Dalu ge," see *Historical Revolutionary Songs* (Peking: Foreign Languages Press, 1971), pp. 9–10.

[42] Hong Qiu, "Nie Er."

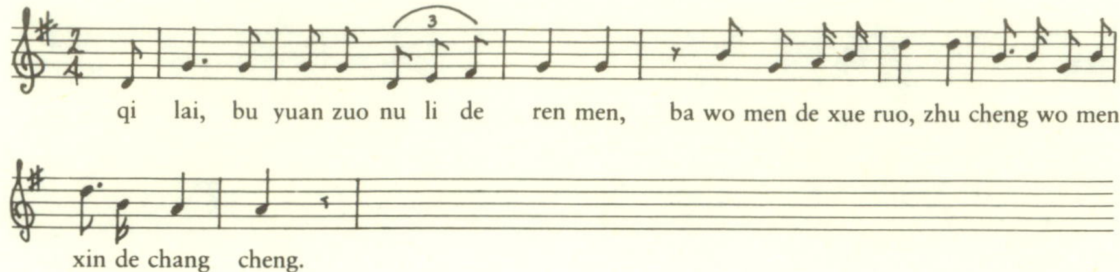
qi lai, bu yuan zuo nu li de ren men, ba wo men de xue ruo, zhu cheng wo men
xin de chang cheng.

EXAMPLE 6. Yiyongjun jinxing qu [March of the volunteers]
Translation: Arise all those who will not be enslaved. / Use our own bodies, / build a new and strong Great Wall.

Unlike Nie, Xian had received a thorough training in composition, having studied at the Paris Conservatoire from 1929 to 1935 under the direction of Paul Dukas and Vincent d'Indy. Xian composed large-scale orchestral works as well as songs. He returned to Shanghai penniless in 1935 and earned a meager salary by writing songs for films. He was soon recruited by Tian Han to join the campaign for anti-Japanese songs as a composer, singer, and conductor. In 1936 alone, Xian poured out some three hundred patriotic songs, some of which, he claimed, took only five or six minutes to write.[43]

Traveling all over China to present the anti-Japanese songs, Xian encountered a great variety of regional folk and popular musical styles, some of which he used in his own music. For example, in "Ding ying shang" [Grin and bear it], whose title came from a popular Cantonese expression, Xian used Cantonese folk tunes to set a text that includes much Cantonese slang. In "Pao guan dong" [Traveling to east of the Pass], he imitated the style of beggar's jingle called *shulaibao* that is widely heard in North China and that is sung to the accompaniment of a pair of wooden or bone clappers.[44]

By uniting Western and Chinese elements, Nie and Xian brought the medium of mass songs to its maturity and, through their association with the anti-Japanese campaign, gave it also the indelible stamp of nationalism.

The War of Resistance against Japan that broke out in 1937 stimulated a further outpouring of songs with patriotic themes. Composers of all ideological persuasions joined forces to create songs supporting the war. Through being sung in war films many of these songs became very popular with general audiences, thus constituting a true mass medium.

The next stage of development took place in Yan'an, where Mao and his comrades had settled in 1935 after the historic Long March. When the

[43] Xian Xinghai, "Xian Xinghai zhaji" [Xian Xinghai's notebook], *Renmin yinyue,* 1955, 8:13.

[44] Ibid.

war broke out, writers, students, and composers headed en masse for Yan'an. The schools that were set up for cadres formally included training in the arts for propaganda use in the curriculum.[45]

In 1939 Xian Xinghai also came to Yan'an, to head the music division of the Lu Xun Academy of Art and Literature. While there Xian wrote the celebrated "Huanghe dahechang" [Yellow River cantata] for mixed chorus and for an orchestra combining Western and Chinese instruments. The cantata had its premiere in Yan'an in 1940.[46] During the Cultural Revolution this work was transcribed and revised (not by Xian himself), to become the internationally known "Gangqin xiezouqu 'Huanghe' " [Yellow River piano concerto]; there is no mention of Xian's name in this revised version.[47] Historically and artistically, the "Yellow River Cantata" is a milestone in contemporary Chinese music. It is by far the most convincing synthesis of Western and Chinese musical idioms. In a single work it unites such diverse techniques and elements as, for example, the Chinese folk antiphonal singing style called *duikou chang,* the Chinese fisherman's work song called *haozi,* traditional Chinese percussive patterns and instrumentation, Hugo Wolf's declamatory recitative style (adapted to the Chinese language), the traditional Western contrapuntal technique of choral writing, and, finally, the atmospheric orchestral effects of the French Impressionistic school.[48] Among the pieces in this cantata, the song "Huanghe chuanfu qu" [Song of the Yellow River boatmen] is frequently sung as a mass song and has had a profound influence on mass songs by later composers (Example 7).

Besides his large-scale works, Xian continued to write short songs in support of the war. Of these "Dadao diren houfang qu" [Go to the enemy's rear] is still popular today (Example 8).[49] Xian died of tuberculosis in a Moscow hospital in 1941, but his influence on the younger generation of composers can still be seen today.

Since composers could not meet the great demand for songs to be used as a propaganda tool in Yan'an, folk tunes were fitted to local vernacular

[45] See Tian Jiagu, ed. *Kangzhan jiaoyu zai Shanbei* [Resistance education in North Shaanxi] (Hankow: Mingru chubanshe, 1938; facsimile reprint, Hong Kong: Yuandong tushu, 1968), p. 30.

[46] Xian Xinghai, "Xian Xinghai," pp. 14–15.

[47] Xian's "Yellow River Cantata" was turned into a piano concerto by the pianist Yin Chengzhong. See Yin Chengzhong, "How the Piano Concerto 'Yellow River' Was Composed," *Chinese Literature* 11 (1974):97–102.

[48] Xian discusses in detail his compositional procedure in his preface to the "Yellow River Cantata" (published with the cantata posthumously). See Xian Xinghai, *Huanghe dahechang* [Yellow River cantata], ed. Huang Luofeng, (Shanghai: Dushu chubanshe, 1947); see also Xian, "Xian Xinghai," pp. 14–15.

[49] See *Historical Revolutionary Songs,* pp. 16–17.

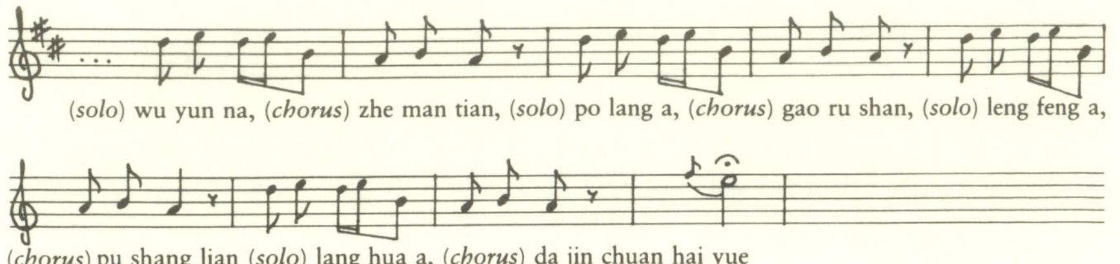
(solo) wu yun na, (chorus) zhe man tian, (solo) po lang a, (chorus) gao ru shan, (solo) leng feng a,
(chorus) pu shang lian (solo) lang hua a, (chorus) da jin chuan hai yue

EXAMPLE 7. Huanghe chuanfu qu [Song of the Yellow River boatmen]
Translation: (*solo*) Dark clouds / (*chorus*) cover the sky, / (*solo*) great waves / (*chorus*) as high as mountains, / (*solo*) cold wind / (*chorus*) cuts our faces. / (*solo*) The water / (*chorus*) rushes into the cabin, hai yue.

texts. In 1942 Mao's celebrated Yan'an "Talks" called for, among other things, the creation of an art medium that would be truly representative of the broad masses of peasants, workers, and soldiers. In response, music personnel in Yan'an assembled a massive collection of folksongs from the northwestern region near Yan'an. One of the songs in this collection was "Xiu jin bian" [A golden embroidered sampler] (Example 9), which was set to a new text anonymously. The song was extremely popular until in the Cultural Revolution, it, along with many other folk tunes, was declared politically unfit. Recently, however, this song was revived and has been republished with the addition of a third stanza commemorating Premier Zhou Enlai.[50]

Another folk idiom that was used for propaganda during the Yan'an period and that had great influence on later songs for the masses is the type of folk theater called *yangge*. Its performance involves songs, dances, and dialogue and is accompanied by an assortment of percussion instruments such as drums, gongs, and cymbals. The music of *yangge* has a lively rhythm, and its melodies are conceived within the Re mode of the diatonic scale. The percussion accompaniment consists of variations on this basic rhythm: . In 1943 the revised "new *yangge*" became the chief cultural and political expression of the Yan'an government and as such influenced other aspects of musical production.[51]

One of the composers who arranged music for the new *yangge* and who also composed songs for the masses was Ma Ke, a chemistry student who turned composer with Xian Xinghai's encouragement. One of Ma's most celebrated theatrical works was his setting for the original version of the musical drama *Bai mao nü* [White-haired girl]. In 1948, while working

[50] The music of "Xiu jin bian" is transcribed here from number notation in *Renmin yinyue*, 1977, 1:52–53 and footnote.

[51] For further information on the *yangge* movement, see David Holm's article in this volume (Part 1); see also David L. Holm, "Report on an Experiment with Yangge Dance and Music," *CHINOPERL Papers* no. 7 (1977), pp. 92–105.

EXAMPLE 8. Dadao diren houfang qu [Go to the enemy's rear]
Translation: Go to the enemy's rear, / chase the aggressors away. / Go to the enemy's rear, / chase the aggressors away.

among the laborers in northeastern China, Ma wrote the internationally known "Zamen gongren you liliang" [We workers have strength] (Example 10). This inspired song expressed his admiration for the proletarian class and his faith in a socialist future for China.

"We Workers Have Strength" quickly caught on nationally among students and workers. Part of the song is strikingly similar to Xian's "Song of the Yellow River Boatmen" (see Example 7), while its rhythm calls to mind the percussion beat of *yangge*. Ma's works were censored during the nine years between 1966 and 1975, and he died in 1976.[52] His works were revived after the fall of the Gang of Four.

DEVELOPMENTS AFTER 1949

Since Liberation, literally thousands of songs for the masses have been produced. However, the medium has shown little musical development since it was brought to its maturity by Xian and Nie and consolidated by Ma Ke and his contemporaries. Later development has been concerned with the ideological refinement of the songs' texts, categorization of the songs according to their political functions and messages, and the perfection of the mechanisms for controlling all song production.

Recently in the thaw following the Cultural Revolution, there have been tentative signs of renewed openness to musical experimentation. One sign was the article in *Renmin yinyue* [People's music] that discussed the merits of Y. R. Chao's compositions and his views on music (see above).[53] Another sign was a reprinting of Mao's talk to a group of music personnel in 1956, in which he encouraged them to develop a new style of Chinese

[52] Qu Wei, "Shenqie huainian Ma Ke tongzhi" [Deeply remember comrade Ma Ke], *Renmin yinyue,* 1977, 4:24–26; see also Qu Wei, "Gequ *Bai mao nü* de dansheng" [The birth of the opera *White-Haired Girl*], *Renmin yinyue,* 1977, 2:12–18. The music for the song "Zamen gongren you liliang" is based on the number notation in *Renmin yinyue,* 1977, 3:53–54.

[53] See Note 21.

zheng yue li nao yuan xiao, jin bian xiu kai liao,
er yue li gua chun feng, jin bian xiu de hong,
jin bian xiu za Mao zhu xi ling dao de zhu yi
jin bian shang xiu de shi jin xing Mao Ze
gao yi xiu Mao zhu xi, ren min de
dong. er xiu zong si ling, ge ming de
san xiu Zhou zong li, ren min de
hao fu qi.
lao ying xiong.
hao zong li.

EXAMPLE 9. Xiu jin bian [A golden embroidered sampler]
Translation: In the first month we celebrate New Year. / Let us embroider in the golden sampler the image of Chairman Mao, / our superb leader. / In the second month Spring wind blowing, / let us embroider in a golden sampler the image of our savior Mao Zedong. / First embroider the image of Chairman Mao, / who is the savior of the people. / Second embroider the image of the commander-in-chief, / who is the hero of our revolution. / Third embroider the image of Premier Zhou, / who is the people's good premier.

music that would fuse Western and Chinese elements.[54] Since this article appeared on the front page of the *People's Daily,* its political significance cannot be ignored; whether it will have a practical impact on musical composition, however, remains to be seen.

Production and Dissemination of Songs for the Masses

The tunes of songs for the masses come from two main sources: individuals and folksongs. Two categories of individual composers are recognized: professionals (*zhuanye*) and amateurs (*yeyu*). The professionals are members of either the National Association of Chinese Music Personnel (established 1949; name changed to Chinese Musicians' Association in 1959) or the Chinese Association of Composers (established 1954). These groups are supported by the state to produce, teach, and perform music and to conduct research. Some professional composers have received formal training in composition, while others gained recognition through avocational activities and were then appointed to be members of either asso-

[54] Mao Zedong, "Tong yinyue gongzuozhede tanhua" [Talks with music personnel], *Renmin ribao,* 9 September 1979, p. 1.

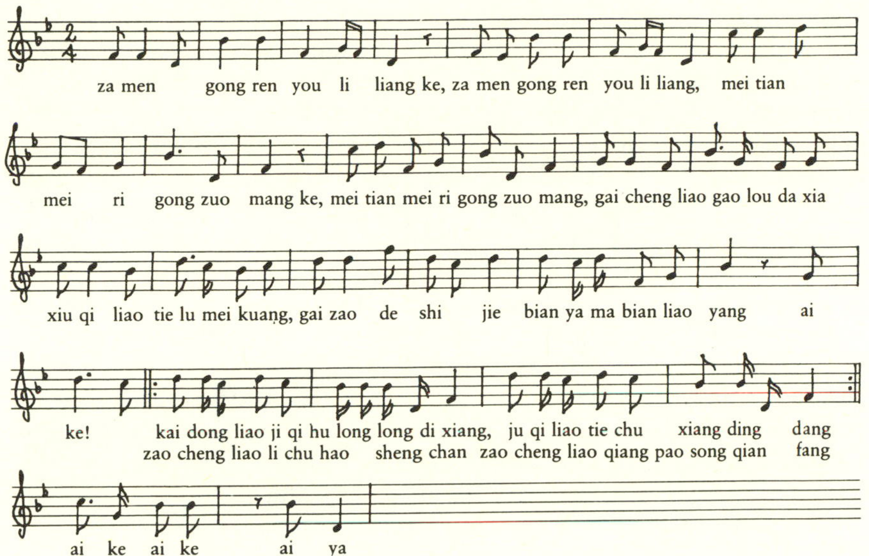
za men gong ren you li liang ke, za men gong ren you li liang, mei tian
mei ri gong zuo mang ke, mei tian mei ri gong zuo mang, gai cheng liao gao lou da xia
xiu qi liao tie lu mei kuang, gai zao de shi jie bian ya ma bian liao yang ai
ke! kai dong liao ji qi hu long long di xiang, ju qi liao tie chu xiang ding dang
zao cheng liao li chu hao sheng chan zao cheng liao qiang pao song qian fang
ai ke ai ke ai ya

EXAMPLE 10. Zamen gongren you liliang [We work ers have strength]
Translation: We workers have strength. / We workers have strength. / We work hard day and night. / We work hard day and night. / We build tall buildings and big mansions. / We repair railroads and dig in the mines. / We change the surface of the earth. / Turn on the engine, / raise the hammer, / manufacture the plough, / produce guns and cannons.

ciation. During the early days of the People's Republic, the number of professional composers was not great; though their number grew as more people joined their ranks, it is still small.

From the early 1960s the government has made a consistent effort to encourage amateurs—i.e., factory workers, peasants, soldiers, and students—to create their own songs. The two basic methods of supplying motivation have been *fudao* ("to assist and coach") and *zhengge pingzhuang huodong* ("to initiate song-writing competitions"). Conducted nationwide, both activities have been jointly sponsored by the Composers' Association and by the Ministry of Culture and are enforced at the provincial and local level by cultural bureaus and units.[55]

Assistance and coaching are provided for musically inclined amateurs in the form of short courses in tune writing and text setting. Conducted by professional composers, music teachers, or cadres conversant with the rudiments of music, these after-work classes emphasize practical instruction

[55] Information gleaned from the following issues of *Renmin yinyue*: 1962, 10:21–23; 1963, 4:12; 1964, 11–12:28–29; 1965, 3:27; 1965, 4:8–10; 1966, 2:2–12, 21, 27.

and teach the simplified "number notation" to facilitate the writing down of compositions. Public forums on the techniques of composition are also held by professional composers, and articles by professionals on how to write songs frequently appear in popular magazines, journals, and newspapers. Further encouragement is provided by periodic song-writing competitions held at the national or local level. The winning songs are frequently published and broadcast or sung in mass rallies. Reports by amateur composers of their procedures or experiences in composing appear in papers and magazines.[56]

The policy of motivating the people to write their own music is but one practical application of Mao's "mass line" theory. Mao maintained that, if they were encouraged to participate in creative activities, the masses could articulate their views. The authorities and the professionals, thus acquainted with the people's preferences, could imitate them and shape artistic media that the people would welcome. On a more practical level, however, one of the factors responsible for official mobilizing of the masses to write songs may have been the fact that there were simply not enough new songs produced by the small number of professionals to fulfill the state's propaganda needs, a situation that resulted in a mass-production method of song composition. This method was evident in the field of literature as well.[57]

Another realization of Mao's "mass line" theory was the sending of professional composers periodically to labor among the workers and peasants, so that the composers could develop a realistic understanding of the workers' needs and could accurately reflect these needs in their compositions. During the Cultural Revolution this policy was carried to an extreme. Professionals, composers included, were subjected to intense reeducation; many were censured or silenced. Those who were allowed to remain in their posts as composers were organized into teams to compose collectively, and no work was considered complete until it was duly revised in the light of mass opinion. Further, collectively composed works

[56] Information about two well-known amateur song writers, Shi Zhangyuan and Li Youyuan (1903–1955) is provided respectively in *Renmin yinyue,* 1961, 1:5, and *Renmin yinyue,* 1978, 1:34–35. Li Youyuan was the composer of the famous song "Dongfang hong" [The east is red]. Other amateurs who have won prizes in song-writing competitions were sometimes invited to write about their experiences. See, for example, Liu Wenjin, "Zai qunzhong douzhengzhong chuangzuo" [Composing amidst mass struggle], *Renmin yinyue,* 1965, 5:10; and Yao Yuxing, "Wo dui yeyu yinyue chuangzuode tihui" [My experience as an amateur composer], *Renmin yinyue,* 1966, 2:28–30.

[57] On practices of collective composing, see *Renmin yinyue,* 1962, 10:9, 21–23; *Renmin yinyue,* 1963, 1:2–3; and *Renmin yinyue,* 1964, 11–12:22–25. On collective efforts in literature, see Lars Ragvald, "Professionalism and Amateur Tendencies in Post-revolutionary Chinese Literature," in Göran Malmqvist, ed., *Modern Chinese Literature and Its Social Context* [Stockholm, 1977], pp. 152–179.

were never attributed to the individuals involved, but bore the name of the composing team, which was usually that of a work unit attached to a factory or commune. The theory was that such a collectivized creative process would totally submerge the individual's efforts into a democratic pool of mass opinion. Thus the gap between professionals and the masses would be eliminated, and the resultant creative product would truly be a work of the masses.

The notion of the collective creative process was widely publicized and highly romanticized during the Cultural Revolution. The idea, of course, was that music should not be a purely mental product, composed only by trained specialists sitting at pianos, but a spontaneous, direct, and collectively created outgrowth of physical labor. Practice, however, differed from theory, according to some of the professional composers who took part in the process. Except for such politically important showpieces as the model operas, for which careful planning was done, most of the so-called collectivized compositions were nothing but haphazard pastiches of unrelated musical phrases or ideas that individuals had suggested at random, frequently during working periods. Some stringent guidelines apparently circulated that prescribed the use of certain melodic or rhythmic figures for works of a certain type. After the Cultural Revolution, this form of random, collectivized composition was evidently discontinued, and the methods used prior to the Cultural Revolution have returned.[58]

The repertoire of songs for the masses also includes a large number of songs whose tunes were derived from folk tunes. In 1955, immediately following Mao's decision to accelerate agricultural collectivization, composers, music researchers, and music instructors were exhorted to go the the countryside. There they were to show their support for Mao's decision by working with the peasants and by collecting folksongs for use in propaganda in support of the policy. The justification for such a massive collecting project, according to Zhou Yang, then the Vice-Minister of Culture, was to "scientifically preserve and systematically organize this national treasure [i.e., folksongs], to revise (*gaizheng*) and enrich (*jiagong*) their contents in order to make them a fitting medium to entertain the people and to educate them at the same time."[59] The theory behind such rhetoric, once again, is the "mass line" concept of "from the masses, to the masses." Thousands of folksongs were accordingly collected, and to their

[58] For information about the actual practice of collective composition during the Cultural Revolution, see Lu Yang, "Yinyue chuangzuo suibi" [Notes on the process of music composition], *Renmin yinyue,* 1977, 7:29–31.

[59] See Minjian yinyue yanjiushi (Folk Music Research Section), "Min'ge gaibian zongjie" [Summary of folksong revision], in Zhongyang yinyue xueyuan minzu yinyue yanjiusuo (Central Music Institute, National Music Research Department), ed., *Minzu yinyue yanjiu lunwenji* [Monograph on folk music studies] (Peking: Yinyue chubanshe, 1956) 1:102.

"revised and enriched" tunes were set new words that bore political messages in a language style closely akin to that of the original folksongs.[60]

Special mention should be made of a large group of songs whose tunes have been borrowed from the folk or popular music of China's many minority ethnic groups and set to Chinese texts. The use of Chinese implies that these songs are aimed at the majority Han race; one may speculate that even the tunes themselves have been sinicized and modernized.

Direction and Supervision of Song Production

The political themes to be propagandized through cultural products, songs included, are dictated by the most important decision-making body of the Chinese Communist Party, the Central Committee. Its decisions are carried out and supervised by the Ministry of Culture with the help of the state-owned mass media, various local cultural institutions, and the associations for music personnel and composers. It was the Party's Central Committee, for example, that in 1955–1956 ordered the collection of folksongs as part of the intensified collectivization of agriculture.

Another case of the Party's direction of cultural production began at the Tenth Plenum of the Eighth Central Committee, which convened in September 1962. At that meeeting, Mao Zedong attacked modern revisionism and proclaimed an intensification of class struggle. In the following month, the editors of the official publication *Gequ* [Song] called for the writing of militant songs reflecting the spirit of class struggle, suggesting that a marchlike rhythm would be appropriate. *Gequ* subsequently published hundreds of songs whose texts and music followed these guidelines.[61] In 1970 Mao issued another statement, this time denouncing the Cambodian coup and attacking the U.S. Shortly after, a song appeared with a text derived directly from Mao's statement. Called "Quan shijie renmin yiding shengli" [People of the entire world will be triumphant] (Example 11), the song was constantly sung and broadcast in China in the early 1970s.[62]

Political regulation is not restricted to newly composed songs. Sometimes old favorites are revived for use in a new political context. In the autumn of 1971, for example, the "Internationale" and another old standard, "San da jilu baxiang zhuyi" [The three rules of discipline and eight points for attention] were repopularized to be sung in rallies criticizing Lin Biao.[63]

These and many other examples illustrate the close control exercised over China's mass media, in which songs play an integral part. Indeed, a

[60] Ibid., pp. 102–120.

[61] *Renmin yinyue,* 1962, 10:9.

[62] I am indebted to Anders Hansson for this information. During the early 1970s, Mr. Hansson served as a cultural attaché to the Swedish Embassy in Peking.

[63] As above.

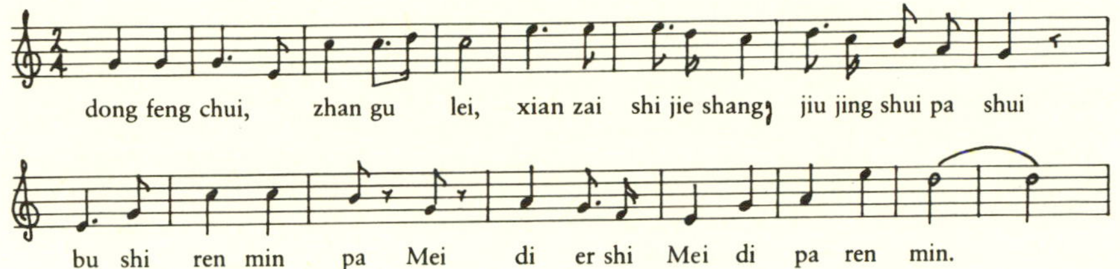
dong feng chui, zhan gu lei, xian zai shi jie shang, jiu jing shui pa shui
bu shi ren min pa Mei di er shi Mei di pa ren min.

EXAMPLE 11. Quan shijie renmin yiding shengli [People of the entire world will be triumphant]

Translation: The east wind is blowing, / the battle drum is sounded. / In the world today, who is afraid of whom? / It is not the people who are afraid of the American imperialists. / It is the American imperialists who are afraid of the people.

chronological survey of popular songs would form an accurate chronicle of political events in the People's Republic of China.

Songs are disseminated and popularized in a variety of ways: by publication in newspapers and in song handbooks with number notation, both of which are distributed widely by governmental organizations; by broadcasting; or by being taught in schools, factories, or communes. Since teaching songs directly is by far the most effective method, it deserves special emphasis.

Songs are taught and sung regularly in schools and universities.[64] In factories and in the countryside, where it is less convenient to have singing sessions, music specialists periodically visit to teach songs. In addition, state-sponsored art troupes are sent to perform for the people and to teach them songs. Many of the songs prepared for the peasants are "revised and enriched" folksongs. The peasants are instructed to sing these new folksongs in a "modern and scientific way," that is, to sing without the special vocal ornaments associated with certain kinds of folksongs. The preferred vocal style was an open-throated manner based on Western voice production.[65]

During periods of intense political campaigning, song rallies are held in public places. Sometimes the masses are exhorted to master a specific group of songs by a certain date as part of their political lesson for a special campaign.[66] Cadres, students, or other music personnel conduct informal song-teaching sessions anywhere people gather: in the cinema

[64] This observation is based on my own experiences as a student in China during the 1950s and on my interviews with Chinese students now studying in this country. Paul Clark also reports that, when he was a student at Peking University in the 1970s, songs were taught to the university students every Wednesday afternoon.

[65] Information gleaned from various issues of *Renmin yinyue.*

[66] For example, in 1961 Lin Biao called for the masses to learn ten songs as part of a political lesson. See *Renmin yinyue,* 1961, 1:12.

before or after the show, on street corners, and in local recreational centers. In rural areas, songs are taught in the field, in communes, or at agricultural fairs.[67]

Categorization of Songs according to Content

The messages of the song texts fall into the following broad categories, some of which may overlap.

Songs of Praise and Exaltation. These include songs praising leaders, the motherland, the Party and other important institutions, model heroes, and socialism in general. By far the greatest number of these songs praise Mao Zedong; the best-known is perhaps "Dongfang hong" [The east is red]. A group of the songs in honor of Mao consists of songs set to Mao's poems as well as to quotations from his writings and utterances. During the Cultural Revolution many such songs were published, but they are now seldom sung.[68] More recently, songs have appeared praising Zhou Enlai, Hua Guofeng, and Deng Xiaoping. Among the favorite topics for songs in praise of the country's institutions are the Chinese Communist Party and the heroism of the People's Liberation Army. The model hero most venerated in song is Lei Feng; a typical song about him is "Xuexi Lei Feng nayang" [Learn from Lei Feng]. This category of song obviously serves the general political goals of raising the consciousness of the masses, of providing them with a firm national identity, and of indicating to them acceptable social and political behavior. Songs about the nation and about Party dogma tend to become perennial favorites; other, more topical songs gain and lose in popularity according to the political fashions of the time or to the fortunes of the individuals involved.

Songs for Special Groups or Work Units. These are songs intended to promote group solidarity among soldiers, students, children, workers, and peasants. Their texts deal with activities associated with each group: songs for workers have titles such as "We Workers Have Iron Shoulders" and "I Dedicate Crude Oil to My Motherland"; songs for peasants are called "The New Faces of the Countryside" or "Sing of the Agricultural Mechanization." In general, songs aimed at peasants derive their tunes from folk music, while those aimed at soldiers, students, and workers have more westernized tunes. But exceptions occur, and groups often sing each other's songs.

Songs that Announce Major Policy Decisions. These songs began to appear with increasing frequency during the Cultural Revolution. Their

[67] Information gleaned from various issues of *Renmin yinyue:* 1963, 3:9; 1963, 6:8.
[68] A fact reported to me by Chinese students now studying in this country.

texts incorporate the key terms of the policy decisions announced in the *People's Daily* and other official Party organs. A typical song is "Heartily Hail the Party's Eleventh Congress," which appeared when the Party validated Hua Guofeng's chairmanship in 1977. Because of the topicality of these songs, their circulation is often short-lived.

Songs of Criticism. These songs denounce failures, errors, deviations, crimes, and shortcomings. Such criticisms are always quite specific and are frequently directed against individuals. For example, the second purge of Deng Xiaoping inspired a song called "Raising the Iron Fist." Its text runs as follows:

The banners are waving,
The wind and thunder are roaring,
The People's Army is marching heroically.
Let us fight against the Rightist-Revisionists' attempt to reverse the verdict.
Raising the iron fist of revolution,
Angrily and loudly denounce Deng Xiaoping.
Resolutely eliminate feudalism, capitalism, and revisionism.
Whoever wishes for restoration is regressing.
We will fight against him with determination.

A song of 1977, "Smashing the Gang of Four into Pieces," has the following lines:

The conspiracy of Wang, Zhang, Jiang, and Yao to usurp the
  Party leadership is despicable.
We are united around the Party.
The crimes committed by the Gang of Four must be avenged.

Songs concerning Foreign Affairs. This category includes two types of songs. The first attacks imperialism. Before China's rapprochement with the United States, a large number of these songs concerned examples of American aggression, from the Korean War to the Cuban missile crisis, the U-2 Incident, and finally the Vietnam War and the invasion of Cambodia.

The second type of song about foreign affairs expresses solidarity with socialist and other nations friendly to China. Some of the titles are almost identical, although the tunes are not. For example, in the 1950s there was a song called "Moscow-Peking," in the 1960s, when Albania was a close ally of China, there was one called "Tirana-Peking," and today there is a song called "Bucharest-Peking."

Songs about Taiwan. These songs either show solidarity with the people of Taiwan or express China's determination to rejoin Taiwan to the motherland. The songs bear titles such as "Taiwan tongbao shi womende qin gurou" [The people of Taiwan are our own flesh and blood] and "Women yiding yao shouhui Taiwan" [We must have Taiwan back].

Musical Form

Mass songs are usually sung without instrumental accompaniment. When instruments are available, however—in a classroom, a radio broadcasting studio, or a well-organized political rally, for example—these songs may be accompanied by a piano, an organ, an accordion, or even a full orchestra or band. Sometimes the instrumental accompaniment simply duplicates the voice line; at other times, if the composer so directs or if the musicians have the necessary competence, simple chords may be added.

Some composers, particularly the professionals, devise melodies that clearly imply a harmonic support. Such musically educated elites may insist that harmonic accompaniment is a sign of modernity. Nonetheless, the concept of functional harmony and the sound of functional chord progressions remain relatively unfamiliar, and hence unimportant, to the Chinese populace. The goverment apparently agrees; most of the official song handbooks I have surveyed suggest no accompaniment beyond the occasional direction to "use drum or cymbal accompaniment here." All the handbooks I have examined use number notation.

Musically, therefore, the mass songs can be characterized as simple tunes with no obligatory accompaniment. The following remarks on some characteristic melodies and rhythms of the mass songs are based on my examination of some five hundred songs.[69]

Some general preliminary remarks are in order. First, regardless of their origin, the tunes fall into two major categories: those inspired by Western concepts of tonality and those inspired by indigenous Chinese folk tunes. Secondly, all the songs are diatonic. Some employ the heptatonic scale and others the hexatonic or pentatonic scales; the latter are always in anhemitonic form (that it, there are no semitone steps in the scale). Finally, most of the songs are constructed in the major mode, but other modal configurations are also present. For example, many songs are based on the sol and re modes (which resemble the Mixolydian and Dorian modes respectively), while a few songs are based on the minor mode.

As a rule, no modulation occurs in any of the songs examined, and

[69] The musical examples discussed and cited in this section come from various Chinese song handbooks and recordings that are readily available in this country. The handbooks I have examined include: *Gequ* [Songs] (Peking: Yinyue chubanshe, 1952–1954, 1965–1966, 1969); *Jiefangjun gequ ji* [Song collection of the People's Liberation Army] (Shanghai: Wenhufa chubanshe, n.d.); *Geming gequ dajia chang* [Let's sing revolutionary songs] (Peking: Yinyue chubanshe, 1964); *Zhandi xin'ge* [New songs from the battlefield]—among many others too numerous to list here.

EXAMPLE 12. Shehuizhuyi jinxing qu [March of socialism] (*no text*)

chromatic alteration of pitch is rare. The handbooks indicate that the tessituras of the songs generally lie in the octave between B below middle C and B above middle C, in other words, in a range comfortable for the average singer, but the range may vary from an interval of a tenth to one of a thirteenth.

These songs are usually not very long, containing only six to eight phrases that divide into two halves. Many songs have more than one verse, all of which, however, are sung to the same tune, i.e., the songs are strophic.

Westernized Songs. The melodic tendencies of these songs usually result from an implied harmony. The basic implied chords are the tonic and dominant triads of the major scale and, to a lesser extent, of the minor scale. Needless to say, such a limited use of underlying harmony produces a simple harmonic rhythm, and the melodic motion that derives from it is often predictable and stereotyped. This predictability is well illustrated in Example 12, "Shehuizhuyi jinxing qu" [March of socialism]. The phrases of this song are determined by the text lines, and each phrase ends either on the tonic or on the dominant note. The melody is, by and large, the tonic triad, i.e., C–E–G in the key of C.

Like hundreds of songs of this type, this one begins on the upbeat with a dotted rhythmic figure ♪.♬|♩ on the dominant and tonic pitches. One possible source of this motif could be the beginning of the "Internationale." The Chinese national anthem, "March of the Volunteers," also uses a similar motif, although the initial skip of a fourth may simply come from the linguistic tones of the words "qi lai" (see Example 6).

This type of westernized tune typically has a marchlike rhythm that is

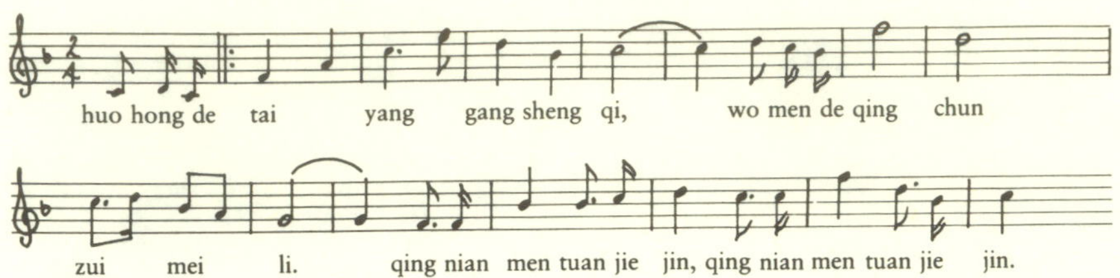
huo hong de tai yang gang sheng qi, wo men de qing chun
zui mei li. qing nian men tuan jie jin, qing nian men tuan jie jin.

EXAMPLE 13. Geming qingnian jinxing qu [March of revolutionary youths]
Translation: Like the early morning red sun, / our youth is beautiful. / Young people closely unite, / young people closely unite.

squarely aligned with the regular beats of the duple meter. The relentless ♩. ♪ | ♩ ♩ ♩ ♩ | ♩. ♪ ♩ 𝄾 | rhythm is only occasionally interrupted and modified by syncopation (the asterisk over measure 13 of Example 12 indicates one such use of syncopation).

The texts, as usual, are written in an easily comprehensible vernacular and generally in prose, as in Example 12. Some texts resemble verse in having a regular number of words in each line, and some even attempt to use rhyme. The ratio of one or two pitches to a syllable results in a predominantly syllabic and declamatory texture.

All the melodic, rhythmic, and textual factors described above contribute to produce a song style totally devoid of complexity. This simplicity is, of course, intentional; it obeys Mao's decree, in his Yan'an "Talks," that mass songs can relay their political messages best by staying simple, plain, and easy to memorize.

Examples 13 and 14 are both in the major mode, the first using the hexatonic scale (with omission of either the fourth or the seventh degree) and the second the pentatonic scale. These two types are very common among westernized songs.

Songs Modeled after Folk Tunes. In this group of songs, the Western concept of tonality does not apply. The folksong styles most commonly found in this category come from the northwest and north-central regions. The tunes of North Shaanxi characteristically use the sol mode (i.e., the Mixolydian mode). Frequently, the overall melodic tendency is a descending contour from the central pitch "sol" down to the "do" below, and then down to the low central pitch "sol." Example 15, which is modeled after a folk tune of North Shaanxi, shows just such a descending melodic contour. However, in three instances (bracketed in the score), this descending contour is inverted and ascends to the high central pitch "sol" instead of falling to the low central pitch "sol." This inversion may be an attempt to tone-paint the text; the first bracketed phrase translates as "Collectiv-

EXAMPLE 14. Gongren jieji goutou ying [Members of the working class are tough]

Translation: The working class is tough, / following Mao Zedong. / March, march, march. / Embracing our mother in our hearts, / cast our glances at the worldwide horizon. / March without delay along the road of revolution.

ized economy shimmering with golden beams" and the second as "The hearts of the Commune members turn toward the Communist Party."

Also characteristic of North Shaanxi's folksongs is the use of the Aeolian mode (A to a of the white keys of the piano; transposed to E in this example as in Example 16). The basic outline of this example is marked in the score as A and B. A appears twice at the beginning; the rest of the tune is made up of B and its modification, labeled B′.

Many of the tunes derived from folksongs use pentatonic scales. Several varieties of the pentatonic mode are found, the most common construction being do–re–fa–sol–la, as used in Example 17. The melody of this song is punctuated by the use of a pair of motives, marked *a* and *b* in the scores. The lively rhythm of this song brings to mind the rhythmic pattern of the *yangge* folk theater.

Example 18 is a song in the Mixolydian mode (G to g of the white keys on the piano; transposed to D in this example), which is commonly found among the folksongs of Gansu province. The melodic outline of this song, a pair of conjunct tetrachords, characterizes this type of folk tune in the D pentatonic mode. Also characteristic is the use of vocables.

Two final examples will illustrate the wide variety of pentatonic modes used in Chinese folksongs. Both Examples 19 and 20 derive from folksongs of Hunan province. The scale used in Example 19 is do–re–me–sol–la, while that used in Example 20 is la–do–re–mi–sol.

SUMMARY

The antecedents of contemporary songs for the masses were the politico-religious songs introduced by Hong Xiuquan, the leader of the Taiping

EXAMPLE 15. Sheyuan xin xiang Gongchan dang [Commune members' hearts turn toward the Communist party]

Translation: As the sunflower faces toward the sun, / commune members' hearts turn toward the Communist Party. / The benefits of people's communes are bountiful, / shimmering with golden beams of collectivized economy. / We poor peasants firmly grasp the seal of authority. / Never will we forget class struggle. / Chairman Mao leads us marching forward. / Commune members' hearts turn toward the Communist Party.

Rebellion who adopted some tunes and the practice of congregational hymn singing from Western missionaries. Since then, the medium has gone through a series of transformations. Immediately after the 1911 Nationalist Revolution, songs carrying didactic messages and modeled after the music of Protestant hymns were used to help foster a new national ideology. Such songs have become a major component in the musical experience of the modern Chinese. Some Chinese composers, motivated perhaps by a sense of nationalism, sought to include Chinese idioms in these didactic songs. Several lines of experimentation developed, but most approaches involved the use of melodies derived from folksongs or based upon the contours of the linguistic tones of the song-texts; the latter approach, used by very few composers, represents the continuation of a traditional technique of song composition.

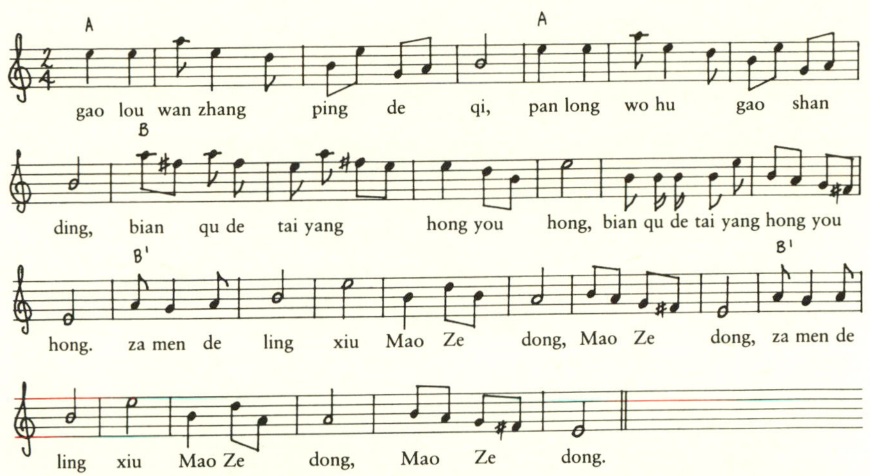

EXAMPLE 16. Womende lingxiu Mao Zedong [Our leader Mao Zedong]
Translation: Like tall buildings rising from the land, / like dragons and tigers reposing atop high mountains, / is our leader Mao Zedong, / who like the sun is radiating red beams in the Yan'an area.

EXAMPLE 17. Renmin gongshe jiu shi hao [People's communes are good]
Translation: Drums and gongs are beaten, / what a joyous sound! / Let us sing heartily. / What shall we sing? / Let us sing praise to the people's communes.

jie fang qu ya mo he hai, da sheng chan ya mo he hai, jun dui he ren min
xi li li li cha cha cha cha suo luo luo luo tai, qi dong yuan ya mo he hai.

EXAMPLE 18. Bianqu shi chang [*or*] Jun min da shengchan [Ten stanzas in praise of the border area (*or*) Soldiers and people produce together]
Translation: In the Liberated Area, he-hai, / soldiers and people, he-hai, / work together, / xi li li li / cha cha cha cha / suo luo luo luo tai / work together, he-hai.

liu yang he wan guo liao ji dao wan,
ji shi li shui lu dao xiang jiang, jiang bian
you ge shen mo xian na, chu liao ge shen mo ren
ling dao ren min de jie fang a yi ya yi zi ye.

EXAMPLE 19. Liuyang he [The Liuyang River]
Translation: How many bends are there in the Liuyang River? / How many miles are there to get to the Xiang River? / Which district is it along the borders of the river / in which a leader for the Liberation was born?

It was during the War of Resistance against Japan that Chinese composers (of all ideological persuasions) first made consistent and systematic political use of these musical experiments. Popularized in war films, or disseminated through the many war mobilization demonstrations taking place all over China at the time, these war songs became an authentic medium for the expression of modern Chinese nationalism. After Mao's Yan'an "Talks" of 1942, music personnel in Yan'an began to collect folksongs in the nearby northwestern provinces. Their distinctive styles were then incorporated into songs for the masses as also were, eventually, those of folksongs collected later from other regions.

Since 1949, songs for the masses have become an integral part of the

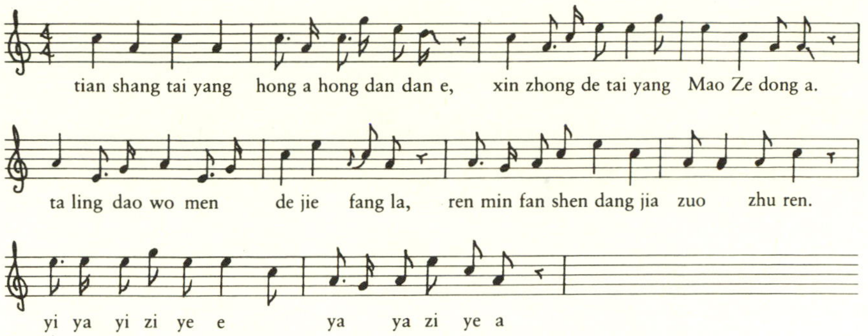

EXAMPLE 20. Tianshang taiyang hong tongtong [The sun in the sky is deep red]

Translation: Like the red sun of the sky, / Mao Zedong is the sun of my heart. / He leads us and liberates us, / making the people to be leaders of our country.

mass media. They impart important and topical political information to the masses, motivate them to participate in current national projects and campaigns, and in general arouse them to an awareness of group solidarity and national consciousness. Songs for the masses, together with their predecessors, make up a repertoire of modern Chinese songs that eclectically combine Western and Russian musical traits with those of indigenous Chinese folksongs. These songs form a chronicle of the vicissitudes through which, over the past hundred years, China has struggled to become a modern nation.

As China emerged from the Cultural Revolution and embarked on a policy of modernization, political campaigns, which occurred so often during the previous decades, were de-emphasized. Likewise, the use of songs as a political tool has also been de-emphasized. In recent years, increased contact with the outside world has incidentally brought about the proliferation of imported popular songs, particularly those from Hong Kong and Taiwan. These songs are introduced either through overseas broadcasts or on cassettes smuggled into China. Sung in a crooning style and with sentimental texts concerned mainly with love and alienation, and with accompaniments reminiscent of the early urban white rock-and-roll of the late 1950s and early 1960s, these songs have gained popularity among certain segments of urban youth. Even in the relaxed mood of the late 1970s, this caused some consternation among Party and government leaders, and over the following years steps were taken to control this new trend.

SIX

Model Opera as Model: From *Shajiabang* to *Sagabong*

Bell Yung

The traditional performing arts in China have never been static but have changed constantly as the needs of society have changed. Sometimes the process has been slow and the reasons behind it complex.[1] At other times the changes have been rapid, drastic, and large-scale and the reasons more obvious. The evolution of Peking opera since the establishment of the People's Republic offers an example of the latter kind of change. The revolutionary model operas with contemporary themes that emerged in the 1960s represent the climax of a series of changes that began in 1949.

It may be helpful here to compare a few salient features of traditional Chinese opera with Western opera. A Chinese opera is not known by its composer but by its place of origin and, of course, by its title. According to a survey conducted in 1957, China has over 350 different forms, or styles, of opera.[2] Each one is identified with a particular province, district, or dialect. Some of these operas are popular over a wide area—Peking opera is heard over most of China—but most are performed in only a small region.

Most of these regional operas have fairly large repertories. The stories on which the performances are based come from historical and semihistorical accounts, myths, legends, and fiction. With few exceptions, the stories have what are called "historical" settings.[3] To a large extent, all

[1] For example, the restructuring of China's social order in the seventeenth and eighteenth centuries contributed to the flourishing of regional opera in many parts of the country during that period. See Tanaka Issei, "Development of Chinese Local Plays in the Seventeenth and Eighteenth Centuries," *Acta Asiatica* 23 (1972): 42–62.

[2] Su Yi, "Quanguo juzhong chubu tongji" [A preliminary listing of operatic genres in China], in *Xiju luncong* [Collected papers on theater], 1 (Peking, 1957): 215–223.

[3] "Historical" generally implies that the story takes place not later than 1911, when the Qing dynasty fell. If set after that time, stories are considered "contemporary."

the regional operas share the same stock of stories, which are familiar to audiences throughout China. The various forms differ in makeup, costume, gestures, and other details. Most important are the differences in the dialects used and in the musical materials.

The music of a Western opera is written by a composer. In traditional Chinese opera, by contrast, the music of all the operas of a particular regional style comes from a pool of pre-existent material identified with that style. No single "composer," in the Western sense of the word, is responsible for any opera. The person who more or less takes the place of the composer is the scriptwriter. Scriptwriters set down the text of the opera and choose from the common pool the musical materials they consider most appropriate. The repertories of most regional styles consist of works transmitted through many generations without a known scriptwriter. As long as they preserve the regional styles, performers can manipulate both the text and the music of the opera.

Most of the regional styles developed their distinctive features during or after the seventeenth century. Since that time, as they have constantly interacted with and influenced each other, their complex musical structures and compositional processes have continued to evolve. Of all these forms, by far the most popular and important has been Peking opera. Beginning as an amalgam of several regional styles popular in Peking during the eighteenth century, Peking opera became a distinctive form by the latter part of that century. By the late nineteenth century, it had spread through a large part of China and was considered the most sophisticated of all the regional styles.[4]

THE DEVELOPMENT OF MODEL OPERA

Throughout its history, people have tried to reform Chinese opera in various ways. One of the best-known recent examples dates from the early twentieth century, when the famous singer Mei Lanfang and his literary collaborator, Qi Rushan, brought literary sophistication into the Peking opera and introduced gestures, movements, and singing styles from the *kunqu* performing style. The results have generally been recognized as an improvement.[5] In Canton and Hong Kong during the 1930s and 1940s, for another example, Western theatrical techniques and music were liberally adopted in the performances of Cantonese opera, largely in response to popular demand.[6]

[4] For a brief history of Peking opera, see Colin Mackerras, *The Chinese Theater in Modern Times* (Amherst: University of Massachusetts Press, 1975).

[5] Chen Jiying, *Qi Rushan yu Mei Lanfang* [Qi Rushan and Mei Lanfang] (Taibei: Zhuanji wenxue chubanshe, 1967).

[6] Bell Yung, "The Music of Cantonese Opera" (Ph.D. diss., Harvard University, 1976).

Since Liberation, China's Communist leaders have undertaken to reform Peking opera yet again, in the light of their policy that literature and art are to be considered primarily a means of achieving political goals. There were attempts to create new theater and reform traditional theater even before the liberation of the whole country. In 1942, after Mao Zedong gave his well-known "Talks at the Yan'an Forum on Literature and Art," a new form of theater called *yanggeju,* with song and dance based upon folk material, was created. Experiments to reform Peking opera were also undertaken during the 1940s. The choice of Peking opera for the first and major experiment in reform was justified by the form's hundred years of prestige, popularity, and wide influence among the masses.

From 1949 to 1955, in the first major phase of change, the government set up committees and agencies in Peking and in other centers throughout the country to oversee the "reform" of Chinese opera in general. Many traditional works were revised, mainly in plot. At the same time, new operas, many with contemporary and revolutionary themes (as opposed to the traditional works, which employed historical settings almost exclusively), were written and staged. Some traditional operas that were considered reactionary were officially banned or their performance discouraged by attacks in the press. This large-scale, hastily executed movement to revise or originate a great number of operas resulted in a lowering of artistic standards, while with the departure from the stage of popular traditional elements attendance fell sharply.

These initial difficulties led directly, in 1956–1957, to the next phase of development, which coincided with the Hundred Flowers movement. The ban on reactionary operas was relaxed, so that many traditional operas were revived in their original form. This liberal policy was enthusiastically received by audiences; and the newly written operas with "correct" political messages were performed far less often than in the previous period.[7]

In 1958 there was another change of policy. Now opera was "to walk on two legs," i.e., to alternate contemporary and revolutionary themes with traditional, historical ones. Opera troupes were instructed to split their repertories between the two forms. "Walking on two legs" represented a compromise: the traditional operas would supposedly draw the audience into the theater, while the new operas would continue to relay their "correct" political messages. External factors intervened, however. In the late 1950s and early 1960s, China entered a period of economic decline caused by, among other factors, the failure of the Great Leap Forward, the withdrawal of Soviet aid, and major natural disasters. The gov-

[7] According to a survey conducted in 1956, operas with historical settings accounted for well over 99 percent of the total repertory. See Tao Junqi, ed., *Jingju jumu chutan* [A preliminary investigation of the repertory of Peking opera] (Peking: Zhongguo xiju chubanshe, 1963).

ernment responded by introducing greatly liberalized economic measures to encourage production and at the same time relaxed its control over literature and art. The policy of "walking on two legs" lasted in theory until 1963. In fact, however, opera troupes began to favor the obviously more popular traditional operas over the newly written ones shortly after 1958.

From 1963 to 1965, the government again tightened its control over the repertory. Reports, speeches, and articles by such prominent figures as Mao Zedong and Jiang Qing denounced many traditional operas as feudalistic, superstitious, and vulgar and urged the revolutionization of the stage so that it would reflect and serve socialism. Peking opera was singled out to be the first form of theater to undergo this metamorphosis. In the summer of 1964, the National Festival of Peking Operas on Contemporary Themes was held in Peking. Twenty-nine troupes, including some from other provinces, staged thirty-five operas. During the next year, scores of other operas with contemporary themes were written and produced, while several newly written historical operas were harshly denounced. As a consequence, all historical operas received far fewer performances and, eventually, ceased to be performed at all. During the Cultural Revolution, attacks against tradition and the past in all areas intensified. By late 1966, only a handful of operas were being performed. These were the five *yangbanxi* ("model operas") with contemporary and revolutionary themes: *Shajiabang, Hong deng ji* [The red lantern], *Zhiqu Weihushan* [Taking Tiger Mountain by strategy], *Haigang* [On the docks], and *Qixi Baihutuan* [Raid on the White Tiger Regiment].[8] In 1966, the term *yangbanxi,* or model theater, generally referred to eight works, including the five operas named above and three non-operatic works: the ballets *Bai mao nü* [The white-haired girl] and *Hongse niangzijun* [The red detachment of women], and the symphonic suite based upon *Shajiabang*. From about 1969, several other works were added to the category of *yangbanxi,* including the operas *Dujuanshan* [Azalea Mountain], *Longjiang song* [Ode to the Dragon River], *Panshiwan* [Bay of Panshi], *Pingyuan zuozhan* [Battle on the plains], and *Hongse niangzijun* [The red detachment of women]; the symphonic suite based on *Taking Tiger Mountain by Strategy*; and songs from *The Red Lantern*. The origin and meaning of the word *yangban* ("model"), as used in the term *yangbanxi* have been studied elsewhere.[9] One meaning is certainly that these five operas were to serve as models for other operas. By the early 1970s, several new operas had been created

[8] For a more detailed discussion of the history of model opera, see, for example, Zhao Cong, *Zhongguo dalude xiqu gaige 1942–1967* [The reform of theater on the Chinese mainland, 1942–1967] (Hong Kong: Chinese University Press, 1969) and Mackerras, *Chinese Theater*.

[9] Hua-yuan Li Mowry, *Yang-pan hsi—New Theater in China* (Berkeley: University of California Press, 1973).

along the same lines as the first group of model operas; furthermore, a large number of regional versions of the model operas, called *yizhi geming yangbanxi* ("adapted"—literally, "transplanted"—"revolutionary model operas"), were produced throughout China. For most of the Cultural Revolution, these models and their adaptations were the only operas staged. After the Gang of Four fell in 1976, however, the model operas, which had been closely associated with Jiang Qing and her artistic collaborators,[10] soon passed out of prominence. They are now hardly ever performed, except as musical excerpts heard occasionally on radio.

THE EVOLUTION OF A MODEL OPERA

The task of creating new operas on contemporary themes presented operatic composers, scriptwriters, stage managers, and performers with many technical problems. For example, such modern characters as worker, peasant, and solider heroes and female revolutionaries had to be represented by the styles of singing and movement of the traditional role types. Composers faced the major difficulty of trying to put music into written notation in a form that had always been transmitted orally and whose notational conventions and structural elements, therefore, had not been subjected to the intense analysis given written genres such as poetry and, in this century, fiction. These difficulties were compounded when it came to the further process of adapting a model Peking opera into, for example, Cantonese opera. The complexity of the problem is indirect testimony to the rich diversity of theater in China and to the strength of regional traditions. The present paper will undertake a detailed technical analysis of one such adaptation: the evolution of the model Peking opera *Shajiabang* into the Cantonese opera *Sagabong*.[11] Specifically, I will compare the musical

[10] Most notable among these was Yu Huiyong, who served as Minister of Culture during the latter part of the Cultural Revolution. Yu played an important role in laying the theoretical groundwork for the model operas. As a result of his political involvement, he committed suicide during the purge of the Gang of Four shortly after the Cultural Revolution ended. Interviews with musicians who worked under Yu during the Cultural Revolution have revealed that Yu was recognized as the source of all the important musical ideas, while relatively minor duties such as orchestration were carried out by his assistants, for the following operas: *On the Docks, Azalea Mountain, Bay of Panshi, Ode to the Dragon River,* and a completely revised version of *Taking Tiger Mountain by Strategy*. There is little doubt that, during the second half of the Cultural Revolution (1969 and after), Yu was the sole creative force behind the model operas.

[11] Names and terms related to the model (Peking) opera are romanized according to the Peking dialect, using the *hanyu pinyin* system. Names and terms related to the Cantonese opera are romanized according to the Cantonese dialect, using the Yale system (but dropping the *h* that distinguishes the low tones from the high ones). For Cantonese romanization, see Parker Po-fei Huang and Gerard P. Kok, *Speak Cantonese* (New Haven: Yale University Institute of Far Eastern Languages, 1960).

elements of the two operas, using as material the published opera scripts, musical transcriptions, and film soundtracks.[12]

Shajiabang began life as *Ludang huozhong* [Sparks amid the reeds], a *huju* (Shanghai opera) with a modern setting created in 1958 by the Shanghai People's *Huju* Opera Troupe. By 1963, after several years of performance and revision, it had established itself as a popular item in the troupe's repertory. In October of that year, the First Peking Opera Company adapted it as a Peking opera, first staging it during the 1964 National Festival mentioned earlier. After undergoing several drastic revisions in 1965 and receiving its present name, *Shajiabang* became one of the handful of model operas.

The story is set in Shajiabang, a town in Jiangsu province. It takes place sometime in the early 1940s. A group of wounded New Fourth Army soldiers, led by Instructor Guo, is hiding from the Japanese and Nationalist troops in the marshes near Shajiabang. Sister A Qing, an underground agent of the Communist Party who runs a local tea shop as cover, protects the wounded soldiers by deceiving Commander Hu and Adviser Diao of the Nationalist forces. Instructor Guo, with courage and determination, and helped by Sister A Qing and other local residents, overcomes all adversities and finally returns to Shajiabang with his troops to annihilate the enemy.[13]

The Script

The script of *Sagabong* is a literal reproduction of that of *Shajiabang*. The songs are identical, and the spoken passages have been changed only slightly, by the addition of Cantonese colloquialisms. This adaptation was poorly done, however: some of the new expressions do not sound idiomatic to a Cantonese ear, while many other parts of the spoken text that should have been altered, if Cantonese were to be consistently preferred, stayed the same. Thus the general effect of the spoken passages in *Sagabong* is artificial and awkward.[14]

[12] *Shajiabang* (script and score of the Peking opera) (Peking: Renmin chubanshe, 1970); *Shajiabang—Yueju changduan xuan* [*Shajiabang*—selection of sung passages from the Cantonese opera version] (i.e., the score of this version) (Hong Kong: Zhaoyang, 1971); *Shajiabang* (the film of the Peking opera, released by Changchun zhipian gongsi [Changchun Film Studio], 1971); and *Shajiabang* (the film of the Cantonese version, released by Zhujiang dianying zhipian chang [Zhujiang Film Studio], 1972).

[13] For more background material and a complete translation of the script, see Lois Wheeler Snow, *China on Stage* (New York: Random House, 1972).

[14] The spoken passages of traditional Cantonese opera are also not totally free of artificiality and awkwardness, due to the heavy usage of literary Chinese. However, the use of colloquialism is consistent within a character type. A comical character generally speaks in a colloquial style, while a more serious character, such as a scholar or a government official, speaks in literary Chinese. Thus, use of colloquialism is one means of characterization in Cantonese opera.

Modes of Speech Delivery

Traditional Peking opera uses two major modes of speech delivery: *jingbai* ("natural speech") and *yunbai* ("declamatory speech"). The former is the street dialect of Peking; the latter differs from the former in having a different set of linguistic tonal inflections and slightly different consonants and vowels. The *yunbai* is delivered in a heightened and artificial manner, with a relatively more drawn-out rhythm than *jingbai*. It is purely a stage speech. Traditional Cantonese opera commonly employs six or seven modes of speech delivery,[15] but in *Sagabong* only the mode resembling the street dialect of Cantonese is used. The other modes were eliminated in obvious imitation of the similar simplification in *Shajiabang*.

Percussion Music

Percussion music, one of the most important musical elements in both Peking and Cantonese traditional opera, serves many functions in a performance. Not only does it accompany every kind of stage movement, from long battle scenes to the roll of an eye, it also reflects the actors' thoughts and emotions, introduces sung passages, and occasionally imitates the sounds of such nonexistent stage props as a boat rocking in water. The percussion instruments of traditional Peking opera are a drum, a pair of clappers, a large and a small gong, and a small pair of cymbals. Cantonese opera uses woodblocks (which take the place of Peking opera's drum and clappers) and several kinds of large gongs and cymbals in addition to those used in Peking opera (which are appropriately called in Cantonese *jing luogu* ["Peking gongs and drums"]).

Percussion music plays a noticeably smaller role in *Shajiabang* than in traditional Peking opera. Several of its functions have been taken over by an enlarged ensemble of string and wind instruments. Similarly, *Sagabong* uses less percussion music than is traditional in Cantonese opera. Furthermore, the two operas are much more alike in their use of percussion music than is any other pair of operas from the respective traditional repertories. In many passages, the percussion score is identical. Another major change in *Sagabong* is the total elimination of Cantonese gongs and cymbals; only Peking gongs and drums are employed.

Tunes in Peking Opera

The adaptation of the model's singing passages into Cantonese was a more complicated task. Peking opera, like most other traditional operas, relies almost exclusively on pre-existent tunes. Peking opera's tunes can be grouped into two basic families, the *xipi* and the *erhuang*. Each family

[15] Yung, "Music of Cantonese Opera," chap. 7.

contains a small number of tunes that share some traits but differ in tempo, rhythm, and melodic detail. Each tune in the family has an established dramatic function: for example, *xipi kuaiban* is a member of the *xipi* family that has a relatively fast tempo and is generally sung during lively or agitated moments in the drama. There is a total of about thirty tunes (or tune prototypes) in the two families; each may be used one or more times in an opera, and each may of course appear in many other operas.[16] The major prototypes in the *xipi* family are:

xipi manban ("slow-tempo *xipi*");
xipi yuanban ("standard-tempo *xipi*");
xipi erliu (literally, "two six," a medium tempo *xipi*; the name could be a homonym for some other, more meaningful words);
xipi liushui ("flowing-water-tempo *xipi*");
xipi kuaiban ("fast-tempo *xipi*");
xipi yaoban (a tune prototype in which the rhythm of the vocal line does not but the instrumental accompaniment does conform to a simple meter or beat); and
xipi sanban (a tune prototype in which neither the vocal line nor the instrumental accompaniment conform to any simple meter or beat).[17]

In Peking, Cantonese, and many other kinds of regional opera, each tune is identified by a name such as the ones given above. Most operatic performances have no musical score; the script lists only the name of the tune prototypes. The performer is expected to know how to fit the text to the standard tunes.

A song passage in any Peking opera consists simply of one or more tunes sung one after the other, occasionally with spoken passages between them. For example, in Act 2 of *Shajiabang,* Instructor Guo sings a passage called "Zhaoxia ying zai Yangchenghu shang" [The morning glow over Lake Yangcheng]. He uses the following series of tunes from the family: *xipi yuanban, xipi erliu, xipi liushui,* and *xipi kuaiban.* The same passage appears in *Sagabong,* with identical lyrics. Its musical treatment will be a major concern of the present study. First, however, a few words must be said about the musical structure of traditional Cantonese opera.

[16] For a general discussion of the musical structure of Peking opera, see Liu Jidian, *Jingju yinyue gailun* [A general discussion on the music of Peking opera] (Peking: Renmin yinyue chubanshe, 1981); Rulan Chao Pian, "Aria Structural Patterns in the Peking Opera," in J. I. Crump and William Malm, eds., *Chinese and Japanese Music-Drama* (Ann Arbor: University of Michigan Press, 1975), pp. 65–89; and Gerd Schönfelder, *Die Musik der Peking-Oper* (Leipzig: Deutscher Verlag für Musik, 1972).

[17] While the etymology of the word *ban* still needs investigation and may not be related to "tempo," the interpretation of, for example, *manban* as "slow tempo" seems at least consistent with the structure of the music.

Tunes in Cantonese Opera

Cantonese opera is related to Peking opera but has a long history of its own.[18] The tunes it uses are much greater in number and quite different from those in Peking opera. Cantonese opera also has two families of tunes, called *bongji* and *yiwong* (often abbreviated as *bong wong*). Musicologists believe that these two groups are historically related to *xipi* and *erhuang*, respectively. The Cantonese forms do indeed share certain characteristics with their counterparts in Peking opera. Each family has a small, fixed number of prototypes that share some traits yet differ in tempo, rhythm, and melodic details. For example, *bongji faaidim* is a member of the *bongji* family, has a relatively fast tempo, and is sung generally during lively and agitated moments in the drama. The melodic details of the Cantonese tunes are, however, quite different from those of Peking opera.

The *bong wong* tunes form one of the two major categories of tunes in Cantonese opera. The other category, *siukuk*, consists of tunes from a wide variety of sources: folksongs from Guangdong and other provinces, popular songs from movies and other media, tunes adapted from the classical *kunqu* and other operatic styles, and newly composed pieces. *Siukuk* naturally shows a great diversity of melodic styles. But before the various songs are performed onstage, they are given the "Cantonese" treatment: their melodic details are modified, their melodic contours adjusted according to the Cantonese musical scale and mode, and the instrumentation peculiar to Cantonese opera added. Above all, pronouncing the lyrics of a song in the Cantonese dialect unavoidably alters the song's melody, especially the vocal attacks and the decays of individual notes, until it sounds more Cantonese. Its use of *siukuk* gives Cantonese opera a strong regional flavor as well as a richer melodic repertory than many other operatic styles.

One major difference between *Sagabong* and traditional Cantonese opera is that the former has no *siukuk* tunes.[19] The passage from Act 2 of *Shajiabang* sung to the sequence of *xipi* tunes listed above is sung to identical texts in *Sagabong*, to the following sequence of tunes: *bongji maanbaan* ("slow-tempo *bongji*"), replacing *xipi yuanban*; *bongji jungbaan* ("medium-tempo *bongji*"), replacing *xipi er liu* and *xipi liushui*; and *bongji faai-jungbaan* ("fast medium-tempo *bongji*"), replacing *xipi kuaiban*.

[18] Mai Xiaoxia, "Guangdong xiju shilüe" [A brief history of Cantonese opera] in *Guangdong wenwu* [Cultural relics in Guangdong] (Canton, 1941), pp. 141–185.

[19] *Siukuk* only became popular in traditional Cantonese opera in the 1920s and 1930s. Opera scripts from before that period use only *bong wong* tunes. *Sagabong*'s elimination of *siukuk*, therefore, may be considered a return to earlier practice.

Bongji tunes have here replaced the *xipi* tunes of *Shajiabang*, just as *yiwong* tunes elsewhere replace the model's *erhuang* prototypes. The pattern of replacement is logical, given the historical relationship between the two pairs of families and the similarity of their respective dramatic functions. Within a family, the choice of tune may depend on its tempo. For example, the relatively slow *xipi yuanban* used first in *Shajiabang* is replaced by the corresponding slow *bongji maanbaan*. A replacement tune may also be chosen because it has a rhythm similar to that of the original tune: *xipi kuaiban* and *bongji faai-jungbaan*, for example, share similar rhythmic patterns. Finally, the tune's dramatic functions may also be an important factor: *xipi kuaiban* and *bongji faai-jungbaan* are generally employed at lively or agitated moments in, respectively, traditional Peking and Cantonese opera.

The Significance of Tune Names

The names of the tunes are much less important in *Sagabong* than in traditional Cantonese opera, because the music of the former is written out in full, either in staff or in number notation. The singers and instrumentalists need simply follow the score. The performers' independence of tune names is reflected by the general disintegration in *Sagabong* of the otherwise rigid correspondence of names to melodies. For example, the fast-tempo *bongji faaidim* of Cantonese opera usually replaces the fast-tempo *xipi kuaiban* of Peking opera to which it has rhythmic similarities. Indeed, where *xipi kuaiban* tunes appear in Acts 2, 4, 5, and 8 of *Shajiabang*, they are replaced in *Sagabong* by tunes whose melodic material identifies them as *bongji faaidim*. However, the script calls these tunes *bongji jungbaan* and *bongji faai-jungbaan*, names that properly refer to two other Cantonese tunes. There are two possible explanations for the change of name. First, the word *dim* is not used in Peking opera and thus may have too much Cantonese or regional flavor. Second, the Cantonese *bongji faai-jungbaan* does have a tempo and a dramatic function like those of *xipi kuaiban*. The performance shows that the singer follows the score rather than the tune titles, which are now only hangovers from the old tradition and apparently do not serve any practical function.[20]

Another example of the alteration of a tune name—or indeed of the imitation of a Peking name, involves the tune known as *gwanfa*. This is one of the most important and frequently used tunes in the *bongji* and *yiwong* families. Like the *sanban* and *yaoban* tunes of the *xipi* and *erhuang* families, *gwanfa* does not conform to any fixed meter or beat but is

[20] Note that tune names in Cantonese opera may vary from region to region and from period to period. I have derived the discussion here from the research I conducted in Hong Kong in the early 1970s and from scripts of operas produced in the previous decades.

rhythmically rather free. The most natural replacement for *Shajiabang*'s *xipi sanban* and *yaoban* would be *gwanfa*. And, indeed, these Peking tunes are replaced with what seems to be a cross between the original tunes and *gwanfa*. But the title *gwanfa* is never used; instead, the Peking titles *sanban* (Act 8) and *liushui* (Act 2) are retained, although they have never before been used in Cantonese opera. *Gwanfa,* as too regional and colloquial a title, has been eliminated.

Tune Identity

Choosing corresponding tunes is not the only problem encountered in turning a Peking opera into a Cantonese opera. When an original text as written for a Peking opera is sung to a Cantonese *bongji* or *yiwong* tune, the tune adjusts itself to fit the text. Is the adjusted tune, we may ask, still the same tune? The situation poses an interesting challenge to the fundamental concept of tune identity.

The concept of "a tune" in Chinese opera is not at all like the Western notion and needs a word of explanation. The same tune sung with different texts can sound like a different tune: certain structural elements of the melody change to accommodate the various texts. Yet other elements of the melody do not change, so that the tune's identity is preserved: the tune may thus be recognized as such in order for it to serve its dramatic purposes. For example, a tune will always be in couplets, but the length (number of beats or measures) of the lines of the couplet may vary. Likewise the cadential notes are fixed, but the melodic contour may be flexible. Whether a structural element is invariant and how much change can occur without the loss of identity depend on the individual tunes and on the operatic style.[21] For example, in traditional Cantonese opera, the *bongji* and *yiwong* tunes generally have invariant lengths: a couplet's melodic line always has the same number of beats. In the *xipi* and *erhuang* tunes of Peking opera, by contrast, the length of a melodic line is relatively more flexible.

Consider the *bongji faaidim* tune of traditional Cantonese opera. Like many other tunes of the *bongji* family, it is in couplet form. Each melodic line carries a textual line of seven syllables. It always has seven beats per line, and the seven syllables are sung to a characteristic rhythmic pattern, called its syllable placement. Example 1 shows this pattern (the crosses represent the syllables in the line):

[21] For a discussion of this issue in relation to Peking opera, see Pian, "Text Setting"; for a discussion in relation to Cantonese opera, see Bell Yung, "Music Identity in Cantonese Opera," in Daniel Heartz and Bonnie Wade, eds., *International Musicological Society: Report of the Twelfth Congress, Berkeley 1977* (Kassel: Barenreiter Kassel, 1981), pp. 669–675.

EXAMPLE 1
Syllable placement of *bongji faaidim.*

First line

Second and subsequent lines

In Act 2 of *Shajiabang* there is a section that begins "*ni dai tongzhi qin ru yijia*" ("you treat your comrades as your own family"); the tune used is *xipi liushui.* In *Sagabong* the tune is called *bongji jungbaan* but is, in fact, *bongji faaidim.* The passage consists of nine couplets, of which the first three are given in Example 2:

EXAMPLE 2
First three couplets of "Ni dai tongzhi qin ru yijia" (*Shajiabang,* Act 2).

line 1 Ni dai tong zhi qin ru yi jia
You treat your comrades as your own family,

line 2 Jing xin tiao li zhen bu cha
Taking care of them with the utmost attention,

line 3 Feng bu jiang xi bu ting shou
Mending and washing without ever stopping,

line 4 Yi ri san can you yu xia
Serving them fish and shrimp three meals a day.

line 5 Tong zhi men shuo si zhe yang chang qi lai zhu xia
Comrades told me, if they keep on living in this style,

Zhi pa shi xin ye kuan ti ye pang
They can't help feeling relaxed and gaining weight—

Lu ye zou bu dong shan ye bu neng pa
No longer able to walk long distances or climb hills.

line 6 Zen neng shang zhan chang ba di sha
How will they ever manage to fight the enemy again in combat?

Example 3 shows the syllable placement for the six lines of text.[22] The crosses represent the syllables; the rhythmic notation above the text line

[22] The transcription here is from *Shajiabang* (script and score of the Peking opera) (Peking: Renmin chubanshe, 1970).

EXAMPLE 3

Shajiabang 7
line 1
Sagabong 7

line 2 7
8

line 3 7
7

line 4 8
8

line 5

22
$21\frac{1}{2}$

line 6 9
$9\frac{1}{2}$

shows the syllable placement of *xipi liushui,* that below, the placement of *bongji faaidim.* The numbers at the end of each line represent the number of beats per line.

Comparison of the syllable placement of the two tunes shows a close similarity. The tunes also have almost the same number of beats per line. The irregular number of beats in the melodic lines is not uncommon for traditional Peking opera, but would be quite unusual in the *bongji faaidim* of traditional Cantonese opera. Such irregularity would jar the ear of a connoisseur; it would probably be considered nothing but a mistake. It is easy to explain this example of irregularity of *bongji faaidim.*

The text of *Shajiabang* contains a large number of *chenzi* ("padding syllables" or "padding phrases"), especially in line 5. The relatively flexible melodic line of Peking opera can accommodate these extra beats. However, the *bongji faaidim* of traditional Cantonese opera almost always has seven syllables per line. An occasional padding syllable (such as the fifth syllable, *qin,* in line 1) can fit into the melodic structure without altering the number of beats in the line. But there is no way to fit the many padding phrases of line 5 into the melodic structure without increasing the number of beats. The only way to retain the original text of *Shajiabang* was to modify the tune by expanding it. Unfortunately, such a procedure violates a crucial, structural criterion of *bongji faaidim.*

This discussion illustrates how, in the process of adaptation into *Sagabong,* the traditional tunes of Cantonese opera could lose their distinctive characteristics. As a consequence, *Sagabong* also loses some of the characteristic features of Cantonese opera.

The Role of Linguistic Tones

What makes a musical genre distinctive is not always something as obvious as the length of a musical phrase or a set of cadential notes. In a tonal language such as Chinese, the relationship between the words and music in opera, especially the relationship between the linguistic tones of the text and the melodic contour, can distinguish some musical genres from others. The nature of this relationship has been an important issue in the study of Chinese vocal music.[23] Regional differences in the treatment of

[23] See Yuen Ren Chao, "Tones, Intonation, Singsong, Chanting, Recitative, Tonal Composition, and Atonal Composition in Chinese," in Morris Halle, ed., *For Roman Jakobson* (The Hague: 1956), pp. 52–59; John Hazedel Levis, *Foundations of Chinese Musical Art,* 2d ed. (New York: Paragon, 1964); Lindy L. Mark and Fang Kuei Li, "Speech Tone and Melody in Wu-Ming Folk Songs," in Ba Shin, Jean Boisselier, and A. B. Griswold, eds., *Essays Offered to G. H. Luce* (Ascona, Switzerland: Artibus Asiae, 1966), pp. 167–186; Pian, "Text Setting"; Yang Yinliu, *Zhongguo gudai yinyue shigao* [Draft history of old Chinese music], 2 vols. (Peking: Renmin yinyue chubanshe, 1981); and Bell Yung, "Creative Process of Cantonese Opera: The Role of Linguistic Tones," in *Ethnomusicology* 27, 1 (January 1983): 29–47.

the text reveal much about how works are composed in the regions' particular genre of opera and about the musical values of the community. Peking opera and Cantonese opera are quite different in this respect. In the process of adaptation, how was the Peking style handled in *Sagabong*?

Chinese is a tonal language: i.e., it uses pitch not only for intonation but also to differentiate syllables, as vowels or consonants do in English. The relative pitch levels, the contour of pitch movement, and the duration of pitch may all have phonemic significance. The term "linguistic tone" refers to these pitch properties of a spoken syllable. Each Chinese dialect has a small number of tonal categories, into which all syllables spoken in that dialect fall. The Peking dialect has four tonal categories, whose characteristics can be transcribed with simple symbols: a simplified time-pitch graph is drawn to the left of a vertical reference line that represents pitch height. Thus, ˥ stands for a tone that begins high, remains high, and ends high. ˧˥ stands for a tone that begins at midpoint, rises, and ends high. ˧˩˧ stands for a tone that begins at midpoint, falls, then rises and ends at midpoint. ˥˩ stands for a tone that begins high, falls, and ends low. Using this schema, the tones of the Peking dialect can be represented as follows:[24]

EXAMPLE 4
Linguistic tones of the Peking dialect.

˥	˧˥	˧˩˧	˥˩
first	second	third	fourth

The syllables of the first two lines in Example 1 have the following linguistic tones:

EXAMPLE 5
First two lines of Example 2 with the linguistic tones of the Peking dialect.

line 1	˧˩˧	˥˩	˧˥	˥˩	˥	˧˥	˥˩	˥
	ni	dai	tong	zhi	qin	ru	yi	jia
line 2	˥	˥	˧˥	˧˩˧	˥	˥˩	˥	
	jing	xin	tiao	li	zhen	bu	cha	

When these lines are spoken, the voice goes through a certain amount of tonal inflection. When the same lines are sung, the syllables follow a melodic line that has a distinct pitch contour. Is there any discernible

[24] After Yuen Ren Chao, *A Grammar of Spoken Chinese* (Berkeley: University of California Press, 1968).

correspondence between the lyrics of the song as spoken and as sung? The following is a transcription of the same two lines as sung to *xipi liushui*:[25]

EXAMPLE 6

First two lines of *xipi liushui* from *Shajiabang* (Act 2).

Comparison between the linguistic tones of the text and the melodic line shows that they behave somewhat differently, and at times independently. For example, the second syllable *dai* (˥˩) has a linguistic tone that drops to a relatively low pitch; it is, however, sung here to a melodic phrase that rises to a high pitch. Of the next two syllables: *tong* (˧˥) and *zhi* (˥˩), the first rises to a relatively high pitch level while the second drops to a relatively low level. But the musical contour shows *zhi* at a higher pitch than *tong*. This lack of apparent correspondence between the linguistic tones of the text and the melodic contour is often found in traditional Peking opera.[26]

The Cantonese dialect has nine tonal categories:[27]

EXAMPLE 7

Linguistic tones of the Cantonese dialect.

˥˧	˨˩	˧˥	˩˧	˧	˨	˙˥	·˧	.˨
Upper Even	Lower Even	Upper Rising	Lower Rising	Upper Going	Lower Going	Upper Entering	Middle Entering	Lower Entering

[25] The transcription here is from *Shajiabang* (script and score of the Peking opera) (Peking: Renmin chubanshe, 1970).

[26] The relationship between linguistic tones and melodic contour in Peking opera involves more than the simple question of correspondence discussed here. See Pian, "Text Setting," for further details.

[27] After Yuen Ren Chao, *The Cantonese Primer* (New York: Greenwood Press, 1947). The symbols for the three entering tones have been changed in this essay from Chao's short, horizontal strokes to dots in order to avoid confusion with the other tones. In phonetic transcription for most Chinese dialects it is common practice to reserve the dots (at various heights) for neutral tones. However, since Cantonese does not have neutral tones, the danger of such confusion does not exist.

These tones have several different pitch levels; flat, rising, or falling contours; and long or short durations (the short tones are marked with dots). The Cantonese version of the two lines we have been considering is:

EXAMPLE 8

First two lines of example 2 with linguistic tones of the Cantonese dialect.

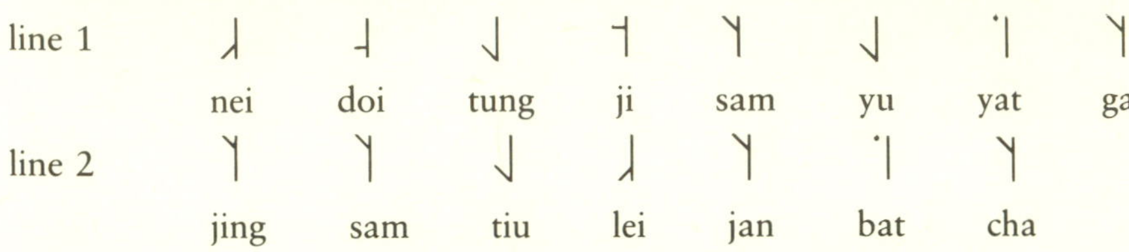

When adapted to *Sagabong,* the text is sung to *bongji faaidim:*[28]

EXAMPLE 9

First two lines of *bongji faaidim* from *Sagabong* (Act 2).

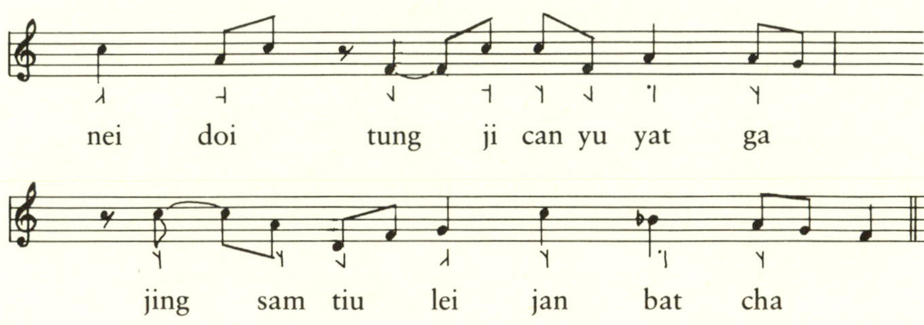

Comparison between the textual and melodic contours shows that they correspond much more closely than in *Shajiabang.* For example, the third syllable *tung* (˨˩) has a low spoken pitch, and its melodic line drops to a low pitch. Similarly, the fourth syllable *ji* (˥) has a high pitch, and its melodic line correspondingly rises to a high pitch. This correspondence holds up in the rest of the line and throughout the other song passages of the opera. In a previous study, I showed that traditional Cantonese opera matches the linguistic tones of the text to the melodic contour of the song according to a rigid rule.[29] To a certain extent, this rule was also observed in the adaptation of *Sagabong.*

Closer inspection, however, reveals that this rule was not always observed as rigorously as it would be in traditional Cantonese opera. At places, the linguistic tones of the text do not match the melodic contour.

[28] The transcription here is from *Shajiabang—Yueju changduan xuan.*

[29] Yung, "Creative Process of Cantonese Opera," p. 37.

For example in line 1, the first syllable *nei* (˩˧) is sung to the note C. Yet the last two syllables of the same line, *yat* (·˥) *ga* (˥˧), whose linguistic tones have a relatively higher pitch than the first syllable, are sung to the note A, a minor third lower. Another example occurs in the last three syllables of line 2, which all have high-pitched linguistic tones but are sung to a descending scale. In traditional Cantonese opera, such singing would be considered a poor performance.

It was perhaps the difficulty of adapting a text in the Peking dialect to Cantonese that necessitated some relaxation of the rule of matching. In traditional Cantonese opera, a line of text must follow certain patterns of linguistic tones and avoid others. One pattern to avoid is a sequence of several syllables that have the same linguistic tone. In Example 8, the last three syllables of line 2 have the following tones: ˥˧ ·˥ ˥˧ . Even though the middle syllable has a different tone from the others, it shares the same pitch height, so that the three syllables are spoken with three consecutive high pitches. This is considered a poor pattern. Another pattern to avoid is parallel sequences of linguistic tones in two consecutive lines of text—especially at the ends of the lines. Such a pattern appears in the last two syllables of line 1 and the last two syllables of line 2, which have an identical pair of linguistic tones.

The reason for avoiding these two tonal patterns is not difficult to understand. Since the melodic contour has to correspond closely to the linguistic tones of the text, a sequence of identical, or near-identical, tones would produce a melodic line that also did not vary in pitch. In Cantonese opera such repetition is not considered esthetically pleasing. Similarly, when two consecutive lines of text have identical or near-identical tonal patterns, the resultant two lines of melodies will be too similar for the Cantonese taste. Since the text of *Sagabong* was not originally designed for Cantonese opera, there are many instances where rules about patterns of linguistic tones are broken. The Cantonese composer, if he wanted to be faithful to the text, had two alternatives. First, he could have broken the rule about matching linguistic tones and melodic contour. Second, he could have adhered to the rule but sacrificed the esthetic principles that govern Cantonese music. In Example 9, the composer compromised, adhering basically to the rule but applying it somewhat less rigidly than in traditional Cantonese opera. The last three syllables of line 2 are evidently sung to a descending scale to avoid repeating the same pitch three times. Even so, the melody in Example 9 is still unusual for Cantonese opera because the pitch contours of the two lines are a little too similar: the linguistic tones of the two lines of text resemble each other more than is generally considered proper.

The brief discussion above shows that, in the process of adapting *Shajiabang* into Cantonese opera, some musical elements of traditional Cantonese opera were incorporated into the new work while others were modified or ignored. The text was the central, determining factor, in deference to which Cantonese idioms and melodies had sometimes to be sacrificed. Also eliminated was such indigenous Cantonese music as that which formed the rich repertory of *siukuk.* Since *bongji* and *yiwong* are historically related and structurally similar to the tunes used in Peking opera, many *bongji* and *yiwong* tunes are retained; however, some of them were so altered that they lost their identity. At times, names of the Cantonese tunes were altered. Finally, many locally popular musical instruments were omitted. One important feature of traditional Cantonese opera that *Sagabong* incorporated is the special rule that the linguistic tones of the text and the pitch contour of the melody should match. Yet, as pointed out above, even this rule was occasionally relaxed in order to accomodate the text.

THE EFFECTS OF MODEL OPERA ON CHINESE MUSIC

In the pages above, I have briefly examined some musical aspects of the adaptation of a model opera into a regional form. Other musical elements, such as vocal style, instrumentation, and tuning systems, as well as such nonmusical elements as costumes, sets, acting, and dancing also need to be studied before the relationship between model and adaptation can be fully understood. Such a study should also extend beyond the pair of works discussed here to the many other adaptations of model operas into Cantonese and other regional operatic styles. The many different forms of regional opera no doubt entail very different problems and solutions for the adaptor. Yet, even given its limitations, the present study allows us to draw some conclusions about the consequences for Chinese music of the system of model operas.

The main consequence of adaptation, when the model has played its role effectively, is that the copy loses many of its regional characteristics. The texts of the adaptations had to be uniform because they had, in the then-current political climate, to follow strictly the official guidelines about "correct" content. Yet, from this brief study of *Shajiabang* and *Sagabong,* we see that regional adaptations also tend to lose their musical identity. Two factors lie behind this loss.

In the first place, model operas were expected not only to present correct political messages but also to meet the highest artistic standards. Thus, adaptors were under pressure to disregard their regions' native style in favor of the model opera's artistic example. We have seen how the creators of *Sagabong* discarded musical materials of indigenous Cantonese origin.

The second influence operated less directly. In Chinese vocal music, perhaps more so than in other cultures, the structure and style of the music are closely related to the verse form of the text and to the linguistic characteristics of the regional dialect. We have seen that this relationship is especially close in Cantonese opera. Yet the text of the model opera, which is adopted almost verbatim, brings with it the verse form and dialectal peculiarities of the Peking dialect. The musical structure of the adaptation will inevitably be affected by elements of the borrowed text that are alien to the regional style.

There may be much to regret if the future development of Chinese opera continues along these lines. The great diversity of regional operatic genres constitutes an immense musical treasure. It is the fruit of centuries of artistic effort and an inexhaustible resource for China and the world. The loss would be irreparable if such diversity were to be forced to fit a single mold.

Throughout the history of Chinese opera, regional genres have constantly interacted with and influenced each other. The model opera *Shajiabang* was itself adapted from a Shanghai-style opera. In some periods, a certain genre gained so much popularity or social prestige that its influence became unusually strong. Notable examples have been *yiyang* opera in the sixteenth century, *kunqu* opera in the seventeenth century, and *pihuang* opera (later known as *jingju* or Peking opera) in the nineteenth and early twentieth centuries. It was not, therefore, really a new idea when, during the Cultural Revolution, Peking opera was made the model for other regional operas. However, two factors distinguish this recent domination from those of the past. First, official pressure was applied both to encourage regional operas to copy the models and to ban the traditional repertory. Second, the model opera has a strong theoretical basis, which not only applies ideological principles to the literary content but also imposes rigorous and extensive restraints on the style, structure, and function of the music.

Between 1966 and 1977, the model operas and their adaptations dominated the musical scene in China. One should not forget that, regardless of their ideological content, the model operas were created after extensive research in music theory and are exceptional works of art in the history of Chinese music. They have undeniably influenced the musical taste both of musicians and, more importantly, of the masses in the period since the Cultural Revolution. Musical and theatrical experiments first tried in the model operas have their offspring today in many genres of Chinese music and drama and such experimentation will, undoubtedly, continue for many years to come.

The appearance in the 1950s and 1960s of an extensive body of music theory, with an emphasis on the analysis of music sound (as opposed to the analysis of the philosophical and social contexts of music) was in itself an important development in the history of Chinese music. One major reason for this development was certainly related to the pressure to create model operas. An important consequence of the theorizing was that musicians' concepts of music and of their compositional procedure began to change. These changes will surely have deep significance for the future of Chinese music.

In the last few years, the political climate in China has once again changed. Among the areas most obviously affected by these changes have been music and theater. Although model operas and their adaptations are rarely seen or heard today, their influence on the future course of Chinese music and theater should not be discounted.

SEVEN

From Romantic Love to Class Struggle: Reflections on the Film *Liu Sanjie*

Wai-fong Loh

The development of the legend of Liu Sanjie [Third Sister Liu] can be traced in several local gazetteers in the Lingnan area of South China and in Ming-Qing writings. Many of the songs she supposedly wrote are still sung in Southwest China, particularly by the minority Zhuang tribe in Guangxi province, and have been further popularized since the film was made in 1961. Twentieth-century field researchers have collected various oral traditions about Liu's life. The reception of the film *Liu Sanjie* can be estimated both from box-office statistics and from articles published from 1961 to 1962 in *Dazhong dianying* [Popular cinema] and more recently in other newspapers and magazines.

The analysis offered here, based mainly on the source materials mentioned above, deals more with the content and style of *Liu Sanjie*, especially with its historical development and ideological implications, than with filming techniques or the director's skill. However, as a film, *Liu Sanjie* exhibits characteristics common to all films. The making of any motion picture entails a high cost, which must be justified either by profit, as has been the case in Hollywood, or by the benefit of the ideology conveyed, as in the case of the Chinese film industry. In either case, a production cannot be considered satisfactory unless it is approved and appreciated by a large audience. The critics' discussions and the audiences' reception of *Liu Sanjie* clearly illustrate a major characteristic of the Chinese film industry. Thus, a few words about the history of film in China are in order here.

The development of the Chinese film industry can be divided into five periods:

In the first period, that of the silent film (1905–1930), all serious film makers were trying both to educate and to entertain. They wanted to effect reforms, and their films attack such feudal customs as arranged marriage (*Nan fu nan qi* [The arranged marriage]), the exploitation of women (*Qi fu* [The abandoned woman]), and family restrictions. The evils of opium smoking (*Heiji yuanhun* [The soul lost to opium]) and bureaucratic corruption (*Tan guan rong gui* [The splendid return of a corrupt official]) were also common themes.

Clearly definable left-wing films began to emerge in the second period, the stage of free experimentation (1930–1949). 1930 was the year in which sound movies were first made in China; in the same year, Xia Yan organized a left-wing film group whose function was to write screenplays. Some typical products of this group were *Kuang liu* [Wild current] by Xia Yan, *San'ge modeng nüxing* [Three modern women] by Tian Han, and *Zhongguohaide nu chao* [The angry tides of the China Sea] by Yang Hansheng. From this stage on, film makers (and viewers) were divided into two intensely hostile camps. Both sides were nationalistic, but the films of the left emphasized class struggle, those of the right theories of universal human nature. There was competition, too, between serious films made to fulfill an educational purpose and those made purely for entertainment. This was probably one of the most colorful stages in Chinese film history.

In the third period, from Liberation to the beginning of the Cultural Revolution (1950–1965), films were subjected to stringent state guidelines. Class struggle became the dominant theme. As the left took over the industry in China proper, the arena of struggle between the left and right esthetic camps moved to Hong Kong, where film audiences usually preferred entertainment to messages.

The fourth period (1965–1977) can be called the stage of internal conflict, in which films were sometimes used to discredit political enemies. This period was also characterized by the intensified "model theater" (*yangbanxi*) movement in film.

The last period, from the Cultural Revolution to the present, to some extent resembles the preceding period. I prefer, however, to consider it as a new stage of free experimentation under state guidance. Film makers have been re-examining the value of China's traditional performing arts and learning from the West's film industry. Their films have been displaying greater variation of theme and style, although almost every film still bears a solemn message.

From the time of the silent movies, serious Chinese film makers and viewers demanded that each film have a solemn, educational theme or message. Only productions sanctioned by traditional performing arts like Peking opera or screenplays adapted from traditional popular fiction were exempted from this demand. The attitudes toward various types of films can be described, in simplified form, as follows: Films of such traditional forms of performing arts as Peking opera were appreciated or, at least, tolerated. Farce, vulgar comedy, and detective or adventure films were usually condemned, although the overwhelming majority of films made during the first two stages were of this type. Most important were the *wenming dianying* ("modern films"), the majority of which were adapted from the stage form called *wenmingxi* ("modern drama"). These films always had a clearly spelled-out social or nationalistic theme, congruent with the views of either the right or the left camp. Documentary films were usually accepted by both the right and the left as necessary and useful. The left, however, was occasionally suspicious or even hostile to documentaries commissioned or made by foreigners about such "strange" Chinese customs as funerals or foot binding.

Liu Sanjie was a product of the third period of Chinese film history. With great skill and imagination, its makers adapted a traditional story to fit a popular but overworked theme, managing in the process to be both entertaining and educational.

THE LEGEND OF LIU SANJIE

Many variants of the legend of Liu Sanjie have been recorded by members of the educated elite, in local gazetteers, and in field researchers' collections. Details included in any particular version seem to depend more on who preserved that version than on when or where the legend was first developed. One of the earliest versions appeared in the seventeenth century in Qu Dajun's *Guangdong xinyu* [New stories from Guangdong].[1] According to Qu, Liu Sanmei (i.e., Liu Sanjie) was born at the turn of the eighth century A.D. in Xinxin, Guangdong. She grew up to become an ingenious woman thoroughly educated in the classics and history and especially good at making up songs. Many singers traveled for a thousand *li* to hear her and to compete with her. Most of them exhausted their repertoire of songs in two or three days and left full of admiration for her. Liu traveled frequently in Guangdong and Guangxi provinces, where she not only learned the dialects of the minority groups but also composed songs in these languages. The songs she made for these groups were always accepted as models. Liu Sanmei "acquired enlightenment" (*de dao*) through music. In Guangdong, the exchange of songs, particularly between two lovers, was an established, ritualistic form of communication. For seven days and seven nights Liu Sanmei and a youth exchanged songs on the top of a hill, until finally they turned into stones (i.e., achieved immortality). The natives of Yangchun district built a temple at the spot, where in later days singers came to offer copies of their new songs and to pray. At one

[1] Qu Dajun (1630–1696), *Guangdong xinyu,* 8:5a–b.

time the keeper of the temple had several boxes of such songs, which other singers would copy.

Another early Qing record, included in the *Gujin tushu jicheng* [Ancient and modern library],[2] describes the mystery of the singing immortal Liu Sanmei vividly and in great detail. She was born (according to this author) in A.D. 705, in Guixian, Guangxi. She was not only well educated but also a descendant of the Imperial clan of the Han dynasty. When her friend Zhang Weiwang, a *xiucai* (civil-service licentiate) from Langling, Guangxi, came to visit her, the natives built a stage for the two to sing on. On the third day the assembly needed more room and moved to the hills. On the seventh day, the songs could no longer be heard from below. A boy dispatched to invite the singers down the hill found them turned into stone. All the natives climbed the hill to offer their prayers. When Liu's betrothed, Lin, went up the hill, he laughed and also turned into stone.

These two variants seem to be folktales considerably remodeled by their educated transcribers, who probably added Liu's educational background and genealogical information. In local gazetteers such as the *Tongzhi Cangwu xianzhi* [Cangwu district gazetteer, Tongzhi period, 1862–1874], Liu appears as a peasant who worked at the spinning wheel and in the field. Versions such as this are probably closer to the "real" Liu Sanjie. This more popular conception can be reconstructed from gazetteers and records of the oral tradition.

The *Yishan xianzhi* [Yishan district gazetteer, 1881] introduces a villain in the person of Liu's brother: "Liu Sanmei loved to sing. Her brother disliked her." In the early 1940s, Chen Zhiliang recorded a related variant from oral tradition in *Guangxi tezhong buzu geyao ji* [Folksongs of minorities in Guangxi]. This version, popular in Yongxian, Guangxi, relates how Liu's brother tried on several occasions to stop her from going out to sing with boys. Each time, she was able to outwit him and escape his domination.

Although the tales recorded by field researchers after Liberation usually depicted Liu as one who loved labor, the tales collected in 1961 in *Guangxi Zhuangzu wenxue* [Zhuang minority literature from Guangxi] offer versions of the legend that treat her duties as obstacles to happiness. The tale told around the Fusui area explains that singing was an activity often enjoyed by people in love. Liu claimed she would only marry a man who could sing better than she, while her brother and mother wanted her to marry a rich man. To prevent Liu from singing, her brother made her carry water in barrels with pointed bottoms, which she could not set down when she wanted to tarry to sing a song. But Liu Sanjie nonetheless managed to stand the barrels on the ground without their tipping. Her brother

[2] *Gujin tushu jicheng*, part 6, *juan* 1440.

then gave her many other tasks, which she always completed, until, enraged, he finally pushed her off a cliff.

In the story popular in the Yishan area, the villain was a member of the gentry who thought that the free way in which Liu sang love songs with young men was against the Confucian moral code. Several tales relate how Liu won song competitions with educated *xiucai*. In one story, three *xiucai* arrive with a shipload of songbooks. When they found that the books offered little help against Liu's natural wit, they threw all the books into the river—or, in another version, burned them.

All but the first two of these variants emphasize one of two main themes. In the first, Liu Sanjie defies the prohibitions of her family (or of Confucianism) and insists on choosing her own lover. Thus presented, the legend is essentially a love story. In the second theme, the victory of Liu Sanjie, the uneducated peasant, over educated *xiucai* seems to challenge the elite values of education and self-cultivation. Either theme makes for a very romantic story. Yet neither theme was adequate for the modern presentation of Liu Sanjie's story. A revolutionary work must emphasize the value of labor, the wisdom of the masses, and above all, class struggle. Contemporary versions of Liu's legend have been submitted to a stringent review procedure. In the late 1950s, the Liuzhou caidiao tuan (The Group for Liuzhou Opera) decided to write a play about Liu. Researchers combed Guangxi province for stories and songs, collecting more than two hundred legends plus dozens of folksongs and melodies. In 1959, after several stages of collective creation, a third draft of the play *Liu Sanjie* was staged as the opera *Geju Liu Sanjie* [Opera of Third Sister Liu]. Other theatrical groups also then experimented with the new work; in April 1960, more than twenty versions were staged in Nanning. Conferences and workshops were held after the performances. In 1961 the Chinese Theater Press published a revised version of the play. In the same year Changchun Studio released a movie based on the CTP version. Thus, although Qiao Yu wrote the script for the film, many people had cooperated in the actual reworking of the original story.

THE FILM *LIU SANJIE*

The film *Liu Sanjie* can best be described as a musical (*gechangpian*), although it has also been called an opera (*geju*) and a feature film (*gushipian*). Its simple story is told and sung in lyrics accompanied by beautifully recreated folk music. In the film Liu is a firewood-cutter who attacks the rich landlords through her songs. One of the landlord's men cuts a rattan vine while Liu is using it to climb a cliff; she falls into the river below, but survives to spread revolutionary ideas down the river by singing to the peasants and fishermen. She runs afoul of another rich landlord, the film's main villain, and falls in love with a fisherman's son. In the end, the lovers evade the landlord's pursuit and disappear into the river mist, presumably to continue preaching revolution through song. Although the film is not set in a specific period, many of the audience probably knew that, according to legend, Liu Sanjie lived in the Tang dynasty.

Many details reveal the industry and skill of the contributors to the film version. First, the tale was transformed from a romantic love story into an educational comedy of class struggle. The conflict between landlords and peasants was emphasized, while the love interest and the song competition were retained—although, of course, revolutionary sentiment became the foundation of the former and the latter was presented as a contest between the landlord class and the peasants.

If it is difficult to convert a mythical romance into a revolutionary story, it is even more difficult to give a revolutionary story the light-hearted tone of a comedy. Revolutionary themes call up violent feelings, yet the violence must not be allowed to spoil the light atmosphere of the story. The early Liuzhou version had one scene in which Liu Sanjie was making an embroidered arrow bag for her lover, and the play ended with the lover killing the landlord with an arrow. This grim conjunction was abandoned by Qiao Yu. Instead, he had Liu Sanjie embroidering a *xiuqiu* (a cloth or silk ball that, when offered by a girl to a man, means the girl promises to marry the man); at the end, Liu and her lover simply evade the landlord's pursuit.

The scriptwriter had very little room to maneuver revolutionary ideology. Insinuation and sarcasm were his most frequent tactics. For example, the early field researchers collected this riddling song:

What has a mouth but won't talk?
What hasn't any mouth but makes a lot of noise?
What has legs but won't walk?
What hasn't legs but travels a lot?

Buddha has a mouth but won't talk.
A gong has no mouth but makes a lot of noise.
A chair has legs but won't walk.
A boat has no legs but travels a lot.

By altering this only a little, the scriptwriter accomplished his task almost perfectly. His version goes:

What has a mouth but won't talk?
What hasn't any mouth but makes a lot of noise?
What has legs but won't walk?
What hasn't legs but travels a lot?

Buddha has a mouth but won't talk.
A gong hasn't any mouth but makes a lot of noise.
A rich man has legs but he won't walk.
His money has no legs but travels a lot.

When, in the film, Liu Sanjie sings the third line of the answer, we are shown the villain sitting in a sedan chair being rushed down the road. The juxtaposition is indeed funny, and the insinuation clear. Overall, however, Qiao Yu shows somewhat more interest in entertainment than in indoctrination. The love story and the hilarious song competition occupy at least as important a role in the film as does class struggle. The scriptwriter even sacrificed such a commendably revolutionary statement as: "If I am right, I dare to scold the Emperor. It doesn't matter whether you are a lord or not"—probably because of its coarseness of style.[3]

Almost all the songs in the film are of high esthetic quality and, with some exceptions during the song competition, refined in both style and content. Comparison reveals that the bellicosity of the early play versions was toned down in the film to the point where even conservative audiences in Hong Kong and Singapore could find the central theme acceptable and amusing. The villain is ugly and stupid but not as evil as most villains in post-Liberation films. This forbearance may mark one instance in which art prevailed over ideological considerations. However, there is no doubt that in *Liu Sanjie* the scriptwriter successfully grafted an alien theme onto a legend, thus bringing the story to a new stage of its existence.

The whole film emphasizes the esthetically rich and tranquil life of peasants and fishermen. The music and songs bear out the same theme. Even hostile critics paid tribute to the beauty of its cinematography and to the composers and musicians who worked on the film. Yet, although they received less attention, the lyricists and the scriptwriters deserve most of the credit for the film's success. While the composers worked with beautiful folk music and songs, the lyricists had to juggle legends, love vows, and revolutionary ideology—a feat they accomplished with elegance. Without losing much of the folksongs' original flavor and beauty, these artists were able to adapt them into songs that preached revolution while matching the quality, both of style and content, of the poetry in the *Shijing* [Book of songs]. Here, for example, is one of the opening songs of the film, with a rough translation:

Shan ding you hua
shan jiao xiang (le)
qiao di you shui
qiao mian liang (le)
xin zhong you liao bu ping shi (le)
shan ge tu huo chu xiongtang (le)

[3] The screenwriter also cut some other coarse couplets. See Zhang Haizhen, "Dianying *Liu Sanjie* de chuli shi zhengquede" [The treatment of the film *Liu Sanjie* is correct], *Dazhong dianying* [Popular cinema] (1962), 2: 19–20.

[Where there are flowers on top of the hill,
there will be fragrance at the foot of the hill.
Where there is water underneath the bridge,
it will be cool when you stand on the bridge.
Where there is injustice that you feel in your heart,
a song will burst out like fire from your breast.]

This song resembles classical poetry in form, but has a simplicity and a concreteness of expression that recall folk poetry. It has the virtue and power of folk wisdom. The logic of human feelings and expression is gracefully interpreted by parallels from nature. Yet in style this song is comparable to a classical poem such as this one, from the *Book of Songs*:

Tossed is that cypress boat,
Wave-tossed it floats,
My heart is in turmoil,
. . . .
My heart is not a stone,
It cannot be rolled.
My heart is not a mat,
It cannot be folded away.
. . . .
O sun, ah moon,
Why are you changed and dim?
Sorrow clings to me
Like an unwashed dress.
In the still of the night I brood upon it,
Long to take wing and fly away.[4]

It may be said that the lyric in *Liu Sanjie* has the same quality as this. The songs of *Liu Sanjie* are not only potently persuasive but also gracefully entertaining; maintaining classical forms, they display a crystal clarity and freshness that are often blended with a certain degree of innocence, as do the poems shown above.

The songs in *Liu Sanjie* are simple and plain, sometimes funny, and sprinkled with socialist ideology; but they are always elegant. They seem to stand, stylistically, at the meeting-point of elite and popular culture, and they were welcomed by both audiences: "the refined and the popular [audiences] can both appreciate them" (*ya su gong shang*). One secret of this dual appeal is the lyricists' trick of hiding sophisticated allusions in plain language. An example is the fifth line of the song cited above: "xin zhong you liao bu ping shi" ["Where there is injustice that you feel in your heart"]. The term *bu ping* has different meanings to different people. To

[4] Translated by Arthur Waley in Cyril Birch, ed., *Anthology of Chinese Literature* (New York: Grove Press, 1965), poem 24, untitled.

the less educated it means *bu gongping,* "unfair" or "unjust." To the more informed, the same term is a clear reference to Han Yu's famous remark, "All things in the universe, when they are not properly balanced, will cry out in protest" (*Wu bu de qi ping ze ming*)[5]. The screenwriter has thus unobtrusively compressed a complicated meditation on the ultimate motivation of poets and thinkers into two words.[6]

The central theme of the film is beautifully spelled out in the last two lines of this song. It is a film about grief and injustice in human life (*renjian bu ping,* "injustice in the world of men"). Such a theme must certainly strike a chord in every human mind—but it is also in line with the song-gathering theory (*cai feng*) developed by the elite political scientists in ancient China. The writers of the play about Liu Sanjie were fully aware that they were applying the techniques associated with this theory.[7] Zheng Tianjian (who was, I suspect, directly involved in creating the version of the play published in 1961) discussed the approach used in the film in his article "On the Creation of *Liu Sanjie.*"[8] He cited examples in which the lyricists skillfully used puns, parables, and narrative in ways both entertaining and instructive, just as the anonymous poets of the *Book of Songs* did. In Chinese history, politicians often fabricated "folksongs" to stir up resentment and resistance. But to the commoner singer a song has quite different functions. Agreeing with the common people, the lyricists of *Liu Sanjie* also present another song with the same elegant form and intuitive logic:

Shan ge bu chang youchou duo
da lu bu zou cao cheng wo
gang dao bu mo sheng huang xiu
xiongtang bu ting bei yao tuo

[If songs are not sung, sorrow will spread.
If roads are not walked upon, weeds will grow.
If steel knives are not sharpened, rust will erode them.
If heads are not held high, backs will bend.]

[5] In "Song Meng Dongye xu" [Preface to poem sent to Meng Dongye], in *Han Changli quanji* [Complete works of Han Yu], (Taibei: Shangwu, 1967), *juan* 5, 5:7–8.

[6] For the conscious use of this allusion, see Zheng Tianjian, "*Liu Sanjie* de chuangzuo" [The creation of *Liu Sanjie*], in Conference on *Liu Sanjie,* ed., *Liu Sanjie* (Peking: Zhongguo xiju chubanshe [Chinese Theater Press], 1964), pp. 143–160.

[7] See Mao's introduction to the *Shijing* in *The Chinese Classics,* vol. 4, *The She King,* trans. James Legge (Hong Kong: Hong Kong University Press, 1960), pp. 34–36, for an explanation of the following terms for techniques used by ancient song writers: *feng, fu, bi, xing.*

[8] He specifically refers to the *fu-bi-xing* approach; see Zheng Tianjian, "*Liu Sanjie* de chuangzuo," p. 10.

Again the words are simple and plain, linking common natural phenomena to more sophisticated human feelings. The music has a serenity that deepens the meaning of the words.

Audiences responded warmly and enthusiastically to *Liu Sanjie,* and it became a great financial success for the distributor and for many theater owners—even though the critics' responses were divided (see below). The sound track could be heard in the streets of Hong Kong for months after the film was first shown. Many viewers (in Hong Kong and elsewhere) went to see the film several times. In China, sheet music with color pictures of the star were distributed to collectors and music lovers. The ultimate compliment came from the right-wing film producers of Hong Kong and Taiwan. They imitated the music and songs of *Liu Sanjie* to produce a rightist version called *Shan'ge lian* [Folksong love story]. This movie was also a financial success and won a prize in Taibei.

Should *Liu Sanjie* be considered a product of folk or of elite culture? In the 1960s, it was generally classified as the former; in fact, the film's name, *Liu Sanjie,* was then almost synonymous with "folksong" (*shan'ge*). Yet Peking opera, also once considered strictly a popular art, is today widely accepted as classical. Movie makers can hire artists of the highest caliber, such as only nobles used to be able to patronize, and make their performances available to millions; in that sense, motion pictures tend to popularize elite culture. Yet these same artists can be employed to perform tales based on folk culture, thus making popular culture elite. The film *Liu Sanjie* is an interesting synthesis of these trends, in which elements of elite culture have been carefully and intentionally presented in popular forms.

THE CRITICISM OF *LIU SANJIE*

For all the care that went into its making, *Liu Sanjie* did not satisfy all its viewers. The first critical article appeared in *Popular Cinema* in October 1961. In it A Yi censured the film for modernizing an ancient immortal. Because Liu was presented in realistic form, "her behavior was necessarily regulated by the principles of the real world, thus affecting her movement, style, and nature to the extent that she looks more like a contemporary woman than like a woman who lived in the ancient society of the Zhuang people. She sounds like a progressive woman during our land reform movement."[9]

In January 1962 three more critical articles appeared in the same journal. One author maintained that the image of Liu Sanjie was both historically and artistically true; the idealistic image, he averred, had been successfully joined to the realistic one. The other two critics agreed with A Yi

[9] *Dazhong dianying,* 1961, no. 10.

that the immortal's image was spoiled by making her too revolutionary. One charged that the peasants presented in the film were too confident and radical. "Could the ideological consciousness of the ancients reach this progressive level?" he asked. He found that only anachronism resulted from the effort to make an ancient legend serve a contemporary purpose. The other critic also protested against the legendary Liu Sanjie being made to look like a contemporary revolutionary. He would rather have seen her flying in the clouds like a fairy.

Popular Cinema published six further articles on *Liu Sanjie* in the following issues. Four attacked the film and two defended it. One of the latter denied that Liu Sanjie had been modernized, while the other suggested that the audiences loved her precisely because she had been modernized. In August 1962 two more hostile articles appeared in *Popular Cinema*. One critic admitted that some viewers liked the film but only, he maintained, for its esthetic aspects. This was the last comment on *Liu Sanjie* to appear in *Popular Cinema*.

These criticisms may have affected the judges of Peking's second Hundred Flowers Film Awards (May 29, 1963). In the contest for Best Feature Film, *Liu Sanjie* came in fourth, following *Li Shuangshuang*, *Huaishuzhuang* [Locust-tree manor], and *Dong jin xuqu* [Eastern march prelude]. It was not even nominated under Best Scriptwriter and Best Director. However, the 180,000 voters who participated in a film festival sponsored by *Popular Cinema* awarded *Liu Sanjie* three first prizes: Best Film Photography for cinematographer Guo Zhenting, Best Film Music for composer Lei Zhenbang, and Best Art Design for Tong Jingwen and Zhang Qiwang. The unusual fact that reports about the Hundred Flowers Film Awards seldom mentioned *Liu Sanjie* suggests that the film was generally considered problematic. It was mentioned only casually once, in reference to "the diversified tastes of our audience." The creators of *Liu Sanjie* were probably aware of its problems. When the Chinese Theater Press published the play in 1961, Zheng Tianjian wrote, "Like other ancient cultural legacies, *Liu Sanjie* has both honey and poison in it."[10] The scriptwriter's decision to allow Liu Sanjie to sing quite a few love songs and to make an embroidered *xiuqiu* for her lover while she was struggling against the class enemy probably cost the writer the votes of both the revolution-oriented voters and the fans of romantic love stories. From this perspective, the film is indeed a victim of the situation.

Judging from audience response, the films of the 1960s were better than most of the films produced during the Cultural Revolution. Critics expressed themselves freely, and their expectations were high. Most of those who wrote on *Liu Sanjie* found its realism distressing; they wanted

[10] Zheng Tianjian, "*Liu Sanjie* de chuangzuo," pp. 143–160.

historical but not ideological accuracy in a legendary story. They especially disliked the modernistic "struggle methods" (*douzheng fangshi*) used in the film. They rejected "stylistic esthetics" (*xingshi mei*), insisting that a historical figure must live within his or her time. Some critics thought that Liu should have had magic powers and that the film should have been wittier and more colorful.

During the Cultural Revolution, *Liu Sanjie* was withdrawn from circulation, as were all films of its period. Afterward, along with many others, it was rereleased by the authorities and enjoyed great popularity because of its mild and artistic approach to its revolutionary theme. Why have audiences generally found the film satisfactory, but not the critics? Perhaps the critics took the matter of motion pictures more seriously than the audiences, and thus their expectations were higher. Also, in committing themselves on paper, the critics may have been overly cautious, sometimes even pretentious, on ideological issues. Yet at the same time, as intellectuals, they paid great respect to traditional content and forms and objected to the imposition of a revolutionary theme on a legend.

Liu Sanjie may well owe its popularity to the lovely scenery of Guilin, to its beautiful folksongs, to the romantic legend of its heroine, and, most of all, to the scriptwriter and the composer's ability to present these elements in a style that both educated and less educated audiences could appreciate. These artists guided the traditional tale of Liu Sanjie into a new stage of its existence. The critics' backwardness in recognizing the film's value may be due to the novelty in the 1960s both of the genre of the film and of film criticism itself.

EIGHT

The Film Industry in the 1970s

Paul Clark

Film enjoys perhaps the largest popular audience of all the cultural media of contemporary China. More people, and a wider range of people, watch movies than read novels, see television, or attend stage performances. Lenin's statement that "of all the arts, film is most important to us" has often been quoted in the People's Republic.[1] Given the significance attached to cinema, it is not surprising that since 1949 much attention has been paid to the development of the art. At the producing end, Chinese film makers, like their colleagues in other parts of the world, are grouped together with producers of what are generally regarded as elite forms of art. The complexity and expense of their genre set film makers apart from artists in the more indigenous performing arts. From its beginnings, the film world of Shanghai had been distant in many senses from the local opera of Shanxi, even if the films made in the revived industry of the late 1940s reached more people than Hua Guofeng's Shanxi opera troupe. These cultural workers operated in two different realms; the insulated, though cosmopolitan, elite world of the film studios, on the one hand, and the popular atmosphere of the traditional opera stage and other popular forms, on the other. The history of Chinese cinema since 1949 has been in part an effort to integrate these two cultural realms.

The problems that faced film makers in the 1970s can be traced back both to the early post-Liberation attempts to effect such a synthesis between high and popular culture and to the tensions between film makers and political leaders. By the mid-1960s, the generation of film makers who had started their careers before Liberation were reaching the peak of their

I should like to thank Bonnie S. McDougall, discussions with whom helped shape many of my ideas on Chinese cinema.

[1] For a recent example, see quotation by He Ling in *Dianying yishu,* January 1979, 1:26.

achievement. They were assisted by a group of younger artists trained, with Soviet help, in the mid-1950s. Three films—*Nongnu* [Serfs, 1964], *Li Shuangshuang* (1962), and *Liu Sanjie* [Third Sister Liu, 1962]—attest to the level these film makers attained. By the time these films were released, however, the outside arbiters of artistic and political orthodoxy were examining the film industry with more than usual attention. In 1966, the supporters of Jiang Qing's cultural policies in effect closed down the industry for almost half a decade.

The first half of the 1970s saw the slow establishment of a new equilibrium between film makers and cultural-policy makers. The arrest, in October 1976, of Jiang Qing and some of her supporters was hailed by Chinese film workers, old and young, as a "second Liberation." Subsequently, however, the film industry had trouble matching the speed with which its less popular sister arts re-established themselves. The political climate allowed audiences and film makers to express their views and through 1979 they continued to criticize harshly the more recent products of the film industry, often motivated by hangovers of "Gang-ness" (*bangqi*) in the new films.

As the decade drew to a close, the Gang of Four years were increasingly put into perspective. Film makers and, to a lesser extent, their audience came to realize that many of the artistic and political problems facing Chinese cinema were of deeper origin. With older film makers returning to prominent positions of artistic and managerial leadership, the historical continuities of Chinese cinema became clearer. The problematical relationships between film and life and between film and politics had certainly been distorted in the period from 1966 to 1976. But perhaps they had never been adequately addressed by Chinese film makers. By the end of the 1970s, a renewed urge to face up to these problems had appeared, particularly among the new generation of cinema workers.

THE IMPACT OF THE CULTURAL REVOLUTION

To gain a proper understanding of developments after 1976, we must first assess the impact of the triumvirate of Jiang Qing, Yao Wenyuan, and Zhang Chunqiao and of their supporters on Chinese film making. In view of the accusations against them that filled film magazines and other print media during the year after their arrest, this should be an easy task. In reality, it is not. The difficulty partly stems from the seemingly haphazard or arbitrary nature of their cultural autocracy in the film world. Such absence of consistency compounds the problem of assessing the impact of the Cultural Revolution. But a careful reading of accounts of studio activities before October 1976 tends to cast doubt on the presumption that that month was a sudden turning-point. As in other fields of literature and the arts, changes in the film world had started before 1976 and have continued to be slow and cumulative.

This is not to underestimate the effects on Chinese cinema of Jiang Qing and her associates. Almost all feature films produced before 1966 were withdrawn from release at the start of the Cultural Revolution. No new feature films were apparently made until the early 1970s, and these were merely celluloid versions of some of the model theatrical works (*yangbanxi*). Speaking in 1978, Yuan Wenshu, the reinstated secretary of the Chinese Film Association, compared the gang's policies to the "three all" (*san guang*) campaigns of the Japanese in North China. He claimed that the film industry was turned into a no man's land and that between 1966 and 1973 only one feature film was made.[2] In January 1973, at a meeting of the Politburo with cultural personnel, Premier Zhou Enlai spoke of the need for feature films. But the response to this call was disappointing, due to further interference from the supporters of Jiang Qing. The works produced before 1974 consisted of film versions of *yangbanxi* or remakes as model films (*yangban dianying*) of such pre-Cultural-Revolution stories as *Nanzheng beizhan* [Fighting south and north] and *Pingyuan youjidui* [Guerrillas of the plain].[3] In 1974, with the release of the children's film *Shanshande hongxing* [Sparkling red star], the pace of film making quickened.

From these changes it appears that by 1973 some members of the older generation of film makers were back at work. *Sparkling Red Star* was jointly produced by two successful directors of the 1950s and early 1960s, Li Jun and Li Ang. Both had been criticized during the Cultural Revolution.[4] The return of such artists to the studios suggests that the Gang of Four was losing effectiveness or was deliberately relaxing its grip on film production in response to the need for more feature films. Reliance had to be placed on those with film experience.

The events of 1975 were at once a reflection of both the destructive influence of the Gang of Four and of its increasing weakness. The latter trend may have precipitated the Gang's more hysterical efforts at control. In 1975 it launched an "antiguild" (*fan hangbang*) effort in film circles. A particular target in that year was the recently completed film *Haixia,* the story of the pre- and post-Liberation experiences of an orphan girl in a South China fishing village. The movie was produced at the Peking Film Studios under the direction of Xie Tieli, who had been severely criticized in 1964–1965. The antiguild efforts seem to have sprung from the realization that film makers would not remain docile producers of model films.

[2] *Renmin dianying,* 1978, 6:3. This calculation excludes *yangbanxi.* The one feature film was *Pingyuan youjidui* [Guerrillas of the plain].

[3] Ibid.; see also part 12 (1971–1976) of a fifteen-part series on post-1949 Chinese cinema by Xueyan and Litao, in *Nanbeiji* 92 (January 1978): 45–50.

[4] *Renmin dianying,* 1978, 2–3:47.

The campaign was, therefore, aimed at wiping out the "cliquish system of the director as the central figure." Before the Cultural Revolution (and since 1976), directors had on occasion done much of the planning for a film, often finding the story, helping produce the script, and working out costs. These powerful directors of the older generation threatened the Gang of Four's influence in the film world when production started under way again in 1975.[5]

Haixia had been made by a production group under Xie's leadership. Jiang Qing and Zhang Chunqiao are said to have written critiques of the film in order to provide ammunition for their supporters in the Ministry of Culture. These latter made several visits to the studios in an attempt to put pressure on the makers of *Haixia*. The producers showed the film to Zhou Enlai and appealed to Mao Zedong, who declared in late July 1975 that copies of director Xie's letter complaining of Ministry pressure should be distributed to members of the Politburo. Even so, the film's release soon after brought more criticism from the Gang of Four.[6]

Three observations arise from an examination of the troubles of *Haixia*. First, the attack on the film appears quite arbitrary; at least it does not focus on the merits of the film itself, although Jiang Qing argued that the heroine looked like a city girl and that the film did not make class struggle its key theme.[7] Generally, however, the criticism concentrated on the people who had made the film. The same is perhaps true of the critiques of another major target of the Gang, *Chuangye* [The pioneers]. The makers rather than the merits of the film were also, arguably, at the center of the post-1976 criticism of *Juelie* [Breaking with old ideas], a so-called "Gang" film released in early 1976. Despite some atypical character development (an initially "bad" teacher undergoes conversion), *Breaking with Old Ideas* was taken to be a film made to the Gang of Four's prescription. More recent listings of such movies, however, do not include *Breaking*, which was withdrawn from release in 1977 when new educational policies very different from those advocated in the film were introduced.[8]

The second observation is that all the reported criticisms of *Haixia* in 1975–1976 seem to have come not from the Peking studio itself but from

[5] This account is drawn from *Renmin dianying*, 1978, 5:16–17 and 1978, 1:12–15. See also *Renmin dianying*, 1977, 10:6–8; 1976, 7:28–32, and the filmscript in 1976, 7:39–64. On the role of directors, see *China Reconstructs* 28, 8 (August 1979): 8. Xie's 1964 film was *Zaochun eryue* [Early spring in February].

[6] *Renmin dianying*, 1978, 1:12–15; 1978, 2–3:30–37.

[7] *Renmin dianying*, 1978, 2–3:30–37.

[8] *Renmin dianying*, 1976, 5, published on 27 September 1976 before the arrest of the Gang of Four, contained the first half of the filmscript of *Chuangye*, pp. 32–64. The attacks on the film are reported in *Renmin dianying*, October 1976, 6:16–33. For a general account of the Gang of Four's control of film making, see *Renmin dianying*, 1978, 8:1–5. For a nonlisting of *Juelie*, see *Renmin dianying*, 1978, 6:4.

outside, from the Ministry of Culture. Such cases as this of *Haixia* suggest that the cultural triumvirate headed by Jiang Qing had few followers among the people actively involved in film production. While by 1979 other things had changed, and the whole system of film production was being re-examined, film workers again complained of obstruction from above, from the Ministry and local agencies.

The third observation occasioned by the *Haixia* episode is the apparent continuity of personnel in the Chinese film world in the 1970s—even if few movies were produced initially. Wang Yang of the Peking studio argued that, in the ten years of the Cultural Revolution, no older film makers matched their pre-1966 levels of artistry. Some middle-aged directors and some young film makers who were fresh graduates of the Film and Drama Academies had not produced a single film by 1979. Wang Yang also pointed out that before 1977, although most filmscripts written since the Cultural Revolution had not been filmed, many older scenarists were engaged in writing, sometimes under orders from the Gang of Four.[9] Thus, while there was a substantial change, or second Liberation, in the atmosphere at the studios, the personnel remained, apparently, largely the same after October 1976 as they had been in the first half of the 1970s.

The lack of substantial change in personnel after 1976 parallels the apparent absence of real change in most of the films made after the fall of the Gang of Four.[10] Film magazines in late 1978 and in 1979 emphasized particularly the problems of the post-Gang feature films, while saying less than before about the Gang itself. A monthly section in *Renmin ribao* [People's daily], which had more authority and a wider circulation than all the film journals put together, was given over to discussions of "What's wrong with the movies?" and "How can films be made better?"

The irony of post-Gang cinema emerges perhaps most sharply in the nine films that depict the struggle against the Gang of Four while using artistic methods close to those endorsed by the Gang itself.[11] Viewers complained about these thrillers' simplistic nature, which they compared to the complexity of their own experiences under the Gang. It is perhaps easier to be simplistic about the pre-Liberation past, of which most filmgoers now have not had first-hand experience. The lingering influence of the Gang of Four

[9] *Guangming ribao,* 23 March 1979, p. 3; *Renmin dianying,* 1978, 4:61–63. In 1976 the Gang of Four had completed eight films about the struggle against "capitalist roaders," thirteen more were in production, and thirty-nine were being written, for a total of sixty films: *Renmin dianying,* 1978, 8:2.

[10] Until the summer of 1979, no feature films made after October 1976 appear to have been publicly released outside of the People's Republic, not even in Hong Kong. An exception is *Dahe benliu,* shown in the United States in June 1979 at the Workshop on Contemporary Chinese Literature and the Performing Arts. In November 1979, a Chinese film festival held in Tokyo included three new feature films.

[11] The films are listed in *Dianying yishu,* 1979, 1:34.

on post-1976 cinema is felt in three areas: scripts, characterization, and, more broadly, the tension between realism and filmism.

Scripts

With the re-orientation of film after October 1976, scripts were at a premium. It usually takes from two to four years for a story idea to turn into a feature film,[12] but the film-starved audiences could not wait that long. Many of the over sixty feature films produced after October 1976 were shot from scripts written a few years earlier. *Baoziwan zhandou* [Battle of Leopard Valley], about a Nanniwan-like production movement in the War of Resistance, was released in the spring of 1978. The filmscript, based on a play of the same title from 1964, had been drafted in 1973. It went through ten rewrites in four years, the last of which extended from March 1977 to January 1978.[13] A similar process produced *Dahe benliu* [The great river rushes on], which starred China's most popular actress, Zhang Ruifang. The film was released to early critical acclaim in 1979. The first of its two parts was based on a screenplay that the creator of *Li Shuangshuang,* Li Zhun, had written in 1975. Within weeks of its release, *The Great River Rushes On* began to be criticized for residual Gang-ness and for its lack of realism.[14]

The need for new scripts was voiced by the film publications in 1978. A new edition of Xia Yan's major work on film adaptation, *Xie dianying juben jige wenti* [Some scriptwriting problems; orig. pub. 1959], was excerpted in *Renmin dianying* [People's cinema].[15] The same magazine carried several articles on scriptwriting in its October/November 1978 issue. In early 1979, there was a total of only forty or so properly trained scriptwriters in the seven feature film studios. The studio leaders called for more, especially younger, personnel to be trained.[16] About half of all scripts were submitted by amateur writers from outside the studios.

Characterization

Closely related to the problem of finding scripts was the question of how to portray characters in the new films. Here, too, there was continuity with the immediate past: both periods had difficulty creating believable heroes and villains. In a long article published in September 1978, the

[12] So He Ling claims in *Renmin dianying,* 1978, 4:6.

[13] *Renmin dianying,* 1978, 4:14–17. For another example, see *Renmin dianying,* 1978, 8:13–14.

[14] Renmin dianying, 1978, 6:5. For the later critical reaction against the film, see below. The stories of the two parts of the film can be found in *Renmin dianying,* 1977, 5–6:65–96 and 1977, 7:36–64.

[15] *Renmin dianying,* 1978, 4:22–27; 1978, 5:18–26.

[16] *Renmin ribao,* 12 March 1979, p. 3.

review group of the Film Section of the Ministry of Culture declared that the influence of the Gang of Four was still "extremely deep." Specifically, the group disapproved of superheroes, with their clean clothes and other Gang accoutrements, and of the tendency to create "meathead enemies" (*caobao diren*), or to replace the "capitalist roaders" of earlier scripts with "Gang followers" in the new productions.[17] The heroine of *Nanjiang chun zao* [Spring comes early on the southern border], one Peking filmgoer complained, indulged in unnecessary heroics. In the best Jiang Qing tradition, she easily persuades the angry masses of the wisdom of her acts with a few well-chosen sentences.[18] Chinese writers after 1976 found it difficult to create good characters with depth, instead of cut-outs whose generalized features serve merely to indicate their rank—worker, poor peasant, or soldier.

In an interview conducted early in 1978, Xia Yan called for characters with an internal momentum and integrity, be they good, bad, or middling. He pointed out that most people in real life are not able to express their heartfelt feelings; film characters, he said, should reflect this attribute.[19] Some progress was made in this direction. *Julan* [The mighty wave] has a hero who gets angry twice, which was a first in the experience of one letter writer.[20] Two members of the Huangpu district film-review group in Shanghai praised the portrayal of the heroine in *Nü jiaotongyuan* [The female liaison agent]. In contrast to earlier heroines, whom everyone (except the enemy) could instantly identify as Communist Party workers, the woman in this film was more subtly portrayed. For instance, she acts in a wisely subdued manner when one of her comrades is killed. Such restraint in presenting characters helped involve the audience with the heroine and her task.[21]

Believable, rounded characters may become more common as more films include "middle characters," in accordance with a major post-1976 shift in artistic themes that recalls similar efforts in the early 1960s. Movies based on their characters' re-education, such as *Li Shuangshuang* (1962), rather than on confrontation between "the enemy and ourselves," should help put heroes and villains in their proper places. More compact and manageable stories may also provide a more suitable context for the sustained portrayal and development of characters. It could be argued, for example, that the juxtaposed portraits of Haixia as pre-1949 orphan and as a contemporary militiawoman substituted, in 1975, for the real character growth that Xia Yan and others are now seeking.

[17] *Renmin dianying,* 1978, 9:2–3.

[18] *Renmin dianying,* 1978, 8:13.

[19] *Renmin dianying,* 1978, 2–3:19.

[20] *Renmin dianying,* 1978, 2–3:59–60. The filmscript is in *Renmin dianying,* 1977, 10:26–64.

[21] *Renmin dianying,* 1978, 5:13–14.

With respect to characters, one new development deserves brief mention. Part 2 of *The Great River Rushes On* features actors portraying Zhou Enlai and Mao Zedong. Such look-alikes began to appear also in stage productions. There may have been some controversy over the decision to include these historical figures in fictional films. Such a debate is implied in an article on the film in *People's Daily* that is subtitled "In approval of the portrayal of Premier Zhou in *The Great River Rushes On*."[22] Certainly, it could weaken the move toward believable characters, for audiences might well be distracted by an urge to assess the degree of resemblance and by admiration for the obvious artifice involved in such portrayals. Watching Zhou Enlai, in *The Great River Rushes On,* address the masses in the pouring rain without benefit of umbrella, this viewer may not have been alone in wondering when the actor's eyebrows would start to melt down his face. These portrayals may undermine the efforts of the other actors in the films. On the other hand, the appearance of a historical figure may lend credibility, at least to the events presented. Indeed, Zhou Enlai's tour of the water-conservation project in this film is accompanied by the kind of music that Chinese television news uses in covering the meetings of national leaders with state visitors. But such intrusions of documentary style into an otherwise fictional story are potentially inhibiting. The development of conventions for the portrayal of real people in films could conflict with the creation of more ambiguous fictional characters. Such portrayals of real people in films and plays may be a short-lived phenomenon.

Realism Versus Filmism

These concerns over scripts and characters relate ultimately to a major question for Chinese, and indeed for all, film makers, the problem of realism. Much has been written criticizing the theories of the Gang of Four, especially the principle of "three prominences" (*san tuchu*). A film or any other work of art is supposed to place concentric emphasis on good characters, on the story's heroes, and on the main hero. This theory and other such rather mechanical devices gave feature films a standardized appearance. One movie-magazine reader characterized Gang and some post-Gang films in this way: "Women correct, men wrong; political workers right, production workers wrong; Party branch secretary right, factory manager and production team leader wrong." Merely seeing the beginning of such a film would enable a viewer to predict the end.[23]

Since the fall of the Gang of Four, film makers have addressed the

[22] *Dianying yishu,* 1979, 3:16; *Dazhong dianying,* 1979, 1:4–5; *Renmin ribao,* 31 January 1979, p. 3.

[23] *Renmin dianying,* 1978, 1:14.

problem of film realism. The most fruitful of such discussions have emphasized the inherent characteristics of film and of film's rendering of reality. What is being sought is not an impossible celluloid copy of reality but a new connection between art and life that recognizes the peculiarities of the medium.[24] Instead of Jiang Qing's "Start from the political line" (*cong luxian chufa*), there is now another slogan, "Start from life" (*cong shenghuo chufa*)—a point of departure likely to generate less stereotyped films. Yuan Wenshu, a realist about realism, renewed the call of the 1950s for a combination of revolutionary realism (*xianshizhuyi*) with romanticism (*langmanzhuyi*); this synthesis, he argued, was approved by Mao and Marx and meshes with Chinese literary tradition.[25]

With these concerns came an increasing emphasis on cinematic art, particularly in 1979 with the vocal emergence of a new generation of film makers. This group has had less grounding in theater, whether traditional or modern, than its predecessors. Its emphasis on "filmism" (i.e., the use of techniques unique to film) was perhaps also a natural reaction from the ten years during which those in control of cultural policy had considered cinema merely an adjunct of the stage. Staginess—the reliance on conventions derived from the stage that do not belong in film—had existed in Chinese cinema before the Cultural Revolution and had been exacerbated under the opera-centered cultural regime of the Gang of Four. Films made after 1976 were hailed in many reviews by film-magazine writers and readers for their use of specifically cinematic techniques to portray characters, concretize situations, and move audiences.[26]

A scene in *The Great River Rushes On* illustrates an awareness of the problem of stage-inspired set pieces in a fluid medium like film. Onboard a fishing boat, the heroine Li Mai relates the bitterness of her life before 1938 to Commander Qin and Song Min of the New Fourth Army. Unlike many such scenes in earlier films, there is an earthy humor, well conveyed by Zhang Ruifang's performance, in parts of the recollection. In earlier films, Commander Qin would have stiffened slightly, looked inspired, clenched one fist, and, gazing at an indeterminate point over the camera lens, told Li Mai that now the Chinese people have Chairman Mao and the Communist Party to lead them against the old order that had caused such misery. Commander Qin does give this standard speech to Li Mai, but not into the camera. As if embarrassed by such a stock situation, director Xie Tieli suddenly takes the camera outside the cabin. We see

[24] See, for example, *Dazhong dianying*, 1979, 1:2–3.

[25] In an article titled "Zhuyi zhenshi" [Pay attention to reality], *Renmin dianying*, 1978, 5:3. On realism, see also *Renmin dianying*, 1978, 4:14; 1978, 6:26; and 1978, 9:1–5.

[26] See, for example, *Dazhong dianying*, 1979, 2:22–23; *Guangming ribao*, 7 April 1979, p. 3.

Commander Qin giving the speech as a small figure in the lighted doorway of the cabin addressing Li Mai within. The standard speech is thus presented indirectly and in a context that places less emphasis on the individual giving it.

A re-emphasis on filmic art is clear in *The Great River Rushes On.* Films such as *Serfs* (1964) had given promise of such artistry, but the promise had been lost for ten years. The opening shots of *Great River,* which fill the screen with the silt-laden river and the bare shoulders and muscles of a river boatman, make a startling departure from earlier films. Unfortunately, this stress on muscle power or on the river is not taken up as a motif for the rest of the film. In the same scene, the relationship between two young people is suggested visually by their joining each other to pull on parallel ropes to raise the sail of their boat.

The story involves a village that is flooded by the Yellow River in 1938; the change of this village's name to Tieniu ("Iron Ox") in the revised script (the original script was written before October 1976) allows for the use of an ancient statue of a cow to lend a sense of place to the film. Superstitious villagers are briefly shown making offerings to the statue as the flood waters draw near. Toward the end of Part 1, children returning from exile to the village start to play around the cow, which is up to its neck in silt. This sense of locality (which is confusingly absent in, for example, two films of 1976, *Zuguo, a, muqin* [My country, oh, my mother] and *Fengshuwan* [Maple tree valley]) helps reinforce the theme of the film: the twenty-year struggle of the villagers to take control—from the river, the Japanese, and the landlords—of their village.

Film's ability to evoke tension, which is often downplayed or lost in Chinese films made before 1976, is used to good effect here. When the young fisherman races back from the river to warn the villagers that the dikes are about to be blown up, music, camerawork, and editing all combine without the usual haste to get maximum effect from his journey.

Part 2 of the film exploits the freedom of transition possible in film, which is familiar to Western but novel to Chinese audiences. Immediately after Li Mai meets Mao Zedong in a quiet, reverential scene with few people, the film cuts to thunderous applause and a shot of row upon row of joyful faces at a huge meeting. Li Mai has just reported her encounter with Mao to the conference.

Cheng Yin, a scenarist and director for over thirty years, noted in 1979 that in its sixty-year history Chinese cinema had still not eschewed the stage's influence.[27] In *The Great River Rushes On,* released in 1979, set-pieces create a staginess at odds with the atmosphere of much of the work. Many scenes feature one actor addressing a large crowd. Such tableaux are

[27] *Renmin ribao,* 24 April 1979, p. 3.

perhaps unavoidable, given scripts that require these speech-giving scenes. But the impression of staginess is often compounded by the directors' efforts to place extras in the crowds in artful ways. The art seems more often drawn from the stage than from film experience.

The impression of set-pieces is sometimes reinforced by sudden changes from one major scene to another. The instant transition between Li Mai's encounter with Mao and her report to the conference, referred to above, is different because it is part of a single episode and underlines the importance to all of the meeting with Mao. Usually, however, a major episode lacks linkage with the following such episode, just as conventional stage dramas present a series of large, self-contained scenes. There are occasional visual links between episodes, as when a shot of a starving refugee gnawing on dry grain is followed by one showing Japanese businessmen cutting a cake or as when a brief scene in which Li Mai and Song Min are lying on a *kang* discussing Song's possible marriage is paralleled in the next scene by the village landlord seated on an opium bed. But a tendency toward a stagelike exposition, large scene by large scene, prevails in the film.

One viewer's contribution to the discussion in 1979 of "What's wrong with the movies?" frequently referred to the playlike nature of many recent films, as seen particularly in their excessive use of dialogue.[28] It has been suggested that the acting techniques need to be adjusted to the needs of the medium. The cast of *The Great River Rushes On* went to work each day repeating the words: "We don't want a play. Don't perform."[29] Scriptwriters also need to write with the special characteristics of the medium in mind, including its freedom of temporal transition. Cheng Yin drew attention to the interdependence of these twin concerns of realism and filmism. He suggested that the way to solve the problems of generalism and falseness in the new films was for film makers to "start out from life" and to use the characteristics of their art to their fullest extent.[30]

FILM RELEASES AND PUBLICATIONS

Chinese film makers gained some respite from their audience's impatience with the standards of many post-Gang feature films by rereleasing films made before 1966. This was part of an effort to re-establish connections with their audience, connections that the misplaced theatricality of Jiang Qing had all but destroyed. In the two years before January 1979,

[28] *Dazhong dianying,* 1979, 3:6–9. On dialogue, see also *Renmin dianying,* 1978, 2–3:57–58.

[29] *Renmin ribao,* 27 January 1979, p. 3; see also Zhang Ruifang in *Dazhong dianying,* 1979, 1:5.

[30] *Renmin ribao,* 24 April 1979, p. 3.

three hundred films made before 1966 were rereleased, while another hundred were awaiting distribution.[31] Such films showed what an earlier generation in the industry had achieved. They also served to illustrate, to both audiences and film workers, some of the strengths and weaknesses of Chinese cinema.[32] Further, films made before 1949 were shown for the first time in almost two decades at the Spring Festival of 1979.[33]

This effort to satisfy the audience's interest in the medium also lay behind changes in film publications over these three years. Beginning in late 1977, more information was provided about film personalities—including writers and directors as well as actors—and about current productions. The January 1978 issue of *People's Cinema* featured New Year's resolutions from thirteen film figures, a device also used before 1966, that serves to legitimize the cinema by conveying the film workers' awareness of their shortcomings, to tell audiences of works in progress, and to announce the reappearance of several old figures.[34] In the same issue of the magazine, readers' letters started to appear on a regular basis. The debate over cinema was not just for the makers of films; film viewers were also being encouraged to take part.

In January 1979 *People's Cinema,* which had been published since March 1976, was replaced by three periodicals. The popularizing function of the magazine was taken up by *Dazhong dianying* [Popular cinema], which included more material on films in progress. For example, the February 1979 issue contained reports from each feature film studio on its current productions and plans.[35] This magazine had the largest readership (an estimated 100 million by 1982) of any periodical in China. Serving as a vehicle for more theoretical discussions, which began to increase in volume and incisiveness at the end of 1978, was *Dianying yishu* [Film arts], which had ceased publication in 1966. More specialized was the revived *Dianying jishu* [Film technique], which carried articles on technical aspects of film production, processing, and projection. In addition to these national magazines, Shanghai, Peking, and other localities published such periodicals as *Dianying chuangzuo* [Film writing] and *Dianying xinzuo* [New film works] that featured film stories and scripts (*dianying wenxue*

[31] *Renmin ribao,* 27 January 1979, p. 3.

[32] See, for example, references to the filmism of *Nongnu* in *Renmin dianying,* 1978, 2–3:57–58.

[33] *Dazhong dianying,* 1979, 2:12–13; *Renmin ribao,* 23 January 1979, p. 3; *Dazhong dianying,* 1979, 4:7–8. A new film, *Baomijude qiangsheng* [Gunfire in the security section], is set in an urban context of the 1940s: *Dazhong dianying,* 1979, 4:14.

[34] *Renmin dianying,* 1978, 1:3–8. From July 1977, *Renmin dianying*'s photo sections began to list the directors, major actors, and other personnel involved in featured films. From November, actors were identified with the parts they played.

[35] *Dazhong dianying,* 1979, 2:3–5.

juben).[36] The last three periodicals were initially bimonthly. By the end of the decade, something like the pre-Cultural-Revolution film-publishing scene had been re-established.

There were other signs of progress in the restoration of the industry. In June 1978 the Chinese Film Personnel Association was revived and then superseded by the Chinese Film Artists' Association.[37] Other meetings of a formal and informal nature were publicized. In March 1979, for example, the heads of feature film studios met in Peking, where they discussed the problem of "What's wrong with the movies" with relative candor.[38]

As well as products of their own film industry made before 1966, Chinese audiences after 1977 had an opportunity to see a greater variety of foreign films. In August and October 1978, for example, Romanian and Japanese film weeks were held in Peking and fifteen other major cities.[39] The Japanese week consisted of three films: a thriller called *The Chase* (*Tsuiho; Zhuibu*), an animal story about fox cubs (*Kori no koji; Hulide gushi*), and *Sandakan #8* (*Sandakan hachi Bokyo; Wangxiang*). Charlie Chaplin's *Modern Times* began playing to packed houses; in some theaters, showings started at six in the morning. Some foreign films shown before 1966, like *The Million Pound Banknote*, were rereleased. During the Spring Festival of 1979, to mark the establishment of full Chinese-U.S. relations, two other American films—Peckinpah's *Convoy* and the science-fiction film *Future World*—were shown.

These showings of foreign films served several purposes for audiences and for film makers. To the general audiences they offered a view of the rest of the world. *Future World*, for example, was cited as an illustration of the rich creativity of the American people and of their well-advanced fascination with science.[40] *Sandakan #8*, the story of a Japanese woman sent in the late Meiji period to work in a brothel in Borneo, provoked a lot of questions about its suitability for young Chinese viewers. The participants in a discussion printed in the first issue of *Popular Cinema* concluded that the film broadened the horizons of adolescents and provided them with a useful class education.[41] For film makers, seeing more foreign films was an opportunity to observe a range of new styles and ways of

[36] *Dianying wenxue juben* are not shooting scripts but hybrid literary versions of what will be or has been filmed. Publication in this form reflects a continuing tendency to regard cinema as a lesser branch of literature.

[37] *Renmin dianying*, 1978, 6:6.

[38] *Guangming ribao*, 23 March 1979, p. 3. In 1979 the major feature film studios were: Peking, Shanghai, August 1st (PLA), Changchun, Xi'an, Emei (Sichuan), and Pearl River (Canton).

[39] *Renmin dianying*, 1978, 8:9; *Renmin ribao*, 28 October 1978, p. 6.

[40] *Renmin ribao*, 23 January 1979, p. 3. A reader's comparison of *Dahe benliu* with foreign films can be found in *Dazhong dianying*, 1979, 4:12.

[41] *Dazhong dianying*, 1979, 1:10–12.

treating subjects. *Sandakan #8*'s portrayal of the past formed a welcome contrast to the tendency to formalize, almost to prettify, the oppression of prerevolutionary society.[42] Certain chase or fight sequences in the Chinese spy thrillers made after 1976 apparently reflect a growing acquaintance with more recent foreign work. An article in the first issue of *Film Arts* discussed the development of montage with references to Western studies on film theory, perhaps for the benefit of the younger film workers who lack much training in film theory.[43] Articles on the Hollywood cinematographer James Wong, on world film festivals, and on the Oscar awards appeared in *Popular Cinema* in early 1979.[44] The opinions of foreign film makers were solicited and publicized. Felix Greene, who had made documentaries in China in the early 1970s, presented the criticisms many Western viewers had of Chinese films in a discussion session in early 1979.[45] Joint ventures were also mooted. The first of these was a Japanese historical drama with a Buddhist theme, *Tianping zhi meng* (Tempyō no iraka; The roof tile of Tempyō). Directed by the maker of *Sandakan #8* with a Chinese assistant director, it was filmed on location in Luoyang, Yangzhou, and elsewhere.[46]

DEBATES ON LONG-TERM PROBLEMS

Despite this flurry of publishing and film screening, at the end of the decade large problems remained for the Chinese film industry. With the new year 1979, film workers began to tackle these problems more directly, in their own journals and in newspapers with wider circulation. The Gang of Four years were set in a broader perspective and more long-term questions addressed. What was earlier identified as Gang-ness was increasingly looked on as perhaps endemic problems for Chinese literature and art, including cinema. As to the question of artistic style, the issue most often discussed was realism, the relationship between art and life. The issue for film production itself was democracy, the relationship between art and politics.

The issue of democracy was closely intertwined with another problem, an apparent tension between generations in the industry. In this respect film circles reflected a trend in society at large where, particularly since

[42] One reviewer praised the way the film involved its audience: *Renmin dianying,* 1978, 12:7–9.

[43] *Dianying yishu,* 1979, 1:50–54. One young scriptwriter, pointing out the weakness of theoretical training, asked that more foreign films be made available: *Dazhong dianying,* 1979, 3:7.

[44] *Dazhong dianying,* 1979, 2:28–29, 32; 1979, 3:30–31. A Chinese delegation attended the Cannes film festival in May 1979.

[45] *Dazhong dianying,* 1979, 3:10–11, 5.

[46] *Dazhong dianying,* 1979, 10: pictorial section; *Renmin ribao,* 9 December 1979, p. 6.

1976, youthful impatience or ambition has been frustrated by the return of older figures to more prominent positions. Although the arrest of the Gang of Four in 1976 was not apparently followed by a major changeover in personnel, film artists who had been prominent before the Cultural Revolution have much greater influence now than in the years immediately before 1976. Young film workers do not appear to have been demoted but many seemed to feel that the older leadership was not taking advantage of the new opportunities for cinema.

The younger film makers appear to have real grounds for complaint. From 1977 to 1979, of 140 graduates in acting sent to film studios, less than half had a chance to perform. At one studio, most of the more than twenty graduates sent there had already abandoned acting as a career. Young directors, at last given an opportunity to make films, were furnished with comparatively inexperienced cinematographers, designers, and other specialists.[47] Presumably, the older, more experienced assistants worked for the more established directors.

Given this situation, it is perhaps not surprising that the younger film workers and viewers took a bolder stand on the relation of art to politics, a topic that exercised film circles in the first half of 1979. It was a key theme in a major article, "Wenyi minzhu yu dianying yishu" [Artistic democracy and film art], which was published under the heading "Dianying weishenme shangbuqu?" [What's wrong with the movies?] in *People's Daily* in January 1979. The article was written by two young film workers, Peng Ning and He Kongzhou. Art is the product of personal creation, Peng and He wrote, and can serve politics in a variety of ways. Art rests on politics but is not equivalent to it. There is a need to foster independent creativity and artistic individuality and to broaden the range of subjects portrayed by film makers, who should be encouraged to work in a freely collaborative manner.[48]

Discussion in the industry on these systemic problems of Chinese cinema concentrated on both self-imposed and bureaucratic inhibitions. Zhou Enlai had called attention to these problems almost two decades earlier, in a speech that he delivered in June 1961 to a forum on literature, art, and films and that was published in the January 1979 issue of *Film Arts* and in other cultural publications.[49] The phrase "a lot of mothers-in-law" (*popo duo*) was used to characterize the current bureaucracy and film censorship. Unlike novels and plays, new films faced a great many obstacles (*guanka*) before release. One young film maker who had worked in the industry for only a year called for the elimination of bureaucratic methods of manage-

[47] See article by the editors in *Dazhong dianying*, 1979, 4:3; *Renmin ribao*, 12 March 1979, p. 3.

[48] *Renmin ribao*, 21 January 1979, p. 3; *Dianying yishu*, 1979, 1:28–33.

[49] *Dianying yishu*, 1979, 1:1–14, esp. p. 9.

ment. He accused some leaders, who were often laymen in matters of art, of wantonly interfering in the writing of scripts and in their production. Between script and release a film had to survive up to ten assessments by the studio and the cultural leadership. He proposed giving local and production sections more self-determination. Otherwise, the lifeless films so resented by audiences would continue to be made.[50] Peng and He, the youthful authors of "Artistic Democracy and Film Art," directed the thrust of their argument against this cautiousness that characterized many film personnel. Many in positions of cultural leadership looked on the current policy of openness (*fang*) not as a long-term opportunity for growth but as a temporary expedient to be followed by renewed "control" (*shou*).[51]

Two general ways to reformulate the relationship between art and politics in film were suggested in the first half of 1979. One involved restructuring the industry, the other, a re-examination of the history of Chinese cinema since 1949.

Restructuring was first publicly suggested by Peng Ning and He Kongzhou in January. They concluded their article on artistic democracy and film with concrete proposals for the systematic reform of the methods of film production. The Film Section of the Ministry of Culture should boldly take up the training of talent. Film studios and artists' collectives (*chuangzuo jiti*), like similar groups set up in 1957 in the first Hundred Flowers period,[52] should cooperate in making films and should enjoy financial independence. To democratize the running of the studios, representative assemblies of film employees should assess and supervise the cadres who manage artistic enterprises.

These specific suggestions, which Peng and He preferred to call a revolution rather than a reform of the industry, seem to have received no public answer. This does not mean, of course, that they had no impact. At the February meeting of the leaders of the national feature film studios in Peking, most speakers who were quoted called for greater studio independence. Producing films and leading creative efforts by the methods used in political administration could only narrow the scope of films. It was a sign of the times that the long newspaper report of the gathering made no mention of the Gang of Four.[53]

The other approach to the problem of the proper relationship of politics and art involved a reappraisal of film making since 1949. An effort was made to differentiate the good from the bad in the thirty years since

[50] *Renmin ribao,* 14 May 1979, p. 3. See also *Renmin ribao,* 13 February 1979, p. 3, article by Han Xiaolei and Huang Shixian; and *Renmin ribao,* 22 January 1979, p. 4, article by Li Derun.

[51] *Renmin ribao,* 12 January 1979, p. 3.

[52] See reference in *Dianying yishu,* 1979, 2:1.

[53] *Guangming ribao,* 23 March 1979, p. 3.

Liberation to provide lessons for a still-troubled industry. Members of the older generation of film makers seemed to share their younger colleagues' concern for artistic democracy (*yishu minzhu*). Xia Yan, the most famous living Chinese film maker, offered three reasons for film's historical problems. First, ideological weakness, in particular, had allowed false, "leftist" interference, which encouraged artistic restrictions. Second, the relationships between politics and art and between quantity and quality had been only superficially addressed. Third, not enough attention was paid to training personnel. Xia called for more rational economic management and for greater concern over quality. Quality had begun to matter more in the effort to produce thirty suitable films to honor the 1979 National Day.[54] In a later summary of historical experience, Li Shaobai derived lessons from the two waves of major production and the two periods of slowdown in the years 1949–1965. The first lesson was that the leadership should approach their task according to the objective reality of cinema and of its laws. The second lesson was that artists' enthusiasm should be encouraged. The periods of moderate political leadership of the industry, when administrative commandism was avoided, had liberated the outlook and energies essential to the development of film.[55]

NEW DIRECTIONS

As the Chinese film industry approached the end of both the thirtieth year since the founding of the People's Republic and of the third year since the arrest of the Gang of Four, there were signs that the earlier talk of a second Liberation was going to be realized in images on the film screen. While the enthusiasm and contribution of older film makers should not be underestimated, many of these signs of real change were associated with more youthful talents.

The younger film makers attempted to broaden the range of subject matter. Instead of such cautious studio attempts to recreate past successes as using *Li Shuangshuang*'s same writer and star for *The Great River Rushes On,* young artists were encouraged by directors and others from the older generation and given more independent experience.[56] These younger workers were perhaps more able than the older directors, now mostly in their sixties, to answer Peng and He's call to "stand in the forefront of the age and answer big social questions." In mid-1979 Peng Ning was working at the Changchun studios on a "film poem" (*dianying-*

[54] *Dianying yishu,* 1979, 1:17–18. See also articles by Zhang Junxiang, Zhang Shuihua, and Yu Min in *Dianying yishu,* 1979, 2:1–14.

[55] *Renmin ribao,* 14 May 1979, p. 3.

[56] *Guangming ribao,* 5 May 1979, p. 3, article by Hai Lang. See also the big emphasis on youth in April 1979's *Dazhong dianying,* p. 5 and pictorial section.

shi), *Lu zai tade jiaoxia yanshen . . .* [The path at his feet extends . . .], about an artist filled with love for his country and people. Described as neither a documentary nor a feature film, the work was in the hands of a young group of artists.[57] Another youthful group was producing *Zuiren* [Criminal], a story of juvenile delinquency after the Cultural Revolution.[58] A third group at the Peking studio was filming *Hunli* [Wedding], about the love experiences of three sisters before and after the Tiananmen Incident.[59]

A promising feature of these new efforts was the film makers' self-consciousness and their concern for their audience. In many places in the new films the makers played on the expectations the audience had built up on its diet of Gang and pre-1966 films. Ten minutes into Part 1 of *The Great River Rushes On,* for example, a rosy-cheeked peasant girl, beaming out of the screen, starts to sing a song. Even for a hardened Chinese audience, this seems a little early for the first of the normal dose of two songs. They discover almost immediately, however, that such expectations are misplaced. This is not a standard musical interlude, but part of a real performance of street theater in Tieniu village by members of a propaganda troupe of the New Fourth Army.

But the problems Chinese film makers have in cultivating an awareness of their audience may stem from the very nature of the medium itself. Film is a popular art only at the receiving end, in terms of the number of people who are its consumers. At the creating end, films are made by special people with special training, spending a great deal of money.[60] Such specialized, elite film makers, particularly when they have little dependence on box-office receipts, may continue to hold assumptions about the nature of

[57] *Dazhong dianying,* 1979, 3:24. When this paper was written in 1979 there was little indication that this enigmatically described film idea would become a center of controversy. The idea became the film *Kulian* [Unrequited love], coscripted by Peng Ning and the fifty-one-year-old poet Bai Hua and directed at the Changchun studios by Peng Ning. Before the completed film (also known as *Taiyang he ren* [The sun and the man]) could be released, *Kulian* became the center of continuing debate on the relationship between politics and art and a target of those who opposed the liberalizing policies of the previous four years. For an assessment of this controversy and a discussion of some of the films made after 1979, see the present writer's "Film-making in China: From the Cultural Revolution to 1981," *The China Quarterly* 94 (June 1983): 304–322.

[58] For the filmscript, see *Renmin dianying,* 1978, 6:39–62. The controversial nature of the script is indicated by the discussion it provoked among film makers and teachers, in *Renmin dianying,* 1978, 7:39–47. It appears that the film was not released.

[59] *Dazhong dianying,* 1979, 3:24.

[60] In late 1979, a concern about budget control became more marked; it emerges, for example, in the conclusion of a film cadre meeting that films should be made according "to artistic and financial laws" (reported in *Dazhong dianying,* 1979, 8: pictorial section). *Dahe benliu* and another major 1979 film, *Cong nuli dao jiangjun* [From slave to general], were both comparatively expensive productions, perhaps reflecting an urge to have such blockbusters restore the industry's standing in the estimation of its audiences.

their "popular" audience long after these are outdated. One viewer, from a teacher-training program in Fengtai district, argued that times had changed. "Some leaders persistently stress that films must achieve the levels reached in the 1950s, and that this would meet the approval of the masses. In fact . . . things from the 1950s will not satisfy the people's needs. Film making should not create limitations for itself (*huadiweilao*), nor stop and look backward (*tingzhidaotui*)."[61] Criticisms that some film makers kept working with material that had been successful for them in the past were not uncommon in 1979.[62]

The fall of the Gang of Four provided a favorable climate for re-assessment of the relations between film makers and their audience. But the difficulties that Chinese film makers had adjusting to their audience's needs made it easier for political leaders to intervene in the industry after 1949. The political leaders could claim that they understood the mass audience better than the film makers. The Gang of Four episode, in this perspective, was merely a heightened version of what had happened before. If Chinese film makers did not know who their audiences were, political leaders could and did inform them.

The problems that Chinese film makers face are further compounded by an imperative of their "popular" art. The films they make are expected to be comprehensible to all viewers, including the humblest peasant.[63] The sense of the re-assessment of Chinese cinema in the late 1970s was that this expectation can make a film less effective both as edification and as entertainment. Differentiating between types of audiences, as when foreign films are shown to largely urban audiences, may be one way to resolve this artistic quandary. The least educated peasant, after all, is not expected to enjoy the sophisticated *baogao wenxue* ("reportage") of a writer like Xu Chi in such a popular medium as *People's Daily.*

A major difficulty is that Chinese film makers may not know who their audiences are. One young film worker publicly argued in 1979 against the tendency to look on mass audiences as "A Dou," that is, as fools.[64] It is not clear how elite film makers determine what the humblest peasant (himself perhaps a myth) can comprehend and wants to see on the screen. A market research poll that surveyed more than six hundred Peking filmgoers in early 1979 was an encouraging sign, at least for urban audiences.[65]

[61] *Dazhong dianying,* 1979, 3:8.

[62] E.g., *Dazhong dianying,* 1979, 4:3.

[63] This imperative was emphasized in discussions with visiting American film makers in 1979, as reporter in Ted Rhodes and Mark Petersson, "The Chinese Film Industry," *Filmmakers Monthly* 12,7 (May 1979): 13–23. I am indebted to Stephen Horowitz for bringing this article to my attention.

[64] *Renmin ribao,* 14 May 1979, p. 3.

[65] *Guangming ribao,* 5 May 1979, p. 3.

By the end of the 1970s, a new generation of film makers was being prepared to succeed the older group who had pioneered film in the People's Republic. The effort to revitalize the Chinese cinema was predicated on harmony between old and young film workers, on a less cautious attitude on the part of the leaders, and on a satisfactory adjustment of the relationships between art, life, and politics. As viewers and film makers become more aware of each other's peculiarities, the Chinese film industry may well proceed in quite unexpected new directions. But whether it would keep the nerve it found in early 1979 and finally embark on a new era remained to be seen.

NINE

Making the Past Serve the Present in Fiction and Drama: From the Yan'an Forum to the Cultural Revolution

Robert E. Hegel

The literature of the May Fourth era was meant to be read by the "Europeanized gentry," Qu Qiubai observed in 1932. Linguistically and culturally, the new creative writing of that period, with its foreign terms, concepts, and structures, was beyond the comprehension of the masses. Literature for the common people, for China's revolutionary masses, should be composed in the living colloquial speech; it should utilize both the strong points of the traditional literary forms and the sensible, straightforward narrative style of the popular storyteller, Qu declared. He even went so far as to call for "a new *Water Margin*" and "a new Yue Fei."[1] Qu was drawing attention to a fact already familiar to other literary critics, among them Mao Dun and Cheng Fangwu: May Fourth writing, geared as it was toward urban intellectual readers, was not well suited to

[1] Qu Qiubai, "The Question of Popular Literature and Art" ("Dazhong wenyi de wenti") (orig. pub. in *Wenxue yuebao* [Literature monthly], 10 June 1932), trans. Paul G. Pickowitz, in John Berninghausen and Ted Huters, eds., *Revolutionary Literature in China* (White Plains, N.Y.: Sharpe, 1976; herafter cited as *Revolutionary Literature*), pp. 47–51, esp. pp. 49–51. *Shuihu zhuan* [Water margin] was apparently compiled (from legends, storytellers' accounts, and earlier written fragments) around 1400, although the extant editions are considerably more recent. See below for a discussion of the work. The best available English translation is Sidney Shapiro, trans., *Outlaws of the Marsh,* 2 vols. (Peking: Foreign Languages Press; Bloomington: Indiana University Press, 1981). Yue Fei was a patriotic general of the Southern Song period. His exploits were common fare for professional storytellers and stage presentations; the first novel about him appeared in the middle of the sixteenth century, although the best-known version of his fictionalized life story is Qian Cai's *Shuo Yue quanzhuan* [Complete tales of Yue Fei] (eighteenth century; recent ed., Shanghai: Gudian wenxue, 1955). See Sun Kaidi, *Zhongguo tongsu xiaoshuo shumu* [Bibliography of Chinese popular fiction], rev. ed. (Peking: Zuojia, 1958), pp. 50–52, for bibliographical notes on the various novels concerning Yue Fei.

function as revolutionary literature for the masses.[2] This conclusion became official Party policy when Mao Zedong gave his "Talks at the Yan'an Forum on Literature and Art" ten years later.[3]

The views of Qu Qiubai and his fellow critics on this question were a manifestation of China's ever-developing nationalism and a tacit condemnation of the iconoclasm of many May Fourth writers' whole-hearted adoption of Western literary models.[4] One of the chief reasons behind this resurgence in cultural pride was articulated by the May Fourth Marxist thinker Li Dazhao, who blamed the sorry state of China since the middle of the nineteenth century on foreign imperialism. This perception was widely influential and seems to have been partly responsible for Mao Zedong's "revolutionary nationalism." Mao was keenly aware that Chinese society could only be transformed on its own terms, by utilizing and preserving the traditional strengths of the great Chinese masses.[5]

Furthermore, to Mao it was an item of faith that the general truths of Marxism-Leninism, such as its analytical methods, should be given "national form" (*minzu xingshi*) by adapting them to Chinese circumstances.[6] As he was to declare in 1956, art "is the manifestation of people's lives, thoughts, and emotions, and it bears a very close relationship to a nation's

[2] Mao Dun, "From Guling to Tokyo" ("Cong Guling dao Dongjing") (orig. pub. in *Xiaoshuo yuebao* [Fiction monthly] 19,10 [1928]), trans. Yu-shih Chen, *Revolutionary Literature,* pp. 37–43; Cheng Fangwu, "From a Literary Revolution to Revolutionary Literature" ("Cong wenxue geming dao geming wenxue") (orig. pub. in *Chuangzao yuekan* [Creation monthly] [1928], trans. Michael Gotz, *Revolutionary Literature,* pp. 34–36.

[3] As C. T. Hsia points out in his *A History of Modern Chinese Fiction, 1917–1957* (New Haven: Yale University Press, 1971), pp. 301–302.

[4] In a recent study, (*The Crisis of Chinese Consciousness: Antitraditionalism in the May Fourth Era* [Madison: University of Wisconsin Press, 1979]), Lin Yu-sheng has examined the radical iconoclasm of several intellectuals (Chen Duxiu, Lu Xun, and Hu Shi) prominent during the May Fourth era. He concludes that the completeness of their rejection of Chinese tradition was itself a function of that tradition. Given a holistically conceived universe where cultural values and political authority are inseparable, any opposition to traditional institutions would entail a rejection of all related values. While Lin's discussion is not limited to creative writing, his more general comments also illuminate both a major strain in May Fourth thinking and the reaction to that iconoclasm among the Marxist thinkers, Qu and Mao, and various writers.

[5] For the chauvinism in Li Dazhao's thinking, see Stuart R. Schram, *The Political Thought of Mao Tse-tung,* rev. ed. (New York: Praeger, 1969), esp. p. 29; for a fuller study of Li, see Maurice Meisner, *Li Ta-chao and the Origins of Chinese Marxism* (Cambridge, Mass.: Harvard University Press, 1967). Mao's nationalism is described by Stuart R. Schram in *Political Thought,* pp. 132–134; examples of writings revealing this tendency can be found in Schram, pp. 161–168, including texts from *Selected Works of Mao Tsetung,* 5 vols. (Peking: Foreign Languages Press, 1967–1977), 2:305–334 and 4:411–424.

[6] See Mao, *Selected Works,* 2:208–210. Li Chi discusses this point in her "Communist War Stories," in Cyril Birch, ed., *Chinese Communist Literature* (New York: Praeger, 1963), pp. 139–157, esp. pp. 139–141. Schram, *Political Thought,* discusses this point on pp. 12, 115–116, with the relevant text quoted on p. 171f.

customs and language. . . . It is no good cutting ourselves off from history and abandoning our heritage. The common people would not approve."[7] Given also the essential role he felt ideology played in speeding the revolution,[8] it is reasonable that Mao should stress the necessity of presenting new political ideas in forms familiar to the mass of China's common people. Probably the best-known formulation of this notion is Mao's frequently cited dictum: "Make the past serve the present; make foreign things serve China" (*gu wei jin yong; yang wei Zhong yong*).[9] This formulation served as a guideline for literary production in China's liberated areas and, subsequently, in the People's Republic to the end of the Cultural Revolution. This essay will explore a few examples of the "revolutionary nationalism" Mao espoused and will uncover elements of traditional literature in the works of contemporary Chinese writers. First, however, a few general observations are in order.

The Marxist theoreticians' cultural pride was shared by literary historians, even those of such different political persuasions as Hu Shi and Lu Xun.[10] While their iconoclasm made them reject as moribund much of the elite literature of old China, especially its essays and erudite verse, their nationalism drove them to search for positive elements in China's literary heritage. What these scholars discovered was protest poetry, vernacular fiction, drama, and the many popular entertainments of the ballad and narrative traditions. Since so many of the stories of fictional and dramatic narratives had circulated for centuries in the broadly popular oral tradition as well, much of the credit for the vitality and creativity of this material

[7] See Stuart R. Schram, ed., *Chairman Mao Talks to the People, Talks and Letters: 1956–1971* (New York: Pantheon, 1974), p. 85; see also Mao Zedong, "Talk to the Music Workers," *Beijing Review* 22,37 (14 September 1979), pp. 9–14.

[8] For Mao's views on the indispensability of intellectuals in revolutionary struggles, see, for example, *Selected Works,* 2:301–303 and 305–334, esp. pp. 321–322. Although Mao states that economics and politics are more crucial determinants of ideology in his "On New Democracy" (*Selected Works,* 2:339–384, esp. pp. 340–341), later in the same essay (p. 382) he declares that culture must "prepare the ground ideologically before the revolution comes."

[9] On Mao's various instructions regarding this point, see Mao, *Selected Works,* 3:81 ("Talks at the Yan'an Forum," 1942); 3:60 ("Oppose Stereotyped Party Writing," 1942); 2:340–341, 380–381 ("On New Democracy," 1940); etc.

[10] I refer to Hu Shi's unfinished *Baihua wenxue shi* [History of vernacular literature] (only the first volume was ever published) (1926–1927; reprint ed., Hong Kong: Yingzhong shuwu, 1959), "Zixu" [Author's preface], p. 9, as well as to the numerous essays on and prefaces to vernacular novels and the like reprinted in *Hu Shi wencun* [Collected writing of Hu Shi] 4 vols. (Taibei: Yuandong tushu gongsi, 1971). Lin Yu-sheng, in *Crisis,* pp. 82–102, discusses Hu Shi as a "pseudoreformist" iconoclast, but he overlooks Hu's work on traditional literature. See also Lu Xun's famous *Zhongguo xiaoshuo shilue,* rev. ed., (1930; reprint ed., Hong Kong: Jindai tushu gongsi, 1965) (published in an English translation by Yang Hsien-yi and Gladys Yang, *A Brief History of Chinese Fiction* [Peking: Foreign Languages Press, 1959]) and Tan Zhengbi's *Zhongguo xiaoshuo fada shi* [History of the development of Chinese fiction] (1935; reprint ed., Taibei: Qiye shuju, 1974).

was ascribed to China's masses. Consequently, the literary works containing these popular stories were generally considered good potential models of national forms, to use the terminology of the time.

However, this blanket attribution of traditional vernacular literature to the masses proved at least partially incorrect and has led to serious misunderstandings of its historical significance. The full implications of this mistake have become clear only recently, as many works previously considered popular have been identified as expressions of traditional elite ideology. Most, if not all, of the more famous classic novels, for example, were demonstrably written by literati for other literati. *Water Margin* is one such work. To nationalistic scholars it seems to record the determination of the masses to resist despotic Confucian authority. This interpretation is valid if one considers only the book's tales of individual heroes, which had been known to illiterate audiences in China for centuries through dramatic adaptation, in legends, and from the tales of countless storytellers. The contribution of these storytellers to the novel as it now stands has been considerable. But the work as a whole is not merely a condemnation of isolated official abuses of power; its latest redactor, Jin Shengtan (1610?–1661), deliberately modified an earlier text to cast doubt on the motivations of its bandit leader and to condemn rebellion in general. An untutored peasant watching a stage presentation of the adventures of one of its heroes, such as Wu Song, would never perceive this broader aim of the work. But an educated person who read the entire novel, including Jin Shengtan's voluminous introductory material and running commentary, would find this conclusion unavoidable.[11] Thus *Water Margin* does not necessarily embody the aspirations of China's masses, in either their traditional form or as perceived through modern, leftist eyes. Furthermore, the work was linguistically beyond the reach of all but the best educated (a point to be examined further below).

In short, the traditional literature to which their nationalistic impulses drew twentieth-century literary historians and writers was, in fact, two different but overlapping bodies of literature. The first included popular entertainments, theatricals (oral works), and adventure fiction in the simple classical prose of the peasantry and of the poorly educated literate population. The second consisted of the aristocratic drama of the southern *chuanqi* tradition and the literati novels of the elite. It is my intention here to examine several general formal features of the traditional narratives that have made them suitable for adaptation to present cultural requirements and then to present specific examples of such borrowing from traditional works by modern writers. Even within this small corpus of material my

[11] See Robert E. Hegel, *The Novel in Seventeenth Century China* (New York: Columbia University Press, 1981), chap. 3, for a discussion of *Water Margin* and its original political message.

observations are highly selective; I hope that further investigations will be made into the ways in which contemporary Chinese writers have made "the past serve the present."

THE LANGUAGES OF TRADITIONAL NARRATIVE

Implicit in the concept of national form are certain notions about the appropriate use of language. Qu Qiubai criticized the Europeanized style used by the May Fourth writers; Mao frequently referred to the spoken language of the peasants as an appropriate linguistic form. However, both of these styles contrast sharply with the languages of traditional written literature. Throughout the Ming and Qing periods, all education in China began with the classical literary language. From moralistic primers the student proceeded to the Confucian Four Books and then to works of history, philosophy, and poetry (the Five Classics and other texts). In this way he prepared for the ultimate goal of education: to become, by way of the imperial civil-service examinations, a government official. No formal school taught students to read the vernacular and, given the increasing divergence over time of the syntax and vocabularies of the static literary language and the dynamic living speech, literacy in the first does not imply fluency in reading the second. It took a high degree of literacy in the classical language to appreciate the most refined Ming and Qing vernacular fictions because they use a very large vocabulary—including both current and literary words—and are heavily larded with verse and with allusions to China's classics of history and philosophy. Strictly speaking, then, such works cannot be considered popular; they were designed to be read by the cultural elite. By contrast, works designed for broader audiences tend to use a grammatically more straightforward version of the classical literary language and a smaller vocabulary than the literati novels.

Evidence of this situation can be found in those novels that went through successive "incarnations" in the hands of old China's writers and editors. For example, the tale of the Tang general Qin Shubao was formulated by the poet and dramatist Yuan Yuling (1599–1674) as *Sui shi yiwen* [Forgotten tales of the Sui] in 1633 and around 1675 incorporated by Chu Renhuo (ca. 1630–ca. 1705) into the better-known *Sui Tang yanyi* [Romance of the Sui and the Tang, first published in 1695]. Early in the eighteenth century, this character became central to yet another redaction, *Shuo Tang quanzhuan* [Tales of the Tang]. In the course of this transition the language of the narrative changed dramatically, from vernacular for the literati readers to a stiff but more concise classical for the less well educated. Moreover, the central figure becomes significantly less complex from version to version. Yuan Yuling's intention had been to exemplify the maturation process while criticizing social ills; in Chu Renhuo's hands Qin

Shubao demonstrates the dilemmas a good Confucian might face in attempting to satisfy conflicting norms of behavior. These two novels were written by and for literati. *Tales of the Tang,* on the other hand, is an anonymous adventure novel and lacks both the moral seriousness and the artistic complexities of the literati novels. Since the tale of Qin Shubao was only one element in Chu Renhuo's rambling narrative, he shortened considerably Yuan Yuling's account; in his turn, the anonymous editor of *Tales of the Tang* compressed the tale even further, so that it became only a rapid-paced sequence of adventures.

Throughout this sequence of novels, levels of art are directly related to levels of language. Not surprisingly, the printing of the text and illustrations also falls dramatically in quality from the second to the third in the series, in direct proportion to the financial resources of the anticipated audience. Thus, in the novel at least, use of the vernacular language does not necessarily identify a work as popular in the sense of being aimed at a mass audience; in fact, just the opposite is the case generally, as it is in this series of novels about Qin Shubao.[12] While traditional oral forms might be appropriate linguistic models for new creation, among the written forms it was the literati novel that came closer to the style required by the Marxist critics than did the more genuinely popular works.

PARALLELS IN WORLD VIEW

The process of "making the past serve the present" in literature was facilitated by parallels in world view between past and present. Both the writers of the Ming-Qing period and the writers of New China perceive the world as fully comprehensible. At least in theory, both groups of writers share the social values of their respective readers and seek to confirm or to exemplify, rather than to impart, these values to them. Both sets of writers perceive humans—collectively, not individually—to be of central importance in the universe, consider humanity collectively responsible for change in physical reality, and agree that there exist easily comprehensible universal principles by which human action should be guided.

Ming and Qing writers held the Confucian view that human events flow in cycles which were traditionally described as alternations of *yin* and *yang* forces. These bipolar continua form the structuring devices in China's old narratives. While one specific continuum might form the background for a particular work (e.g., the continuum from political unity through disunity to final reunification in *Sanguo zhi yanyi* [Romance of the Three King-

[12] For a detailed discussion of how relationships among language, ideology, and publishing can identify literati—as opposed to more broadly popular—fiction, see Hegel, *The Novel in Seventeenth Century China,* particularly chaps. 1 and 2. *Forgotten Tales of the Sui* is discussed in chaps. 4 and 5, and *Romance of the Sui and the Tang* in chap. 6.

doms] and other old historical novels), very often in these works images and action are significant on a number of levels simultaneously. Examples include *Xi you ji* [Journey to the west] and *Hong lou meng* [A dream of red mansions].[13] A character in an old prose work has the choice whether to participate in, hence to facilitate, the flow of events or to withdraw and perhaps therefore to impede that flow. Such is the choice that confronts the wily strategist Zhuge Liang in *Three Kingdoms,* for example. References to the "will of Heaven" *(tianming)*, fate (*shu*), and the like aside, the Confucian world view imparted a humanistic bent to the old fiction. As Mao Zonggang (fl. 1650–1675) observed at the beginning of his version of *Romance of the Three Kingdoms*: "Empires wax and wane; states cleave asunder and coalesce." That is, in the traditional view, no state nor stage of political development could last indefinitely; it is the nature of political rule to be transient. But all historical novels of the Ming and Qing, like *Three Kingdoms,* demonstrate that such changes are due to the strengths and weaknesses, the successes and failures, of people—humans make themselves and their insitutions. They are not, like Job, the helpless victims of some capricious higher force. Although there is cyclical alternation between poles, the direction of events is no more externally predetermined in Confucian fiction than in Chinese Marxism; contemporary fiction lays no more stress on collective action than did the literati novels of the Ming and Qing.[14]

Confucian values place the greatest emphasis on social order, that is, order maintained through the strictly hierarchical organization of society. Essentially, any act was "right" that promoted community harmony on these terms, while a "wrong" act did just the opposite. Characters in old

[13] See Andrew H. Plaks, "Allegory in *Hsi-yu chi* and *Hung-lou meng,*" in Plaks, ed., *Chinese Narrative: Critical and Theoretical Essays* (Princeton: Princeton University Press, 1977), pp. 163–202. Plaks terms this "bipolar complementarity."

[14] While this point deserves considerably deeper investigation than is possible in a study of this length, the following observations are relevant to further considerations: Students of Marx and subsequent Marxist thinkers regularly confront the issue of determinism versus voluntarism in Marxist thought; it would appear, at least superficially, that each major Marxist thinker has presented conflicting views on this issue. Mao Zedong, as prime example, had full confidence in the inevitable success of socialism in China as the next step after feudalism and capitalism in the evolution of political and social systems. In his words, "The supersession of the old by the new is a general, eternal, and inviolable law of the universe" ("On Contradiction," *Selected Works,* 1:333). In his sinification of Marxism, Mao came to stress voluntarism in social and political development, hence the tremendous importance he placed on the role of the intellectual and artist in furthering the revolutionary cause. The role of art is to mold ideology and, once equipped with this new set of values, humankind will choose to bring society to a "predetermined" higher stage of development—by an act of collective *will.* This contradiction is exemplified in Mao's Yan'an Forum speeches, as elsewhere. For a discussion of human responsibility for "fate" in Confucian terms, see Hegel, *The Novel in Seventeenth Century China,* chap. 4.

popular fiction are presented as occupying specific social roles, the responsibilities of which they fulfill either well or badly. This practice made it easy to construct models, type-characters specialized by their social functions and moral stances, which two were intimately related. Popular fiction and drama—often in pointed contrast to works designed for elite audiences—for the most part presented only models; onstage, clearly defined role categories limited character complexity even further. Popular fiction and drama emphasized action over any complexities of interaction among these relatively stiff type-characters.

In reality, however, a single individual could occupy many social roles simultaneously, a fact that literati novelists utilized to impart a convincing degree of complexity to certain characters in their more artistic works. Some of the more memorable scenes of old literati novels involve characters who, realistically, find themselves caught between the conflicting demands of overlapping roles. In *Romance of the Three Kingdoms,* Zhuge Liang must choose between loyalty to his leader Liu Bei and his commitment to preserve the latter's state. If he chooses the second alternative, he must depose Liu's incompetent son, thus disobeying his friend's implicit charge to protect the young sovereign. Near the end of *A Dream of Red Mansions,* Baoyu decides he must postpone becoming a Buddhist monk and accepts his filial duty to take the imperial civil service examinations. Qin Shubao also finds himself caught between personal and political loyalties in *Romance of the Sui and the Tang.*[15] Traditional popular novels simply ignored such difficult moral questions in favor of complicated plots and contrived coincidences.

It was old China's literati novelists whose work was the more didactic. The vernacular fiction of the Ming and Qing developed a conventional simulated context for narrative: a professional storyteller speaking to his listening audience. This "storyteller's manner," as it has been described, allows the narrator to indulge in moralizing asides to the reader, comparing the action in the narrative with model events in the past and discussing the morality of a character's acts. Passages of verse are interpolated into the prose narrative of literati fiction to serve the same end, interrupting the action to allow the reader to ruminate over the more profound implica-

[15] Note the quandary faced by Zhuge Liang in *Sanguo zhi yanyi,* chap. 85, and C. T. Hsia's insightful discussion of this scene in his *The Classic Chinese Novel* (New York: Columbia University Press, 1968), pp. 57–62. Baoyu's act of conciliation occurs at the end of *Hong lou meng,* chap. 119; see, again, Hsia, *Classic Chinese Novel,* pp. 287, 290–292, 294–295. Qin Shubao's dilemma is in *Sui Tang yanyi,* chap. 55; see Robert E. Hegel, "Maturation and Conflicting Values: Two Novelists' Portraits of the Chinese Hero Ch'in Shu-pao," in Curtis P. Adkins and Winston L. Y. Yang, eds., *Critical Essays on Chinese Fiction* (Hong Kong: Chinese University of Hong Kong Press, 1979), pp. 115–150. Perry Link discusses the similarities between modern popular literature in China and the West in his study of fiction of the 1910s and 1920s, *Mandarin Ducks and Butterflies: Popular Fiction in Early Twentieth Century Chinese Cities* (Berkeley and Los Angeles: University of California Press, 1981).

tions of the tale. One must not assume that these moralizations were superfluous to the meaning of traditional fiction, simply because they are conventional; literati authors regularly addressed contemporary political and social concerns in their novels.[16] Again, by contrast, the more popular works kept editorial asides and verse interpolations to a minimum in order to avoid slowing down the rush of events and boring the less educated readers.

Contemporary Chinese writing parallels certain important aspects of this tradition, particularly of the more artistic novels. In contrast to the May Fourth writings (and to some products of the Hundred Flowers and post-Cultural-Revolution periods, including Liu Xinwu's stories),[17] which point to newly perceived problems with missionary zeal, most post-Liberation writings seek to confirm views already introduced through social change, in political study, and in the other media. Inherent in all Marxist political statements is the proposition that the universe is comprehensible, that humans are central therein, and that by collective effort humans can and do transform the world. Whatever promotes solidarity and strength for progressive social change is good; any act or view that thwarts progressive change is bad. Class struggle is observable and predictable, according to the Marxist theorem; and class struggle becomes a basic structuring device in much fiction of the People's Republic, as alternations of *yin* and *yang* had been previously. Likewise, contemporary fiction merely *demonstrates* this concept; *proof* of its validity is as unnecessary now as was proof of the *yin* and *yang* principle in Ming and Qing times.

Confucian works were often set in a general time in the past. Traditional historical fiction devoted little effort to achieving authenticity; the customs and institutions depicted in these works conflated elements of the nominal time setting with elements from the author's own time, a procedure justified by the universality of Confucian values.[18] Marxist works,

[16] For example, various late Ming novels condemned, in thinly veiled terms, imperial extravagance, the abuses of power by court eunuchs, and the prevailing fashion of heedless self-indulgence during their time; see Hegel, *The Novel in Seventeenth Century China,* chaps. 3–5.

[17] The fact that Liu Xinwu's stories (e.g., "Ban zhuren" [The class teacher], *Renmin wenxue* [People's literature], November 1977; trans. in *Chinese Literature,* January 1979, pp. 15–35) appeared well after the Gang of Four had become fair game for censure might reasonably lead one to conclude that his work, too, merely confirms the readers' beliefs. Clearly, given the mixed response the stories provoked in the Chinese press, not all readers agreed with Liu's views on the Gang's effect on China's youth; see *Beijing Review* 22,3 (19 January 1979), pp. 7, 27.

[18] *The Scholars* (*Rulin waishi*), composed aroung 1750, is a noteworthy example; although set in the previous dynasty, it describes the examination system as it was in the author's own time. See the "Appendix" in Wu Ching-tzu, *The Scholars,* trans. Yang Hsien-yi and Gladys Yang (Peking: Foreign Languages Press, 1957), p. 717.

however, must be dated precisely, in order to pinpoint the specific stage in history from which the class struggle will progress through the narrative. Amenability to interpretation in terms of the alternation of *yin* and *yang* must have been an implicit criterion in the selection of subject matter for traditional novels. Recent writers, too, have had to choose material to fit their world view. War is an extremely common topic because, like other intense political struggles, it entails the replacement of the old social relations by a new order, of the chaos of foreign aggression by national security, and other such climactic changes.[19] The essential differences between old and new fiction here lies in their views of concluding events: old fiction brought society in a circle, from order through disorder back to social tranquility, through warfare; new fiction must show social progress in the making.

PARALLELS BETWEEN CHARACTERIZATION PAST AND PRESENT

Characterization in narrative has been a central concern of Marxist theorists. Mao Zedong specifically addressed this aspect of writing:

> Life as reflected in works of literature and art can and ought to be on a higher plane, more concentrated, more typical, nearer the ideal, and therefore more universal than everyday life. Revolutionary literature and art should create a variety of characters out of real life and help the masses to propel history forward.

But in his next breath Mao discussed popularization and the elevation of cultural standards:

> Popular works are simpler and plainer and therefore more readily accepted by the broad masses of the people today. Works of a higher quality, being more polished, are more difficult to produce and in general do not circulate so easily and quickly among the masses at present. . . . In present conditions, therefore, popularization is the more pressing task.[20]

The traditional models Mao would have chosen for contemporary writers to study, it may be inferred, would not have been the literati novels of Ming and Qing times but the more popular works, which were less ideologically ambiguous and had more action. Zhou Yang elucidated this point by calling on authors to model their new creations on the entertainment forms of the semiliterate.[21] Thus, the attention of writers was drawn to

[19] For Mao's comments in "On Contradiction" on the supersession of the old by the new, see *Selected Works,* 1:333.

[20] See Mao, *Selected Works,* 3:82.

[21] Zhou Yang had advocated the adaptation of popular forms of mass entertainment to fit China's new needs even before the Yan'an Forum; see Merle Goldman, *Literary Dissent in Communist China* (1967; reprint ed., New York: Atheneum, 1971), pp. 15, 49.

those works whose characters tended to have fixed attributes. While the younger writers in Yan'an responded enthusiastically to this call, the question of appropriate models was to figure in most literary debates following Mao's "Talks at the Yan'an Forum."

Mao had called for writers to integrate themselves with the masses and to base their works on socialist realism. The popularization and further development of reportage, *baogao wenxue,* was one consequence. Writers like Liu Baiyu reported on battles in which they personally participated. The immediacy of these thinly fictionalized accounts made reportage an essential part of the new writing of the 1940s. The adaptation of *yanggeju* and of other local dramatic forms marks another important trend in the new popular literature. The opera *Bishang Liangshan* [Driven to join the Liangshan rebels], praised by Mao Zedong, and the one-act play *Fuqi shizi* [Man and wife learn to read], by Ma Ke are examples of such adaptation.[22] Here old type-characters were replaced by new models—workers, peasants, and soldiers—sexual innuendo was deleted, and the slogans and techniques of the new political drives were fitted to the familiar songs.[23]

Experiment produced a number of successful applications of socialist realism to traditional fictional forms. Among these were the works of Zhao Shuli. His *Li Youcai banhua* [The rhymes of Li Youcai, 1943] begins in a matter-of-fact tone, introducing its principal character by place, name, nickname, age, and social status. The approach is rather more like the biographical sketches of literati historiography and literary anecdote (and like Lu Xun's "A Q zhengzhuan" [The true story of A Q]) than like the old vernacular fiction. The more literate examples of the latter frequently summarized the events that preceded the appearance of the protagonist or surveyed the moral principles the tale was meant to exemplify. Some of Zhao Shuli's characters are types, such as the grasping landlord, for instance. As in old fiction, particularly in the novels and *huaben* (vernacular short stories) of the Ming and Qing times, the action of Zhao's narrative is interrupted by verse segments—here, Li Youcai's own rhymes—that comment with insight and sarcasm on the morality of the action. Significantly, Li Youcai is set apart from the action, rather like the interlocutor (*fumo*) in plays of the old *chuanqi* tradition of aristocratic drama or like the narrator of a Ming-Qing novel. Zhao's innovation lies in providing this traditionally anonymous narrator/interlocutor with a personality.

Most of the characters in *The Rhymes of Li Youcai* are rather realisti-

[22] See Hsia, *History,* p. 303. Mao's comment of 9 January 1944 was reprinted in *Hong qi* [Red flag] (September 1967), p. 2. The Ma Ke piece appears in *Yanggeju xuanji* [Selected *yangge* plays] (Peking: Renmin wenxue, 1957), pp. 221–233, and, translated by David Holm, in *Revolutionary Literature,* pp. 74–80.

[23] Holm, in *Revolutionary Literature,* pp. 72–73.

cally complex in their struggles with old ways of thinking and feudal patterns of behavior. Zhao Shuli's short story "Chuan jiabao" [The heirloom, 1949] paints its protagonists in a similarly realistic fashion; neither the backward old lady nor her progressive daughter-in-law is either wholly villainous or wholly heroic. Although there is no question about the author's political convictions in these works, it is problematic whether these characters are "more typical, nearer the ideal" or are simply realistic portraits of northern Chinese peasants. Zhao's major characters resemble the central characters in old literati novels to the extent that they have *both* good (progressive) *and* bad (feudal/traditional) attributes and actions. The old lady in "The Heirloom" possesses concrete evidence of class struggle; her battered box of rags serves as a valuable symbol of the sufferings of the peasants under the old society. While the younger woman has more collective consciousness, both characters suffer from a degree of egocentrism. Neither woman attempts to understand the other; the heroine is certainly not corrupted, nor is the older woman wholly reformed, by the time the story reaches its conclusion. Neither selflessness nor selfishness remains unqualified by the characters' convincing foibles or strengths, and the contrast of values is left unresolved by the writer. This ambiguity perhaps reflects the efforts of the Party's leadership at that time to form a united front among all contemporary points of view.[24]

Such politically and morally complex characters fall within the vaguely defined area of the "middle character" (*zhongjian renwu*), because of their realistic combinations of positive and negative traits. Although the definitive call for writers to concentrate on figures of this sort was not issued until 1962 (by Shao Quanlin), Zhao Shuli and others, particularly Liu Qing in *Chuangye shi* [The builders, 1960], had developed evocative middle characters long before. In 1964, at the same time as they were strenuously disagreeing among themselves about the peasants' readiness for land collectivization, Party leaders officially denounced Shao and his theory. This did not stop writers from producing characters who exemplified ideological ambiguities or complexities: until the Cultural Revolution, no major writer would portray heroes and villains simplistically.[25] It is in this area that several major fictional works of the People's Republic

[24] *Zhao Shuli xuanji* [Selected works of Zhao Shuli] (Peking: Kaiming shudian, 1951), pp. 76–93; translated in Chao Shu-li, *The Rhymes of Li Yu-Tsai and Other Stories* (Peking: Foreign Languages Press, 1966), pp. 69–88.

[25] Joe C. Huang (*Heroes and Villains in Communist China: The Contemporary Chinese Novel as a Reflection of Life* [London: Hurst, 1973]) discusses Shao Quanlin's theory against the background of the struggles within the Party's leadership over agricultural policy (pp. 281–284). Huang analyzes several characters that Shao cited as model middle characters (pp. 273–281). A major collection of materials concerning the Shao Quanlin case is "Guanyu 'xie zhongjian renwu' de cailiao" [Materials on "Creating middle characters"] *Wenyi bao* [Literary gazette], 9 September 1964.

show a close affinity to traditional literati novels. In the artistically more refined novels of the Ming and Qing periods, stereotyped characters demonstrate the conceivable extremes of behavior and exemplify the desired moral message. But it is the middle characters, not the stereotypes, that reveal the author's serious perceptions of their society; it is the middle characters of both old and new fiction that are deliberately depicted realistically, in contrast to the one-dimensional exemplars.

However, heroes and villains, ultimately based on less refined traditional works, did find a place in the new writing. Villains are easily drawn from observation: the writers Liang Bin and Ouyang Shan, at least, found that it was not difficult to individualize them.[26] Nor was the hero a problem for many writers, particularly those who wrote about the time of the War of Resistance and the Civil War. Most war literature focuses on the heroic acts of heroic individuals acting selflessly—they are, at once, appropriate models in times of struggle and the easiest for the writer to create. In wartime, behavior often approaches the ideal. Wartime writers could utilize the spoken language in the format of reportage to create effective literature. Significantly, the political message in such writing is as explicit as Confucian morals ever were in old fiction; the characters here become as one-dimensional as on the traditional stage. And such war stories could be as effective as any traditional work—peasant readers preferred a clear distinction between wrong and right in their entertainments.[27] War literature being a form of heroic fiction, its heroes and villains belong to predictable types. They include:

> the resourceful Party member outwitting the enemy by his intelligence and bravery. The landlord, who is uniformly a traitor, may be given an opportunity to reform, but his confessions are to prove mere subterfuge and he is eventually lost beyond redemption. . . . at least one scene of torture where the grim endurance of the high-minded Party member or the defiance of the village people under Communist leadership are depicted in sharp contrast with the Chinese traitor's cowardly treacherousness in administering torture or carrying out other orders of their Japanese masters. While the landlord is a lost soul, the poor man who has wavered or erred is usually given a chance to repent and reform.[28]

As Li Chi observes here, it is the peasant who serves as the middle character in war literature. But the need for such characters is slight when the struggle is so clear-cut—with Eighth Route Army, Party, and patriotic elements

[26] Huang, *Heroes and Villains,* p. xiv, n. 8, quoting Liang Bin from *Renmin wenxue* [People's literature] (June 1959), p. 23, and Ouyang Shan from *Xingdao ribao* [Xingdao daily], 13 October 1966.

[27] Huang (*Heroes and Villains,* pp. 323–327) summarizes the findings of surveys conducted in a number of rural villages in 1962 and 1965.

[28] Li Chi, "Communist War Stories," pp. 139–157, esp. pp. 141–142.

fighting to the death against invaders, their puppets and collaborators, and reactionaries. The heroic fiction produced before the Cultural Revolution, then, drew its characterizations from traditional forms of popular entertainment that emphasized type-characters and rigid role categories.

Significantly, fiction by People's Liberation Army (PLA) writers came to prominence just before the Cultural Revolution, in *Ouyang Hai zhi ge* [The song of Ouyang Hai, 1965, rev. ed., 1966]. Although the novel has no villains as such, its hero is the perfect embodiment of selfless devotion to the Party's goals and is utterly lacking in moral or political complexity.[29] The character Ouyang Hai thus forms a perfect transition between the heroic literature of the years before the Cultural Revolution and the model operas that followed it. Of the operas first designated as "models" (*yangbanxi*), all but one, *Haigang* [On the docks], are set in wartime; their stories were adapted, appropriately, to a tradition of Peking opera that emphasizes type-characters and rigid role categories. The amalgamation of war literature with traditional opera thus produced an art form with none of the moral complexity of Ming-Qing literati novels; in the area of characterization, at least, the Cultural Revolution spelled the end of the complexity that modern fiction had shared with the old literati fiction for most of a decade.

ADAPTATIONS FROM TRADITIONAL NARRATIVES IN *DAUGHTERS AND SONS*

Xin ernü yingxiong zhuan [Daughters and sons; literally, New tales of men and women heroes] was written in 1949 by the husband-and-wife team of Kong Jue and Yuan Jing.[30] Although its portraits of the initially weak and befuddled peasantry owe something to the May Fourth variety of realism, socialist realism is responsible for the quick maturation of these characters into militia heroes of the War of Resistance. Many elements of traditional vernacular narrative are to be found in this work. Most obviously, the chapters in *Daughters and Sons* use poems, songs, or slogans as epigraphs to set the mood for the action that follows. In this the authors followed a precedent in Ming and Qing fiction that was popularly sup-

[29] Huang, *Heroes and Villains*, pp. 292–319; the novel was first published by the Jiefangjun wenyi she; the revised edition was published by Renmin wenxue, Peking, in 1966. See C. T. Hsia's comments on this character in his "Communist Literature since 1958," in Hsia, *History*, pp. 509–532, esp. pp. 527–528.

[30] 1949 is the date on Guo Moruo's preface in Yuan Jing and Kong Jue, *Xin ernü yingxiong zhuan* (Peking: Zuojia, 1963). Tsai Meishi (*Contemporary Chinese Novels and Short Stories, 1949–1974* [Cambridge, Mass.: Harvard University East Asian Monographs, no. 78, 1978], p. 161) notes that Kong and Yuan are divorced. Kong was expelled from the Party and the Writers' Association in 1952 for his immoral conduct.

posed to derive ultimately from the traditional storyteller.[31] Here as in old fiction these quotations serve to retard the pace of the action, thus building suspense while allowing the reader to contemplate the broader implications of what is to come. The narrative, which generally proceeds quickly, is also deliberately slowed by descriptions of place and by a love affair—a format common in such old adventure novels of the literati tradition as the *Romance of the Sui and the Tang*.

Verse (or song) is rarely interpolated in *Daughters and Sons*; the few examples have a rather more sophisticated value than that of merely building suspense. In Chapter 5 the protagonist, Niu Dashui, is to be married to a young woman in a neighboring village. As he rides along a dike on a borrowed horse to collect his bride, he hears a youngster on a boat singing a springtime love song. Dashui's romantic mood is shattered, however, when he arrives at his destination to find a detachment of Japanese soldiers raping and pillaging. His bride is among their victims. The springtime song here provides a much crueler irony than an old literati novel is ever likely to have presented.[32] Likewise, these contemporary authors seem much more conscious than their predecessors several centuries before of the effect of abrupt changes of pace.

Daughters and Sons also borrows several scenes from well-known traditional novels, particularly *Water Margin*. *Daughters and Sons* is set in a liberated area of Hebei during the War of Resistance. In the rural villages and towns surrounding Baiyang Lake, local peasants grow reeds as a cash crop; the reeds grow tall as a man and are interlaced with a maze of narrow waterways familiar only to local inhabitants. When Japanese forces begin to sail across the lake to raid the surrounding communities, the peasant militia, led by Party cadres, repeatedly ambush them, scoring sweeping successes despite the enemy's superior arms. These scenes in the modern novel clearly recall the similarly stirring scenes in *Water Margin*, where the bandit rebels use just such swamp warfare to foil a number of attacks by imperial armed forces on their Liangshan base.[33] In both novels the invaders are annihilated, defeated by the working people's knowledge of the marsh that supports them.

The protagonists of *Daughters and Sons* are youthful militia heroes. But among the secondary characters is a figure reminiscent of, if not copied

[31] Li Chi, "Communist War Stories," p. 146.

[32] See Yuan and Kong, *Xin ernü*, pp. 70–71; Sidney Shapiro, trans., *Daughters and Sons* (Peking: Foreign Languages Press, 1958 and 1979), pp. 78–79. (Shapiro omits the words of the song here.) He first published his translation, under his Chinese name Sha Po-li, in New York (Liberty Press, 1952).

[33] Huang (*Heroes and Villains*, pp. 33–35) notes the strong influence of *Water Margin*'s heroes and scenes in Liang Bin's *Keep the Red Flag Flying* (*Hong qi pu*, 1958; rev. ed., 1959); in pp. 133–134 Huang notes adaptations from *Water Margin* and *Romance of the Three Kingdoms* in Ai Xuan's *The Thundering Yangtze* (*Dajiang fenglei*, 1965).

from, the traditional theater. The long plays of the southern *chuanqi* tradition are regularly introduced by a learned old man with a long beard. This interlocutor (the *fumo*) summarizes the plot of the play and comments directly—for the benefit of the audience—on the moral message to be derived therefrom. The interlocutor may enact this role again, later in the play. In Chapter 6 of *Daughters and Sons,* an unnamed old man "with a long white beard" speaks for the peasants in praise of the militia's victory over the Japanese. Appropriately, the old man is described as one of the "enlightened gentry" (*kaiming shishen*), an educated man whose values are congruent with those of both the authors and the protagonists.[34] Similarly, in Chapter 10 an old man facilitates an exchange of prisoners between the militia and the Japanese puppet forces. The narrator simply describes the Japanese treatment of their prisoner: "They pounced on Dashui like cruel beasts of prey. For hours they subjected him to every horrid device their sadistic minds could contrive." It is left to the "interlocutor" to react on behalf of the reader, to demonstrate *how* the reader should respond. On seeing the prisoner, the old man "recoiled in dismay." Only later is the victim's condition described—in realistically gory detail; the old man has been used to shape the reader's response in advance.[35] Both of these elderly figures are anonymous and are clearly distinguished from the peasant heroes of the work.

Daughters and Sons adapted two other scenes from old Chinese fiction. Both involve famous tricks and stratagems by which a relatively disadvantaged hero overcomes a rapacious and powerful villain. In Chapter 14 of the modern work the rapist of Dashui's bride, the Japanese commander Iino, forces a puppet mayor to arrange a marriage with an attractive woman he has seen. In fact, the woman is an underground agent for the guerrillas and a Party member. In a grotesque scene, the "groom" becomes helplessly drunk at his wedding feast, and a young militiaman disguised as the bride shoots him dead as he approaches the marriage bed—but not until the villain has fondled the young man's leg.[36] Variations on this scene appear in several traditional works, among them *Water Margin* and the ever-popular *Journey to the West.* In Chapter 4 of *Water Margin,* Lu Zhishen takes the place of an unwilling bride and thrashes the would-be groom, a miserly local bandit leader. Monkey rids a landlord family of an unwanted son-in-law in Chapter 18 of *Journey to the West*; he disguises

[34] *Daughters and Sons,* p. 86; *Xin ernü,* p. 78.

[35] *Daughters and Sons,* pp. 144–145, 148, 149; *Xin ernü,* pp. 134, 136, 138.

[36] *Daughters and Sons,* pp. 199–203; *Xin ernü,* pp. 182–185. It is also noteworthy that the spectators in the streets nearby, peddlers and the like, are all disguised guerillas—another idea borrowed from *Water Margin.* In Chapter 41 of that work, disguised bandits rescue a pair of their friends from execution by this means. (I use here the chapter-numbering system of the seventy-chapter version edited by Jin Shengtan in the seventeenth century.)

himself magically as the girl in order to entice the Pig, Zhu Wuneng, within reach of his mighty cudgel. In both cases, the would-be lover whets his appetite by touching the supposed object of his desire just before the trap is sprung.[37]

A second stratagem, apparently borrowed from or at least very similar to an episode in *Romance of the Three Kingdoms,* appears in Chapter 18 of *Daughters and Sons.* There a young woman is found to have two lovers, both puppet leaders and jealous of each other. The Communist resistance convinces this woman, herself a former member of the village Woman's Association, to play one villain off against the other until one is killed.[38] In Chapters 8 and 9 of *Romance of the Three Kingdoms,* a loyalist plots to use the maiden Diaochan as a means to estrange the despot Dong Zhuo from his adopted son Lü Bu. Both fall in love with her, and in his jealousy the younger man slays the elder. The episode is known in its traditional theatrical versions as "the stratagem of interlocking rings" (*lianhuan ji*).

As with this second example, modern users of traditional scenes and techniques clearly modify them to a substantial degree. The bottles may be old, but the wine is decidedly new. This tendency is clear in the story of the villain Zhang Jinlong, a ne'er-do-well and local bully who first serves as a sharpshooter in a big landlord's gang of thugs and later becomes a leader in the puppet armed forces. Initially, however, underground Party members attempt to recruit him for the people's militia. At first he acquiesces but subsequently sets himself up in a town where he and his cronies spend their time gambling, drinking, and whoring. Reprimanded for his misdeeds, Jinlong raids a fortified city to prove his worth to the resistance. Almost singlehandedly he manages to steal into the center of town to rob and kill the defenseless head of the merchants' association.[39]

This raid is strongly reminiscent of, and probably copied from, the acts of individual daring so common in the adventure novels of the swordsman (*wuxia*) tradition, popular since the middle of the Qing period.[40] An early example of such a feat comes, again, in *Water Margin.* In Chapter 30 of that novel Wu Song takes his revenge on a local despot who had plotted to have him arrested and executed. The rough hero sneaks into the general's house to kill everyone he encounters, even going as far as to steal, gratuitously, all the valuables he finds. It is significant that neither attacker is satisfied with simply killing his victim; both behead the lifeless corpses. In

[37] One is reminded of a similar trap laid by Wang Xifeng for Jia Rui in *Hong lou meng,* chap. 12. There a male cousin disguises himself as Xifeng; the suitor is shamed and exposed to the cold and damp for his presumptions.

[38] *Daughters and Sons,* pp. 251–256; *Xin ernü,* pp. 228–235.

[39] *Daughters and Sons,* pp. 103–106; *Xin ernü,* pp. 94–96.

[40] See James J. Y. Liu, *The Chinese Knight-Errant* (Chicago: University of Chicago Press, 1967), esp. pp. 116–137.

Water Margin Wu Song's murderous rage is justified, even if he carries his vendetta beyond those who had wronged him. Jinlong, however, has no such justification; he commits cold, calculated murder. As a consequence, he is sternly criticized for disobeying orders, for self-seeking adventures, and for killing a potential ally. A scene that in the original novel praises revenge against the abuses of the powerful thus becomes in its adapted form the vehicle for a clear differentiation between the value of individual causes, whatever their justification, and the collective good—here, the united front against Japanese aggression.

ADAPTATIONS OF EARLIER LITERATURE IN *TRACKS IN THE SNOWY FOREST*

Famous scenes from traditional fiction also appear recast in *Linhai xueyuan* [Tracks in the snowy forest, 1956]. Here the novelist Qu Bo (b. 1923) adapts another *Water Margin* episode, the tiger-killing scene from Chapter 22. In the earlier novel, the valiant fighter Wu Song passes through a mountainous region on his way home. With the braggadocio typical of traditional swordsman heroes, Wu Song imbibes five times the recommended amount of a powerful local wine and then sets off to cross a ridge. The area, however, is the home of a man-eating tiger. No sooner does Wu Song succumb to the effects of the wine and lie down for a nap than the tiger attacks. Wu Song's poorly aimed blow breaks his cudgel against a branch. After a long and arduous struggle, Wu Song manages to kill the beast with his bare hands. The speed of the cat's attack had left no time for reflection; now, with the tiger dead at his feet, Wu Song finally begins to quake with fright. Soon he encounters a group of hunters who take him to a nearby settlement, where he presents the tiger to the local authority and becomes an officer in his army.

Qu Bo's version of this story is similar in many details. In *Tracks in the Snowy Forest,* Yang Zirong is a PLA scout sent out alone to the lair of a group of reactionaries and thugs who have turned to banditry in the traditional mold. Yang travels in disguise, assuming the identity of a bandit captured previously by the PLA. He crosses a mountainous region of China's northeastern provinces, riding on the bandit's horse, which is far more important to him as a means of validating his disguise than as mere transportation. Appropriately, the tiger here is attracted to the horse; the threat is not to the man but to his mission. Therefore, Yang Zirong must stop the tiger at all costs. Yang takes careful aim with his rifle while the tiger is still comfortably far away, but the bullet is a dud. Like Wu Song, Yang Zirong is thus deprived of his primary weapon, and the tension of the scene mounts accordingly. Yang uses his Mauser pistol to shoot a clip of bullets at the attacking beast; this only angers the tiger. Then Yang fires again with his rifle and misses; he fires again and again until, finally, he lodges a bullet in the tiger's brain as it lunges directly at him. As did Wu Song, Yang Zirong stamps on the beast to prove that it is dead, then falls limp with fright. A few moments later, bandit scouts discover him; Yang uses his killing of the tiger as yet another reason for the "authorities" (here, the bandits) to treat him with respect.[41]

From beginning to end, the scene is less fantastic than its prototype in *Water Margin,* but the essential stages in the struggle are unmistakably similar. The major change is the context: Wu Song drinks copiously to prove his individual mettle, whereas Yang Zirong's reflections on his grudges against local despots and all those who oppress the working people gives his tiger killing political significance. As if to acknowledge his source, Qu Bo has Yang declare, "Interesting—on my way to Tiger Mountain I've had to cross a Jingyang Ridge."[42] Jingyang Ridge was the site of Wu Song's encounter with the tiger in *Water Margin.*

Water Margin's heroes are individualized to only a minor degree; its villains are even more wooden embodiments of self-indulgence, craft, and cruelty. Qu Bo's villains are similarly one-dimensional. Without exception they are ugly. Xu Damabang ("Horse Cudgel Xu"), for example, has "horsy eyes . . . stubble half an inch long covering his face . . . . a big stout body. . . . He is the incarnation of an evil spirit."[43] His wife Hudiemi ("Butterfly Enticer") is a "hideous witch. . . . Her face [is] . . . like a dried-up ear of corn—long, thin and yellow, with a mouthful of gold teeth." Furthermore, she constantly "twitches her hips" (*pigu niule liangniu*) to show her sadistic excitement over the cruel treatment of the peasants.[44] While other writers, Zhao Shuli among them, describe their villains in more convincing terms, Qu Bo seeks from the outset of his work to set his villains apart from normal humanity. "Butterfly Enticer," he notes, had "looks [that] were enough to turn your stomach." She speaks in shrieks and screeches; she is also grotesquely painted with cosmetics. It goes without saying that she is morally reprehensible as well; although the fact is irrelevant to the plot, Qu Bo frequently mentions her aggressive prom-

[41] Chu Po, *Tracks in the Snowy Forest,* trans. Sidney Shapiro (Peking: Foreign Languages Press, 1962), pp. 196–202; Qu Bo, *Linhai xueyuan* (Peking: Renmin wenxue, 1957; reprint ed., 1977), pp. 202–204. Qu notes that he completed the novel in eighteen months of part-time writing, from February 1955 to August 1956, in his "Guanyu *Linhai xueyuan*" [On *Tracks in the Snowy Forest*]; *Linhai,* p. 579. This essay is dated September 1958.

[42] *Linhai,* p. 204; the English version ignores the allusion; see *Tracks,* p. 199. Qu Bo, in his "Guanyu *Linhai xueyuan,*" p. 580, acknowledges that, although modern novels such as *How the Steel Was Tempered* (*Gangtie shi zenyang lianchengde*) inspired him, he knew the classics, *Water Margin, Three Kingdoms,* and *Shuo Yue quanzhuan* [*Complete tales of Yue Fei*] so well that he could recite sections from memory.

[43] *Tracks,* pp. 21–22; *Linhai,* p. 21.

[44] *Tracks,* p. 22; *Linhai,* p. 23.

iscuity.[45] Furthermore, she and her brothers use their father's prisoners as living targets for pistol practice and to train their guard dogs.[46] Surely this woman's match has not been seen in Chinese literature since Daji had pregnant women ripped open in the sixteenth-century fantasy-adventure novel *Fengshen yanyi* [Investiture of the gods]. As a political commissar describes Xu and Butterfly Enticer, "These are no ordinary enemy remnants. They're the worst types of savages."[47]

Another of Qu Bo's villains disguises himself as a Taoist priest. His neck is "nearly as thick as his head"; he is having an affair with a woman whose dress and manner are "an odd mixture of the city and the country" (*cheng bucheng, xiang buxiang*).[48] This blend of styles becomes yet another mark of villainy, that these characters attempt to conceal their motives and their morals, that they add subterfuge to murder, mayhem, rape, and the various other atrocities they perpetrate on the working people. Given any realistic detail, these characters would appear as sadists who delight in the suffering of others. But realism in any proportion seems not to be Qu Bo's goal in creating this group of characters. Instead, they serve only as convenient devices in the development of the plot toward its inevitable conclusion, the victory of the PLA and militia forces over the bandits. Thus, as the plot progresses, the villains turn from cruel masterminds into bumbling fools.

Initially in *Tracks in the Snowy Forest,* the bandits stage lightning attacks on isolated villages, fleeing before PLA detachments can arrive. Caught off guard in the first such raid, the victims are apparently unarmed; the bandits suffer no casualties but the peasants are decimated, their leaders tortured to death, their animals slaughtered, and their houses burned. The PLA arrives to find the people immobilized, frozen by the rage that, unconvincingly, had not prompted them to resist in any successful fashion. Even the land-reform leader, older sister of the protagonist Shao Jianbo, had been captured easily. Jianbo himself is at first emotionally paralyzed by the outrage.[49] This is the first in a series of occasions in which the diabolically clever villains outwit or outmaneuver the PLA heroes. Three-gun Zheng, a professional thief in league with the reactionaries, is a crack shot. By contrast, Yang Zirong empties a pistol at a tiger without hitting it once. At least in these scenes, the "heroes" are unheroically weak and the villains decidedly stronger.

However, Yang Zirong is a key character here. An accomplished storyteller as well as an experienced scout and fearless fighter, he can recite

[45] *Tracks,* pp. 23–25; *Linhai,* pp. 23–24.
[46] *Tracks,* p. 27; *Linhai,* p. 26.
[47] *Tracks,* p. 34; *Linhai,* p. 33.
[48] *Tracks,* p. 141; *Linhai,* p. 142.
[49] *Tracks,* pp. 6–9, 28–33; *Linhai,* pp. 5–9, 27–31.

from *Romance of the Three Kingdoms, Water Margin,* and *Yue Fei*;[50] the reader is prompted by this fact to see these heroes—and this novel—as full inheritors of this heroic tradition. Thus, after initial setbacks the PLA fighters predictably score easy victories over their foes: Yang Zirong works to find the bandits' location, then captures one of their messengers (Chapter 4); "Tank," Liu Tanke, scours the mountains alone, then overtakes an opium peddler in a frantic footrace (Chapter 5). Tank is as great an athlete as his predecessors in old China's military romances; he even describes himself with the traditional term "*haohan*" ("good fellow"). When his adversary pulls a knife, Tank kicks it out of his hand and drives it point first into a tree.[51] The villains appear shrewd, but in fact each one's subterfuge is foiled by the insightful Shao Jianbo; every villain soon becomes ridiculous, no longer frightening.

With the help of the local population, the PLA handily captures the bandits on Breast Mountain (Chapter 8). The struggle against the bandits on Tiger Mountain takes a long time to come but presents few setbacks for the heroes; the villains are totally convinced that Yang Zirong is the bandit he pretends to be, and he springs a totally effective trap for them. Yang has even become a good shot by this time.[52] During the bandits' raid on the train in Chapter 18 a few heroes fall, but far more bandits.[53] At this point, the narrative slows, and fighting becomes less important. An innocent love affair develops between the PLA commander Shao and a young medical worker, amid the victory celebrations and the planning for the future. One bandit chief is taken after five minutes of fighting (Chapter 25); another battle takes half a minute (Chapter 33).

The conclusion, when it comes, is anticlimactic. The villains described in such fearsome terms at the beginning of the tale, including Three-gun Zheng, are captured easily, their reported prowess left unconfirmed by their actions. Like those in the truncated version of *Water Margin,* the villains here become merely the background for the heroic actions of the PLA. In fact, the novel ends with the words, "A new struggle has begun . . ." (*Xinde douzheng kaishile . . .*).[54] Qu Bo here prefigures a sequel; his work thus becomes a single, multisegmented episode in the saga of the broader revolutionary struggle. To this extent, *Tracks in the Snowy*

[50] See *Tracks,* p. 58; *Linhai,* pp. 54–55. Yang proves his ability as a storyteller in chapter 17: *Tracks,* pp. 226–228; *Linhai,* pp. 234–236. Although Shao Jianbo is the chief autobiographical figure, Yang's feats of memory clearly recall Qu Bo's: see note 42 above.

[51] *Tracks,* pp. 71, 78; *Linhai,* pp. 67, 73. Huang (*Heroes and Villains,* pp. 143–144) discusses this character and his vitality. This vitality did not survive the process of translation.

[52] See chaps. 15, 17, 19, and 20. *Tracks,* p. 233 and *Linhai,* p. 241, note that Yang deliberately aims his shots very close to the bandits who used to trick him—even though he is shooting from a considerable distance and in the predawn gloom.

[53] *Tracks,* pp. 250–252; *Linhai,* pp. 259–262.

[54] *Tracks,* p. 549; *Linhai,* p. 572.

Forest is seemingly meant to join the tradition of popular novels that follow successive generations of heroes, who each battle similar villains through time.

That Qu Bo wants his readers to link his novel to the earlier tradition of military romances, that he is "making the past serve the present," is demonstrated in several ways. First, like the warriors of *Water Margin,* many of the PLA officers here are known by descriptive nicknames. "Tank" has been mentioned above; another athletic scout is known as "Longlegs" ("Changtui"). Even the pretty medic, Bai Ru, has the nickname "Xiao Baige" ("Little White Dove"). Despite the love affair between their commander and Bai Ru, most of the PLA men show no more interest in romance than did their predecessors in *Water Margin.* They treat Bai Ru in a comradely fashion, for the most part; when her sex is even acknowledged, it only provides the basis for schoolboyish teasing. Like the women warriors in *Water Margin,* this woman proves herself equal to the men in endurance, valor, and selfless devotion to the mission.

Water Margin remains well known largely because of the famous scenes that have been, over the centuries, adapted to the stage. In Chapter 35 of *Tracks in the Snowy Forest,* entitled "Xueshang daxia" [Great swordsmen on the snow], Shao Jianbo recounts the highlights of the men's adventures to his superior officer as if they were the topics of plays. He enumerates all the most exciting and dramatic incidents, which were, with few exceptions, individual exploits not collective movements. Since Qu Bo prefaces this list with references to famous episodes from *Romance of the Three Kingdoms,* there can be no doubt that the parallels here are deliberate, that he was deliberately placing his work within the tradition of Ming and Qing vernacular fiction. Indeed, the superior officer exclaims, after hearing Shao's account, "Your exploits would make a beautiful novel!"[55] And ironically, just before his downfall, the last bandit leader explains his failure through an oblique reference to *Three Kingdoms.* In the classic, he says, each of the three contending states had as advantage one of the cosmic triad: Heaven or time (*tianshi*), Earth or location (*dili*), and the support of Man (*renhe*). Having none of these, the bandit mourns, he is doomed to failure.[56]

While other heroes approach the traditional *xia* swordsman in their unflagging strength and courage, Shao Jianbo is clearly a different sort of character, a product of the present and not the past. While others carry out their hair-raising adventures alone, Shao's attention is always riveted

[55] *Tracks,* p. 508; *Linhai,* p. 534. Huang (*Heroes and Villains,* p. 135) notes that *Linhai* was criticized—e.g., in *Changjiang wenyi* [Yangtze literature and art] (April 1959), pp. 68–69—for its author's poorly disguised narcissistic depiction of Shao, his autobiographical hero.

[56] *Tracks,* p. 539; *Linhai,* p. 563.

on his larger responsibilities. To this extent, he is the perfect PLA leader. He is shaken by the the death of his sister but hardly less so by the loss of his class brothers and sisters; he gladly accepts responsibility; he is quick of wit, farsighted, determined, kindly; he encourages others to think and to act creatively; he is selfless and oblivious to personal discomfort. He adheres strictly to regulations without being mechanical; he depends heavily on his fellows for wisdom.

Shao does make mistakes. The omniscient narrator recounts the mental turmoil that Shao suffers when, for example, he allows a train to run straight into the brigands' ambush and sends a relief column too late. Shao torments himself with guilt over the injuries and deaths he has unwittingly caused.[57] With lesser characters, such mistakes might impart a convincing degree of complexity. But with Shao Jianbo, as later with Ouyang Hai, the hero's response to a mistake in judgment is only further proof of his superiority. Although Shao reacts realistically to his personal loss when his sister dies at the beginning of the novel, by the end he is pure paragon:

> Under these dangerous circumstances, apparently surrounded by an enemy four times his [sic; read "its"] strength, hemmed in by a dense network of fire, the small detachment stood like an indestructible rock, like an evergreen which feared neither ice nor frost. Jianbo gave his commands, calm and unruffled. For he knew that the slightest show of panic on his part would cause his men to lose their fighting determination, their steadiness, their courage. He had to be the immovable Mount Tai in his men's hearts, the helmsman in the storm, the pure metal in the fires of the crucible. Only thus would he be worthy of the name of People's Liberation Army commander, only thus would he deserve the name of Communist.
>
> Calmly and carefully he examined all the circumstances he needed to know . . .[58]

Shao Jianbo in *Tracks in the Snowy Forest* is a hero of a new type, a hero for the problems of the socialist age. He is a model of selfless devotion to the cause of the masses, dedicated to wiping out the forces of exploitation and oppression. He also is young, talented, and handsome. The young female member of the PLA detachment loves him deeply and, presumably, passionately; his demonstration of concern makes her blush furiously. Were he and the other characters in the novel to be compared to the role categories of the old Peking opera, one might see in Shao Jianbo something of the *wusheng,* the young man of martial bent whose gentle good looks mask his prowess in arms. His comrades resemble more the *jing* role, the fierce-faced and mature but rough-mannered military hero. The bandits, at least after their first introduction, function as evil *chou,* or

[57] *Tracks,* pp. 254, 302; *Linhai,* pp. 263–264, 318.

[58] *Tracks,* pp. 455–456; *Linhai,* pp. 482–483.

clowns; they are objects of scorn as well as mirth. Without question, the moral stance of each character in this modern work is as immutable as that of the role categories in the old theater.

A FURTHER ADAPTATION FOR THE STAGE

As limited as was the realism in Qu Bo's novel, the stage version of the story was even more idealized. The Peking opera *Zhiqu Weihushan* (initally known in English as *Taking the Bandits' Stronghold* and later as *Taking Tiger Mountain by Strategy*) appeared in 1958, soon after the publication of the novel.[59] Its earliest version seems to have followed the novel closely; it was later criticized for a scene in which Yang Zirong sings "obscene ditties" as he ascends the mountain to the bandits' lair. The final rewriting of *Taking Tiger Mountain,* finished in July 1970, offers a striking example of the "three prominences" theory of artistic construction proposed by Jiang Qing and Yao Wenyuan, a theory that took to further extremes the theme of "revolutionary romanticism" developed in the 1950s.

The revolutionary model opera, an exemplum for all other literary production during the decade from 1966 to 1976, narrates Yang Zirong's solo mission on Tiger Mountain in detail. Prefaced to this adventure is only enough action to provide a minimal context: the rapacity of the bandits and the evolution of a strategy to destroy them. In the earlier versions of the opera, each character was named: the commander Shao Jianbo, the medic Bai Ru, and others. Shao was an important singing character as well. The bandit villains were also accorded a reasonably large amount of

[59] Goodwin C. Chu and Philip H. Cheng ("Revolutionary Opera," in Godwin C. Chu, ed., *Popular Media in China* [Honolulu: University Press of Hawaii, 1978], p. 85) note that the play's first version was produced by the Shanghai Peking Opera Theater in 1958. Its Yang Zirong was played "much in the traditional swordsman style of the old Chinese opera." The play initially had only a brief run; it could not compete with the favorite traditional romantic play *Liang Shanbo and Zhu Yingtai* (Chu, p. 97). Hua-yuan Li Mowry gives a brief history and synopsis of the play in her *Yang-pan hsi—New Theater in China* (Berkeley: University of California Center for Chinese Studies, 1973), pp. 68–71. On p. 114, n. 8, Lowry notes that in 1957 the Peking Opera Troupe of Peking had staged a play, based on the same chapters of *Linhai,* entitled *Capturing the Hardened Bandit Vulture by Strategy* (*Zhiqin guanfei Zuoshandiao*). See Tao Junqiu, *Jingju jumu chutan* [A preliminary bibliography of Peking operas] (Peking: Zhongguo xiqu chubanshe, 1963), pp. 503–504. For comments on the process of revision, see "Strive to Create the Brilliant Images of Proletarian Heroes," written by the *Taking Tiger Mountain by Strategy* Group of the Peking Opera Troupe of Shanghai, *Chinese Literature,* January 1970, p. 62 (translated from *Hong qi* [Red flag], November 1969, pp. 62–71). Martin Ebon (*Five Chinese Communist Plays* [New York: Day, 1975], p. 155) notes that in translation the bandit leader's name changed from "Eagle" to "Vulture." However, neither the play nor the bandit changed names in Chinese.

dialogue on stage.[60] But, in the successive revisions, these characters lost their individuality and even their names, which were replaced by mere titles. The emphasis clearly shifts to the heroism and craftiness of the single PLA scout, who becomes the "perfect, lofty proletarian hero."[61] The heroic personalities of Shao Jianbo and the other fighters fade away as, in successive revisions, they do no more than fulfill plot functions.

The model opera's portrayal of Yang Zirong certainly deserves a more detailed study than is possible in a survey such as this. In the hands of the novelist Qu Bo, he wasted many bullets killing a single tiger; in his latest development, he drops the beast in its tracks with a few shots. Here realism disappears; so, too, does all visible trace of Qu Bo's debt to *Water Margin,* leaving only an unconvincing paragon of socialist virtue. Yang Zirong's resemblances to the traditional swordsman were sternly condemned by Jiang Qing and her collaborators. In the original novel, Yang is under the strictest orders to maintain his bandit disguise at all times. Thus, as he ascends to the bandit lair, Yang practices being reckless, haughty, and even vulgar in order to make his act convincing. Surely an experienced reader would see this realistic performance as further proof of Yang's dedication to the peoples' cause, and, in fact, he makes no compromise with the outlaws in *Tracks in the Snowy Forest.* To Jiang Qing and her group, however, this point seemed too subtle for a viewing audience to grasp. Thus Qu Bo's character, as he first appeared on the stage, was denounced as "a filthy-mouthed desperado and a reckless muddle-headed adventurer reeking with bandit odour from top to toe."[62]

Qu Bo, rather convincingly, had Yang acknowledge the bandit Eagle as his leader; the later Peking opera versions have him "hold the initiative" and "lead Vulture [i.e., Eagle] by the nose round and round the stage."[63] Furthermore, this scout, as the principal hero, stands "head and shoulders

[60] See *Zhiqu Weihushan* (Shanghai: Shanghai wenhua, 1965). This is the earliest version to which I have had access; it differs considerably from the 1967 version, which was merely polished to form the "model" edition of 1970. See "Taking the Bandits' Stronghold," *Chinese Literature,* September 1967, pp. 129–181; a slightly different version in Ebon, *Five Communist Chinese Plays,* pp. 155–210; *Taking the Bandits' Stronghold* (Peking: Foreign Languages Press, 1969); "Taking Tiger Mountain by Strategy," in *China Reconstructs* 19,2 (February 1970); *Zhiqu Weihushan* (Hong Kong: Sanlian shudian, 1969) (reprint from *Hong qi,* November 1969, pp. 32–61), translated as "Taking Tiger Mountain by Strategy," in *Chinese Literature,* January 1970, pp. 3–57, and reprinted in John D. Mitchell, ed., *The Red Pear Garden* (Boston: Godine, 1973), pp. 203–285. The final version of 1970 was published in Peking by Renmin wenxue in 1970 and translated into English as, again, *Taking Tiger Mountain by Strategy* (Peking: Foreign Languages Press, 1970).

[61] Hung Ping, "A Fine Peking Opera on a Revolutionary Modern Theme," *Chinese Literature,* August 1967, p. 187 (translated from *Hong qi,* August 1967, pp. 60–65).

[62] "Strive to Create," p. 62. Huang (*Heroes and Villains,* pp. 145–147) discusses briefly how Qu Bo's character was ossified to serve the purposes of the model opera.

[63] "Strive to Create," p. 69.

above the masses" and even above all other heroes. In his development, Yang Zirong thus exemplifies one trend initiated in contemporary Chinese fiction by Mao's Yan'an "Talks": a simplification in the name of popularization and an even more cautious use of specific traditional models.[64] As a consequence, Yang Zirong and most of the other characters in the model opera version became just as stereotyped as any on the traditional stage or in old popular adventure novels. The adaptations were thus selective and, most importantly, reminiscent of the general features of earlier popular literature.

In conclusion, one can discern in these few contemporary works significant elements of traditional narratives and narrative techniques. It was common enough in the old fiction and drama to borrow scenes and type-characters. Recent examples of this sort of borrowing can be found in *Daughters and Sons* and *Tracks in the Snowy Forest,* the sources for which include the classic novels *Water Margin* and *Romance of the Three Kingdoms.* But here the model from the past is the literati novel, a literary pastime of the old elite. The emphasis on action without moral introspection that was characteristic of the more popular novels of the Qing period is reflected in contemporary works such as the multitude of war tales. Dogmatic interpretations of Mao Zedong's "Talks at the Yan'an Forum" shifted the model for characterization from the literati novels to the adventure tales and popular dramatic works written for less well-educated audiences of the past. While middle characters in more realistic works of recent Chinese fiction parallel the complex characters of the artistically refined old works, the heroes of revolutionary model opera are more like those of the traditional theatrical forms.

In 1942, Mao Zedong called on writers to set their highest priority on "popularization." To some writers, this meant "simplification," the deletion of ambiguity and of all moral or political complexity. By writing in a version of the spoken language rather than in the more artificial literary medium of Ming-Qing adventure novels, Party-directed writers from the 1940s to the 1970s followed the practice of the old literati novels to a certain extent. Their increasingly overt didacticism certainly owes more to literati novels than to more popular fiction. But, in terms of characterization, contemporary works of this period moved ever closer to the often wooden exemplars of the old popular fiction and drama, in which every

[64] One might speculate on the implications of the diminished role the PLA commander plays in the model opera. The opera places less emphasis on formal leadership, discipline, and the like, and at the same time glorifies the possibilities for individual initiative when the hero holds "Mao Zedong Thought" in his mind and is "at one with the masses." This schema certainly suggests a new chain of command that would bypass formal structures—such a system as did indeed develop during the Cultural Revolution.

character is fully revealed in moral terms at his or her first appearance. This movement toward "revolutionary romanticism" and the "three prominences" idealized heroes and villains to a degree congruent with that of Confucian moral tales. But, to the extent that the characters were simultaneously deprived of their human complexity, they became as predictable as their predecessors in older works and, hence, less appealing to mature, experienced readers. The greater seriousness with which certain works of fiction have approached moral and political questions since 1976 is unquestionably a reaction against this simplicity. Consequently, the influence of the elite vernacular fiction of the Ming and Qing periods may again become discernible—if the past continues to be made to "serve the present."

TEN

A Notable Sermon: The Subtext of Hao Ran's Fiction

Michael Egan

Contemporary Chinese literature presents a unique challenge to literary criticism. In China, as in the West, concepts of stability and change help to define works of literature and literary periods. Points of identity and of difference between and among texts form the basis of any historical discussion of literature. In the European tradition, when one speaks of the Classical or Neoclassical periods, or of the Renaissance, Romantic, or even Beatnik eras, one is referring to a unit of time that has been substantially, perhaps even primarily, defined by literature.[1] A historical approach to Chinese literature also yields well-defined periods, as well as types of forms, genres, and subject matter that can be placed in relation to one another by analysis of their similarities and differences, both structural and thematic. This is as true for contemporary Communist literature as it is for the Chinese classics. Any student of contemporary Chinese literature almost automatically classifies a work of fiction as having been written by a member of the May Fourth generation, or as belonging to the Hundred Flowers period, the Great Leap Forward, or the Great Proletarian Cultural Revolution. The most recent categories of fiction in this catalogue are Gang of Four and post-Gang-of-Four literature.

But the historical taxonomies of Western and traditional Chinese literature reveal a fundamental difference from that of post-Liberation China. While it is true that contemporary Chinese literature has helped to define and express the thought of the periods mentioned, the changes in literature came about not as the result of any "natural" generic growth and development (insofar as any literature can be said to develop "naturally" within

[1] From a series of symposia on history and literature, conducted by Ralph Cohen at the University of Toronto in March 1979.

its social, political, and economic context) but as the direct result of changes in Party policy that were imposed from above. While the reflection of societal structures in Western or bourgeois works of fiction may be haphazard or unconscious, in contemporary China the relationship between a work of art and its political basis in historical materialism is obvious and undisguised. Historical categories in Communist Chinese literature are extrinsic and artificial; society defines literary parameters before literature has a chance to define and reflect society.

This fact adds yet another difficulty to the already formidable task facing the Western reader of Chinese literature. Hans Robert Jauss wrote that "in the triangle of author, work and reading public the latter is no passive part, no chain of mere reactions, but even history making energy. The historical life of a literary work is unthinkable without the active participation of its audience."[2] Since no work of art or of literature can function, much less endure or succeed, if it does not speak for and capture a public, the test of effectiveness becomes very important. Do the mechanisms of a literary text work? If so, how do they work? Further, if we are to call a literary work (any or all of Hao Ran's novels discussed below, for example) successful, for whom is it successful? Does a contemporary text have the same meaning for a Chinese as for a Western reader, who might have no special knowledge of China and who might have to approach the text in translation? Even among Chinese readers, later generations (political as well as chronological) will probably have more problems to solve than the original readers. The linguistic and political codes of the text will be most accessible to its contemporary readers. The codes used by successive generations of readers will, with the passage of time, diverge more and more from the code of the text. If the difference in code between reader and text is drastic, as is the difference between a contemporary Western reader and the political, linguistic, and social code of a Communist Chinese novel, the dislocation can be extreme. Even to a Chinese reader, the changes in the literary code from period to period since 1949 must have been distracting.

Many of these changes can be seen in the work of Hao Ran, a writer who more than any other represented the Chinese literary establishment over the ten years from 1964 to 1974. This paper will look at the three major works he wrote during this time: the long novels *Yanyang tian* [Bright sunny skies] and *Jinguang dadao* [The road of golden light] and the short novel *Xisha ernü* [Sons and daughters of Xisha].

In his study of these two long novels, Wong Kam-ming has made the case that one of the chief differences between *Bright Sunny Skies* and *The*

[2] Hans Robert Jauss, "Literary History as a Challenge to Literary Theory," in Ralph Cohen, ed., *New Directions in Literary Theory* (Baltimore: Johns Hopkins University Press, 1974), pp. 11–41. Quote from p. 12.

Road of Golden Light is that the plot of the former is most concerned with "class struggle" and that of the latter with "line struggle."[3] That is, the main focus of the plot in *Bright Sunny Skies* is on the development of the characters' powers of awareness and cognition, which will then permit them to recognize and deal with class struggle when it occurs in their village. In *The Road of Golden Light,* the plot is based upon the implementation of the correct line for developing cooperatives and collectivization. Both novels are extremely and self-consciously political, with no apologies.

For all that the novels share great similarities, however, when questions of response and popularity are raised it seems that *Bright Sunny Skies* is more accessible and more enjoyable than *The Road of Golden Light.*[4] Yet *Bright Sunny Skies* is no less overtly political, in intent and execution, than *The Road of Golden Light.* In one of the many, many references to the political nature of *Bright Sunny Skies,* Hao Ran has said that he was ready to begin work on the novel but his seniors at the *Red Flag* editorial office advised him to wait.

> "Study the communiqué issued by the Tenth Plenary Central Committee of the Communist Party, at the end of its Eighth Session," they told me. And I did. . . . They sent me back down to the countryside again in November of that year to learn from real life. A month later I returned to my office, thinking that at last I must be ready to begin my novel.
>
> But more study awaited me at *Red Flag.* I had to review the Anti-Rightist Movement and struggle in 1957 and the Chairman's statements on that movement. . . .
>
> I must be ready now, I thought. But no, the leadership insisted that I study some foreign material first . . . on the second General Assembly of the Soviet Russian Communist Party, the stuff on Greater Democracy championed by Khrushchev and his gang. I discovered the world wide implications of the class struggle and the subtlety of the devious attacks we must be on guard against.[5]

The argument that *Bright Sunny Skies* might be esthetically more effective because it is less overtly political does not work; both novels are equally and unremittingly political. If the problem of the relative effectiveness of these two novels is defined as lying in the relationship between text and reader, rather than between author and text, the questions become:

[3] Wong Kam-ming, "A Study of Hao Ran's Two Novels: Art and Politics in *Bright Sunny Skies* and *The Road of Golden Light,*" in Wolfgang Kubin and Rudolph G. Wagner, eds., *Essays in Modern Chinese Literature and Literary Criticism* (Bochum, FRG: Brockmeier Press, 1982), pp. 117–149.

[4] This subjective statement reflects both my own subjective response to the texts and the views of readers, both Chinese and Western, who were questioned on the topic.

[5] Quoted in Kai-yu Hsu, *The Chinese Literary Scene* (New York: Vintage, 1975), pp. 92–93.

How do Hao Ran's novels communicate with their readers? How does a work of literature get its message across? In the words of Michael Riffaterre, "Literature is made of texts, not intentions; . . . texts are made of words, not things or ideas."[6] What literary devices does Hao Ran use to encode the text's message to its readers? And is it possible that Hao Ran uses different codes in his various novels?

Structurally, *Bright Sunny Skies* and *The Road of Golden Light* have a great deal in common. Both are very long, episodic novels, with large casts of characters. Both texts owe a great deal to traditional Chinese fiction and share the techniques of omniscient third-person narration, complete with rhetorical intrusions. However, an examination of the two texts might show significant differences in the way their respective messages are encoded.

Hao Ran is justifiably famous as a master of characterization. Both Joe C. Huang and W. J. F. Jenner have written about the skill with which Hao Ran can bring characters to life on the printed page. Hao Ran's technique deserves re-examination, however, because it varies from novel to novel, and each variation speaks to the reader in a different way.

Joe Huang has pointed out the importance of the love affair between Xiao Changchun and Jiao Shuhong in *Bright Sunny Skies*.[7] His insight that "*Bright Sunny Skies* is a novel of harsh political struggle, but is considerably humanized by an interlacing love story"[8] is invaluable. As Huang writes:

> Xiao Changchun, as a socialist hero, seems to have two sides; the public side which satisfies ideology, and the private side which gives life to an artistic image. He is painted as a man of tough fiber in dealing with matters of a political nature. Yet at the private level, in his relations with relatives, friends, and neighbors, and in love, he proves to be a man of warm feelings.[9]

It is not only the love between Xiao Changchun and Jiao Shuhong that humanizes the highly political plot of *Bright Sunny Skies*. Xiao also encounters a temptation to adultery in the person of the backward and misled woman, Sun Guiying—although "temptation" is perhaps not quite the *mot juste*, because there is not the slightest chance that the stalwart and upright Party Secretary will succumb to Guiying's transparent blandishments. Nonetheless, the attempted seduction in Chapter 74 is extremely interesting.

[6] Michael Riffaterre, "The Stylistic Approach to Literary History," in Ralph Cohen, ed., *New Directions in Literary Theory* (Baltimore: Johns Hopkins University Press, 1974), pp. 147–164. Quote from p. 147.

[7] Joe C. Huang, "Hao Ran, the Peasant Novelist," *Modern China* 2,3 (July 1976): 369–396.

[8] Ibid., p. 385.

[9] Ibid.

First of all, Guiying is a wavering "middle" character, a poor peasant and orphan whose whole life is a history of suffering. Her father was killed during the Japanese invasion and her mother was forced to become the mistress of a fat, sixty-year-old butcher. At the age of thirteen, while her mother was ill, she was raped by the butcher.[10] The reader is not surprised to learn that, given this background, she was soon applying makeup. Blossoming into an "evil flower," she took a job as a waitress in a teahouse. She is often described as muddle-headed and as easy prey for bad people. At the same time, her great suffering and class background give her the potential for reform and redemption, if only she can be influenced by the right people. She has been tricked by the evil landlord Ma Zhiyue into marrying his protégé, Ma Lianfu, with whom she is quite disappointed. Thus, she is an easy victim for Ma Zhiyue's wife, who wants to entrap and discredit Xiao Changchun by having Guiying seduce him.

Ma Fenglan, the panderess, is described very unflatteringly by the author. She is fat and smelly and waddles like a duck. Her legs are like two white radishes, and she does not wipe the rheum from her eyes.[11] She passionately hates the revolution because she lost everything, including her dowry and first betrothed, during land reform. Damningly, she had sexual relations with Ma Zhiyue before being married to him. So, however much these evil character traits may endear her to the reader, no good can be expected from her. She is irredeemably bad.

The reader is not surprised when, through a series of elaborately calculated moves, Ma Fenglan fans the flames of Guiying's passion for Xiao Changchun (with whom Guiying had fallen in love from afar while she was still working in the teahouse). First she suggests that Xiao is attracted to Guiying, then gives her a handkerchief, saying that it is a present from Xiao. Finally, while Guiying's husband Ma Lianfu is at an irrigation worksite, she rouses Guiying to fever pitch with suggestive conversation. She implies that Xiao is ripe for a fall after three years of being a widower: "Ma Fenglan pretended to sigh, 'Ai! Men are all the same! Secretary Xiao's been a bachelor for three years, how do you think he stands it? I suffer for him. Why should you laugh? It's true!' "[12]

After Ma Fenglan departs, the narrative reveals the state to which Guiying has been aroused:

> In the last few days the crafty and cunning daughter of a landlord, Ma Fenglan, had been stuffing kindling into her head. The exchange of words that they had by the river yesterday was like pouring oil on dry kindling. And when she had returned home, the handkerchief which had flown into

[10] Hao Ran, *Yanyang tian* (Peking: Renmin wenxue, 1972), pp. 836–841.
[11] Ibid., pp. 963, 1263.
[12] Ibid., p. 964.

> her hands heated the kindling and dried it out even more. An intense flame leapt up inside Sun Guiying and clouded her senses.[13]

Thus, the careful process of incitement is very neatly described by the elaborate development of the kindling imagery. When the kindling bursts into flame, the result is a foregone conclusion:

> Pretending to be lying down on the *kang*, Sun Guiying said in a soft voice, "Do come in and sit down."
>
> Xiao Changchun entered the room but as soon as he saw Sun Guiying's face and the expression in her eyes he began to have doubts about her. . . .
>
> Sun Guiying curled up on the *kang* and whispered softly and coquettishly, "Elder brother, I've no use for a doctor. Can't you do something for my illness?"
>
> Xiao Changchun saw through the woman's intention instantly. He was indignant, yet he found her vulgar display laughable. He pretended not to have heard what she had just said and turned to walk away. . . .
>
> With one leap, Sun Guiying darted to the door, blocking Xiao Changchun's exit. "What's the hurry? Now that Lianfu's not home, can't you even sit for a while in my house?"
>
> Xiao Changchun did his best to restrain his anger. His thoughts took a new turn and he stood still. . . .[14]

The attempted seduction ends when Xiao tells her, with proper righteousness: "You've got it all wrong. I, Xiao Changchun, am not this kind of man." Having rebuffed her, Xiao softens the blow by giving her a little homily intended both to educate her and to put her bizarre behavior into perspective:

> Calm down and think things over. You're not entirely to be blamed for your less than honorable first thirty years. They have been thrust upon you from the old society; you are but a victim. But we are now living in a new society. It's not like the past anymore. You'll have to decide where you want to go and what you want to do. You ought to take the new road of light which is socialism. And for the next thirty years, stand up, transform yourself, and become a working woman."[15]

Even though Xiao's relations with the women Sun Guiying and Jiao Shuhong are very different, there is still a basic and revealing similarity. The man is the more advanced politically, and his superior position is one of tutelage. A relationship between persons of opposite sexes is used, over and above its universal human interest, to convey an ideological message. The technique occurs more than once in *Bright Sunny Skies*. Han Baizhong and his wife Jiao Erju are another couple who are used for didactic pur-

[13] Ibid., p. 965.

[14] Ibid., pp. 970–971.

[15] Ibid., p. 972.

poses. They are portrayed with warmth, skill, and sympathy. Han Baizhong gives Erju the task of winning over her brother's wife, who has been associating with bad people. The couple's interdependence and closeness is neatly and economically depicted:

> [Han Baizhong] was some distance from his house when he realized that Jiao Erju was not home. When the Elementary Agricultural Cooperative was first set up, their house was used as the office. Ever since that time, they fell into the habit of never barring their gate, day or night. When someone was at home, the doors were kept wide open; when no one was there they were only pulled shut. Unlike city folks who left notes for their mates when they were out of the house, neither of them could read or write. Like the busy people they were, husband and wife would run home to eat and hardly have time to put down their chopsticks before having to run out of the house again. Even if they had been literate neither of them would have thought to check the table top for a note. However, they had their own way to communicate. There was a piece of chalk in a crack in the brickwork. They would use it to scratch a symbol of their destination on the gate. For the fields, a square; for the temple, a roof-like triangle. For a visit to Ma Cuiqing's house the character for woman was used; for doing the laundry a few wavy lines. All they had to do was take one look at the symbol to know instantly where the other person was.[16]

This passage, along with other, similar material, establishes the context within which several important political struggles are carried out. Erju, the political inferior of her husband, is educated by him and learns the correct way to approach people about their backwardness. Before she knows better, she tries to win people over by methods such as bribery or matchmaking, and the people she tries to educate are in-laws or relatives.[17] Thus, the novel's political themes and problems are constantly posed in personal terms that have an immediate impact upon the novel's audience, whatever its level of political sophistication. Even a Western audience, unfamiliar with or possibly hostile to communism, would have no trouble identifying with, and thus being drawn into the plot by, a husband-wife theme, in-law problems, seduction, or a love interest. The political struggles themselves are of the most accessible sort. They have to do with conquering what are recognized as universal character traits and flaws: greed, envy, jealousy, and selfishness. Political debate and practice in *Bright Sunny Skies* are not matters of power struggles, factionalization, and ideological hairsplitting. They are, rather, presented in the form of such practical problems as family disagreements and misunderstandings, of a sort that would not be out of place in American popular media.

Bright Sunny Skies uses other methods as well to insure audience re-

[16] Ibid., pp. 512–513.
[17] Ibid., chap. 39.

sponse. The seduction scene quoted earlier presents remarkable parallels to traditional Chinese literature. Wu Song and Jinlian ("Golden Lotus") play out similar scenes in *Shuihu zhuan* [Water margin] and *Jin Ping Mei* [Golden lotus], complete with matchmaking, firewood and stove imagery, and the punchline "I am not this sort of man."

Characters are often presented in a way that should strike a responsive chord in a traditional Chinese audience. Ma Fenglan is drawn as a typical villainess; Jiao Erju, a positive character, is the portrait on the other side of the traditional coin. She is first described as a forty-year-old woman, coarse and strong like the trunk of a locust tree. Her father died when she was very young. Because her feet were never bound, she bears the nickname "Big Feet Erju." Footbinding has become symbolic of the enslavement of women in the old society, and the emphasis on Jiao Erju's unbound feet is used to hammer this point home.[18] At first, her big feet are a source of suffering to her; insecurity about them inclines her to reject a marriage proposal, and she is taunted:

> Those whose tread is like thunder's crack,
> Will always have hardship on their back.[19]

Later, however, her big feet prove to be her salvation. They enable her to flee from Landlord Ma and escape to Peking. When her husband is hurt, she saves the day by pulling a rickshaw to earn their livelihood. Her whole story (from nickname to exploits) is very evocative, because it is based on an emotional subject matter that a Chinese readership can instantly identify with.

Throughout the novel, language also causes reverberations. There are frequent implicit and explicit references to Buddhism. Sun Guiying, in her regret over the fiasco of her attempt at seduction, thinks, "She had committed a crime against Xiao Changchun, and a whole lifetime could never wash away her sins."[20] When Jiao Shuhong went to struggle with Guiying, "She walked up to Sun Guiying with a serious and solemn face looking like the God of Plague."[21] When Guiying is won over, this dialogue takes place:

> "How quickly you change. You sound like you've just ended a vegetarian fast," said Ma Cuiqing.
>
> Angrily Sun Guiying said, "End a vegetarian fast? If I were in your shoes I'd go to their front door and curse them for eight generations."[22]

[18] Ibid., pp. 55–59.
[19] Ibid., p. 57.
[20] Ibid., p. 1244.
[21] Ibid., p. 1246.
[22] Ibid., p. 1250.

When people in the novel die, they go to meet King Yama.

Hao Ran is famous for his "peasant language." His characters often speak with an earthy coarseness that all can respond to: "Is there anyone who'd put rouge on their backside instead of their face?";[23] "That bitch Ma Fenglan, all water stinks that drifts downstream from her";[24] "Flies flock to the sound of a fart";[25] and "The children are all big eaters like their father—they eat a pot and shit a *kang*."[26]

Sometimes older novels are referred to directly, as in "I feel like Pigsy holding a mirror to his face to discover that he's non-human both inside and out."[27] Sometimes the reference is indirect, as when a bloody oath might recall the exuberant excesses of *Water Margin*: "If they're really short of grain, you can pluck my eyeballs out and stamp on them like bubbles."[28]

The quotations cited here do more than demonstrate the vitality of Hao Ran's prose and the skill with which he uses language. They constitute a rich matrix in which are imbedded the nuggets of Hao Ran's ideological message. The references to Buddhism, to human and family life, and to general situations that may be familiar to readers of early texts need not be specific in order to create a context of convention and presupposition with which a reader can identify. Further, it does not greatly matter if these conventions and presuppositions cannot be traced to their sources and positively identified; they still constitute a general intertextuality that serves as a sort of sounding board against which the text at hand, *Bright Sunny Skies,* can reverberate. These conventions reside not necessarily in the text but in the reader, whose response is activated by the text.

Readers encounter a general intertextuality, which Roland Barthes has described:

> I [am] not an innocent subject, anterior to the text. . . . This "I" which approaches the text is already itself a plurality of other texts, of codes which are infinite or, more precisely, lost (whose origins are lost).[29]

Intertextuality is less a description of a work's relation to particular prior texts than it is an assertion of a work's dialogue with its readers, a dialogue instituted by activating codes that a reader has already consciously or unconsciously absorbed. The study of intertextuality is not necessarily the investigation of sources and influences, as traditionally conceived; it

[23] Ibid.
[24] Ibid., p. 1249.
[25] Ibid., p. 514.
[26] Ibid., p. 518.
[27] Ibid., p. 525. The reference is to a character in *Xi you ji* [Journey to the west].
[28] Ibid., p. 514.
[29] Roland Barthes, *S/Z* (New York: Hill & Wang, 1974), p. 10.

might include anonymous discursive practices or codes whose origins are lost.[30] Insofar as *Bright Sunny Skies* can be called successful, it succeeds because it activates codes that are shared by its audience. Many of those codes are accessible to a Western as well as to a Chinese audience. The intertextuality of *Bright Sunny Skies*—that is, the relationship between the text and its codes and the discursive practices of its culture—helps to articulate that culture and its possibilities.

In *The Road of Golden Light,* a reader can detect a substantial change in Hao Ran's use of signs and codes. Stylistically, the novel is similar to *Bright Sunny Skies,* and Hao Ran still demonstrates his mastery of colloquial language. Some areas of similarity to and difference from traditional fiction, along with Hao Ran's reliance on traditional storytelling techniques, have already been commented on by Cyril Birch.[31] Certainly, Hao Ran's characteristic use of language and of traditional devices lends an air of continuity to the later novel. Moreover, the novels' common generic form—their length, semi-episodic nature, and large casts of characters—itself constitutes one type of intertextual relationship with traditional fiction. Nonetheless, the literary structures of *The Road of Golden Light* seem to be based on a different set of assumptions than those of *Bright Sunny Skies.*

For instance, references to Buddhism or to traditional culture in the everyday speech of the characters have been eliminated or greatly reduced. In a work written after the Cultural Revolution had begun and stricter demands for revolutionary correctness were being made, there might be two reasons for this. If the positive characters or heroes used such modes of speech, it would denote a certain backwardness in their thinking, thus making them less worthy of emulation. Second, there is in the very use of prerevolutionary modes of discourse a code that is perceived as being in opposition to the correct practice of revolutionary literature. The symbolic structure of *The Road of Golden Light* is supposed to refer to revolutionary goals and glory, not to remind readers of an undesirable past.[32]

Characterization in *The Road of Golden Light* has also changed, although there are many similarities between that novel and *Bright Sunny Skies.* Both novels have as hero an outstanding Party member, whose story functions as a unifying plot element, stringing together and giving continuity to a multitude of incidents. The political development of the hero, as he learns more and more about class and line struggle, provides the main moral

[30] See Julia Kristeva, *Semeotiké* (Paris: Editions du Seuil, 1969), pp. 146–180.

[31] Cyril Birch, "Continuity and Change in Chinese Fiction," in Merle Goldman, ed., *Modern Chinese Literature in the May Fourth Era* (Cambridge, Mass.: Harvard University Press, 1977), pp. 385–404.

[32] For an excellent discussion of symbolism in *The Road of Golden Light,* see Wong Kam-ming, "Study of Hao Ran's Two Novels."

lesson of each text. Thus, *The Road of Golden Light* can be read as a quest, a sort of revolutionary, Communist updating of *Pilgrim's Progress,* with a hero who evolves and distills a set of rigorous moral standards.

However, modes of characterization seem to have changed in *The Road of Golden Light* in at least two ways, and each change has had an important effect on reader response. The villains in *The Road of Golden Light,* while still familiar to the reader, are recognized because they are flat, clichéd figures, not because they seem like old friends from old novels. While the behavior of a woman such as Ma Fenglan in *Bright Sunny Skies* is totally stereotyped and predictable, she is nonetheless lovingly depicted; she is an endearing troublemaker whose behavior starts a familiar but enjoyable story cycle. That the cycle's most recent incarnation comes in a Communist context might even serve to heighten the reader's curiosity: how will the tale work itself out in its modern guise?

The archvillain of *Bright Sunny Skies,* Pigtail Ma, may not be a familiar figure from traditional literature, but he is very human and well motivated; it is perhaps too easy to identify with and understand him. He is driven to desperation by the loss of the familial burial site, and his economic motivation is very strong. His idea that grain should be distributed not to each according to his needs but to each according to his work, or in proportion to the amount of land he has contributed to the collective, was not expressed only by a few fictional and reactionary blackguards. Pigtail Ma's ideas on land reform and grain distribution were also held at the highest Party levels.[33] His fear for his own soul and for the souls of his ancestors, and his greed (understandable in the context of the Party debates of the 1950s), humanize him and provide him with motivation that makes his behavior comprehensible, if not forgivable.

By way of contrast, the negative characters in *The Road of Golden Light* seem to have no reason for their evil natures but their class background. Fan Keming is one-dimensionally evil by nature and is much less interesting than Pigtail Ma. Other bad elements in *The Road of Golden Light*—Feng Shaohuai, Qin Fu, and Zhang Jinfa, for example—lack all but the most transparent sort of motivation. The evil they work is banal and, ultimately, boring.

Kinship is another area where intertextual filiations with traditional works seem less strong in *The Road of Golden Light* than they were in *Bright Sunny Skies.* An example is the relationship between the former's main hero, Gao Daquan, and his brother Erlin. The pair had been through a lot together; they had seen friends and loved ones die because of the

[33] "Resolution of the Central Committee of the Chinese Communist Party on the Establishment of Peoples' Communes in Rural Areas" (29 August 1958), in Robert Bowie and J. K. Fairbank, *Communist China, 1955–59: Policy Documents with Analysis* (Cambridge, Mass.: Harvard University Press, 1962), pp. 454–456.

oppression of the old society and known grinding poverty because they had been landless. After working their way from Shandong to Hebei, they were finally given land by the Party, to which each was wildly grateful. Love of the soil is the great bond between them:

> Even though the land they trod on hadn't received its spring plowing, it was already soft and moist; it warmed their hearts.
>
> Gao Erlin laughed with delight. "In our old home the unplowed land was hard as a board; here it's soft like a cotton quilt, makes me want to lie down for a nap. . . . Sometimes I'm afraid this is only a dream. . . ."
>
> Gao Daquan replied to his younger brother: "You and I may never have dreamed of this, but the old revolutionary comrades thought it all out. So many people shed their life blood to liberate the poor peasants. Remember that this land was bought with the blood of heroes. Remember them, and you'll know that this good land didn't just drop into our hands; they paid for it with their lives, and the Communist Party gave it to us."[34]

For all their shared experience and love of land, the brothers grow apart for ideological reasons. However, their previous closeness does not make their estrangment more poignant, it only makes it seem improbable. Erlin, rather than work for a mutual-aid team and help to establish collectivization, elects to go it alone. He tries to advance himself economically through his own individual efforts. After being manipulated by the malign Feng Shaohuai into marrying Feng's cousin, he goes to work for Feng as a hired carter. There he is open for exploitation by bad elements.

Erlin's relationship to Gao Daquan does not have much effect on the reader's reaction to his plight. In *Bright Sunny Skies,* a universal loyalty to kinship and blood relationships was part of the code of intertextuality between work and reader; in *The Road of Golden Light,* the intertextuality relies more on the reader's *political* sophistication to trigger emotional and esthetic response:

> Gao Daquan said to his brother: "That's all fine. But if you can't tell good people from bad, the right path from the wrong path, you'll be misled, and never get anywhere. Erlin, am I getting through to you?"
>
> Erlin looked at his brother and glanced away, "Don't worry, I'm not stupid. . . ."
>
> "Stupid or not stupid, your mind has been on wealth and you haven't been seeing things clearly. When you have time, visit some families who have joined mutual aid teams; listen to them, study their ideas. Then look at what they're wearing and see what they're eating and what they've got stored up. Compare what they have now with what they had before they joined the mutual aid teams, with what you have since you've taken the wrong road. Then it'll be really plain that socialism is best; the shining road will be clear to you."[35]

[34] Hao Ran, *Jinguang dadao* (Hong Kong: San lian, 1974), 1:325–326.
[35] Ibid., 2:495.

It would seem from this passage that the two brothers differ simply on the question of which line to adhere to (ironically, when Erlin turns heretic because of his selfish desire for greater personal wealth, Daquan seeks to reform him by appeal to his greed). There is no motivation, no human drama, save that which sprouts from political seeds.

The sad tale of Liu Wan and his wife provides another example. Liu Wan had "resolutely" stood with Gao Daquan at the time of land reform but, after getting his share of land and a cow, he, like Erlin, became selfish and preoccupied with self-interest:

> When the slogan "Build up the family fortune" (*fa jia zhi fu*) was going around, he took the revisionist slogan to heart, and made money by traveling to neighboring villages to sell his labor.[36]

Liu Wan's father had been a doctor and his family had previously been well off. But the family fell on evil days, the property was divided, and poor Liu Wan got only two *mu* of poor land, which he soon had to mortgage.[37] Transparently, this checkered class background prepares the reader for Liu Wan's irresponsible behavior. For all of his faults, though, he is a good man; when he goes wrong and joins a bogus mutual-aid team it is because he has been tricked by Zhang Jinfa and Feng Shaohuai. Members of the false mutual-aid team really only work for themselves; they think their families will grow richer if they rely on their own resources and refuse to share. Only rich peasants and unscrupulous scoundrels can make this system work, however, and Liu Wan finds himself in a terrible fix. After delaying plowing (due to Feng and Zhang), he sows too late; then the rainy season arrives and his plot is overgrown with weeds. At the same time, his wife gives birth. He is frantic; he has to cook, care for his wife, care for his children, care for his cow. And the rains never let up; they are flooding his fields. His agony as he is forced to watch his precious crops die before his very eyes is almost unbearable. It would take five days of weeding to clear his fields.[38]

Liu Wan is a well-drawn and human character. The reader can identify with all his emotions; his flaws serve to humanize him. Tormented with worry, he is yet a proud man. He tries to get the bogus mutual-aid team to help him; when they refuse, he is too stubborn to admit his errors and seek help from the Party. Liu Wan's wife tells him that Party Secretary Gao is eager to help, but Liu Wan says he doesn't have the "face" to ask. Liu Wan's story is told in an almost naturalistic fashion and with great intensity. He cannot sleep, and his thoughts are as tangled as a ball of string; he has nightmares. He gets up early, eats a meager breakfast without tasting

[36] Ibid., 2:449–500.
[37] Ibid., 2:511–512.
[38] Ibid., 2:571.

it, and goes off to his fields to do as much as he can by himself. As he toils, the sweat pouring off of him, he sees someone working with him in the field, laboriously and clumsily hoeing with a trowel. It is his wife, squatting over the seedlings, only four days after giving birth. She refuses to stop and Liu Wan returns to his labor, emotionally overcome, his mind a mixture of warmth and bitterness.

The day is stifling, the sun blazing. Suddenly clouds gather, a wind springs up and there is a rumble of thunder. They rise to go home before the deluge, but the wife's legs buckle and go numb. She is very sick. Gao Daquan and members of the good mutual-aid team are summoned, but it is too late. Liu Wan's fields will be taken care of by the mutual-aid team, but his wife cannot be saved. Gao Daquan is at her bedside. Her last words are:

> "Too late, too late. . . . If only we'd followed you, and joined your mutual aid team earlier, how much better things would be. . . . Too late."
>
> Gao Daquan replied, "It's not too late. In the fall we'll start an agricultural cooperative, and you and Liu Wan are invited to be its first members."
>
> The sick woman shook her head. "I won't live to see the day." Her eyes shining with light, she asked him, "Party Secretary, please take care of our two children, of my husband . . ."
>
> "Don't worry, we're bitter fruit from the same vine. We'll take the socialist road together."
>
> A smile came over the face of the sick woman, and she slowly closed her eyes.[39]

Hao Ran seems to totally destroy the effect of some of his best writing by following it with some of his worst. The reader is genuinely moved by the desperation and suffering of Liu Wan, yet the death of his wife is presented in such a way that it is almost trivialized. She is killed off to punish him for having taken a wrong line and to provide him with the moral lesson he needs so that he can reform:

> "I've killed her! I've killed her! Oh . . ." Gao . . . comforts him, "Uncle, uncle, set your heart at rest. You aren't entirely to blame. It wasn't you who killed her, it was the path that you took; following it cost her life."[40]

Hao Ran spells it out through the mouth of Party Secretary Gao: a human relationship did not kill her, politics did. This speech does not ring true. Despite the power of Hao Ran's prose, the death scene is too contrived to be convincing. Granted, Liu is a stubborn man, and his fear of losing face is a legitimate one. But he knows that losing his crops means starvation for his family, and he knows that he is working his wife to

[39] Ibid., 2:585–586.
[40] Ibid., 2:586.

death. And *we,* the audience, know that nothing will happen to him if he changes his mind, denounces the baddies, and joins a proper mutual-aid team. So the entire melodramatic buildup, effective as it is, is meaningless, even counterproductive. Liu Wan, like Gao Erlin, has an escape hatch all along. That he is too stupid to use it weakens him as a character; the reader's response to him is one of frustration.

The reason that the subplots such as those about Liu Wan and Gao Erlin do not work is that at first the characters rely on "traditional" filiations to arouse reader response. A family or kinship situation, the battle of a farmer with the elements, or a feud, or fear of death—all can provide subtexts that are universal, identifiable by all readers. But the type of fiction that Hao Ran is writing requires him to switch these filiations—in midstream, as it were—from personal to political codes. The result is a strangely alienating, almost discontinuous form of literature. It has an unfamiliar subtext and seems to stand in isolation from the development of Chinese literary history, divorced from its literary past, despite the fact that Hao Ran always strives to "make the past serve the present." His use of traditional literary structures only underscores the radical departure that his texts have taken in their mode of discourse.

Hao Ran's novels provide an interesting example of literature in transition. The difference between *Bright Sunny Skies* and *The Road of Golden Light* can be defined in literary as well as political terms. Just as the plot moves from class struggle in one novel to line struggle in the other, the textual filiations and affiliations go from the (relatively) humanistic, universal, and traditional in *Bright Sunny Skies* to the didactic and political in *The Road of Golden Light.* There are extremely few literary allusions in the latter work, but there are a multitude of political allusions. Didactic and mimetic functions have been merged to such an extent that the subtext of the novel is predominantly political in nature, and the reader's intertextual response is most often activated by political texts and political codes, rather than by literary or esthetic ones. If the text provides one element of a relation, thus requiring the reader to supply the remaining portion on his own, that reader requires a political rather than a literary education.

Although the struggles in *Bright Sunny Skies* work themselves out on an individual basis and are quite accessible to the reader, there is at least one important intertextual link that assumes political knowledge: the problem of how to allocate the fruits of labor. A reader need not, however, be aware of Party controversies in order to appreciate the novel in a number of ways. The work has a rich intertext that functions esthetically as well as politically.

Quoting Harold Bloom in regard to Hao Ran is instructive. What happens when

> one tries to write or to teach or to think or even to read without the sense of tradition? Why, nothing happens at all, just nothing. You cannot write or teach or think or even read without imitation, and what you imitate is what another person has done, that person's writing or teaching or thinking or reading. Your relation to what informs that person is tradition.[41]

Strong hints of where Hao Ran stands in the literary tradition can be found in *Bright Sunny Skies,* but in *The Road of Golden Light* textual filiations are almost entirely political.

This is not necessarily to say that they are ineffective. The overtly political nature of daily life in China creates for the Chinese reader a political, instead of a literary, tradition that would be activated by the novel. For instance, we can presume that the Chinese audience would be familiar with the background of *The Road of Golden Light*: the rural situation in 1953, immediately after the first land reform, was unsatisfactory. Although the peasants were free from debt and had been given their own land, the smallness of the farm units and the fragmentation of plots made for very inefficient agriculture and hindered the adoption of modern technology. Further: "No sooner had land-reform been completed than there reappeared the traditional practice of usury; better off and more economically efficient peasants began to lend money to poorer and less efficient ones, and in some cases the debtors were forced to sell their lands to their creditors."[42]

When seeking the subtext behind a villain like Feng Shaohuai, it is perhaps more fruitful to look to modern political history than to traditional literature.

The organization of mutual-aid teams, the progression of lower cooperatives to higher cooperatives, and the Party's sensitivity to "peasant individualism" are all part of the political tradition, and knowledge of that political tradition is necessary for any sort of reader response to *The Road of Golden Light.*[43] Maurice Meisner's history of collectivization from 1953 to 1957 reads almost like a plot outline of *The Road of Golden Light.* Meisner quotes Mao:

> Many poor peasants, due to their lack of means of production, still remain in poverty, some of them having contracted debts; others are selling their land or renting out their land. . . . If this situation is allowed to develop further, there will come increasingly more serious [class] polarization in the rural areas."[44]

[41] Harold Bloom, *A Map of Misreading* (New York: Oxford University Press, 1975), p. 32.

[42] Maurice Meisner, *Mao's China: A History of the People's Republic* (New York: Free Press, 1977), p. 141.

[43] Ibid., chap. 10.

[44] Ibid., p. 143.

The rise of a kulak class, the "inclination of the Party's own rural cadre to succumb to petty bourgeois 'peasant ideology',"[45] are all themes of *The Road of Golden Light*; for instance, the bad cadre Zhang Jinfa is petty-bourgeios peasant ideology personified. Many peasants refused to join mutual-aid teams, preferring to try their luck in the "private sector"—hence Gao Erlin. Many peasants tried to avoid the entire process; in *The Road of Golden Light,* the reader is given the sham mutual-aid team of Feng Shaohuai, and the barrenness of his and Zhang's approach is symbolized by the series of dry wells they dig, hoping to show up Gao Daquan's correct policy. There is no reason to doubt Hao Ran when he writes, as he did of *Bright Sunny Skies*:

> When I wrote this book, I hoped to be able to write about the customs, lives and reality of the people. While I wanted to be able to convey the vision of workers, peasants and soldiers, I especially wanted to put the novel in the hands of the peasants. . . . But I didn't write well. . . . I wrote a first draft and returned to the peasants for [criticism and correction].[46]

Hao Ran has made many such statements, but in *The Road of Golden Light,* at least, he relied more on historical sources than on peasant informants for the foundation of his work.

The major trend in the development of Hao Ran's fiction from *Bright Sunny Skies* to *The Road of Golden Light*—the increasing ascendance of the political rather than the literary subtext—continues in *Sons and Daughters of Xisha,* which seems to have almost no subtext at all. Again, character and characterization provide a key to Hao Ran's work. Even in *The Road of Golden Light,* some negative characters had good traits as well as bad. Zhang Jinfa, Wang Youqing, and Gu Xinmin all have a positive side to their natures, for all that they are evil persons.[47] In *Sons and Daughters of Xisha,* no such ambiguities exist. Volume 1 of the novel tells the tale of the people's struggle against Japanese aggression in the South China Sea. The Xisha fishermen are heroic under the leadership of the Chinese Communist Party, and their adversaries—the traitors, despots, and Japanese invaders—are totally evil. The two proletarian revolutionaries, Zheng Liang and Grandpa Wei, are never less than perfect. Volume 1 also presents the childhood history of A Bao, heroine of Volume 2.

Volume 2 has two parts. The first records how, in 1959, the Saigon government attacked five Chinese fishing boats, drove them ashore, and captured over eighty fishermen. They are imprisoned and mistreated but finally released due to Chinese pressure. Other Saigon attacks on the Xisha

[45] Ibid., p. 145.

[46] Hao Ran, "Ping changpian xiaoshuo *Yanyang tian*" [On the novel *Bright Sunny Skies*], *Guangming ribao,* 23 October 1965.

[47] Joe Huang, "Hao Ran," p. 390.

islands also provide background. The actual setting of the novel is the Xiangyang Commune on one of the islands.

Fifteen years pass. In the second part of Volume 2, Xisha has changed and modernized, but there is still confrontation between the fishermen and the Saigon troops. With the growth of socialism, contradictions between positive characters decrease; they are never as serious as in Volume 1 and are more easily solved. The emphasis is on depicting the modernization and economic progress of Xisha and the fighting spirit and patriotism of the fishermen. The climax of the novel is a great battle scene in two parts. A Bao is victorious in the land battle, and Fu Hailong (commander of a PLA warship and A Bao's husband) conquers at sea.

Conflict in *Sons and Daughters of Xisha* is almost impersonal. Characters have so little motivation that they make the people in *The Road of Golden Light* seem models of complexity; compared to *Xisha, Bright Sunny Skies* is a rich text indeed. In the three novels the reader can see Hao Ran's increasing adherence to a formulaic mode of writing imposed by Party policy. The doctrine of the "three prominences" promulgated by Jiang Qing holds complete sway over *Sons and Daughters of Xisha.* All characters, including villains, give prominence to positive characters, who yield in turn to heroic characters. Heroic characters bow in turn to the main hero. Jiang Qing started developing this scheme for reformed Peking opera in 1964; by the 1970s her theory had a stranglehold on the novel as well as the stage.[48]

Sons and Daughters is a perfect example of the three prominences theory in action. Conflict and contradictions serve as challenges for heroes and heroic characters to respond to. Each victory is a synthesis that resolves the relevant ideological contradiction. The plot is used only to advance characterization by showing how heroic thought and action can overcome any obstacle. The heroine's attempt to resolve contradictions earns her sufficient prominence that her character and ideology are allowed to emerge.

A Bao is, of course, the heroine of the novel. She is at the pinnacle of a pyramid, resting on heroic secondary characters like He Wangli and Zheng Taiping. They also support Party policy, socialism, and the development of Xisha, but occasionally they may waver slightly or be caught in a minor contradiction. Such occasions serve merely to thrust A Bao forward, and she solves the problem with a glib slogan like "We must rely on our own strength" (*zili gongsheng*) or "We must show some backbone" (*ying gutou*). The base of the pyramid is formed by the class enemies One-Eyed Crab (Duyan Xie) and Big Pumpkin (Da Nangua). One-Eyed Crab used to own the fishing fleet and to exploit the fishermen; Big Pumpkin is the

[48] Beverley Lum, "A Report on the Principle of 'the Three Prominences' " (unpublished manuscript), pp. 1–5.

leader of the Saigon troops. There are other heroes too. Fu Hailong and Zheng Liang, A Bao's father, fall between her and the secondary characters, and help taper the pyramid to its summit.

Heroes who are paragons are very familiar by now, so we are not surprised to learn that A Bao has been "tempered by bloody and fierce revolutionary struggle."[49] Never before, though, have villains been so completely stereotyped. One-Eyed Crab is an unreconstructed traitor, a renegade without scruples. He has refused to change, despite the many opportunities offered by the People's Government. He keeps his backward mentality and longs for the good old days, which were joyful because he could do bad things whenever he wanted to. He is only waiting to strike a blow against the revolution and restore feudal conditions; he squirms "like an ant in a hot pan."[50]

A Bao instantly recognizes him as a class enemy; in *Sons and Daughters of Xisha,* class enemies do not go undetected for hundreds of pages, as they do in *Bright Sunny Skies,* or have the opportunity to put their bad policies into action, as in *The Road of Golden Light.* There is instant recognition; the battle lines are clear from the very start.

A Bao, as the main heroine, is ideally beautiful, just as the bad characters are deformed. She is a flat, static character who is presented as perfect and who remains perfect. She cannot be fooled for a minute, so she never has to learn anything, unlike Gao Daquan in *The Road of Golden Light.* She represents the Party and is a model for the masses. When she is forced to talk to "bad eggs" she speaks with contempt (in the work no effort is made to convert such people); when she talks to peasants, she tries to educate them. The plot of *Xisha,* in keeping with the three prominences, is breathtaking in its simplicity. It develops two main contradictions that are resolved in such a way as to make A Bao's heroism even more prominent. *Xisha* is a model of dialectical oversimplification—thesis: A Bao is presented as a heroic model; antithesis: the evil One-Eyed Crab contacts the troops of the Saigon government; synthesis: A Bao discovers and destroys him. Then the whole process is repeated over again; the second climax is the Chinese islanders' victory over the invading Vietnamese.

The leader of the Saigon troops, Big Pumpkin, is if possible even more one-dimensional than One-Eyed Crab. He drinks, swears, and smokes opium, and his room is filled with pictures of naked women (as opposed to the villain's Buddhist icons in *Bright Sunny Skies*). He is such an exact opposite of A Bao that the novel has no suspense whatsoever. It is a straightforward morality play—good versus evil—and the result is a foregone conclusion. There are not even any Party lines for political scientists

[49] Hao Ran, *Xisha ernü* (Peking: Renmin wenxue, 1974), p. 5.
[50] Ibid., pp. 9–10.

to trace. The multidirectional subtext of *Bright Sunny Skies* became one-directional in *The Road of Golden Light*; in *Sons and Daughters of Xisha*, Hao Ran seems to have written a novel with no filiations at all. Chairman Mao is quoted ("Villains will neither change nor die voluntarily"),[51] and readers will recognize the format of *wuxia xiaoshuo* (swordsman novels). Everyone remembers that the Chinese and South Vietnamese were on opposite sides in the Vietnam War. Otherwise, *Xisha* seems almost bereft of filiations. The result is a flat novel in comic-book style that elicits very little in the way of reader response. Moreover, the response it does elicit may not be the one Hao Ran desired: *Sons and Daughters of Xisha* reads very successfully as camp or pop art.

Hao Ran's three novels are written in three distinct styles. One has real roots in China's literary and cultural past as well as in the political present; one has political rather than literary or esthetic allusions; and one is so unremittingly political that it reduces the idea of socialist literature (or even of "revolutionary romanticism") to caricature. It is unlikely that this sequence reflects Hao Ran's normal development as an artist; almost certainly, it is the result of a political line imposed from above by cultural bureaucrats (Hao Ran himself is, or was, something of a cultural bureaucrat). Such radical changes in literature and its presuppositions must present difficulties to any audience, even to one familiar with day-to-day political undercurrents. His growth as an artist may often lead an author to challenge his readers by writing in a radical new style, so that he risks losing them in order to lead them to a new epiphany. Hao Ran seems to have done just the opposite; he changed his style in order to decrease the possibilities of his fiction. It will be interesting to see which of Hao Ran's works will survive the tests of time and rereading.

[51] Ibid., p. 103.

ELEVEN

Contemporary Chinese Poetry and Its Search for an Ideal Form

Kai-yu Hsu

Chinese poets since 1949 have almost constantly been engaged in controversies over the shapes new poetry should assume and how the new forms should be integrated with new content.[1] Two factors can account for this preoccupation. First, poetry as a genre focuses the writer's attention on verse forms because as a lyrical, imagistic medium, poetry requires a greater economy and therefore a more careful deployment of words than the detailed, discursive novel. Second, the recent, rather dramatic move in twentieth-century Chinese poetry from classical Chinese with its condensed syntax to the modern vernacular has created a need for freer prosodic schemes: a new diction requires new forms. In the following section I review several typical contributions to the discussions about poetic form. Most of these discussions, it will become apparent, finally brought forth the truth that poetic form could not be isolated from the other aspects of poetry—its language, imagery, feeling, and thought—and many disputants concluded that the traditional dichotomy betweeen form and content was an abstract construct that ignored the essential unity of a poem.

THE RECURRING DEBATES

Preoccupation with form goes back to the 1950s, when a wave of arguments echoed the earlier intense debate between poets of the Crescent

At the time of the author's tragic death, revisions for the publication of this paper had not yet been made. With the kind permission of the author's widow and following the wishes of the author in earlier correspondence, I have revised the paper in line with usual editorial practice.—*BMcD*

[1] Bonnie S. McDougall, "Poems, Poets, and *Poetry* 1976: An Exercise in the Typology of Modern Chinese Literature," *Contemporary China* 2, 4 (Winter 1978: 76–124) offers some insights into the role of the poet vis-à-vis writers of other genres.

School and left-wing writers in the late 1920s and early 1930s. The background to the 1950s debate was a new emphasis, following the 1942 directive in Mao Zedong's "Talks at the Yan'an Forum on Literature and Art," on Chinese folksong as a source of formal inspiration for the poets of the new society. The debate was complicated by the then-current practice of writing a rather shapeless kind of verse loosely referred to as "free verse". It began with He Qifang's 1954 essays on contemporary formalist poetry, published in *Zhongguo qingnian* [Chinese youth], in which he called for further experimentation with definite prosodic schemes and regular stanza forms. If the poets of modern China did not cultivate such modern forms, he maintained, the rich music that gave classical Chinese poetry its characteristic beauty would be lost. This was the same argument Wen Yiduo had advanced in 1926, and it was supported by other noted poets and writers from the 1930s such as Bian Zhilin, Zhu Guangqian and Wang Li.[2] Despite their polemic, however, free verse had continued to be the most often-used mode.

In the 1960s Guo Moruo addressed the same issue, calling for a concentrated effort to "complete the literary revolution started at May Fourth by going further in giving poetry a national and popular character."[3] Guo urged the new poets to use new forms developed since the time of the May Fourth movement. These were principally Western free verse as championed by Whitman, "liberated quatrains" where the traditional five or seven syllable line could be plumped out with unaccented syllables and the whole line arranged in a sense-grouped metrical pattern; and, less frequently, imitations of short stanza forms such as those favored by the Victorians Dante Gabriel Rossetti and Thomas Hardy. One of the pioneers of free verse in China, Guo Moruo continued to support it as a suitable vehicle for new poetry.

The problem of poetic form began to appear in print again soon after the end of the Cultural Revolution. Thus in 1977, the leading critic Feng

[2] He Qifang, "Guanyu xiandai gelüshi" [On modern regulated poetry], *Zhongguo qingnian* [Chinese youth] 10 (1954): 14–19. See also He's follow-up articles, "Guanyu shige xingshi wentide zhenglun" [The debate on the question of form in poetry], *Wenxue pinglun* [Literary Review] 1 (February 1959): 1–22; and "Zai tan shige xingshi wenti" [More on the question of form in poetry], ibid. 2 (April 1959): 55–75. See also Feng Zhi, "Guanyu xinshide xingshi wenti" [On the question of form in new poetry], ibid. 1 (February 1959): 34–38; Bian Zhilin, "Tan shigede gelü wenti" [On the question of regulated forms in poetry], ibid. 2 (April 1959): 79–83; and Wang Li, "Zhongguo gelüshide chuantong he xiandai gelüshide wenti" [The tradition of regulated poetry in China and the question of contemporary regulated poetry], ibid. 3 (June 1959): 1–12.

[3] Guo Moruo, "Guanyu shigede minzuhua qunzhonghua wenti" [On the question of giving poetry a national character and a mass character], *Shikan* [Poetry journal] 7 (July 1963): 60–62. Translated in Kai-yu Hsu, *The Chinese Literary Scene* (New York: Vintage, 1975), pp. 32–35.

Mu in an obituary article on Guo Xiaochuan commented that Guo's most lasting contribution to contemporary Chinese poetry was his explorations in new poetic forms in the 1950s and 1960s.[4]

In January 1978, a hitherto unpublished letter by Mao Zedong to Chen Yi, written in 1965, was given extensive publicity in the Chinese press. Mao spoke of his dissatisfaction with the lack of progress in new poetry since the May Fourth movement and called for poets to develop new forms based on classical Chinese poetry and folksong. Mao's advice to modern poets was that poetry should be compact, in a neat and attractive form, and rhymed.

Zang Kejia, the stalwart of modern Chinese poetry who had returned to public life in 1975, reminded his audience of Mao's advice when he spoke before the third session of the Third Congress of the Federation of Writers and Artists in May 1978.[5] Zang declared that every word and line of poetry should be hammered and chiseled until it was perfect. He cautioned against inspirational free-flow and upheld the value of well-wrought short lyrics over loosely structured, lengthy verses. In a striking reversal of his opposition in the 1930s and 1940s to Crescent-style estheticism, he even cited Wen Yiduo's theory of 1926 that the three beauties of a poem were the musical, the pictorial, and the architectural.[6]

Toward the end of 1978 a campaign was launched to support more open poetry forums. It was part of a wider movement to encourage more variety in the arts, and official support for this movement was indicated in convincing fashion by the publication in February 1979 of a speech made by Zhou Enlai to music workers in 1961. 1961 was a year of renewed experiment and achievement in many areas of Chinese society. Zhou Enlai was the hero of the nation's intellectuals and artists, so the publication of this speech was a significant event in the outburst of literary creativity that took place from the winter of 1978 to the spring of 1979. While the unofficial literature of this period attracted most Western interest, the official literary world was also to some extent revitalized.

In what was billed as the most important conference on poetry in thirty years, over one hundred writers and critics gathered in Peking from January 14 to 20, 1979, to review the state of the art and to assess its most

[4] Feng Mu, "Buduan gemingde zhan'ge he songge" [Unceasing revolutionary battle songs and eulogies], *Shikan* 10 (October 1977): 80–89.

[5] Zang Kejia, "Zai min'ge, gudian shige jiqushang fazhan xinshi" [Develop new poetry on the basis of folk song and classical poetry], *Shikan* 7 (July 1978): 80–84.

[6] Wen Yiduo's letter to Zang Kejia, dated 25 November 1943, in *Wen Yiduo quanji* [Complete works of Wen Yiduo] (Shanghai: Kaiming, 1948), *Gengji* [Section G], pp. 53–55; and Zang Kejia, "Wen Yiduode shi" [Wen Yiduo's poetry], *Renmin wenxue* [People's literature] 7 (July 1956): 119–125. For Wen's own theory, see his *Quanji* [Complete works], Dingji [Section D], pp. 245–254.

pressing needs.[7] The event, sponsored by *Shikan* [Poetry journal] under its chief editor Yan Chen and associate editors Zou Difan and Ke Yan, featured a galaxy of well-known poets. Included were Feng Zhi (who began writing in the 1920s); Zang Kejia (the 1930s); Ai Qing, He Jingzhi, and Li Ji (from the 1940s); Li Ying, Liang Shangquan, and Zhang Zhimin (the 1950s); and Ning Yu, Xu Gang and others of the 1960s and later. Two specific conclusions about form and content emerged from the conference: (1) The overall goal of the poet must be to help advance the four modernizations (of agriculture, industry, defense, and science and technology). Whatever the form the poet chooses, every poem should be, in effect, a heroic marching song toward this national goal. (2) Within this framework, all kinds of subject matter and poetic forms must be allowed to compete freely for the people's approval. "It is permissible for the poet or the reader to prefer certain forms, but intolerable for the authorities to exclude any forms," the conference report solemnly declared. It went on to praise a large selection of poems written during the first half of the twentieth century for their attempts to liberate the content and form of poetry at the same time, not just to invent new forms.

The conferees agreed tacitly that poetic form could not be dealt with separately from feeling, subject matter, and thought. "As poets emphasize the thought content of their work, they must at the same time pay serious attention to artistic techniques so that their creation will not be only momentarily popular but read and remembered forever as gemlike poetry." The report criticized most of the new poetry as too plain, "not easily differentiated from prose," and pleaded for poets to distill the poetic quality from ordinary language because "poetry, after all, is poetry, and revolutionary poetry is not just a compilation of revolutionary slogans."[8]

THE UNDERLYING ISSUES

Several issues underlie the periodically revived discussions over poetic form: can or should the classical poetic diction be completely eliminated? Which kind of poetry is most needed, the purely lyrical verse that stresses intensity of feeling or the dramatic narrative that may be able to compete with the novel and the stage in recounting revolutionary experiences? Should poets actively pursue freely invented verse forms, or should they make the best use of the familiar quatrains—the mainstay of both classical Tang verse and of the ageless Chinese folksong?

First, in their search for an appropriate poetic language for the twentieth century, many poets first turned away from the classical poetic diction

[7] Benkan jizhe [Our own reporter], "Yao wei 'Sihua' fangsheng gechang" [Raise our voices to sing of the "Four Modernizations"], *Shikan* 3 (March 1979): 4–15.

[8] Ibid., pp. 12–13.

inherited from pre-May-Fourth days and then also rejected the westernized vocabulary and syntax used experimentally by the poets of the 1920s and 1930s. They charged that the former was too archaic and esoteric, while the latter smacked of a Europeanized bourgeois taste—both alien to the proletariat, which is taken to generally include peasants, workers, and soldiers. In 1964 the poem "Raodao" [Detour] appeared, which described in a style reminiscent of the love poems of the 1930s a rendezvous between two lovers. It was roundly denounced; criticism in the press raged for months.[9] The main objection was to its language and imagery; and a folksong was suggested as the correct model:

My lover digs a furrow and I plant the sprouts,
A new coat of green covers the entire mountainside.
My lover hauls manure and I load it in the cart,
With my whole heart I follow him wherever he goes.
The sun sets now and birds return to their nests,
Soon the day will be done and people will go home.
I'll forge a chain and I'll forge a lock,
And I'll lock up the sun to keep my lover around.

But there has been no lack of defenders of China's classical poetic diction, one of whom was none other than Mao Zedong himself. In his letter of 1965 to Chen Yi, Mao suggested that the poet think through images, an idea advanced by Liu Xie as far back as the sixth century in his *Wenxin diaolong* [The literary mind and the carving of dragons][10] and also by Zhou Enlai in his speech of 1961. Mao pointed out that poetry, unlike prose, relies upon metaphor, simile, and allusion and only rarely upon narrative descriptions of factual events. This is where, asserted Mao, the Tang poets succeeded and their followers in the Song dynasty failed. Mao's objection to Song lyrics, many of which used prosaic vernacular elements, and his praise of Li He imply his rejection of the use of plain language in poetry. But Mao advised Chen Yi and every other aspiring poet to avoid archaic allusions. His advice revived an argument over whether or not to use the well-polished epithets and well-wrought images inherited from traditional elite poetry. What appears a well-polished epithet to an erudite reader may very well seem an archaic allusion to another reader, went the argument.

The reverse of the question, whether plain talk should be admitted into poetry, has been debated as far back as the Song dynasty, when poets began to incorporate some colloquialisms into their works. One of the more recent debates on this issue took place between Lin Shu (1852–

[9] Hsu, *Chinese Literary Scene*, pp. 35–42.

[10] Liu Xie, *The Literary Mind and the Carving of Dragons*, trans. Vincent Yu-chung Shih (New York: Columbia University Press, 1959), pp. 195–198.

1924), the pioneer translator of Western fiction, and Cai Yuanpei (1868–1940), the enlightened educator.[11] Lin had insisted that one must be a good student of traditional Chinese literature before one could write good *baihua* ("vernacular") literature, while Cai had strongly disagreed. In practice, however, traditional epithets and the current proletarian vernacular have been juxtaposed many times since 1949; the older poets, such as Zang Kejia, tend to incorporate more traditional expressions in their works, and the younger ones, such as Li Ying, fewer. There have also been extreme examples of each approach.

The second issue in discussions on poetic form was whether to strive for the lyrical in the short, highly condensed, and well-wrought verse that makes the classical Chinese poetry beautiful or to capture the drama of modern China in full-blown epics. The report on the January 1979 poetry conference in Peking urges poets to strive for the most sincere expressions of feeling and for the most honest accounts of fact, which is in effect an invitation to both short lyrical and long narrative poems. While it should be no problem for new poetry to accomodate both types of works, China's new poets are often found debating among themselves the direction to pursue. Representative of the new worker-poets, Li Xueao has moved from the shorter lyrics of his *Taihang luhuo* [The fire in a forge in the Taihang Mountains, 1965] to long, narrative poems in his *Yingxiong song* [Odes to heroes, 1973]. A good number of the more promising newcomers in poetry in the 1970s also started with long poems.[12] The needs of the time and most writers' views of the function of poetry indeed put certain pressures on the poets. Even as early as the 1920s, Wen Yiduo discussed the problem and opted for the shorter lyrical poems. By 1943, however, he had decided that the longer narrative poems were ideally suited for the time. In the interval, he had stopped writing poetry himself. Bian Zhilin, one of the finest lyrical poets of the 1930s, followed a similar path, and he, too, stopped writing. Was Wen Yiduo being prophetic when he said, in the early 1940s, that Chinese poetry had run its course and from there on it must become closer to the novel and drama?[13] The same concern continues to motivate the new poets today.

Third, the question of which stanza forms are most suitable for the new Chinese poetry was complicated by questions of national and cultural identity. In the May Fourth era, the new poets agreed that they must reflect the spirit of the time and make use of local color. Later their advocacy was

[11] Shi Jun, ed., *Zhongguo jindai sixiangshi cankao ziliao jianbian* (Short edition of reference materials on the intellectual history of modern China) (Peking, 1957), pp. 1009–1020.

[12] Feng Jingyuan, "Gangsisheng yao" [Cable Song], in *Shikan* 1 (January 1976): 60–61, is a good example. Translated by Bonnie S. McDougall in Kai-yu Hsu, ed., *The Literature of the People's Republic of China* (Bloomington: Indiana University Press: 1980), pp. 923–925.

[13] Wen, *Quanji*, Jiaji [Section A], p. 205; and Jiji [Section F], p. 30.

translated into two issues: how to make poetry popular (belonging to the common folk) and how to retain a national character in poetry. Torn between innovation and adherence to tradition, even Guo Moruo, in statements made in 1963, wavered between urging new poets to seek new forms and urging them to adopt the time-tested pentasyllabic and heptasyllabic quatrains common to most of the authentic Chinese folksongs.

THE RECORD OF PERFORMANCE

All the arguments about the most appropriate form for new Chinese poetry notwithstanding, the poets of the People's Republic have established a record of performance that demonstrates an admirable ingenuity with a large variety of schemes. These can be grouped as follows:

Free Verse

The free verse of short irregular lines, a la Mayakovsky, eclipsed other new poetic forms on the eve of Liberation.[14] Tian Jian experimented with it in the 1940s in his "Renminde wu" [People's dance] and "Ta ye yao sha ren" [She, too, wants to kill].[15] However, the form's popularity has fallen off since Liberation. Perhaps the nervous drumbeat rhythm lost its appeal once the all-out war for national survival was over. Even Tian Jian has turned away from it toward narrative poems with a more measured cadence, such as his "Tie daren" [Big iron man].[16] But Mayakovsky's style has certainly not disappeared completely.[17] Zhang Zhimin, author of *Sibuzhao* [Can't kill him] and of other well-received anthologies in the 1940s and 1950s, published a poem of 483 lines entitled "Anzhao renminde mingling" [By the people's order]. It reads in part:

You, my comrade readers!
Please stay calm, stay calm!
Written under my pen
Is not a poem
But a historical exposé—
A suit filed by the people!
Forgive me, a citizen
—of New China
Feeling—
Ashamed, hurt!
Because it happened

[14] Wen, *Quanji,* Xinji [Section H], pp. 574–585.

[15] Tian Jian, *Ta ye yao sha ren* [She, too, wants to kill] (Shanghai: Xiwang she, 1947).

[16] Tian Jian, "Tie daren" [Big iron man], *Shikan* 7 (July 1964): 4–7.

[17] Translations of Mayakovsky's poems appeared again in *Shikan* 11 (November 1978): 74–81.

—in my motherland,
On the bank of the Yangtse
—of the twentieth century,
In the stone-walled city
—of nineteen seventy-six.[18]

The poem concerns a victim of the Gang of Four's tyranny who was imprisoned because he had dared to mourn the death of the late premier, Zhou Enlai. The enjambment accentuates the stressed words and suggests a voice choked by emotion. The Chinese language lacks the conjugations and declensions that the Russian Mayakovsky exploited to achieve dramatic turns of phrase in poems such as his famous short work on Lenin's death.[19] But Zhang Zhimin has manipulated the breaks in his lines to good effect and has partially made up for his linguistic disadvantage by placing his rhymes only at the end of strategic lines. In the original Chinese for the passage above, "calm," "citizen," and "city" (which in Chinese is the final word of the stanza) carry the rhyme.

He Jingzhi's "Zhongliu dizhu" [The rock in mid-torrent] uses the same form. The poem was inspired by the sight of a monolith standing dramatically in the midst of the turbulent Yellow River at the Three-Gate Gorge between Shanxi and Shaanxi provinces. He delivers a moving tribute to the strength, endurance, and unconquerable spirit of this rock:

Oh, not to remember the past
I come to the Gorge of Three Gates
  Straddling over where King Yu jumped his horse
See, yellow water rolling, rolling
  Hear, excavator thud-thud.
Makes my
  Eyes full
    of hot tears swelling
  Body full
    of blood boiling, a thousand degrees![20]

The first poem Ai Qing published after the Cultural Revolution, "Hong qi" [The red flag], also comes close to this form:

Red fire,
Red blood,
Red the wild lilies,
Red the azalea blooms, a red flood,

[18] *Shikan* 12 (December 1978): 74–81.

[19] V. V. Mayakovsky, *Poetry* (Moscow: Khudozhestvenaya Literatura, 1964), p. 11.

[20] He Jingzhi, *Fangge ji* [Singing aloud] (Peking: Renmin wenxue chubanshe, pp. 22–24. Translated by Wai-lim Yip in Hsu, *The Literature of the People's Republic of China*, pp. 361–363.

Red the pomegranate in May,
Red is the sun at the birth of day.
But most beautiful of them all,
  the red flags on forward march![21]

In this eighty-one-line poem of eleven stanzas, Ai Qing uses many of the poetic devices that had made him famous in the 1940s. There is the calculated redundancy of "red" in the first stanza, "fire" in the sixth and seventh stanzas, and "forward, attack!" in the ninth stanza. The exclamation marks make the lines sound like commands. There is the familiar parallelism:

Seeing it, the exploiting class
Becomes scared, and they tremble all over;
Becomes enraged, and they grind their teeth,
. . . .
Seeing it, the proletarian class
Becomes elated, and they jump for joy.

The end-of-line rhyme on the word "qi" in "hong qi," which recurs again and again in the poem, underscores the theme of the opening stanza as well as concluding the poem by appearing in the very last line of the final stanza. This rhyming device sustains the one end-rhyme throughout the work, in spite of the interruptions of other rhyming words in between, so that the key rhyme functions like a refrain to uphold the thematic image.

The Long Song

Fangge, or long song (literally, a boldly-sung song), is further development of the free verse discussed above. It basically follows the free verse style, except that it tends to have longer lines. The long-song style has been gaining in popularity because it enables the poet to be both lyrical and dramatic; it accommodates flights of imagination as well as relatively detailed development of character and plot. Thus, it combines the advantages of free verse and of the new *ci-fu* style to be discussed later.

Ai Qing's "Gangdu zan" [Ode to the steel capital] illustrates the versatility of this form. In this seventy-four-line poem, Ai Qing describes how he came to the steel capital of China at Anshan after visiting the Daqing petroleum center. He rhapsodizes about the beauty of the furnaces, the brilliance of molten steel, and the symphony of such a gigantic plant all ablaze, alive, and astir. Again there is much parallelism and repetition for rhythmic effect as well as for emphasis:

[21] *Wenhui bao* (Shanghai daily), 30 April 1978. Translated by Kai-yu Hsu, in Hsu, *The Literature of the People's Republic of China,* pp. 917–918.

The wind of steel, the rain of steel
The thunder of steel and the electricity of steel.
What suddenly strikes
  Is the compressed air blowing into the revolving furnace,
    producing a geyser of steel all rose in color;
And the blossoms of steel, peerless in their brilliance,
    Describe the fireworks over Peking on the eve of a festival . . .
. . . .
Here, people's will is stronger than steel
Here, light shines from people's ideal
Here, no room for hesitation or wavering
Here, motherland's heart is throbbing.[22]

Ruan Zhangjing expanded this form into a two-thousand-line long poem, "Baiyun Ebo jiaoxiang shi" [White Cloud Ebo Symphony, completed in 1963], which depicts the transformation of a barren, rocky knoll on the southeastern edge of the Gobi Desert in Inner Mongolia into a productive commune.[23] It recounts a romantic legend of an early hero who gave his life to provide water from a fresh spring. Later, a more progressive elder who wanted to develop this sacred site had to brave the anger of his conservative fellow herdsmen, who felt that change would be a desecration. It is a story poem, but its dramatic dialogues and lyrical passages are effectively cast in the long-song style.

Folksong

Other song forms inherited directly from Chinese folk tradition have found favor with many poets. Li Ji and He Jingzhi had extensive exposure to many of these forms during their years in the countryside (Li Ji, for example, was for some years a professional folk-drama performer); the two have done much to bring new themes and subject matter to village theaters and street-corner recitals. Li Ji's famous "Wang Gui yu Li Xiangxiang" [Wang Gui and Li Xiangxiang][24] and He Jingzhi's "Hui Yan'an" [Return to Yan'an][25] are new examples of the time-honored folksong form known in North China as *xintianyou,* or "follow-heaven-roam." The name suggests that the singer follows what comes naturally to his mind and mouth as he sings. In this form the basic stanza is a rhymed couplet.

[22] *Shikan* 11 (November 1978): 9–11.

[23] Ruan Zhangjing, *Baiyun Ebo jiaoxiang shi* [White cloud Ebo symphony] (Peking, 1964). Translated in part by Kai-yu Hsu, *The Literature of the People's Republic of China,* pp. 677–681.

[24] Li Ji, *Wang Gui yu Li Xiangxiang* [Wang Gui and Li Xiangxiang] (n.p.: Xinhua shudian, 1949). Translated by Yang Hsien-yi and Gladys Yang (Peking: Foreign Languages Press, 1978).

[25] He Jingzhi, *Fangge ji,* pp. 1–5. Translated by Kai-yu Hsu in *The Literature of the People's Republic of China,* pp. 363–365.

The lines are long and segmented by sense-groups. A single rhyme may be sustained throughout the song, or the rhyme may change as often as desired. The *xintianyou* is basically a narrative form, and Li and He follow this tradition. Aside from them, few contemporary poets have published new works in such relatively strict forms. The moment the poet relaxes somewhat from these strict folksong forms, he is turning to the new long song described above. With a little more regularity in its rhythmic pattern and rhyming, long song could very well serve as clapper-verse, to be sung to the accompaniment of a pair of clappers and of a string of small bamboo slabs.

By far the most popular form of new poetry written since 1949 has been the folksong pattern that has a basic stanza of four pentasyllabic or heptasyllabic lines. This form, which is seen all over the country, allows enough free variation within or between stanzas to suit any theme or any singer. The rhyming is usually *a a b a, a b a b, a a a a,* or, rarely, *a a b b.* Most of the thousands of songs collected during the Great Leap Forward campaign of 1958, the largest harvest of such folksongs in the history of the People's Republic, are in this form.[26] Nearly one-half of all the works anthologized since 1949 are written in this form, which is also used in almost all song contests. A typical piece reads or chants like this *a a b a* quatrain:

Feng shou shan ge | *duo you duo.*
Feng shou shan ge | *yong ma tuo.*
Qian ma dao le | *Zunyi xian.*
Hou ma hai zai | *Erlang he.*

Bumper crop songs, many and many.
Bumper crop songs, with horses carry.
Front horse has reached Zunyi county.
Rear horse still at Erlang River.[27]

or, with the addition of a fifth line:

Yugong tie qiao | *wo shou nei,*
Wo ba Taihang | *dang gu lei;*
Kuai ma jia bian | *xue Dazhai,*
Xiang gu hai xu | *jia zhong chui.*
Lei de Taiyang | *fang guanghui.*

[26] *Hong qi geyao* [Songs of the red flag], compiled by Guo Moruo and Zhou Yang (Peking: Hong qi zazhi she, 1959) presents the most representative of these songs. Translated by A. C. Barnes (Peking: Foreign Languages Press, 1961).

[27] *Hong qi geyao,* p. 209; Kai-yu Hsu, *Twentieth Century Chinese Poetry* (Ithaca: Cornell University Press, 1970), p. 442.

Foolish old man iron pick, seize in hand,
I take Mt. Taihang, as drum to beat;
Fast horse add whipping, study Dazhai,
Loud drum still need, add heavy stick.
Beat Taihang so that issue light shine![28]

"Wode shan'ge shizai duo" [Many, many are my songs] is a typical folk-song duet sung by a man and a woman:

Woman: *Lou ti duo le | nan shang lou,*
Shan ge duo le | nan qi tou;
Na ge qi tou | chang yi shou
He ta yi nian | chang dao tou.

Stairs too many, hard go up,
Mountain song too many, hard begin;
Which one begin, sing one song,
With him one year, sing to end.

Man: *Zhao zhao ri ri | xiang chang ge,*
Wo de shan ge | shi zai duo;
Jiu pa mei men | bu hui chang,
Jiu pa mei men | bu gan huo.

Morning morning day day, want sing song,
My mountain song, really many;
Only fear sisters not know how sing,
Only fear sisters not do work.[29]

The New Ci-fu *Style*

The form known as the new *ci-fu* style, which has been very effectively cultivated by poets such as Guo Xiaochuan and Li Ying, has actually been experimented with since May Fourth times. The traditional *ci-fu* style called for basically hexasyllabic lines, interspersed with tetrasyllabic lines to break the monotony and to effect the changes in pace necessary in a long poem. The basic prosodic unit remained the quatrain, with *a b a b* end rhymes, but occasionally there could be a heptasyllabic line and a different end-rhyme pattern to provide variety. The new *ci-fu* style has a varying number of quatrains in rather long, segmental lines. The pauses in each line create the same rhythmic effect as the stressed syllables in the traditional *ci-fu* poem. The Crescent poet Xu Zhimo used it to rhapsodize about his little garden in "Shihu hutong diqihao" [No. 7, Stone Tiger

[28] *Shikan* 1 (January 1978): 27.
[29] *Shikan* 2 (February 1964): 28.

Lane],[30] Wang Tongzhao used it for an ode to the wind that howls over the Inner Mongolian desert,[31] and even Zang Kejia found it suitable in 1934 for his lament on autumn.[32] All these poems owe much to one of the traditional characteristics of *ci-fu*—a sweeping but well-cadenced outpour of feeling anchored on one object or one single impression around which the poet builds a kaleidoscopic web of associated images.

Among the more recent successful uses of this form is Guo Xiaochuan's "Ke zai Beidahuangde tudishang" [Carved on North Wasteland].[33] The sixty-eight-line poem in seventeen quatrains starts with a sonorous declaration:

Jicheng xiaquba, women houdaide zisun!
Zhe shi yibi yonghengde caichan—qianqiu wangu changxin;
Gengyun xiaquba, weilai shijiede zhuren!
Zhe shi yipian shenqide tudi—renjian tianshang nanxun.

Inherit it, go on, our future children and children's children!
This is a perpetual endowment—a thousand autumns, ten thousand past years, always new;
Till it, go on, future world's masters!
This is a sacred miraculous land—on earth, in heaven, hard to find.

The perfectly symmetrical arrangement of the lines tends to reinforce the cadence, as repeatedly pushing a swing at exactly regular intervals amplifies its arc. The number of syllables and the syntactical structures in lines 1 and 3 are identical, as are those of lines 2 and 4. The bisyllabic expressions in the second halves of lines 2 and 4 contribute to the regularity of the cadence, and the last rhyming word in this first stanza of the poem carries a rising tone, which compels a lower voice in preparation for the next stanza. Over half of the stanzas end on a rising tone, including the very last stanza of the poem; the effect is of a continuing, unfinished song. Since the last stanza repeats the opening stanza, the feeling is that the poet has but chanted one cycle of a song that has endless cycles still to come.

Structurally, every stanza in this poem follows the same pattern. The melody is ponderous but the rhythmic effect is very contagious:

This land once was an abandoned mother,
And the waters in the lake, her eyes gazing at the closing dusk.
This land once was an innocent exile,
Cocking his ears, the empty valleys, to await the sound of every footstep.

[30] Hsu, *Twentieth Century Chinese Poetry*, p. 85.

[31] Ibid., p. 262.

[32] Ibid., p. 285.

[33] Guo Xiaochuan, *Ganzhelin qingshazhang* [Sugarcane forest] (Peking, 1963), pp. 3–7. Translated by Kai-yu Hsu in *The Literature of the People's Republic of China*, pp. 685–687.

This is a magic land, one not easily found in heaven or on earth. The thematic stage, the wasteland of North China, is seen in its past as a forgotten mother or an exiled citizen. It is thus ready to undergo its present heroic and dramatic transformation when the revolutionaries come to develop it, making the desert bloom and restoring the land to its deserved glory.

Using freer rhyming schemes but keeping this general form, Li Ying has written many noteworthy verses. His "Gaoshan shaosuo" [Lookout post on mountaintop] carries on the *fu* tradition, although perhaps in miniature, since it contains only forty lines. But it has all the trappings of *fu*, with its extensive imagery built around a single object:

> Since when
> Did this immense sea suddenly cease rolling;
> Severe, majestic, and craggy at their extreme
> Are the mountains, these frozen waves.
> Lo! Look at them, each thrusting into the sky,
> Black, dark brown, and through them, patches of steel gray.
> Over there, on the steepest peak
> Perches in majesty an outpost of our warriors.[34]

Younger poets are following this lead. Yu Li's fifty-two-line "Ke zai Bancangshanshang" [Carved on Bancang Mountain] is a worthy echo of Guo Xiaochuan and Li Ying. Even the title parallels that of Guo's poem quoted above.

> On Bancang Mountain, the morning glow is like a commuter,
> Rising with the sun, every day, reporting for duty punctually.
> Up the mountain it unfurls a sky full of bright clouds to decorate the orchards,
> Down the mountain it pours countless shafts of rays to dye the Dazhai flags red.
>
> On Bancang, the morning glow stays close to us,
> As we walk over that mountain trail, there stands the house where she once stayed.
> That tree, those flowers, will talk with you, intimately:
> Comrades, can you see that flame leaping over there?[35]

The "she" in the poem refers to Yang Kaihui, Mao Zedong's wife, whose martyrdom became a legend particularly in the years following the downfall of Jiang Qing. The poem is built around the image and story of a woman in a way that provides a most rewarding contrast to Feng Zhi's

[34] Li Ying, *Honghua manshan* [Red flowers all over the mountain] (Peking, 1973), pp. 6–8. Translated by Kai-yu Hsu in *The Literature of the People's Republic of China*, pp. 937–938.

[35] *Shikan* 3 (March 1977): 66–67.

"Weiman" [The drape].[36] Feng's poem illustrates early May Fourth romanticism: soft sentiment, personal devotion, love at first sight and love eternal, fatalism, and so on. The work by Yu Li cited above, however, exemplifies contemporary revolutionary romanticism, whose heroic, exaggerated commitment to a sociopolitical cause excludes the individual's concern over his or her private affairs.

Traditional Forms: Shi, Ci, *and* Sanqu

Traditional forms of Chinese poetry are still very much in vogue among certain groups of writers. The *shi* form, perfected during the Tang dynasty, has been perpetuated in three major modes. The ancient style has a varying number of tetrasyllabic, pentasyllabic, or, less often, heptasyllabic lines; the rhyme usually falls on the even-numbered lines. The so-called modern style—modern because it became popular in the seventh century—is further divided into the *jueju* ("cut-short verse"), with quatrains of pentasyllabic or heptasyllabic lines, and the *lüshi* ("regulated verse"), with eight pentasyllabic or heptasyllabic lines each having strict prosodic and rhetorical requirements. The standard regulated verse, such as written by Du Fu, presents two perfectly matched parallel couplets in the second and third pair of lines. Most of the great Tang poems are in one or the other modern *shi* form.

The *ci* form reached its zenith during the Song dynasty. Each *ci* (sometimes translated as "a lyric in irregular meter"), is a song either adapted from a popular tune or composed by the poet-musician. Once the tunes became established, later poets had to write lyrics to them, deploying the words (syllables) to fit the exact musical requirement of each line. Some great masters of *ci* did alter the tunes to achieve new musical effects, and their innovations have become established as variations on the theme. But most writers just accomodate themselves to the existing tunes, of which some 400 are still extant—though only as patterns, not in the form of musical notation.

Chinese poets have been writing in *shi* or *ci* forms from the Tang–Song era down to the present day. Most of the older contemporary poets, such as Mao Zedong and Zhao Puchu, have never written verse in any other form, while May Fourth poets such as Guo Moruo, Feng Zhi, and Rao Mengkan, if they continued to write poems at all, put their occasional verses in these forms. Old revolutionary leaders, generals, and statesmen, from the late foreign minister Chen Yi to General Zhang Aiping, have been passing poems in these styles privately among their friends and from time to time publishing a few of them. Some new writers have also tried these forms, although most of their attempts, even when undertaken seri-

[36] Hsu, *Twentieth Century Chinese Poetry*, pp. 143–148.

ously, sound like playful *dayoushi,* or doggerel. Interest in these old forms was so noticeable in 1979 that a proposal was made in Peking to found another national poetry journal devoted exclusively to *shi* and *ci.*[37]

Mao Zedong's advice to use not these forms but well-formulated images from traditional poetry, confusing though it may be, has encouraged such practitioners as Zhao Puchu or Ye Jianying (Ye is most senior surviving Red Army commander and a former acting head of state). Zhao's expert *shi* and *ci* are frequently published in the national press, but his efforts violate just about every rule the May Fourth writers tried to establish about clarity, plain talk, avoidance of obscure allusions, and so on. Witness Zhao's poem on Zhou Enlai's death:

A great star falls from midsky,
All four seas surge in startled waves.
The last thread of hope severed,
Leaves us in perpetual sorrow.
Your dedicated life was in travail to the very end,
And care and toil worked hardship on your years.
Who in history could measure up to your statesmanship?
Your loyal heart shared the sun's glory.
Selfless, your merit rose high by itself,
Humility only added to your heroic stature.
The huge roc soars on great winds
While the tiny wren in weeds could only eye you with envy.
I, though ashamed of my feeble ability,
Have striven to offer my limited best.
Often I thought of your kind teaching,
Of it I always reminded myself in my life.
I mourn today, not because of our private friendship,
My tears are shed for a national sorrow.[38]

Though this is a competent poem couched in rather graceful language and cast in the mode of ancient-style *shi,* with pentasyllabic lines, in it Zhao has used a number of traditional images and expressions that are not immediately clear to the uninitiated. The big roc and the wren in the weeds come from the *Zhuangzi,* the second oldest Taoist text (it is perhaps two thousand years old), which requires a high level of literacy. It is true that Mao Zedong's poem of 1965, "Niaor wenda" [The birds' dialogue], put these allusions into circulation. However, there are other lines equally or more obscure. (Clarification of these obscurities in translation is unavoidable.) *Sun ling meng* in the sixth line and *hengju wei zisong* in the sixteenth line, translated above as, respectively, "worked hardship on your

[37] Interview with Bi Shuowang, head of the foreign liaison committee of the Chinese Writers' Association, 17 September 1979, in Iowa City.

[38] *Shikan* 1 (January 1977): 14–15.

years" and "I always reminded myself in my life" (or, "I always reminded myself throughout my quiet life"), are certainly not *baihua* (plain talk). The other poem Zhao published with this one is even worse; he had to provide four footnotes to clarify three of its ten short lines.

Among the new imitations of traditional styles we cannot forget those posted at the spontaneous demonstration in memory of Zhou Enlai in Tiananmen Square on April 5, 1976. Some of them, such as the following which is admittedly one of the very best of the collection, come close to being inspired poetry. The immediacy of the experience and the intensity of feeling are effectively communicated in simple but forceful images; and the language, while very compact, flows freely:

Yu bei | wen gui jiao,
Wo ku | cai lang xiao.
Sa lei | ji xiong jie,
Yan mei | jian chu xiao.

I sorrow, I hear ghosts howl,
I cry, the wolves laugh.
I shed tears mourning the hero,
My eyebrows raised, I draw my sword.[39]

But some of the other poems strike a note more comic than somber, closer to a light-hearted nursery rhyme than to a dirge written in sorrow or in anger. As such they are quite inappropriate for the occasion:

Zongli xingxiang | zhen weida,
Renmin jingyang | diren pa.
Weihe sheng pa | si ye pa?
Zhi yin renmin | liliang da.

The premier's image is truly great,
The people respect him, the enemies fear him.
Why do they fear him, in life as well as in death?
Just because the people's strength is great.[40]

Furthermore, this is inadequate as a poem because it fails to arrest the reader's imagination with any evocative imagery. It is singable, with its repeated rhyming words, but, as with numerous other insignificant folk-songs in the same form, there is not much else in it.

Sanqu, or "free songs," the arias of Yuan drama, have a direct lineage from *ci,* but are greatly enriched by the tunes used in folk drama. Origi-

[39] *Shikan* 11 (November 1978): 30.

[40] Ibid., p. 32. Translations of some of these poems are in *The Tiananmen Poems,* edited and translated by Xiao Lan (Peking: Foreign Languages Press, 1979).

nally a suite of songs arranged to present characters and to carry a story line, *sanqu* later developed into an independent poetic form. Ma Zhiyuan's (fl. 1330) elegant *xiaoling* (little tunes) were the forerunners of *xiaodiao* (small songs), the more prosaic and bluntly, sometimes even coarsely, expressive popular songs of the cities and countryside.

The singable quality of *sanqu* has been effectively exploited by the contemporary poet Liu Zheng, who specializes in satirical and humorous verse. During the Cultural Revolution he remained silent, but his satires, though limited in their targets, have returned since 1976. One of his poems is cast as a scene in a modern *zaju* (Yuan "vari-drama"):

> Calling on the flies,
> Asking the ants,
> Scooping dry all the outhouses,
> Searching through all garbage piles.
> Ah, finally, we've found you!
> Let's not bother about your turning in a blank bluebook,
> You have the greatest courage in opposing the tide.
> Clearly you are number one in the world,
> How can we flunk you?
> Come, come, come,
> Come backstage and let us teach you in secret a scheme to get on top of the world with one leap.[41]

These lines are sung by four characters, the Four Tyrants (Gang of Four), who enact onstage their scheme to pick an ignorant but obedient applicant to serve as their lackey. The verse refers to an actual controversy over a student who, upholding the Gang of Four policy of rebellion, refused to hand in his bluebook during a college entrance examination; at the time he won the case with the support of the Gang of Four faction.

Sets of Poems

Zushi, or sets of poems, have appeared frequently in recent publications. There are no formal requirements for such sets, except that the poet generally writes them on or around one subject, such as a trip to a memorable site. The set, "Zhungeer yangguang" [Sunshine at Zhungeer],[42] which Yu Li published in January 1979, includes four poems. Each has four quatrains, all of which are related to an experience in northern Xinjiang. Liang Shangquan's "Hexi zoulang bubu ge" [Songs step by step along the corridor west of the Yellow River Bend], also published in January 1979, has nine poems. They vary in length and form but were all inspired by the poet's visit to the frontier region on the ancient silk road.[43]

[41] *Shikan* 11 (November 1977): 61–62.
[42] *Shikan* 1 (January 1979): 42–45.
[43] Ibid., pp. 49–53.

COMMON THEMES SINCE 1949

Like all the other literary genres, poetry has had to respond fully to the political needs and campaigns of the time: the anti-rightist campaigns to suppress the opposition; the rectification campaigns to heighten political vigilance; the youth-rustification campaigns to send young students to the countryside and keep them there; the ephemeral literary thaw known as the Hundred Flowers movement; and, currently, the Four Modernizations movement. The poets have been adapting whatever they write to reflect the ongoing political line. Some succeed in turning out poetry that is good despite its obvious political message; others produce pieces not much more than occasional poems, obviously written simply because there was an official occasion calling for such expressions. Thus, in the issue of the national *Poetry Journal* published in August 1976, only a few weeks before the downfall of the Gang of Four, panegyrics praising Mao appeared on forty-four of its ninety-six pages, and condemnation of Liu Shaoqi and Deng Xiaoping stood out prominently in ten of its twenty-four poems. Four months later, the same journal had become conspicuously more modest about Mao but overgenerous with its adulation of Zhou Enlai, Deng Xiaoping, and Hua Guofeng.

Serious revolutionary experiences are usually recounted in longer poems. Tian Jian's "Qianli si" [Thoughts, thousands of miles away][44] tells of the bitter experience of a poor peasant who had to sell his wife and three daughters; Zhang Zhimin's "Leitai" [Contest platform][45] portrays a memorable segment of the history of land reform; and Zou Difan's "Lao daniangde kang" [The old aunt's *kang*][46] depicts life in the countryside on the eve of Liberation.

Most noteworthy are the verses that focus on some aspect of proletarian life and that ring with genuine joy and excitement. These feelings are tangible in Tang Datong's songs of river boatmen, in Li Ying's lyrics on a day in a soldier's life, and in Feng Jingyuan's works on the tempering of steel. The Paul-Bunyanesque stature of the porter in such a new folksong as "Wo shi yige zhuangxiegong" [I'm a longshoreman][47] can be most attractive, as can the folk humor of "Yige hongshu gunxia po" [A sweet potato rolls off the hill].[48] Demanding that barren rocks grow grain, building dikes to harness troublesome rivers, and other equally impressive feats performed by heroic common people are perennial subjects. Legends of

[44] *Shikan* 1 (January 1964): 4–7.

[45] *Shikan* 8 (August 1963): 4–16. Translated by Kai-yu Hsu in *The Literature of the People's Republic of China*, pp. 653–664.

[46] Hsu, *The Chinese Literary Scene*, pp. 200–202.

[47] Hsu, *Twentieth Century Chinese Poetry*, p. 451.

[48] Ibid., p. 454.

ethnic minorities, some in translation, have stayed in favor, as have accounts of visits to frontier areas.

By the end of 1976, a few satirical and humorous verses had returned following the bleak days of the Cultural Revolution. Love poems, however, have been few since 1949, and the very few such pieces printed have aroused controversies similar to that which surrounded the poem "Detour," cited above. The recent discussions of the role of love in literature have been accompanied by a few new love poems.

AT THE END OF THE 1970s

The search continues for ideal forms that will allow poets to develop their voices fully, and there has been a rich variety of innovations. The cautious liberalization of the late 1970s holds out a promise to the 1980s. Classics, both Chinese and Western, have been reissued: works of proven worth that had been blacklisted during the Cultural Revolution have been republished, and a stream of selected contemporary Western poetry is appearing in Chinese bookstores. Shakespeare is once again popular, and T. S. Eliot need no longer be read in secret. The trend is indeed encouraging, though not without impediments.

While ideological dicta are likely to remain overall guidelines, they are now susceptible to a rather wide spectrum of interpretations. Zhou Enlai's speech of 1961 did not contradict the Yan'an "Talks," but its release in 1979 encouraged a clamor for the relaxation of controls that in other times could easily have caused another wave of purges. What if times change? Barely two months after the publicizing of Zhou's speech, the "Democracy Wall" in the populous western district of Peking had become a center of controversy. The official attitude which first tolerated or even encouraged the unofficial literature and political statements pasted up on the wall soon changed. The editors of the more outspoken journals have been arrested, tried, and condemned. By the end of the year, Democracy Wall had been removed to a more remote spot. On January 1, 1980, Deng Xiaoping accused some protesters of using democracy to camouflage their goal of disrupting the nation's unity and progress.[49] So long as literature, like every other human endeavor in China, must serve only one political purpose—which, at the moment, is the four modernizations—the specter of brutal control through mob action that reached its frightening worst during the 1960s could raise its ugly head again at any time.

Critics have begun to break the habit, established in 1949, of referring constantly to the Yan'an "Talks on Literature and Art." Until very recently, every word uttered by Mao on literature in general and on poetry

[49] *China Daily News* (New York), 8 January, 1980, p. 4.

in particular echoed through these critics' essays. The handful of poems that Mao allowed to be published were given the most thorough and diligent critical attention, as though they were the highest and only models of poetry for the nation to emulate. Inspired by Mao's letter to Chen Yi, some critics started referring to the classical tenets laid down by such old authorities as Zhong Hong (fl. ca. 504, author of *Shipin*) and Liu Xie (fl. ca. 530, author of *Wenxin diaolong*).[50] This trend leaves us still eagerly awaiting the formulation of some new, valid artistic criteria. Indeed, at times we may wonder if some of the new critics are sufficiently familiar with classical Chinese poetry. One of them even praised as fresh and new a few lines that Chen Yi had copied from the eleventh-century poet Li Zhiyi. These lines form the lyrics to a popular song that every Chinese person (outside the PRC) has known for years.[51]

Poets today stress the importance of imagery. I have discussed elsewhere the promising development of visceral rather than intellectual responses to such beautiful but stock images inherited from classical Chinese poetry as the arrival of autumn and the fading of flowers.[52] The development is promising because it raises new evocative power from old images. Unfortunately, here too the poetic well threatens to run dry too soon. A newcomer, Jiang Zhou, sees pearls when he looks at the electric light in a commune:

Now our commune's power plant towers high,
The pearls fall into our village from the sky.[53]

Twenty years ago, in *Songs of the Red Flag,* other proletarian poets had seen the same pearls, as have many others in between.[54] Another new-

[50] An example is Xie Mian's review of the poems published in *Shikan* during 1976–1977: *Shikan* 3 (March 1978), pp. 83–88. In the early 1960s, the journal even carried a column of "poetry talk," which reprinted some traditional reading notes written by erudite scholars and poets in high-flown *wenyan* (the classical Chinese language).

[51] *Shikan* 8 (August 1977): 88. The eleventh-century poet's verse is (roughly translated):

You live at the river's source;
I live at the river's mouth.
Every day I think of you but cannot see you,
Though we drink from the same river.

Chen Yi's poem reads:

I live at the river's source;
You live at the river's mouth.
With unlimited feeling between us,
We drink from the same river.

[52] See introduction in Kai-yu Hsu, ed., *The Literature of the People's Republic of China,* pp. 8–9.

[53] *Shikan* 11 (November 1978): 59–60.

[54] Chai Qingshan, "Dengde xiagu" [Valley of lamps], in *Zhan you han* [The battle is still intense] (Peking, 1974), p. 171.

comer, Bao Yutang, wrote a poem entitled "Gehai chunchao gungun lai" [The springtide rolls on and on in the sea of songs],[55] in which he saw the Goddess of Mount Wu startled by the new society. Mao saw much the same vision in 1956, in his poem "Youyong" [Swimming], and other proletarian poets have also invited the lady into their verses.[56] The carrying pole, which became an impressive image of proletarian heroism in 1958, has since found too many pale imitations.[57] Such examples could be multiplied ad infinitum. Small wonder that, at times, the writers themselves complain of "collisions"—of two poets writing on the same theme, using the same form and the same images.[58]

The push towards popularization in poetry in the 1950s and 1960s was a mixed success. The so-called "debates" on form continued to keep alive the issue of which path vernacular literature should follow, but failed to resolve it. Certainly in this period a wide variety of poetic forms flourished, including classical, folk, popular, and modern. The same is true, to a lesser extent and in reduced quantity, of the seventies, especially after 1975.[59] Post-1949 Chinese poetry is also distinguished by the extremely wide range of authors whose work has found its way into the official media, from elderly generals to student protesters, from senior intellectuals to workers and peasants. In this sense, poetry continues to be a "popular" art in China in a way now almost unknown in the West. The search for an ideal form, in poetry as in everything else, will never be realized, but perhaps the discoveries made in the course of searching are what really matter. In this light, the tireless (though at times tiring) talk about poetic forms holds promise for the future of poetry in China.

[55] *Shikan* 12 (December 1978): 38–39.

[56] See Huang Shangxiao's poem, for example, in *Tiaoshan danhai gen dang zou* [Carrying the mountain and sea on my shoulders I follow the Party] (Peking, 1974), p. 11.

[57] Ibid., p. 10, and in *Shanghai min'ge xuan* [Selected folksongs of Shanghai] (Shanghai, 1973), p. 84.

[58] *Shikan* 8 (August 1977): 89.

[59] Hsu, *The Chinese Literary Scene,* pp. 165–264, and McDougall, "Poems, Poets, and *Poetry* 1976," especially pp. 93–99.

Part III

Three Decades in Historical Perspective

TWELVE

Writers and Performers, Their Works, and Their Audiences in the First Three Decades

Bonnie S. McDougall

The essays in this volume suggest a common theme around which a general cultural history of the period 1949–1979 can be constructed: the attempted transformation, consciously implemented by the new state, of an elitist, author-centered culture (i.e., one designed by authors) into a mass, audience-centered culture (i.e., one designed by or for the audience). This transformation could be carried out in three ways: by controlling authors, by controlling their work, or by controlling their audiences. All three ways have been tried. Authors and also performers became state functionaries under Party or other control, so that their intellectual and artistic autonomy could be undermined by political demands. Such audience-centered genres as the performing arts were given new respectability as legitimate elements in the creation of a new national culture and even, at one time, almost completely supplanted the more author-centered literary arts. The audience to which writers and artists were to address themselves was first defined extremely narrowly and then declared to be the only audience. Furthermore, the official conception of the needs and wants of that audience was more often based on theory than on ascertainable fact.

In pursuing this new national culture, writers, performers, and Party leaders turned increasingly to Chinese traditional culture for legitimation, inspiration, and concrete models. This tendency first began during the War of Resistance to Japan (1937–1945), was formalized during the Yan'an period (1942–1947), received new encouragement during the Great Leap Forward (1958–1959), and culminated in the Cultural Revolution and its

I wish to thank T. D. Huters for having read through this paper and offered many valuable suggestions, most of which have been gratefully adopted. He bears no responsibility for any errors that remain.

aftermath (1966–1976). This "great return" (to use Cyril Birch's expression) was a highly selective one, as many of the essays in this volume point out, and non-Chinese elements were not easily discarded from even the most radical creations of the new culture. Nevertheless, from the perspective of the 1980s, China's search for precedents from its popular tradition to use in creating a new, modern, national, and popular culture was the most significant underlying trend of the preceding three decades.

THE BEGINNINGS, 1949–1966

Writers and Performing Artists: Social and Political Roles[1]

Literature and its related performing arts were mobilized to support the new state in China early in 1949, even before the formal promulgation of the new People's Republic. Writers and performers who had distinguished themselves in the previous decades were given assurance of an honored place in the new society. The cordiality shown toward them was part of a general policy to welcome intellectuals, even though some of the performers were not intellectuals in the sense of having received a scholastic liberal-arts or professional education. Many who, like Hou Baolin, were masters of the popular performing arts had not hitherto been included in the limited circle of writer-intellectuals from the May Fourth tradition. But no matter whether their former positions were elevated or humble, the writers and performers were offered security and welcome in the new society. The great majority accepted the offer.

Over the decade and a half leading up to the Cultural Revolution, it began to appear that for some, especially among the famous May Fourth figures, this acceptance had been limited or partial. Some, like Shen Congwen and Qian Zhongshu, abandoned their writing careers, voluntarily or otherwise, and disappeared into the relative obscurity of universities

[1] There is a great dearth of information about the material and social conditions of Chinese writers and performers (especially the latter), which seriously hampers the study of their political role and artistic production. In this section, I have relied heavily on Franz Schurmann, *Ideology and Organization in Communist China,* 2d ed. (Berkeley: University of California Press, 1970), for information on intellectuals in the administrative apparatus, from which I have extrapolated writers' conditions. For a close-up of the workings of the apparatus on the provincial level, see Ezra Vogel, *Canton under Communism: Programs and Politics in a Provincial Capital, 1949–1968* (Cambridge, Mass.: Harvard University Press, 1969). For a general history of writers as state and Party functionaries, see Lars Ragvald, *Yao Wenyuan as a Literary Critic: The Emergence of Chinese Zhdanovism* (Stockholm: Stockholm University, Institute of Oriental Languages, 1978) and "Professionalism and Amateur Tendencies in Post-Revolutionary Chinese Literature," in Göran Malmqvist, ed., *Modern Chinese Literature and its Social Context* [Stockholm: Nobel Foundation, 1977], pp. 152–179. For the ideological and political debates of the 1950s, see D. W. Fokkema, *Literary Doctrine in China and Soviet Influence, 1956–1960* (The Hague: Mouton, 1965), and Merle Goldman, *Literary Dissent in Communist China* (Cambridge, Mass.: Harvard University Press, 1967).

and museums. Many continued to play a role in public literary life but as academics, critics, and literary bureaucrats rather than as creative writers. This group included some of the most distinguished names of the 1930s: Mao Dun, Wu Zuxiang, Ding Ling. Only a handful, such as Zang Kejia and Tian Jian, kept up their creative writing past the first few years of the new society. Others, such as Guo Moruo and He Qifang, soon abandoned their May Fourth identities and, as often as not, cast their sporadic contributions to the national press in the traditional styles.

As the writers and performers settled down in their new positions and began to exercise the new functions delegated to them by the state, some were able to consolidate their previous power, some achieved new eminence, and others were banished from the (geographic or political) center as scapegoats when their and their colleagues' stumbling experiments in policy formation failed. Nevertheless, what is remarkable about the Chinese literary and performing arts establishment (with a few important exceptions) is that, up to their common engulfment in the Cultural Revolution, they all, from distinguished leaders to humblest novitiates, remained loyal to the interests of the state and to its rulers. None of them offered opposition except, as during the Hundred Flowers movement of 1956–1957, at the express invitation of the state. The most noteworthy literary attack on state power came not from the professional creative writers but from politically active intellectuals such as the historian and vice-mayor of Peking, Wu Han, and the Party organizer and journalist, Deng Tuo.[2] In line with Chinese tradition, much of Wu Han's and Deng Tuo's political criticism was in literary form—a fact that, incidentally, underlines the failure of writers in this regard.

The organization and administration of control or censorship over Chinese writers and performers has not been systematically described or analyzed. Some Western scholars speak loosely of censorship as emanating from a single unit at the center, though this does not seem to be the case either on the mainland or in Taiwan.[3] On the mainland, directives to

[2] For literary and other dissent in the 1950s and early 1960s, see Fokkema, *Literary Doctrine*; Goldman, *Literary Dissent*; Peter Moody, *Opposition and Dissent in Contemporary China* (Stanford: Hoover Institution Press, 1977); Bonnie S. McDougall, "Dissent Literature and Contemporary China: Varieties of Official and Non-Official Literature in and about China in the Seventies," *Contemporary China* 3, 4 (Winter 1979): 49–79. For Wu Han and Deng Tuo, see Timothy Cheek, "Deng Tuo: Culture, Leninism and Alternative Marxism in the Chinese Communist Party," *China Quarterly* 87 (September 1981): 470–491.

[3] The official policy of the Republic of China is that there is no censorship either before or after publication. However, the Government Information Office of the Executive Yuan has a publications department that "supervises and controls" publications and a motion pictures department that censors films. According to the constitution, the national budget must allot 15 percent of its expenditure to educational programs, scientific studies, and cultural services; this policy indicates a considerable level of state involvement in cultural affairs (*China Year-*

writers and performers, and the pressure to observe these directives, are apparently sent from the center down in several different ways and are implemented at different levels with varying degrees of severity.

One important control mechanism is the recruitment of writers and artists into the state's cultural apparatus and the supervision of their activities through the professional associations. The Ministry of Culture and other governmental institutions, such as the universities and academies, are dominated by a mixture of famous literary figures (Mao Dun, Guo Moruo) and Party personnel with a background in the arts (Lin Mohan, Zhou Yang, Yu Huiyong). The professional associations, such as the Chinese Writers' Association, are described as voluntary mass organizations, though in fact membership is strictly by invitation only. The professional associations are nominally responsible to the Chinese National Federation of Writers and Artists, but this umbrella organization possesses little substantive power. Instead, it is believed that the associations, like the academies, are supervised by and responsible to the Party's Central Committee.[4] Writers and performers who accept membership in the associations and carry out the tasks assigned to them by the state are quite generously rewarded.[5]

A second control mechanism is the recruitment of writers and performers directly into the Party itself. Unlike its counterpart in the U.S.S.R., the Party leadership in China has always included men of some literary cultivation. Such men had received a traditional elite education in their childhood, together with some Western education in the 1910s and 1920s. Similarly, many writers and literary critics of the 1930s threw in their lot with the Communists before 1949 and acted as leading Party spokesmen after 1949. There is, therefore, a considerable overlap in literary and Party personnel through the post-Liberation period.

A third important control mechanism is the public campaign, which usually involves an attack, organized by the Party cultural authorities, on a

book, 1978 [Taipei: China Publishing Company, 1978], pp. 282, 258, 648, 662). For instances of censorship in Taiwan, see articles by John Israel, Mei Wen-li, and Lucy H. Chen in Mark Mancall, ed., *Formosa Today* (New York: Praeger, 1964), and Mab Huang, *Intellectual Ferment for Political Reforms in Taiwan, 1971–1973* (Ann Arbor: University of Michigan Center for Chinese Studies, 1976).

[4] Howard L. Boorman, "The Literary World of Mao Tse-tung," in Cyril Birch, ed., *Communist Chinese Literature* (New York: Praeger, 1963), p. 28.

[5] Only scattered information is available about the methods and scales of payment. The subject is treated in Paul Bady, "The Modern Chinese Writer: Literary Incomes and Best Sellers", *China Quarterly* 88 (December 1981): 645–657, and in Ragvald, *Yao Wenyuan,* passim. Apart from royalty payments, salaries, trips within the country and abroad, and other special perquisites, rewards could also include publication of a writer's collected works, such as those for Guo Moruo, Ye Shengtao, Mao Dun, and Ba Jin in 1957–1958: see Fokkema, *Literary Doctrine,* p. 149 et passim. Performers were also treated as national celebrities, and the more famous were made members of the National People's Congress.

specially targeted scapegoat. The scapegoat and his or her associates may be punished extremely harshly to serve as a warning to others, and the evidence is that this form of intimidation is successful. Thus, control or censorship is exercised in manifold and often subtle ways and is largely administered by writers or Party officials with some literary experience. The mixture of rewards for conforming with many kinds of pressure and the fear of public attack and punishment has proved a very effective control device.

The process of absorbing intellectuals in general into state organs began very soon after the new state's establishment. Between October 1949 and September 1952, over two million people were recruited into the new administrative system. The Party had to look beyond its own resources to find administrators for the new state bureaucracy. These were drawn from three major sources: worker and peasant activists, new graduates of higher and middle schools, and the old intelligentsia. The Party may have wished otherwise, but it needed the old intelligentsia to cope with the greatly expanded state apparatus.[6] Writers had their special functions as professional intellectuals: staffing publishing houses and editorial boards, teaching and conducting writers' workshops, publicizing the policies and achievements of the new society within the country, representing their country abroad, and receiving foreign visitors at home. Performing artists shared in these or similar activities. How useful the cultural workers were in most of these functions depended on their level of professional skills and on their observable social prestige. Hence, their living conditions and salaries were appreciably higher than those of the average worker.[7] As members of a professional intelligentsia, they benefited from the respect that experts or specialists had enjoyed since China became interested in Western technology in the twentieth century. This respect had been further reinforced after 1949 when the Party set the ideological goal of rapidly creating a fully industrialized modern society in China.[8] The writers also inherited from traditional Chinese culture the ancient respect accorded masters of the written word.[9]

Two elites were growing up in China in the 1950s: the red elite of the Party cadres, who had political power, and the expert elite, whose education gave them exclusive knowledge. In 1956, out of a total population of over 600,000,000 only 3,840,000 were classified as intellectuals (defined as graduates of higher middle schools and up); of these, 500,000 were

[6] Schurmann, *Ideology and Organization,* pp. 167–168.

[7] For some information on duties and remunerations of writers in the 1950s, see Ragvald, "Professionalism," pp. 153–156, 157–158, 160.

[8] Schurmann, *Ideology and Organization,* p. 51; Vogel, *Canton under Communism,* pp. 127–128.

[9] Fokkema, *Literary Doctrine,* p. 58.

classed as "technicians" and only 100,000 as "higher intellectuals."[10] Writers (numbering less than 1000) and performers were presumably included in the latter group, along with university professors and so on.[11] Thus, the higher intellectuals constituted only about .1 percent of the total population, while Party membership formed a significantly higher 1.79 percent. The percentage of Party members was, therefore, roughly equivalent to that of the gentry elite in the old society.[12]

The existence of these two elites, political and expert, was a constant source of tension throughout the 1950s and 1960s. The "thought reform" campaign of the early 1950s was an unsuccessful attempt to merge the two into a single group of educated, politically committed state functionaries. Zhou Enlai recognized the failure of this policy in a speech of January 1956, in which he promised more autonomy and better conditions to intellectuals in return for their support of Party policies. Zhou's speech had been foreshadowed by a series of articles by intellectuals in *Renmin ribao* [People's daily]. The articles had called on the cadres to improve their attitudes toward intellectuals and for improvements in intellectuals' working conditions—in particular, for more pay and better equipment.[13]

As a mark of the Party's new hospitality toward intellectuals, in the period between Zhou's speech and the end of the Hundred Flowers movement in 1957, they were recruited into the Party itself at a higher rate than any other social group (49 percent of the recruits over this period were intellectuals). In 1956 intellectuals constituted some 11.7 percent of Party members; by 1957 this had risen to 14.78 percent. An occupational survey of the Party in 1956 showed that people in cultural and educational positions formed 3.8 percent of the Party membership; presumably this figure also increased in 1957.[14] According to Zhou Enlai in 1956, only some 40 percent of the 100,000 higher intellectuals actively supported the Party; however, the overwhelming majority of intellectuals had already become "government workers in the service of Socialism."[15] By the mid-1950s, the intellectuals had already formed a small but well-entrenched social elite

[10] Schurmann, *Ideology and Organization,* pp. 8, 11–12, 51, 93, 96, 132–139.

[11] Ragvald, "Professionalism," pp. 160, 167; Liu Baiyu, "Wei fanying wenxue chuangzuo er fendou," *Wenyi bao* 5–6 (March 1956): 29–33.

[12] See Chung-li Chang, *The Chinese Gentry: Studies on Their Role in Nineteenth Century Chinese Society* (Seattle: University of Washington Press, 1955), esp. pp. 137–141.

[13] The most detailed and up-to-date study on the years 1956–1957 is Roderick MacFarquhar, *The Origins of the Cultural Revolution: 1. Contradictions among the People 1956–1957* (London: Oxford University Press, 1974), on which I have relied heavily for the next few pages. For the Zhou Enlai speech, see pp. 33–35. See also Ragvald, "Professionalism," pp. 158–160, 167–170.

[14] Schurmann, *Ideology and Organization,* pp. 132–139.

[15] MacFarquhar, *Origins,* pp. 34, 93.

and had made progress toward penetrating the political elite. The ideal of a "red and expert" class seemed feasible.[16]

Among the other practical measures taken after Zhou Enlai's speech to encourage intellectuals were improvements in their living and working conditions; salary increases; reductions in their political, social, and administrative duties; and reductions in unemployment among the group. The Hundred Flowers campaign, launched shortly afterward, was designed to permit greater cultural variety and enjoyment, as an encouragement both to the creative writers and performers and to their intellectual audience. Nevertheless, with a few bold exceptions, intellectuals and writers showed considerable reluctance at first to take advantage of the apparent relaxation.[17]

A further and very important concession to non-Party intellectuals was Mao's willingness, first expressed at the Eighth Party Congress in September 1956, to encourage them to criticize Party members. This policy was soon given new urgency by the troubles in Eastern Europe later in the same year. There is evidence that Zhou Enlai, Deng Xiaoping, and Chen Boda supported Mao's liberal line, while Liu Shaoqi, Peng Zhen, Lu Dingyi, Peng Dehuai, and lower-ranking Party members like Deng Tuo (then chief editor of *People's Daily*) took a more authoritarian and sectarian line in their disinclination to allow open season on Party members. (Government workers, on the other hand, were considered fair game.) With opposition from within the leadership, therefore, Mao's new "rectification campaign" was officially under way by May 1, 1957. Its aim was to correct bureaucratic, sectarian, and subjective work styles among Party cadres, and testimony was earnestly solicited from non-Party intellectuals.[18]

Although the rectification was designed by Mao to promote criticism of the Party, it stirred up so much criticism of and outright opposition to the Party and its policies that the Party officials who had been suspicious about it from the very beginning were able to redirect it into an "antirightist" attack on the intellectuals who had spoken out.[19] Wu Han, presumably with the backing of his patron, Peng Zhen, wrote the first denunciation of "bourgeois rightists"—those who had accepted Mao's invitation to speak out in the "blooming and contending" of May and June 1957.[20] The number of "rightists" among students and intellectuals was estimated as about three

[16] Schurmann, *Ideology and Organization*, pp. 98–99.

[17] MacFarquhar, *Origins*, pp. 35, 51–56, 75–77, 83–85, 92–96, 200, 209.

[18] Ibid., pp. 112–116, 177–183, 186–199, 200–217, 241–249; Vogel, *Canton under Communism*, pp. 188–199; Goldman, *Literary Dissent*, pp. 187–191.

[19] For the antirightist campaign, see MacFarquhar, *Origins*, pp. 261–310; Schurmann, *Ideology and Organization*, p. 91; Fokkema, *Literary Doctrine*, pp. 147–151; Goldman, *Literary Dissent*, pp. 203–242; Ragvald, "Professionalism," pp. 170–172; Jack Chen, *Inside the Cultural Revolution* (New York: Macmillan, 1975), pp. 118–122.

[20] MacFarquhar, *Origins*, pp. 271, 277–278.

hundred thousand. Not all, but perhaps the majority of rightists were intellectuals; the term obviously took in more than just the "higher intellectuals." Mao estimated that about one-third of the rightists were primary-school teachers.[21] In the rectification and antirightist campaigns, several thousand Party members were expelled, including such Party intellectuals as Ding Ling, Ai Qing, and Feng Xuefeng. Some of the rightists, including these three, were given severe and lengthy punishment. A small percentage (26,000) had their rightist labels removed in October 1959; many others had to wait another twenty years.[22] Since the intellectuals, including writers, were the best-known and most articulate critics of the Hundred Flowers period, their suppression attracted a good deal of world attention. However, the majority of the famous intellectuals, such as the May Fourth writers, were still able to hold on to their official positions.

By the close of 1957, even Mao had lost his enthusiasm for using non-Party intellectuals to help reform the Party. The majority of the intellectuals, he found, had not yet undergone a true transformation of outlook but constituted a separate group with its own values: traditional gentry and Western values learned before 1949.[23] The criticisms they brought forward in May and June revealed not only the gap between Party ideals and practice, but pointed to an even greater gap between Maoist ideals and practice and the values of the senior intellectuals.

After 1957 the writers' social position as an elite group was more open to attack, since their autonomy threatened both the Party elite and Mao's wish to curb that elite. The next great campaign, the Great Leap Forward of 1958–1959, was accompanied by another great wave of hostility against intellectuals as professionals. They were accused of demanding exclusive control of technology, a charge that led, by extension, to attacks on professionalism in the arts. Those acting as state functionaries in the middle tier of organization were an especially easy target for the utopian radicalism of the Great Leap. Lao She and Ba Jin, despite their great prestige among their fellow intellectuals, also came under attack at this time, but their seniors, such as Mao Dun and Guo Moruo, survived these attacks as they had the antirightist campaign.[24]

The Great Leap Forward saw a new upsurge in encouragement to amateur writers, in striking contrast to Soviet policy toward writers and artists

[21] Ibid., pp. 314, 405.

[22] Ibid, p. 314; Chen, *Inside the Cultural Revolution,* p. 119. For the rehabilitation of rightists in 1978, see below.

[23] MacFarquhar, *Origins,* pp. 297–298; Schurmann, *Ideology and Organization,* pp. 16, 171; Goldman, *Literary Dissent,* pp. 201–202, 240.

[24] Schurmann, *Ideology and Organization,* pp. 72, 91; Fokkema, *Literary Doctrine,* pp. 192–196, 208–210; Goldman, *Literary Dissent,* pp. 262–263.

at that time.[25] Old May Fourth figures like Zhou Yang and Guo Moruo were quick to associate themselves with amateur writing and with the concomitant revival of interest in the native popular tradition (see below). They thus emerged with their reputations enhanced. However, the dislocations caused by the economic failure of the Leap forced the abandonment of further ambitious plans for mass writing. Professional writers were also affected by the hardships of the "three hard years" (1960–1962), but their living standards improved somewhat, relative to those of the general population, and the policy of sending intellectuals to the countryside was relaxed.[26] It was also a period of realignment in political and ideological positions. The two elite groups, Party and professional, found a common interest in maintaining a professional technical and cultural establishment against the populist line of Mao and his supporters. Mao, however, had retreated to the "second front" of Party leadership after his setbacks from the Hundred Flowers and Great Leap Forward campaigns, and in these three years the Party apparatus was dominant.

The professional writers did not use their improved status and the new relaxation, therefore, to criticize the Party, as in the 1950s. (Intellectuals such as Wu Han and Deng Tuo, however, were able to publish devastatingly satirical attacks on Mao and his policies, often in literary form.) The professional writers were concentrating on raising literary standards by creating a new definition of their audience that would allow them to address their social peers and by extending the permitted subject matter beyond the Party-imposed model of conflicts between heroes and villains. Both of these moves by writers were strongly opposed by a new group of Party-trained intellectuals—people like Yao Wenyuan who retained the spirit of radical utopianism from the Great Leap and who opposed the restoration of May Fourth intellectuals to social prestige and middle- and upper-level power in culture and education. In the early 1960s, these radicals were not permitted to express unduly harsh criticisms of writers, nor had they the political power to enforce their ideas.[27]

When Mao made his comeback to the front line of Party leadership in 1962, it was the field of literature and art to which he directed his principal attention. In the summer of 1962, he made an open attack on the literature of the last few years: "The use of novels for anti-Party activity is a great invention."[28] He did not name any particular novels or authors at

[25] For the changing policy toward amateurs in the 1950s, see Ragvald, "Professionalism"; Fokkema, *Literary Doctrine,* pp. 192–196, 202–205, 208. See discussion below on the revival of interest in the native popular tradition.

[26] Ragvald, "Professionalism," pp. 178–179.

[27] Ragvald, *Yao Wenyuan,* pp. 146–161.

[28] Mao's speech at the Tenth Plenum of the Eighth Central Committee (24 September 1962), in Stuart Schram, ed., *Mao Tse-tung Unrehearsed: Talks and Letters, 1956–1971* (Penguin, 1974), p. 195; released for publication in China in 1967 (see Yao Wenyuan article, p. 31, cited in footnote 39, below). See also Chen, *Inside the Cultural Revolution,* p. 150.

this point, but two years later he made further attacks on the professional arts establishment: "We must drive actors, poets, dramatists and writers out of the cities and pack them all off to the countryside. . . . We must not let writers stay in the government offices. . . . Whoever does not go down [to the countryside] will get no dinner; only when they go down will they be fed." And in 1965: "Today's philosophers can't turn out philosophy, writers can't write novels, and historians can't produce history. All they want to write about is emperors, kings, generals and ministers."[29] The denunciation of writers whose works were published in the 1950s and early 1960s began, and the movement to repudiate "middle characters" (*zhongjian renwu*: characters who are neither villains nor heroes), defended in the early 1960s by professional writers, got under way.[30]

At the same time, attacks on the Ministry of Culture and on traditional theater were being made by Mao personally, with the assistance of his wife, Jiang Qing, and of the army leadership under Lin Biao. In January 1965, Mao Dun was dismissed as Minister of Culture, signaling the imminent destruction of the cultural elite. In April 1966 the whole Ministry was abolished, most theaters closed down, and publication of literary works came almost to a standstill. The Party's cultural authorities, like Zhou Yang and Lin Mohan, came equally under attack. The situation at its worst continued for another five years, and it took more than another five years to restore cultural activities to their previous level. In this ten-year period, the survival of the intellectual elite, both as a group and as individuals, was in extreme jeopardy. With one outstanding exception, author-centered culture was replaced with an audience-centered and anonymous culture. The exception, of course, was the work of Mao himself.

When writers were swept out of their positions of power and prestige during the Cultural Revolution, it was not because they had offered opposition to the status quo, but because of the loyalty they had shown to the now-discredited state organs and Party elite—a loyalty for which they had, in many cases, received substantial rewards. It seems inherently unlikely that such a mass dismissal of writers and performers could have resulted merely from the whim of a small clique of radicals or of a few frustrated writers and performers. To some extent, there was a social basis for the anger that younger members of Chinese society felt against professional intellectuals and the literary and arts establishment. As Schurmann points out, by the 1960s there was still not a unified elite to replace the traditional gentry in exercising authority at all levels, nor was there a common culture that could produce such an elite. The educational level of the great

[29] Mao's remarks at the Spring Festival, summary record, 13 February 1964, in Schram, *Mao Tse-tung Unrehearsed*, p. 207; speech at Hangzhou, 21 December 1965, ibid., p. 237.

[30] See Joe C. Huang, *Heroes and Villains in Communist China: The Contemporary Chinese Novel as a Reflection of Life* (London: Hurst, 1973), pp. 253–254, 266–284.

masses of Chinese people was still very low. According to the 1964 census figures, only 1.735 percent of the population could be counted as "intellectuals" (i.e., as having a senior secondary or higher education), and illiterates and semiliterates still constituted 38.1 percent of the population. Although the failure of the Great Leap Forward had united the intellectual and political elites against the Party populists, there was still no common goal for the two elites. The social elite of intellectuals, with its links to the past and to the West, was cut off from the political elite that was trying to create a new society with little connection to either the past or the West.[31] But when Mao and the clique around him urged the breaking up of established hierarchies of power during the Cultural Revolution, both elites were equally discredited. Neither had a strong enough power base to establish supremacy over the other or to offset Mao's personal prestige as a spokesman for the masses. The disaffection of the Party does not concern us here; but why was it so easy to estrange the intellectuals, including writers and performers, from the rest of society?

In traditional Chinese society, despite their enormous differences in social position and personal wealth, the gentry and the peasantry still shared a common culture; they occupied different ends of the same sociocultural spectrum. The May Fourth writers removed themselves from this common cultural bond by deliberately choosing alien cultural values. Nevertheless, by adopting the Western role of the writer as the "universal intellectual" who fights for social justice and for all oppressed classes or groups,[32] the May Fourth writers achieved a new position in Chinese society. They may not have won universal acceptance within their own culture, but they were considered articulate, prolific, respected, and influential by the younger generation. After 1949, the writers again became part of the establishment, but now they did not share a common cultural or social outlook with the other major elite group or with the masses. At the same time, as functionaries of the state, they lost their role as "universal intellectuals" speaking out on behalf of the masses against state power. Instead, they grasped the opportunity to exercise the state power that their predecessors had wielded in imperial China but that had been denied them in the chaos of the early twentieth century. They may in fact have only enjoyed the outward show of power rather than the substance, but as their interests in some ways overlapped with the interests of the Party elite, this probably came to matter less.

It may be wrong to condemn these writers and performers for their decision to join the state and Party apparatus. As Czeslaw Milosz points

[31] Schurmann, *Ideology and Organization,* p. 12.

[32] For the "universal intellectual," see Michel Foucault, "Truth and Power," in Meaghan Morris and Paul Patton, eds., *Michel Foucault: Power, Truth, Strategy* (Sydney: Feral Publications, 1979), pp. 29–47, esp. pp. 41–47.

out in his discussion of Polish writers who acted similarly, "We must not oversimplify, however, the gratifications of personal ambition; they are merely the outward and visible symbols of a recognition that strengthens the intellectual's feeling of belonging."[33] Huters' analysis of the internal and external pressures on writers to support the change of government shows how the ground was prepared for them. It must also be kept in mind how difficult it was after 1949 to refuse to cooperate actively with the authorities. However, to the younger urban generation of the 1960s, the older writers could seem simply part of the establishment, enjoying the privileges of the elite and unconcerned with the problems of the rest of society. They had even failed in their primary duty as writers. The quality of the works produced by these writers or of the works whose production they supervised and praised was mediocre to downright bad. There was hardly a single work of written literature produced in the 1950s and early 1960s that had a genuine claim to literary distinction. The performing arts fared slightly better, though in general the same perceptions could apply. (Some figures who represented the older tradition, such as Hou Baolin, still held the respect and affection of the older urban audience.)

The Party's welcome to writers and performers in 1949 had its built-in reservations, just as had the artists' acceptance of the welcome. Despite the two groups' mutual distrust and the ups and downs of the 1950s and early 1960s, it was not the Party nor the writers and performers who pulled the other down: both elites fell from grace together, and when they regained power in the 1970s, they did so, again, together.

The Audience: Homogenization of High and Popular Culture

One of the most notable features about the literary and performing arts in contemporary China is that the cultural authorities have insisted on postulating a single, mass, homogeneous audience for cultural products. In traditional Chinese culture, as in other advanced traditional cultures throughout the world, at least three levels of audience were tacitly acknowledged. In China these were: the elite level of the highly educated who, ideally, acted simultaneously or successively as scholars, poets, and government officials; the low level of the illiterate peasantry, whose culture was largely oral and localized; and an intermediate level of the semi-educated, who lived in urban areas and enjoyed a variety of oral and written literary forms. The products associated with each of these levels can be labeled high, intermediate, and low. To some extent, they can also be distinguished by genre: at the elite level, the favored genres are poetry and nonfictional prose written in the literary language (*wenyan*); at the intermediate level, short stories and novels in the vernacular (*baihua*),

[33] Czeslaw Milosz, *The Captive Mind* (Harmondsworth: Penguin, 1980), p. 9.

opera, popular songs, and storytelling; at the low level, folksong and village opera, including various performing genres such as *yangge* (a kind of folk theater) in Shaanxi and *bangzi* (clapper opera) in Shanxi, Shaanxi, and other areas of northern and central China, all performed in local dialects (*tudihua*). The low and intermediate levels can be jointly described as popular.

Attempts to distinguish these two or three levels of cultural products based on their intrinsic features have been inconclusive.[34] Even the most obvious distinction, the three levels of language, is far from forming an absolute criterion. Vernacular expressions can be found in some kinds of literary poetry, and literary poetry can be found in vernacular fiction and opera; local dialects cannot be sharply distinguished from the standard vernacular on linguistic or literary grounds and may be utilized in novels whose audiences reach beyond the given locality. In regard to subject matter, although popular-level characters do not as a rule play major roles in high literature, elite characters are very common in popular literature; and there are fundamental similarities of theme and philosophy that reach across all levels. The myth that popular literature is structurally less complex than elite literature was demolished long ago. Looking from the genres back to their audiences, we find considerable overlap, as elites (unofficially) enjoy fiction and opera, and storytellers roam between city and countryside. A similar overlap exists between the writers and composers of the cultural products. Finally, there are numerous examples of a low or intermediate form, such as the vernacular short story or some kinds of song, being reworked by authors of a higher cultural level for an elite audience. Not only can it be said that cultural communication spanned the social and esthetic differences between high and popular levels but that, in spite of the readily discernable extremes, there was a vast common ground shared by traditional culture as a whole.

The distinction between high and popular culture can shed light on the whole culture of a given society, yet to define what the terms mean is extremely difficult. A full investigation would have to examine the social

[34] For a finely elaborated but concise outline of the three streams and of their interaction in fiction and drama, see Patrick Hanan, "The Development of Fiction and Drama," in Raymond Dawson, ed., *The Legacy of China* (Oxford: Clarendon Press, 1964), esp. pp. 116–119, 143. For a more detailed study see Hanan, *The Chinese Short Story: Studies in Dating, Authorship, and Composition* (Cambridge, Mass.: Harvard University Press, 1973), esp. chaps. 8 and 9 (pp. 170–214). For the discussion in this section I am also deeply indebted to the seminar and conference on high and popular culture conducted in 1978/1979 at Harvard by Patrick D. Hanan, Howard S. Hibbett, and Benjamin I. Schwartz. In particular, I have benefited greatly from the papers and comments by Milena Doleželová-Velingerová, Perry Link, and Edwin McClellan as well as from those by Hanan, Hibbett, and Schwartz. At the time of writing, the proceedings of the seminar and conference have not been published.

backgrounds of authors and audiences, the production and distribution of cultural products, their critical reception, and the author's intentions and anticipated audience (as inferred from the text). Our ignorance of most of these factors in contemporary China seriously hampers our attempts to construct such a well-rounded picture, although the essays contained in this volume, by beginning such an attempt, afford valuable clues.

Even if we adopt the simplest criterion for distinguishing between high and popular culture—namely, the social composition of the audience—there still remain numerous problems. As Benjamin I. Schwartz has pointed out, it is simply too crude to identify high culture as the culture of the ruling class and low culture as the culture of the masses. Even in traditional China, where during major nonforeign dynasties the ruling elite was as nearly as possible equivalent to the educated elite, the bearers of the high culture were not necessarily the spokesmen for the ruling class but may well at times have been in opposition to it. The ruling class, for its part, may be more comfortable with middle-level or popular than with high culture, as is frequently the case in Western societies.[35] In contemporary China, two groups lay claim to elite status: the political elite and the educated elite. Each inherited some values of the traditional gentry and each espoused some modern Western values, but in either case the mix produced a different result. Culturally, it seems that the political elite, or parts of it, preferred traditional Chinese elite forms and popular forms such as literary poetry and Chinese opera, while the educated elite preferred westernized forms such as new poetry and spoken drama (*huaju*). The cultural authorities within the political elite generally shared the education and tastes of the educated elite, and so had divided loyalties when it came to formulating cultural policies and to allocating resources. (During the Cultural Revolution, they were replaced by Party-trained intellectuals and populist leaders who did not share the older intellectuals' cultural values.)

It is also necessary to distinguish the traditional popular audiences from the mass audience today. The popular audience in the past either paid for its entertainment and enjoyed the privilege of choice, or else, especially in rural areas, created its own entertainment. It was subject to pressure to conform to Confucian and other traditional values, and at times its entertainments were severely censored, but in the countryside effective control by the state was limited. The mass audience in contemporary China exercises very little choice, either over what it pays for or over what it is allowed to create for itself. Its choice is circumscribed by an authority that is more concerned with what the masses should have than with what they

[35] From a statement by Benjamin I. Schwartz circulated at the seminar on high and popular culture, Harvard University, 1978.

want; and at times of political crisis, the range of offerings becomes very limited indeed. The situation in Western countries is somewhat comparable in that a mass audience, whose choices are controlled by a relatively small and centralized group interested in appealing to the lowest common denominator, is replacing the traditional popular audience. The Western mass audience, however, operates in an open society and has more options both within and outside the mass culture.

The fact of the Party's control over both author and audience also interferes with the standard distinction between a creator-oriented culture (high culture) and a user-oriented culture (popular culture). Neither category is really applicable in a controlled society. Such a culture cannot be fully creator-oriented, since some functions of the creator (e.g., the choice of content) have been taken over by a third element, the Party. Nor can the culture be fully user-oriented, since the audience's preference may be ignored by the same third element, which prefers to promote its own values.[36] The existence of such problems is not a reason to abandon the high/popular distinction; rather, it suggests fruitful new lines of research into the whole cultural scene of contemporary China.

An observer surveying the range of literary products in China, both written and oral, at the beginning of the twentieth century would find their differences more apparent than their similarities. Some May Fourth writers were therefore ambivalent about traditional culture. Despite the general atmosphere of iconoclasm, there was still a strong tendency, at least in theory, among the left and liberal sections of the movement to exempt popular culture from the scorn they poured on the classical tradition. It was iconoclastic enough to declare, as did Hu Shi, that the "little tradition" was the true cultural mainstream of China, while classical literature was a mere parasite or an empty shell. Nevertheless, in practice few writers consciously borrowed from the little tradition; both in their creative and their critical writing they preferred to choose from among an array of Western models. Most of these Western models were themselves addressed to a highly literate audience, although in the West by the late nineteenth and in the twentieth century, improved and near-universal education had encouraged a considerable merging of elite and nonelite audiences.

The May Fourth writers based their hopes for a national literature on a similar universalizing of education in China that would produce a similar merging of audience levels. In their time, this was starting to happen; they drew their audience from both elite and intermediate levels. In absolute terms, this new composite audience was smaller than either of the audiences it drew from, but this was—or so they hoped—merely a temporary

[36] Perry Link advanced an argument along these lines at the conference on high and popular culture, Harvard University, 1979.

phenomenon. As Guo Moruo remarked, his task was to write as best he could, and it was the task of the educators to create an audience for him.

The turmoil of the twentieth century allowed no such hopeful future to materialize. Although compulsory and universal education was a policy of the Nationalist government, it did not reach the mass of the peasantry in the vast interior. The solemn self-consciousness of the May Fourth writers placed another barrier between them and their potential audience: it is hard to think of even a reform-minded student reader of the 1920s being content with an unrelieved diet of May Fourth writing. Apart from sheer lack of literacy, several factors stood between these writers and the national audience they sought: the reformist or revolutionary nature of their messages, the unfamiliarity of the literary conventions they adopted, and their perceived lack of technical skill.

The May Fourth writers recognized by the early 1930s that their adoption of a highly westernized idiom had placed a barrier between themselves and a wider audience. What separated them even more from all levels of traditional writers and performers was their inability to entertain or intrigue their audiences with the kind of technical skills that dazzled the audiences of traditional storytelling, opera, and literary and folk poetry. Many of the May Fourth writers, in fact, were extremely interested in developing technical skills, and some were notably successful in doing so: Lu Xun, Wen Yiduo, Mao Dun, and Cao Yu come to mind. Others may have failed to reach such levels of achievement but were nonetheless seeking new modes of expression. To an inexperienced audience, however, an unfamiliar technique often seems mere lack of technique. The Shanghai audience that booed Shaw's *Mrs Warren's Profession* off the stage was only able to perceive its lack of traditional stage effects. Similarly, the May Fourth writers failed to find formal structures of interest to them in popular literature. In the late 1930s and the 1940s, the high tide of patriotism that swept the country helped to break down cross-generic prejudices, particularly the May Fourth writers' prejudice against the popular arts. At the same time, twenty years of reformist education was beginning to produce a wider middle-level audience.[37] By the 1950s, some success had been achieved in creating a new literary language intermediate between the westernized May Fourth mode and the informal rural or local style developed in the Yan'an period. This was a very important step toward audience homogeneity.

Further progress, in the 1950s and 1960s, toward universal education and national unity was countered by the conflicts between special groups that the stabler conditions of the new society inevitably produced. The narrow target audience of "workers, peasants and soldiers" that Mao defined in Yan'an for Communist writers was now, theoretically, the audi-

[37] I am grateful to T. D. Huters for suggesting this interpretation of the 1940s.

ence for all writers. However, in his revised version of the "Talks" (1953), Mao redefined his terms slightly to subtly broaden the audience: in several places, "workers, peasants and soldiers" became "masses of workers, peasants and soldiers" or "laboring people" or, again, "workers, peasants, soldiers and popular masses" became simply "popular masses."[38] By 1956, Lu Dingyi's Hundred Flowers speech had redefined the aim of literature as "to serve the working people as a whole, intellectuals included"; in 1960, Zhou Yang could ask, rhetorically, "Whom should literature and art serve if not the laboring masses of workers and peasants, and their intellectuals?"; and in 1961, a *People's Daily* editorial attributed to Zhou Yang stated that: "The whole people (*quanmin*) with the workers, peasants and soldiers as the main body within the people's democratic united front are the audience for our artistic and literary services and other work."[39]

Widening the audience range was a code for the redevelopment of audience hierarchies. Both Chinese and Western writers have noted that the quality of literary works rose in periods of relaxation such as 1956–1957 and 1959–1962, when an audience including intellectuals was permitted.[40] Welcome as this broadening was to the intellectuals, it dismayed those whose concern was for the cultural enrichment, along correct political lines, of the masses. Thus each period of relaxation was followed by a countertrend that refocused attention on the masses (the nation's cultural resources were too limited to focus on both audiences simultaneously). During the antirightist campaign, surveys of low-income groups revealed that the great majority of the people was not reached by the literature and art emanating from the center; shortly after, the amateur-writing and mass-poetry movements were launched. Again, in 1962–1965, reader research was carried out in the villages, and in 1966, the national press demanded that literature address an audience of workers, peasants, and soldiers.[41] A central policy of the Cultural Revolution was to reduce the

[38] See my *Mao Zedong's Talks at the Yan'an Conference on Literature and Art* (Ann Arbor: University of Michigan Center for Chinese Studies, 1981), appendix 1.

[39] Lu Ting-yi [Lu Dingyi], "Let Flowers of Many Kinds Blossom, Diverse Schools of Thought Contend!" (Peking: Foreign Languages Press, 1957), pp. 19–20; Chou Yang [Zhou Yang], "The Path of Socialist Literature and Art in China" (Peking: Foreign Languages Press, 1960), p. 8; *Renmin ribao,* 15 March 1961, editorial attributed to Zhou Yang by Yao Wenyuan in his "Ping fan'geming liangmianpai Zhou Yang" [On the two-faced counter-revolutionary Zhou Yang], *Hong qi* (1967), 1, pp. 14–36, translated in *Chinese Literature* (1967), 3, pp. 24–71.

[40] Huang, *Heroes and Villains,* p. vii; *China Handbook* Editorial Committee, *China Handbook Series: Literature and the Arts* (Peking: Foreign Languages Press, 1983).

[41] Ragvald, *Yao Wenyuan,* p. 106 and n. 15; Huang, *Heroes and Villains,* pp. 323–327. For the Cultural Revolution rhetoric, see, for instance, the speech by Jiang Qing at the 28 November 1966 rally in Peking of 20,000 workers in the field of literature and art, reported in *Hong qi* 15 (13 December 1966), pp. 5–13, and translated in *Chinese Literature* (1967) 2, pp. 3–17.

target audience to its Yan'an prototype by prohibiting outright the publication, circulation, and performance of material not specifically designed for that audience. Again, Mao's poems were a significant exception.

The creation of a worker-peasant-soldier culture was a task whose overwhelming complexity was hardly envisioned in the early post-Liberation days. For want of an alternative, the cultural authorities and producers were drawn mostly from the May Fourth writers and artists. As Huters points out, they were hardly suited for the task, and as the new group of writers and performers was trained under the guidance of the old, it tended to assimilate similar attitudes. Amateur writers, encouraged by handsome remuneration beyond their normal wages, aspired toward professional status; nonprofessional products were the object of professional criticism and audience indifference. Even the Party's own cultural authorities were ambivalent about the egalitarianism implicit in the Party's policy on mass literature and art. However, under pressure from the populist elements in the leadership, several more or less effective devices were experimented with, as described in the essays in this volume. Many of these were direct or indirect borrowings from traditional literature and art.

A new literature and art gradually emerged, therefore, in the 1950s and 1960s, which were able to carry the Party's message in a way compatible with the mass audience's literary and artistic expectations. Among the devices used were: the adoption of formal stylistic traits, such as the storyteller narrative voice; the incorporation of dialect and colloquial expressions into narrative as well as dialogue; the creation of heroic models rather than the complex middle characters; the central and heroic position given to workers, peasants, soldiers, and forceful female characters; the substitution of traditional "realism" for May Fourth naturalism or critical realism and of mimetic, representational description for verbal, presentational description; the avoidance of anything too overtly intelligent, imaginative, or experimental in favor of the plain solemnity of ritualistic culture; the insistence on overt explanation and the absence of ambiguity; and the elevation of the performing arts to equal respectability with written literature.

Most of these devices could be learned by studying the traditional popular culture, and, since in the 1950s and 1960s such research was undertaken, we may assume that the cultural authorities and producers consciously applied it. The presentational barrier between producers and audiences having thus been lowered, or partially lowered, the all-important political and social message of the contents had presumably become more palatable to the mass audience.

At the same time, the very fact that popular literature and the performing arts were now subjects of academic research helped to make them more respectable in the eyes of intellectuals. Knowledge of their complex structures may also have contributed to their rise in status. Moreover, several decades of exposure to Western literature and westernized Chinese literature had by now made the whole range of traditional Chinese culture seem more homogenous—Peking opera and classical poetry no longer seemed worlds apart. Finally, the re-evaluation of social hierarchies made it permissible, even desirable, for intellectuals to admit their liking for certain kinds of popular culture such as the traditional theater.[42] In short, not only did borrowings from the traditional written and performing arts make the new arts more acceptable to the masses; the process involved in the borrowing made the traditional popular arts more acceptable to the intellectuals. The populist goal of achieving a unified national audience did not seem to be beyond reach.

The Cultural Product: Literature and Performing Arts

During the 1930s and 1940s, the literature of the May Fourth movement had established itself as the newly emerging elite literature, edging the old classical literature away from the center though not off the stage altogether. Its elite nature was tacitly acknowledged by the Communist government when in 1949 it appointed the top May Fourth writers to positions of social leadership, published their works in collected editions, and imposed social functions and duties on other May Fourth writers. Most of the new fiction, drama, and poetry of the 1950s and early 1960s fit firmly within the May Fourth tradition. Zhou Erfu's *Shanghaide zaochen* [Morning in Shanghai, 1958] and Yang Mo's *Qingchunzhi ge* [Song of youth, 1958] were obviously successors to Mao Dun's *Ziye* [Midnight, 1933] and Ba Jin's *Jia* [Family, 1931] with the added political interpolations required by the new government. However, this modified form of the May Fourth tradition, while dominant, was not the sole contributor to national publications or to the stage. The native classical and popular traditions challenged its monopoly, and oral literature, with its new respectability as a popular art, similarly challenged the dominance of written literature.

The encouragement of popular tradition was essentially a political tac-

[42] My own fairly extensive theater-going in Peking in the early 1980s gave me the impression of an interesting hierarchy among theater-goers. *Kunqu* performances seem to attract students, intellectuals, and the better-off, while the audience for Hebei *bangzi* is obviously from the lower classes. The audience for Peking opera, especially when a famous performer is featured, is of an only slightly lower level than the *kunqu* audience, and *pingju* audiences seem to be of a slightly higher level than *bangzi* audiences. Spoken drama attracts a different sort of audience, obviously younger than the others. *Kunqu* audiences also include younger people, but *bangzi* audiences are generally rather older. *Xiangsheng* in the better theaters attract a mixed audience; daytime storytelling in humbler surroundings attracts what seem to be the elderly and the unemployed. It is likely that a similar situation existed in the 1950s and early 1960s.

tic, whose groundwork was laid during the Yan'an period of 1942–1947. The May Fourth movement and its late Qing predecessor had prepared the way for a renewed interest in Chinese popular culture, and their adoption of the vernacular novel and short story as their main form of literary expression was an important precedent. On the whole, however, May Fourth writers felt that they had little to learn from popular tradition in the important areas of style and structure. Taking their cue from Western studies of folklore, the May Fourth intellectuals tended to approach folk literature along anthropological and psychological lines. Researchers and writers such as Fu Sinian and Shen Congwen made valuable academic studies and collections of folk literature in the 1930s, but folk elements were used in creative writing only as embellishments (as Mao sarcastically put it), rather than as living models for contemporary adaptation. Having rejected the dead weight of one native tradition, the May Fourth writers were not about to be saddled with another; instead, they turned toward the outside world. The debate on "national forms" in the late 1930s showed that many Party intellectuals were equally resistant.

When Mao directed writers to adopt folk forms, he was probably more moved by political than by literary considerations; the forms he enumerated in the "Talks" were not conspicuously noted for their intrinsically literary or traditional nature. The immediate result of the "Talks" was the redirection of May Fourth writers into research on folk literature and art and the encouragement of the younger, more flexible writers and composers to produce literature and art based on folk material. At the same time, however, and going beyong Mao's actual directives (which he had addressed to professionals), members of the folk themselves began to produce new works in line with the spirit of the directives. Some of these early attempts, such as the new *yangge* discussed by David Holm in this volume, had few literary pretensions; others, such as the work of Zhao Shuli and Li Ji, probably surpassed the expectations of the cultural leadership, creating a sense of euphoria that persisted into the early post-Liberation period.

At the opening of this new stage, the existing forms of traditional popular art were collected for preservation and new material was produced on their model. This reformist attempt was not successful at all levels. Traditional opera, for instance, remained resistant to internal reform as it had in the 1920s and 1930s. The lack of information about its complex, unwritten rules of composition defeated the reforms of outsiders. The most that could be done was to sift through the repertoire for those pieces whose messages were not too blatantly incongruous with the official goals of the new society. Especially in the first few years, the policy of New Democracy allowed traditional opera to continue as a major form of entertainment: the need for national unity temporarily overrode narrower political demands.

In fiction, the new folk elements introduced by Zhao Shuli and used successfully by other writers of the early Communist period seemed to gradually lose their freshness and charm as writers were drawn to the variety of sophisticated techniques from the West. This powerful attraction enticed Zhao Shuli, for one, away from the native elements to a more neutral, "international" style. The model of the Soviet Union was particularly important in the 1950s in enhancing the prestige of "socialist realism," interpreted as Western-style realism at the service of centrally (externally) determined goals.[43] A simplified form of folk poetry was popularized, which was actually a simplified form of classical literary poetry, but only a few, more ambitious, attempts were made to emulate the more structurally complex and independent forms of folksong and narrative art. An exception was *xiangsheng,* an urban performing art involving one or more performers in a lively comedic narrative or dialogue (see the essay by Perry Link in this volume). Film was strongly associated with the May Fourth elite culture and remained so, with the appropriate concessions made to the new political directives (see the essay by Wai-fong Loh above).

The temporary eclipse of Yan'an populism in the arts soon after Liberation was due to several factors. First, the inheritance of state power made the Party newly conscious of the centuries-old traditions of the Chinese state, including the glories of the elite arts. In his revised edition of the Yan'an "Talks" (1953), Mao accordingly inserted the following sentence: "We should take over the rich legacy and excellent traditions in literature and art that have been handed down from past ages in China and foreign countries, but our aim must still be to serve the popular masses." Similarly, he altered "the old forms of the feudal class and the bourgeoisie" to read "the literary and artistic forms of past ages," and "absorb these things" became "take over all the excellent tradition in literature and art." Secondly, as the first quotation hints, the powerful influence of the U.S.S.R. also shifted attention away from the native tradition. Although a certain amount of Western literature still circulated in China during the 1950s, Soviet literature was the main channel through which Chinese writers were able to maintain contact with the Western literature that had dominated the Chinese literary world in the first half of the twentieth century. Thirdly, the writers, artists, and Party intellectuals who constituted the bureaucracies also felt the mantle of China's imperial glory on

[43] At the 1960 ACFLAC Congress, most of the works singled out for praise "came not from the popular entertainers of the style of Chao Shu-li [Zhao Shuli], but from writers schooled in the earlier leftist traditions": Cyril Birch, "The Particle of Art," in Birch, ed., *Communist Chinese Literature,* p. 9. For the changing emphasis in the work of Zhao Shuli and others in the 1950s, see Cyril Birch, "The Persistence of Traditional Forms," in Birch, ed., *Communist Chinese Literature,* pp. 77–83. For the importance of Soviet socialist realism, see Fokkema, *Literary Doctrine,* pp. 109–118.

their shoulders. Both populism and the May Fourth tradition seemed irrelevant to those inheriting the grand literati tradition.

Not all of the Party leaders watched this trend with approval, and reaction was mixed when in early 1957 Mao allowed his classical-style poetry to inaugurate the new periodical *Shikan* [Poetry journal]. His motives are not entirely clear: he may have felt impelled to assert his authority over the cultural bureaucracy or he may have wished to encourage older and non-Party intellectuals (as opposed to the May Fourth figures in the Party establishment). Modestly disclaiming his own value as a cultural model, Mao publicly urged others not to follow his example. However, in the succeeding years, in restricted and private speeches or letters, he made his contempt for May Fourth or "new" poetry very clear.[44] It is hard not to believe that these forcefully expressed opinions circulated more widely at the time, and publication of classical-style poetry in books and journals was common from the late 1950s on. At the same time, the poetry campaign of 1958 inaugurated a new drive to encourage folk poetry.[45] The national anthology of poems, culled from the millions gathered across the whole country, was restricted to just 300 poems, as in the ancient *Shijing* [Book of songs]; the introduction by Zhou Yang and Guo Moruo explicitly compares the two works. The relationship between the classical and folk traditions was thereby introduced into popular circulation, as it had already been incorporated into the discourse of academic literary studies.

The preservation and study of the national theatrical heritage was also a central part of the Hundred Flowers campaign to attract the support of intellectuals.[46] Apart from Mao's personal initiatives on behalf of classical and folk poetry, the attention of the literary heritage movement after the Eighth Congress turned toward various forms of popular theater: spoken drama, regional operas, Peking opera, and *quyi,* the minor performing arts. The formerly distinct native traditions became merely different aspects of a common culture, especially once such traditionally ambiguous forms as the vernacular novel and Peking opera became important bridges between the traditional cultures.

Despite the discreet though firm support Mao provided, from the Hundred Flowers through the Great Leap Forward, and despite the lip service the cultural establishment paid to popular culture, the new generation of writers, including those from the masses, showed a distinct preference for

[44] For Mao's views on poetry, see my "Poems, Poets, and *Poetry* 1976: An Exercise in the Typology of Modern Chinese Literature," *Contemporary China* 2, 4 (Winter 1978): 79–80, 96–97.

[45] See Ragvald, *Yao Wenyuan,* pp. 114–117; Fokkema, *Literary Doctrine,* pp. 202–205, 208; Schram, *Mao Tse-tung Unrehearsed,* pp. 123–124; Goldman, *Literary Dissent,* pp. 243–271.

[46] Fokkema, *Literary Doctrine,* pp. 197, 205.

the more glamorous international style. The case of the modern drama (*wenmingxi,* literally "civilized theater") or spoken drama illustrates how the international style was employed in a nonpopular performing art, bypassing the genuinely popular performing arts such as Peking opera. The modern drama had been the slowest of the new westernized forms to win popular acceptance, even in the cities. Although it first appeared in China several years before the May Fourth movement, and a second attempt was made to popularize it in the early 1920s, modern drama did not achieve its first genuine success until the mid-1930s. Its greatest acceptance came only under the very special circumstances of occupied Shanghai during the war (see the essay by Edward Gunn in this volume), where the two factors that seemed to weigh most heavily in its favor were the absence of a competing performing art (i.e., of traditional opera and the cinema) and its incorporation of elements from opera. In the 1950s and early 1960s, the co-existence of modern drama and traditional opera epitomized the tendency toward cultural diversity that undermined the national goal of a unitary mass culture. On the one hand was opera, a traditional form highly popular at different audience levels but highly resistant to revolutionary modernization (i.e., to the introduction of new character types as vehicles for the new political messages). On the other hand was the drama, a modernized form patronized almost exclusively by the urban intelligentsia and obviously designed to transmit a modern revolutionary content. The rural *yangge* movement, so important in the 1940s, almost disappeared from the national stage.[47]

After the relative relaxation of the period from 1959 to 1962, Mao again attempted, as in 1957, to assert his cultural leadership by allowing the publication of a new batch of his classical-style poems in 1962. This time they were published in *Renmin wenxue* [People's literature], a magazine with a much larger circulation than *Poetry Journal.* The following year, Mao commenced his attack on the Ministry of Culture, and the movement for new revolutionary operas on contemporary themes was launched in 1963.[48] Mao was continuing his two-pronged attack on the Party and on the state cultural establishment, using classical-style poetry to discredit the bare "modern" style of the establishment's new poetry and attacking the persistence of unreformed popular culture to discredit whatever populist tendencies were part of establishment policy.

[47] For a concise summary of the three trends in Chinese theater in the 1940s, see Jack Chen, *The Chinese Theater* (New York: Roy, 1948). For a more general survey of twentieth-century China, see Colin Mackerras, *The Chinese Theatre in Modern Times, from 1840 to the Present Day* (London: Thames and Hudson, 1975).

[48] For a description of skirmishes in the theater world in the early 1960s, see Chen, *Inside the Cultural Revolution,* pp. 135–140, 155–164.

THE "GREAT RETURN": THE CULTURAL REVOLUTION AND ITS AFTERMATH (1966–1976)

Misinformation about the Cultural Revolution is still a serious problem in the understanding of contemporary China. Now anxious to discredit it, the Chinese themselves are making the same kind of errors about it as Western observers. It is common to hear from both Chinese and Western sources that the sole literary or artistic product of those years was "eight model operas". There has also been a failure to understand the reform of Peking opera and its relation to the Chinese tradition. The following section is an attempt to set the record straight. We must first distinguish between the three phases of the ten-year period. It consisted of the Cultural Revolution proper, 1966–1969; the transition, 1969–1971; and the recovery, 1972–1976.[49]

The cultural products of the Cultural Revolution proper fall into three categories: the model revolutionary theatrical works (*yangbanxi*), together with similar model art works such as the "Rent Collection Courtyard" sculptural tableaux, wall posters, and oil paintings; Mao's classical-style poems; and a small number of undistinguished works of written literature and minor performing arts, mostly by new or anonymous authors. Of these three categories, the first two had existed before the Cultural Revolution, at least in some form; the third category, original with the period, did not survive its aftermath. These products were forced on the population at large: there was no alternative to them. This does not necessarily mean, however, that they were disliked. At least three or four of the original five model operas won some measure of genuine popularity.

Model Theatrical Works

The history of the model theatrical works is problematic, and their future uncertain. The earliest and most famous of the works were performed at the Festival of Peking Operas on Contemporary Themes in 1964, as "revolutionary Peking operas on contemporary themes" (*geming xiandai jingju;* "contemporary" here means, roughly, twentieth-century). All were based on pre-existing texts, from novels, films, or local operas, and had worker, peasant, and soldier heroes and heroines. *Zhiqu Weihushan* [Taking Tiger Mountain by strategy] was based on an episode from a novel about the Civil War, which was itself a loose borrowing from a traditional vernacular novel. *Shajiabang* and *Hong deng ji* [The red lantern] were based on Shanghai operas. Some of these works were selected as *yangban,* "models," for future attempts, since their creation was a bold

[49] For information on cultural conditions in this decade I am greatly indebted to Anders Hansson, cultural attaché at the Swedish Embassy in Peking, 1971–1973. In particular, I have relied heavily on his unpublished paper, "Transplanting Model Operas" (1977).

new experiment in the production of written scripts for a previously unwritten medium. By the end of 1966, eight "revolutionary model theatrical works" (*geming yangbanxi,* or *yangbanxi* for short), as they were now known, formed the official canon.[50] (Since only five of the eight were actually operas, it is more correct, if cumbersome, to describe them as "theatrical works.")

By 1976, these eight works had expanded into eighteen, many of them variants of the original eight.[51] The concept of "model work" developed as local opera forms began to be encouraged later in the Cultural Revolution. As early as 1969, when the Cultural Revolution proper was winding down, work started on the "transplanting" (*yizhi*) or adapting of the model Peking operas into local operas, as with the Cantonese opera version of *Shajiabang* (see the essay by Bell Yung in this volume). In addition, new local operas were produced and old ones rewritten in the spirit of the model operas. In 1974 and 1975, no fewer than forty-eight regional forms were revived through the transplantation of model operas, including such widely differing kinds as the old "classical" *kunqu* (or *kunju*), the rather frivolous Hunan *huaguxi* ("flower drum opera"), and opera forms of such national minorities as Uighurs and Tibetans. There were good reasons for reviving local opera. Although Peking opera is the most prestigious and widespread form of Chinese opera today, the local styles enjoy great local popularity, especially in areas where the Peking-based "common language" is not readily understood. Local opera was, therefore, a potentially superior vehicle for propaganda and also helped satisfy the more diversified cultural needs of the early 1970s. Nevertheless, just as in the creation of the model operas, transplanting, creating, or rewriting local operas involved many difficulties, which were aired in the national press in the early and mid-1970s. Some of the later model Peking operas were themselves influenced by regional forms, such as *Dujuanshan* [Azalea Mountain], which uses responsorial singing, a characteristic of Sichuan and Chaozhou opera.

The concept of model works was discredited with the fall of the Gang of Four in 1976. However, some, if not all, of the operas themselves will undoubtedly survive; some were staged in part or in whole in the late

[50] As listed in *Renmin ribao,* 9 December 1966, p. 4. They were performed as a group in May 1967 for the twenty-fifth anniversary of the Yan'an Forum and released on gramophone records for National Day, October 1 of the same year. A statement to that effect in *Chinese Literature,* (1967), 12, notes that the records were "produced with the strong support of the Cultural Revolution Group under the Party's Central Committee" (p. 22). For information on the term *yangban* and the early history of *yangbanxi,* see Hua-Yuan Li Mowry, *Yan-pan hsi: New Theater in China* (Berkeley: University of California Center for Chinese Studies, 1973). For a list of the model works, see Bell Yung's article in this volume.

[51] Information on *yangbanxi* in the following paragraphs is from Hansson, "Transplanting Model Operas."

1970s. One of the major criticisms of the model works was that they monopolized the stage; this monopoly has now come to an end and, after a decent interval of time, the operas may regain some popularity. Another problem was their small number, due probably to the serious problems the writers, composers, and performers faced in adapting to modern conditions a form so tightly bound to the past. Probably the most serious criticism concerned the extension of the model concept into nontheatrical genres, so that poetry and fiction, for example, were expected to follow the theories developed for theatrical works.[52] The most controversial of these theories was that of the "three prominences" (*san tuchu*), which took shape during the late 1960s. At the time of the fall of Lin Biao, the theory changed slightly with the general de-emphasis on genius and individual heroism, but the main point was still the same: in characterization and presentation, the most heroic and most positive aspects should be the primary focus of attention.[53] In opera, this meant the highlighting of exaggerated characters; what was lost in subtlety was made up for in bold theatrical effects, action, and spectacle. The development of new role stereotypes, after their initial novelty had worn off, allowed the audience and performers to concentrate on the traditional skills of singing and stage movement—presumably contrary to the intentions of the cultural authorities. On the whole, the theory of the three prominences was not out of keeping with the spirit of traditional Chinese theatre.

The model nature of *yangbanxi* was established by the publication of "definitive" versions in *Hong qi* [Red flag], the organ of the Chinese Communist Party Central Committee. The script of *Tiger Mountain* was published first, in November 1969. Books recorded the script, musical score, detailed descriptions of costumes and stage properties, stage directions, and so on, indicating that the established model was to be followed with little deviation. This activity marked a radical departure from the unscripted and performer-oriented staging of traditional opera. The approved stage versions were as a rule performed by one of the major Peking opera troupes of Peking or Shanghai. The film versions that followed in the 1970s tended also to follow closely the stage versions, even to using the same props.

The main Western elements in the model works were the semirealistic, semisymbolic, and elaborate stage settings, the Western-style orchestration, and Western musical instruments (these instruments, including the piano, were considered more forceful and better suited to express contemporary heroism than were the traditional Chinese instruments). Some gestures asso-

[52] See, for example, articles in *Shikan* (1976), 4, pp. 15–16, 22–25, 25–27; (1976), 5, pp. 86–87; (1976), 6, pp. 86–87; (1976), 7, pp. 87–89; (1976), 8, pp. 75–76; (1976), 9, pp. 82–85.

[53] Beverley Lum, "A Report on the Principle of the 'Three Prominences' " (unpublished manuscript).

ciated with the international proletarian movement, such as the workers' clenched-fist salute, were also incorporated into the stage movements of the Peking operas. Other model works, such as the ballets, the symphonic suite *Shajiabang,* and the "Gangqin xiezouqu 'Huanghe' " [The Yellow River piano concerto] owe much more to Western or international styles.

The choice of traditional opera as the chief subject of reform was a positive contribution to narrowing the gap between high and popular culture. Although Peking opera retained its central position as the original and most widely seen form of model opera, the local operas came much closer to it and to each other, thereby losing much of their provincial nature; similarly, *kunqu* probably lost its "classical" flavor. When model works were staged in more remote areas, it was sometimes difficult or even impossible to recreate the model exactly, as rural and provincial conditions continued to lag behind the larger cities. An attempt was made to overcome this rural deprivation by sending city opera companies on tour for periods of up to six months. From one point of view, which local audiences and the cultural historian might share, the narrowing of the gap between regional forms is destructive. If homogeneity is the price of survival, is survival still desirable? On the other hand, even if the model theatrical works and their regional variations turn out in the long run to be an experiment that failed, the boldness of the undertaking and the work of its creators and performers can still evoke admiration.

The Classical Revival

The classical revival of the late 1960s and early 1970s was again stimulated by the publication of Mao's classical-style poems. By 1968, the *Mao Zhuxi shici* [Poems of Chairman Mao] had a circulation of 92,000,000 copies.[54] Although this did not quite match the record set by *Mao Zhuxi yulu* [Quotations from Chairman Mao, popularly known in the West as the "little red book"] or *Mao Zedong xuanji* [Selected works of Mao Zedong], the poems' impact must still have been immense. As classical verse, these poems are not particularly obscure in language or allusion, but they are difficult enough to make commentary a necessity and memorization a useful exercise in poetry training. Others among the old revolutionary generals in the Party leadership had published classical poetry before the Cultural Revolution, and in its aftermath, and into the late 1970s, such displays from the leadership became commonplace. Hua Guofeng and Deng Xiaoping are unusual in having declined to emulate their predecessors in this, though Hua did release facsimiles of a folksong copied down in his own handwriting in 1977.[55] Apart from the old generals, a few of the older intellectuals, including such pioneers of the vernacular in May Fourth days as Guo Moruo,

[54] See *Peking Review* (1969), 2.

[55] McDougall, "Poems, Poets, and *Poetry* 1976," pp. 106–107.

Mao Dun, and Ye Shengtao, also published poems in the classical style in the aftermath of the Cultural Revolution. Another boost to classical learning came during the anti-Confucian movement of 1973–1975 when, as part of the Legalist-Confucian debate, many classical texts from the Warring States down to the Qing dynasty were printed in cheap pamphlets for mass study. Some unexpected figures turned up as Legalists and, hence, as writers worthy of study, such as Liu Zongyuan, Li He, and Li Shangyin.[56] Although this vogue did not last long, it was another sign of the continued relevance of the classical tradition.

The real vitality of the tradition was dramatically revealed in the sudden outpouring of poetry occasioned by the Qingming 1976 remembrance at Tiananmen for the late Premier Zhou Enlai.[57] These poems either mourn Zhou Enlai or angrily attack the clique of Zhang Chunqiao, Jiang Qing, and Yao Wenyuan (and probably Mao as well). If the collections are at all representative, we may conclude that the majority of the poems written for this occasion were in classical style; moreover, that they are arranged in the various collections primarily by formal metrical type shows an editorial awareness of formal values in even the most highly charged political verse.

Given such a spontaneous return to the classical tradition by the younger generation, there is good reason to expect its further vitality. In the unofficial journals of 1978–1979 (see below), which, like their Tiananmen predecessors, were produced chiefly by the young, classical and vernacular poetry mingle as in the official literary magazines. Now that the leadership does not set its own verse as a national study goal and that the older generation is reduced in size and power, some of the popular knowledge of classical poetic forms may diminish. However, the increased emphasis on higher education and on the treasures of the Chinese past may create a new educated elite, who may initiate a new wave of classical composition. What may remain unique to China, apart from the mixture of classical, folk, and modern poetry, is the extraordinary range of people who still express themselves in verse: from elderly generals to student protesters and from senior intellectuals to workers, peasants, and soldiers. In this sense, poetry continues to be a "popular" art in a way now almost unknown in the West.

Further Restorations in the Early 1970s

The restoration of order in 1969, after the battles of 1967 and 1968, was largely effected by the People's Liberation Army (PLA), and subsequent events in the PLA continued to affect cultural developments. The fall of Lin Biao in 1971 was followed by a further relaxation in literature and

[56] See, for instance, Liang Xiao and Wen Jun, "Lun Li Shangyinde 'Wu ti' shi" [On the "without title" poems of Li Shangyin], *Lishi yanjiu* [Historical research] (1975), 2. pp. 76–83.

[57] For a discussion of these poems, see McDougall, "Dissent Literature."

the arts, so that at the Spring Festival in 1972 a number of reprints of older and modern books were released, together with some new titles.[58] Strictly speaking, the post-Cultural-Revolution thaw began before the fall of the Gang of Four.

Professional *quyi* (minor performing arts such as *xiangsheng*) returned to the stage in 1972. Over the next four years, there was a gradual increase in the number of books and cultural magazines released per year,[59] and 1976 started out promisingly with the inauguration of five national journals for literature and the arts. The film industry also enjoyed renewed activity during the period from 1972 to 1976 (see the essay by Paul Clark in this volume), and new operas (model and other) were created and transplanted.

Many of the new titles published in this period were re-issues or new works by previously unknown authors, and amateur writers continued to receive encouragement from the authorities. The three traditions—classical, popular, and Western—continued to co-exist, but the popular tradition was more prominent than in any period since the Yan'an days. This resurgence was apparent in such areas as the revival of local opera described above, the publication of folk and classical poetry in the national *Poetry Journal,* and the folksy narrative style adopted in many short stories. One factor behind the continuation of the three traditions was the increased control of the authorities over the content of literary and performing works. With no choice in this respect but some choice in matters of form and style, a writer who selected a traditional genre could at least find some challenge to his or her professional skill. In this way, the native tradition offered a relatively safe harbor for writers seeking a temporary refuge. Nevertheless, as in the 1950s and 1960s, the international style in fiction and poetry still exerted a strong attraction, especially on the younger generation. The only major modern form that failed to make a comeback in the aftermath of the Cultural Revolution was the spoken drama.

The most notable figure in the literary world was the novelist and former peasant, Hao Ran. His short stories from the 1950s and 1960s and his novel *Yanyang tian* [Bright sunny skies] were among the first to be released in 1972, and his novel *Jinguang dadao* [Road of golden light] was the first major new work since the Cultural Revolution proper. Other figures who gradually reappeared between 1972 and 1976 include He Jingzhi, He Qifang, Zang Kejia, Feng Zhi, and Tian Jian. Some had old

[58] McDougall, "Poems, Poets and *Poetry* 1976," p. 80 and n. 7.

[59] According to Jack Chen, seven hundred novels were before the publishers in 1973, six hundred of them by amateur writers: *Inside the Cultural Revolution,* p. 403. See also Chai Pien, *A Glance at China's New Culture* (Peking: Foreign Languages Press, 1975), pp. 27–41.

works republished, and most of the poets produced poems or essays celebrating the new Hundred Flowers.

Nevertheless, the pace of improvement was very slow, and Mao was not the only leader to express impatience. Several times, decisions were made to increase the quantity of literary production, and the section of the leadership responsible for cultural matters became very defensive. The debates between the Zhou Enlai–Deng Xiaoping group (Deng being one of the first cadres to be rehabilitated in 1973) and the Zhang–Jiang–Yao group increased in intensity. It focused especially on such questions as the revival of the literature of the seventeen years before the Cultural Revolution, the appropriateness of the *yangbanxi* as a model for nontheatrical literary works, and the current slow growth in literary and art production.

The problem of slow growth could be attributed to three related causes. First, the gradual rehabilitation of literary and art workers in the early 1970s was limited in the number of people who were allowed to reappear and in the degree to which their former incomes and privileges were being restored. If one section of the leadership was bent on restoration of power to the rehabilitated, another was equally determined not to permit their former power to be restored. Since the latter group (Zhang, Jiang, and Yao) were in control of the cultural media, they were able to limit the effectiveness of these older writers and artists. Secondly, the intimidation of writers and artists during the Cultural Revolution (see below) had been far more intense than in the previous antirightist movement and, with many of the Cultural Revolution leaders still in power, these rehabilitated workers were understandably cautious in responding to new demands for their professional skills. Finally, the new cultural authorities had not been wholly successful in their plan of replacing the older professional writers and artists with amateurs from the ranks of the workers, peasants, and soldiers. Without senior teachers, critics, and editors, without material incentives, and without much time to learn the needed skills, the new generation was under a severe handicap. Moreover, the experience of their elders may well have had an inhibiting effect on these fledgling talents.

The clash between these two factions came to a head in 1976. The Zhang–Jiang–Yao group became pre-eminent after the death of Zhou Enlai and the fall of Zhou's supporters, such as Deng Xiaoping and the Minister of Education, Zhou Rongxin, after the Tiananmen incident at Qingming. The summer of 1976 saw some relaxation of tension with Hua Guofeng, a compromise figure, as the new premier, but the earthquake in July and the death of Mao two months later showed that this unity had been an illusion. The group now known as the Gang of Four (Zhang, Jiang, Yao, and Wang Hongwen) was expelled, possibly at gunpoint and certainly with the support of the PLA. Their chief ally in cultural innovation and administration, the composer and Minister of Culture, Yu

Huiyong, is said to have committed suicide, and Hao Ran, their chief cultural hero, underwent a lengthy period of detention and interrogation before being allowed to publish again.

Two other groups of writers, however, still claim our attention. In the first half of the 1970s, the attention of the Western world was suddenly directed toward the apparent existence of "dissent literature" in China. Newspaper accounts of novels and poems in private or underground circulation were substantiated by the publication of such material in Hong Kong, although the Hong Kong versions themselves received surprisingly little publicity.[60] Secondly, the publication of the stories of Chen Jo-hsi (Chen Ruoxi), first in Chinese in Hong Kong and Taiwan and then in English translation in the U.S., provided foreign readers not only with a sensitive and shocking view of the Cultural Revolution but with some of the finest writing to have come out of China for many years.[61] Chen Jo-hsi's stories were followed by a political thriller by the pseudonymous Hsia Chih-yen (Xia Zhiyan), first in Japanese and then in English translation.[62] Unlike Chen's stories about the problems and terrors of everyday life for teachers in Nanking, Hsia's novel offers dramatic glimpses into high-level political and military circles in Peking and into the underground life of "sent-down" youth in the city. Also unlike the subtle delicacy of Chen's stories, Hsia's novel is written in a flashy best-seller style of little literary merit. Whether either or both of these works can be described as dissent literature is a subject of debate; both were, after all, written and published outside China. Moreover, Chen Jo-hsi was born in Taiwan and educated in the United States; during her six years in China she was regarded as an outsider. Whereas the authenticity of her account of life in China has been amply confirmed, her literary sensibility and style set her apart from mainland writers.

However, if neither Chen Jo-hsi nor Hsia Chih-yen could write or circulate their work in China, others have done so, and it is their expressions that we should look to for truly native dissent writing. Underground literature in China was the direct result of the Cultural Revolution: deprived of works emanating from the center, these young writers created their own. Their works, hand-copied, mimeographed, or orally transmitted, are the most perfect example in contemporary China of the fusion between author and audience: untouched by state or Party intervention, this effort was truly an example of writers serving the people. Some of this literature was

[60] Bonnie S. McDougall, "Underground Literature: Two Reports from Hong Kong," *Contemporary China* 3, 4 (Winter 1979), and "Dissent Literature."

[61] Chen Jo-hsi, *The Execution of Mayor Yin and Other Stories from the Great Proletarian Cultural Revolution* (Bloomington: Indiana University Press, 1978).

[62] Hsia Chih-yen, *The Coldest Winter in Peking: A Novel from inside China* (New York: Doubleday, 1978).

written primarily for entertainment; some was for private solace or personal expression; some was direct political and social protest. The uniquely central position of literature, and of poetry above all, has nowhere been demonstrated so fully and passionately as in the outpourings of poems at Tiananmen in 1976, which circulated underground before reaching first limited and then open publication in China in 1977 and 1978. Although their circulation obviously suited the purposes of a faction within the then leadership, it was nonetheless a spontaneous phenomenon. Private individuals wrote the poems, copied down others' poems, circulated these copies among their close friends, found ingenious hiding places for them in their homes, and refused to hand them over to the authorities.

The Persecution of Writers during the Cultural Revolution

One of the most notorious aspects of the Cultural Revolution was the relentless persecution of most of the prominent writers of the previous decades. Many lesser-known people from literature and the arts, people from intellectual and educational circles, and people with no special claim to fame at all were caught up in this wave of terror. If hundreds of thousands were involved in the rectification and antirightist campaigns, millions were probably caught up during the Cultural Revolution. Many Western observers have been particularly horrified at the fate suffered by some of China's erstwhile leading writers, such as Ba Jin and Lao She.[63] It is easier for us to reconstruct in our imagination the tragedy of someone whose voice speaks to us in familiar tones and whose outlook and interests are close to our own. And yet it is more than just class sympathy or the rhetorical power of the victim that impels us to pay special attention to the persecution by the state of its writers and artists. A state that represses or persecutes its intellectuals, writers, and artists is equally apt to extend such repression to other groups who offend its conventions. Brutality toward a group we can identify is an index of possible brutality toward those whom we cannot identify. Beyond this, there is also the particular distress we feel at the repression of the sensitive and the articulate, regardless of the moral or social worth of their lives or work. The systematic destruction of an existing culture, even if undertaken to clear the way for the growth of a new one, is perhaps always a net loss for the whole of humanity. And if that new culture fails to materialize, or shows only weak and sporadic growth, the poignancy of our loss is even more profound. Even before the Cultural Revolution, there were several instances where individual writers or groups of writers were vigorously persecuted. The rancour of these

[63] See, for example, Paul Bady, "Death and the Novel—on Lao She's 'Suicide' " and "Rehabilitation: A Chronological Postscript," *Renditions,* 10 (Autumn 1978): 5–14, 15–20; Olga Lang, "Introduction" to Pa Chin, *Family* (New York: Doubleday, 1972), pp. xxiv–xxvi.

persecutions was considerable and cannot be easily explained. Historical factors may be part of the reason. Literary persecutions were not unknown in imperial China, where there was a strong tradition of mutual contempt among writers. In more recent times, the persecution of writers by the Nationalist Party in China and by the Communist Party in the U.S.S.R. set precedents for the Chinese Communist Party to follow. Setting writers to persecute other writers was a tactic adopted in the U.S.S.R. and in Yan'an China. Its use in China after 1949, when writers were more deeply involved in competition for state and Party positions, was probably a major factor in the peculiar bitterness of post-1949 persecutions. Referring more broadly to the social basis for the persecutions in the Cultural Revolution, Stuart R. Schram has commented as follows: "It would be unduly simplistic, and unfair to the social category to which many of the readers of this journal [*China Quarterly*] belong, to say that urban intellectuals (who were the main bearers of the Cultural Revolution) are nastier, more vindictive, and more given to factional fighting than peasants, but I suspect that the difference in atmosphere between the two movements [urban and rural] was not wholly unrelated to this difference in their social basis."[64]

Regrettable as it may seem to socialist idealists, it appears from the Chinese example in this century that writers and artists need either actual or prospective social leadership or else material security in order to flourish. They can survive, as creative writers and artists, through material poverty and political oppression—if, at the same time, they have a politically and socially significant role to play. They can survive, if not as producers then as figureheads, in periods of intense political control—if, at the same time, they can enjoy material rewards and assured social leadership. But denied security and denied a political or social role as a group, then regardless of the rewards that may yet be won by the individual, very few artists are prepared to accept the risk.

NEW DIRECTIONS: AFTER THE FALL OF THE FOUR

The fall of the Gang of Four in October 1976 was immediately followed by a sustained campaign against the Gang and their policies and supporters of the last few years. The campaign at this point did not attack the Cultural Revolution; its products, such as the *yangbanxi*; or its prime leader, Mao Zedong. It consisted instead of very bitter and personal invective against the Gang and their followers. Literature and art, as usual, were pressed into service, and although a new element of spontaneous enthusiasm can perhaps be detected in this work, it was basically yet another predictable instance of the leadership's manipulation of the arts.

[64] Stuart R. Schram, "To Utopia and Back: A Cycle in the History of the Chinese Communist Party," *China Quarterly* 87 (September 1981): 407–439, esp. p. 427.

In 1977 and 1978, the campaign against the Gang of Four shifted into a new phase. As the excessive rhetoric began to level off, new and more fundamental targets for criticism were found. The Cultural Revolution was declared officially over and, as its policies were gradually discarded, its procedures and aims were openly denounced, and the infallibility of Mao Zedong and the validity of his deification became open to debate. In literature, the first open sign of the new and more profound approach to the problems of the immediate past was the "exposure" short story, "Ban zhuren" [The class teacher], published by Liu Xinwu in November 1977. Though this was evidently printed with the approval of at least some of the leadership, the next such story did not appear until the following summer, and after some difficulty. This story, "Shanghen" [The scar; sometimes mistranslated as The wound or The wounded] by Lu Xinhua, like "The Class Teacher," introduced elements into literature that had been absent for a decade or more: intellectual protagonists, questioning of the philosophic basis of populist and antirightist movements, problematic or unresolved endings, and the insinuation that tragedy could be an appropriate mode in a socialist society.[65] These issues were debated in the national media during 1978 as other examples of "scar literature," including spoken drama, were published. But the debate was one-sided, and when official sanction was finally bestowed at the end of 1978, it came as no surprise. In 1979, scar literature increased not only in quantity but also in the profundity of its exposure of social ills in China, going back even to the period before the Cultural Revolution. The defects of the movement's quality, however, as in the case of its predecessors, are apparent in its longwindedness, didacticism, sentimentality, and banal writing style.

Along with scar literature came the "unofficial literature" published in privately printed and circulated magazines and pamphlets. Known as "popular publications" (*minban kanwu*), they began to appear at the end of 1978 and flourished most vigorously in the spring of 1979. Most of these publications were primarily political, and the literary material in their pages differs only in content, not in style, from scar literature.[66] However, some of the magazines devoted to literature were truly different. The most notable of these was the magazine *Jintian* [Today], which ap-

[65] See Bennett Lee, "Introduction" to Lu Xinhua et al., *The Wounded* (Hong Kong: Joint Publishing Company, 1979), pp. 1–7; Geremie Barmé, "Flowers or More Weeds? Culture in China since the Fall of the Gang of Four," *Australian Journal of Chinese Affairs* 1 (January 1979): 125–133; Kam Louie, "Discussions on 'Exposure Literature' since the Fall of the 'Gang of Four'," *Contemporary China* 3, 4 (Winter 1979); and McDougall, "Dissent Literature."

[66] Peter Chan, "Popular Publications in China—A Look at *The Spring of Peking*," *Contemporary China* 3, 4 (Winter 1979); Qian Yuxiang, "History, Be My Judge!" trans. by Virginia Mayer Chan in *Contemporary China* 3, 4 (Winter 1979): 128–140; and McDougall, "Dissent Literature."

peared in nine issues between December 1978 and September 1980.[67] It contained the most remarkable poetry published in China since 1949, by young writers such as Bei Dao (Zhao Zhenkai), Mang Ke, Gu Cheng, and Shu Ting. Some of these poems were written as early as 1972 and circulated among friends; others were written after 1976 but were still unacceptable in the official media. Poetry was *Today*'s chief accomplishment, but it also published fine short stories by Shi Mo and Ai Shan (also pseudonyms for Zhao Zhenkai) and Wan Zhi (Chen Maiping).

The year 1979 was a confused period in Chinese literature and arts. On the one hand, the unofficial literature that had surfaced the previous year was gradually suppressed, so that by the end of 1979 it had virtually disappeared from the streets. On the other hand, writers and performers of older generations were being restored to public life and even to positions of cultural and social leadership. The extension of rehabilitation to the scapegoats of the 1950s led to some odd confrontations: Ding Ling and Ai Qing, for instance, appeared on the same platform as their former persecutor, Zhou Yang. However, the mood of 1979 was one of conciliation under the Party's banner. A pass into the official world was even extended to the unofficial writers, and a few poems by Bei Dao and Shu Ting appeared in the official press.

The restored intellectual and political elites found themselves in an even closer partnership than before. Both were anxious to eliminate the remnants of leftism from the state and Party bureaucracy and to revive the concept of an orderly and stable society run by a small elite. Nevertheless, tension still existed between them. The Fourth National Congress of Literary and Art Personnel, held in October–November 1979, revealed a wide range of attitudes among Party leaders, Party cultural authorities, and the writers and artists themselves.[68] Some of the participants recognized their past shortcomings and apologized for them; others could only express bewilderment and grief. In some cases the record was subtly altered. Yang Hansheng's list of writers and artists "hounded to death" by the Gang of Four included writers who had died after the latter's fall, such as He

[67] See Bonnie S. McDougall, "A Poetry of Shadows," in Bei Dao, *Notes from the City of the Sun* (Ithaca: Cornell University China-Japan Program, 1983) and David S. G. Goodman, *Beijing Street Voices: The Poetry and Politics of China's Democracy Movement* (London: Marion Boyars, 1981).

[68] Some of the documents from the Fourth Congress are in Zhongguo wenxue yishu jie lianhehui, ed., *Zhongguo wenxue yishu gongzuozhe disici daibiao dahui wenji* [Documents from the Fourth Congress of Chinese Literature and Arts Personnel] (Chengdu: Sichuan renmin chubanshe, 1980). Translations of some of these and other documents from the Congress are in Howard Goldblatt, ed., *Chinese Literature for the 1980s: The Fourth Congress of Writers and Artists* (Armonk, N.Y.: Sharpe, 1982).

Qifang and Guo Xiaochuan—on the grounds that the Gang's activities hastened or indirectly caused their deaths.[69]

Although the newly rehabilitated writers and artists immediately plunged into new work, not much can be expected from the senior generation, given their advanced age, poor health, and dismal record of achievement in the past. The reappearance of such writers from the Hundred Flowers period as Wang Meng and Liu Bingyan holds more promise. Their proven talent, courage, and ability to mature in adversity has already given their work a strong new voice. Together with the scar and unofficial newcomers, these writers are producing the most interesting literature to come out of China since 1949. The old literary establishment of the period before the Cultural Revolution is back in power, but its ranks are greatly thinned by natural attrition and political persecution, and it was deprived for most of a decade of the chance to mold its successors.

In many ways, the situation at the end of the 1970s resembled that at the beginning of the 1950s. The system of rewards and punishments was revived, and criticism was allowed only within centrally controlled limits. The new leadership offered active encouragement to the formation of new educational and cultural elites. The rural population was encouraged to enrich itself, and though its educational opportunities were limited, there was less control over its recreation. Both the political elite and the new, upwardly mobile intelligentsia had a distinctly Western orientation. Although the traditional theater flourished, the trend toward borrowing from the popular tradition to create new works of literature and art was quiescent. If the movement toward modernization continues as promised, then it is Yan'an populism, not the May Fourth or Western-oriented tradition, that is likely to be only a passing phase in the cultural history of twentieth-century China.

[69] The number of deaths among writers and artists during the Cultural Revolution is obviously a sensitive topic. Between the years 1966 and 1979, the membership of the Writers' Association dropped from 1,059 to 865. Most of the decrease must be due to deaths, and most of these deaths occurred between 1966 and 1969. Roughly 150 writers dead in three years is a very large figure. However, we cannot rule out natural attrition, since some of these writers were born around the turn of the century and the average life expectancy for a Shanghai Chinese male in 1964 (most of the senior writers are urban men) was 69.3 years. It is remarkable that frail elderly gentlemen like Ba Jin, Mao Dun, and Guo Moruo were able to survive.

CONTRIBUTORS

PAUL CLARK recently completed the Ph.D. degreee in History and East Asian languages at Harvard. He was in Peking as an exchange student from New Zealand from 1974 to 1976 and is the author of *"Hauhau": The Pai Marire Search for Maori Identity*. His thesis topic was Chinese film making and film audiences since 1949.

MICHAEL EGAN has a doctorate in modern Chinese literature from the University of Toronto, where he wrote his dissertation on the short stories of Yu Dafu. The author of several articles and book reviews about Chinese literature, he is a freelance writer who divides his time between Toronto and Ottawa.

EDWARD GUNN is assistant professor of Chinese literature at Cornell University. He has published a book-length study, *Unwelcome Muse: Chinese Literature in Shanghai and Peking, 1937–1945*, and *Twentieth-Century Chinese Drama: An Anthology*.

ROBERT E. HEGEL is associate professor of Chinese language and literature at Washington University in St. Louis. He is the author of *The Novel in Seventeenth Century China* and of several articles in both English and Chinese on Ming-Qing fiction.

DAVID HOLM is lecturer in Chinese at Macquarie University in Sydney. He is the author of a number of articles on the Chinese performing arts and on the genesis of Chinese Communist Party cultural policy in Yan'an during the 1940s.

KAI-YU HSU (d. 1982) completed his undergraduate degree at Tsinghua and his Ph.D. at Stanford. From 1959 to 1982 he was professor of world literature at San Francisco State University. Recent publications include: *The Chinese Literary Scene: A Writer's Visit to the People's Republic* (1976), *The Literature of the People's Republic of China* (1980), and *Wen I-to* (1980).

T. D. HUTERS teaches Chinese language and literature at the University of Minnesota. His publications include *Qian Zhongshu* (Twayne, 1982) and *Revolu-*

tionary Literature in China: An Anthology (M. E. Sharpe, 1977), of which he is co-editor.

PERRY LINK is associate professor in modern Chinese literature at the University of California, Los Angeles. Publications include *Mandarin Ducks and Butterflies: Popular Fiction in Early Twentieth-Century Chinese Cities* (Berkeley: University of California Press, 1981). He is currently researching contemporary Chinese fiction and drama in its social context.

WAI-FONG LOH is a graduate of New Asia College at the Chinese University of Hong Kong and received his Ph.D. at Harvard. He is now an assistant professor of Chinese history at Harvard and specializes in the institutional and socio-economic history of China.

BONNIE S. MCDOUGALL has taught Chinese language and literature at the University of Sydney and at Harvard University. Recent publications include the translation of *Notes from the City of the Sun* by Bei Dao and *China Handbook Series: Literature and the Arts*. She spent three years as editor and translator at the Foreign Languages Press, Peking, and is currently engaged on a history of modern Chinese poetry.

ISABEL K. F. WONG was born in China. She received her university education in Australia and in the United States. While finishing her doctoral dissertation for Brown University on *kunqu* music theater, she is also serving as a visiting faculty member at the University of Illinois, Urbana-Champaign. In 1982 she conducted research on music in China with a grant from the Committee on Scholarly Communication with the People's Republic of China.

BELL YUNG was born in Shanghai and raised in Hong Kong. He received a Ph.D. in Physics from the Massachusetts Institute of Technology, and a Ph.D. in Music from Harvard University. In January 1981 he joined the faculty at the University of Pittsburgh. His publications on Cantonese opera, Cantonese popular narratives, and music of the seven-string zither have appeared in *Ethnomusicology, Chinoperl Papers,* and the *New Groves Dictionary of Music and Musicians*.

Glossary

阿庆	A Qing
阿义	A Yi
阿英	A Ying
艾青	Ai Qing
艾珊	Ai Shan
安源路矿工人俱乐部部歌	"Anyuan Lukuang gongren julebu buge"
按照人民的命令	"Anzhao renminde mingling"
阿史那	*Ashina*
巴金	Ba Jin
巴人	Ba Ren
白毛女	*Bai mao nü*
白茹	Bai Ru
白骨精现形记	"Baigujing xianxingji"
白云鄂博交响诗	"Baiyun Ebo jiaoxiang shi"
班主任	"Ban zhuren"
梆子	*bangzi*
板眼	*banyan*
包玉堂	Bao Yutang
豹子湾战斗	*Baoziwan zhandou*

把式 *bashi*
北島 Bei Dao
卞之琳 Bian Zhilin
逼上梁山 *Bishang Liangshan*
碧血花 *Bixue hua*
梆子 *bongji*
梆子快点 *bongji faaidim*
梆子快中板 *bongji faai-jungbaan*
梆子中板 *bongji jungbaan*
梆子慢板 *bong ji maanbaan*
补缸匠 *bugang jiang*
采风 *cai feng*
财狂 *Caikuang*
曹禺 Cao Yu
草包敌人 *caobao diren*
参军 *canjun*
常宝华 Chang Baohua
常凤篆 Chang Fengzhuan
常贵田 Chang Guitian
Chao, Y. R. *see* Zhao Yuanren
陈白尘 Chen Baichen
陈迈平 Chen Maiping
Chen Jo-hsi *see* Chen Ruoxi
陈若曦 Chen Ruoxi
陈志良 Chen Zhiliang
成仿吾 Cheng Fangwu
成荫 Cheng Yin
称心如意 *Chenxin ruyi*
衬字 *chenzi*

褚人獲	Chu Renhuo
传家宝	*Chuan jiabao*
创业	*Chuangye*
创业史	*Chuangye shi*
传奇	*chuanqi*
辞赋	*ci-fu*
崔嵬	Cui Wei
错觉式	*cuojue shi*
大雷雨	*Da leiyu*
大马戏团	*Da maxituan*
打到敌人后方去	"Dadao diren houfang qu"
大鼓	*dagu*
大河奔流	*Dahe benliu*
代言体	*daiyanti*
大路歌	"Dalu ge"
道白	*daobai*
打油诗	*dayoushi*
邓拓	Deng Tuo
刁(参谋长)	Diao (Adviser)
丁玲	Ding Ling
顶硬上	"Ding ying shang"
顶灯	*Dingdeng*
逗哏的	*dougende*
东方红	"Dongfang hong"
东进序曲	*Dong jin xuqu*
对对联	"Dui duilian"
杜鹃山	*Dujuanshan*
二簧	*erhuang*
二人台	*errentai*

范克明 Fan Keming
凡石 "Fan Shi"
放歌 *fangge*
放下你的鞭子 *Fangxia nide bianzi*
费穆 Fei Mu
冯景元 Feng Jingyuan
冯牧 Feng Mu
冯少怀 Feng Shaohuai
冯雪峰 Feng Xuefeng
冯至 Feng Zhi
封神演义 *Fengshen yanyi*
枫树湾 *Fengshuwan*
风絮 *Fengxu*
风云儿女 *Fengyun ernü*
副末 *fumo*
夫妻识字 *Fuqi shizi*
腐蚀 *Fushi*
改行 "Gaihang"
钢都赞 "Gangdu zan"
钢琴协奏曲"黄河" *Gangqin xiezouqu Huanghe*
高大泉 Gao Daquan
高二林 Gao Erlin
高腔 *gaoqiang*
高山哨所 "Gaoshan shaosuo"
高原彩虹 "Gaoyuan caihong"
歌海春潮滚滚来 "Gehai chunchao gungun lai"
歌唱片 *gechangpian*
歌剧 *geju*
革命歌曲 *geming gequ*

顾城 Gu Cheng
顾仲彝 Gu Zhongyi
关帝 Guandi
广东新语 *Guangdong xinyu*
广西特种部族歌谣集 *Guangxi tezhong buzu geyao ji*
贯口 guankou
郭(指导员) Guo (Instructor)
郭沫若 Guo Moruo
郭启儒 Guo Qiru
郭小川 Guo Xiaochuan
郭鎮鋌 Guo Zhenting
果园城记 *Guoyuancheng ji*
故事片 *gushipian*
古装戏剧 *guzhuang xiju*
滚花 *gwanfa*
海港 *Haigang*
海霞 *Haixia*
海燕 "Haiyan"
韩百仲 Han Baizhong
旱船 *hanchuan*
浩然 Hao Ran
贺敬之 He Jingzhi
何孔周 He Kongzhou
何其芳 He Qifang
黑籍冤魂 *Heiji yuanhun*
恒居帷自讼 *hengju wei zisong*
河西走廊步步歌 "Hexi zoulang bubu ge"
红灯记 *Hong deng ji*
红色娘子军 *Hongse niangzi jun*

侯宝林 Hou Baolin

Hsia Chih-yen *see* Xia Zhiyan

胡(司令) Hu (Commander)

胡风 Hu Feng

胡适 Hu Shi

话本 *huaben*

花鼓灯 *huagudeng*

花鼓戏 *huaguxi*

槐树庄 *Huaishuzhuang*

话剧 *huaju*

黄自 Huang Zi

黄佐临 Huang Zuolin

荒岛英雄 *Huangdao yingxiong*

黄河船夫曲 "Huanghe chuanfu qu"

黄河大合唱 "Huanghe dahechang"

蝴蝶迷 Hudiemi

沪剧 *huju*

婚礼 *Hunli*

江舟 Jiang Zhou

江南滑稽 *Jiangnan huaji*

焦二菊 Jiao Erju

焦淑红 Jiao Shuhong

接受对象 *jieshou duixiang*

金圣叹 Jin Shengtan

京锣鼓 *jing luogu*

京白 *jingbai*

京剧 *jingju*

京派 *Jingpai*

金光大道 *Jinguang dadao*

今天 *Jintian*
决裂 *Juelie*
巨澜 *Julan*
柯灵 Ke Ling
柯岩 Ke Yan
刻在板苍山上 "Ke zai Bancangshanshang"
刻在北大荒的土地上 "Ke zai Beidahuangde tudishang"
柯仲平 Ke Zhongping
空城记 "Kong cheng ji"
孔厥 Kong Jue
快而不乱 *kuai er buluan*
狂流 *Kuang liu*
昆剧 *kunju*
昆曲 *kunqu*
蓝苹 Lan Ping
老大娘的炕 "Lao daniangde kang"
老舍 Lao She
雷振邦 Lei Zhenbang
擂台 "Leitai"
雷雨 *Leiyu*
李长之 Li Changzhi
李广田 Li Guangtian
李涵秋 Li Hanqiu
李季 Li Ji
李健吾 Li Jianwu
李景汉 Li Jinghan
李俊 Li Jun
李麦 Li Mai
李求实 Li Qiushi

李双双	*Li Shuangshuang*
李少白	Li Shaobai
李学鳌	Li Xueao
李瑛	Li Ying
李有才板话	*Li Youcai banhua*
李准	Li Zhun
梁斌	Liang Bin
梁上泉	Liang Shangquan
梁上君子	*Liangshang junzi*
连环记	*lianhuan ji*
林默涵	Lin Mohan
林海雪原	*Linhai xueyuan*
立体	*liti*
刘白羽	Liu Baiyu
刘宾雁	Liu Binyan
柳翠	Liu Cui
柳青	Liu Qing
刘三姐	*Liu Sanjie*
刘三妹	Liu Sanmei
刘坦克	Liu Tanke
刘万	Liu Wan
刘心武	Liu Xinwu
六艺	*Liu yi*
刘征	Liu Zheng
柳州采调团	Liuzhou caidiao tuan
卢新华	Lu Xinhua
鲁迅艺术文学院	Lu Xun yishu wenxue yuan
路在他的脚下延伸	*Lu zai tade jiaoxia yanshen*
芦荡火种	*Ludang huozhong*

罗常培 Luo Changpei

Luyi *see* Lu Xun yishu wenxue yuan

Ma, Sitson *see* Ma Sicong

马凤兰 Ma Fenglan

马季 Ma Ji

马可 Ma Ke

马思聪 Ma Sicong

马之悦 Ma Zhiyue

慢而不断 *man er buduan*

芒克 Mang Ke

茅盾 Mao Dun

毛宗岗 Mao Zonggang

帽子工厂 "Maozi gongchang"

梅兰芳 Mei Lanfang

梅萝香 *Mei Luoxiang*

郿鄠 *Meihu*

梅花三弄 "Meihua sannong"

民办刊物 *minban kanwu*

明末遗恨 *Mingmo yihen*

民众剧团 Minzhong jutuan

民族形式 *minzu xingshi*

木魚 mu yu

娜拉 *Nala*

难夫难妻 *Nan fu nan qi*

南疆春早 *Nanjiang chun zao*

南音 *nanyin*

南征北战 *Nanzheng beizhan*

聂耳 Nie Er

宁宇 Ning Yu

牛大水	Niu Dashui
扭秧歌	*niu yangge*
农奴	*Nongnu*
弄真成假	*Nongzhen chengjia*
女交通员	*Nü jiaotongyuan*
欧阳海之歌	*Ouyang Hai zhi ge*
欧阳山	Ouyang Shan
欧阳予倩	Ouyang Yuqian
排门子	*pai menzi*
跑大场	*pao dachang*
跑关东	"Pao guan dong"
跑驴	*paolü*
彭宁	Peng Ning
捧哏的	*penggende*
皮黄(戏)	*pihuang* (*xi*)
平地茶园	*pingdi chayuan*
平原游击队	*Pingyuan youjidui*
弃妇	*Qi fu*
齐如山	Qi Rushan
钱杏村	Qian Xingcun
钱钟书	Qian Zhongshu
千里思	"Qianli si"
乔羽	Qiao Yu
秦(司令员)	Qin (Commander)
秦瘦鸥	Qin Shouou
清宫怨	*Qing gong yuan*
青春	*Qingchun*
青春之歌	*Qingchun zhi ge*
秦腔	*Qinqiang*

秋海棠	*Qiu Haitang*
奇袭白虎团	*Qixi Baihutuan*
曲波	Qu Bo
屈大均	Qu Dajun
瞿秋白	Qu Qiubai
曲艺	*quyi*
绕道	"Raodao"
饶孟侃	Rao Mengkan
任广	Ren Guang
日出	*Richu*
肉中血	*rouzhongxue*
阮章竞	Ruan Zhangjing
	Sagabong see *Shajiabang*
赛金花	*Sai Jinhua*
三突出	*san tuchu*
三个摩登女性	*San'ge modeng nüxing*
三番四斗	*sanfan sidou*
三千金	*San qianjin*
傻公子	*sha gongzi*
沙家浜	*Shajiabang*
山歌恋	*Shan'ge lian*
上海剧艺社	Shanghai juyi she
上海的早晨	*Shanghaide zaochen*
伤痕	"Shanghen"
闪闪的红星	*Shanshande hong xing*
善意的规劝	*shanyide guiquan*
少剑波	Shao Jianbo
邵荃麟	Shao Quanlin
沈从文	Shen Congwen
生而不紧	*sheng er bujin*

石揮 Shi Hui
石默 Shi Mo
师陀 Shi Tuo
时代 *Shidai*
诗刊 *Shikan*
熟而不油 *shu er buyou*
舒婷 Shu Ting
数来宝 *shulaibao*
说唐全传 *Shuo Tang quanzhuan*
死不着 *Sibuzhao*
小曲 *siu kuk*
宋敏 Song Min
宋之地 Song Zhidi
隋史遗文 *Sui shi yiwen*
隋唐演义 *Sui Tang yanyi*
苏联之友社 Sulianzhiyou she
孙桂英 Sun Guiying
损龄梦 *sun ling meng*
她也要杀人 "Ta ye yao sha ren"
太行炉火 *Taihang luhuo*
贪官荣归 *Tan guan rong gui*
探亲 *Tan qin*
唐大同 *Tang Datong*
唐杰忠 *Tang Jiezhong*
田汉 Tian Han
田间 Tian Jian
甜姐儿 *Tian jieer*
天朝赞美歌 "Tianchao zanmei ge"
铁大人 "Tie daren"

啼笑因缘 *Tixiao yinyuan*
同治苍梧县志 *Tongzhi Cangwu xianzhi*
蜕变 *Tuibian*
推车 *tuiche*
秃子尿床 *Tuzi niao chuang*
外插花 *waichahua*
万家宝 Wan Jiabao
万之 Wan Zhi
王贵与李香香 "Wang Gui yu Li Xiangxiang"
王侉子 Wang Kuazi
王力 Wang Li
王了一 Wang Liaoyi
王蒙 Wang Meng
王苹 Wang Ping
王任叔 Wang Renshu
王统照 Wang Tongzhao
汪洋 Wang Yang
围城 *Weicheng*
帷幔 "Weiman"
文天祥 *Wen Tianxiang*
闻一多 Wen Yiduo
文明戏 *wenmingxi*
文学季刊 *Wenxue jikan*
文艺复兴 *Wenyi fuxing*
物不得其平则鸣 *Wu bu de qi ping ze ming*
五更调 "Wu geng diao"
吴晗 Wu Han
吴天 Wu Tian

吴祖光 Wu Zuguang

吴组缃 Wu Zuxiang

误会法 *wuhui fa*

夏衍 Xia Yan

夏之炎 Xia Zhiyan

冼星海 Xian Xinghai

相面 "Xiangmian"

相声 *xiangsheng*

小场子(戏) *xiao changzi* (*xi*)

肖长春 Xiao Chang chun

小二哥 *xiao erge*

小姑贤 *Xiaogu xian*

瞎子算命 *Xiazi suanming*

谢铁骊 Xie Tieli

戏剧与方言 "Xiju yu fangyan"

戏剧杂谈 "Xiju zatan"

新儿女英雄传 *Xin ernü yingxiong zhuan*

心中有了不平事 *xin zhong you liao bu ping shi*

新中国剧社 Xin Zhongguo jushe

信天游 *xintianyou*

熊佛西 Xiong Foxi

兄妹开荒 *Xiongmei kaihuang*

西皮 *xipi*

西皮二六 *xipi erliu*

西皮快板 *xipi kuaiban*

西皮流水 *xipi liushui*

西皮慢板 *xipi manban*

西皮散板 *xipi sanban*

西皮摇板 *xipi yaoban*

西皮原板 *xipi yuanban*
西沙儿女 *Xisha ernü*
绣金匾 "Xiu jin bian"
徐迟 Xu Chi
许大马棒 Xu Damabang
徐刚 Xu Gang
许广平 Xu Guangping
徐志摩 Xu Zhimo
巡按 *Xun'an*
雅俗共赏 *ya su gong shang*
严辰 Yan Chen
阳翰笙 Yang Hansheng
杨绛 Yang Jiang
杨沫 Yang Mo
杨子荣 Yang Zirong
样板(戏) *yangban* (*xi*)
秧歌 *yangge*
(鸚哥、秧哥、阳歌、扬歌)
秧歌剧 *yanggeju*
艳阳天 *Yanyangtian*
Yao Hsin-nung *see* Yao Ke
姚克 Yao Ke
姚蓬子 Yao Pengzi
夜店 *Ye dian*
夜上海 *Ye Shanghai*
叶圣陶 Ye Shengtao

引力	*Yinli*
宜山特种部族歌谣集	*Yishan tezhong buzu geyao ji*
宜山县志	*Yishan xianzhi*
弋阳腔	*Yiyang qiang*
英雄颂	*Yingxiong song*
义勇军进行曲	"Yiyongjun jinxing qu"
移植革命样板戏	*yizhi geming yangbanxi*
友谊颂	"Youyi song"
于会咏	Yu Huiyong
于力	Yu Li
于伶	Yu Ling
袁静	Yuan Jing
袁于令	Yuan Yuling
韵白	*yunbai*
臧克家	Zang Kejia
张庚	Zhang Geng
张恨水	Zhang Henshui
张金发	Zhang Jinfa
张金龙	Zhang Jinlong
张瑞芳	Zhang Ruifang
张生戏莺莺	*Zhang sheng xi Yingying*
张世文	Zhang Shiwen
张曙	Zhang Shu
张伟望	Zhang Weiwang
张志民	Zhang Zhimin
赵丹	Zhao Dan
赵慧明	Zhao Huiming
赵朴初	Zhao Puchu
赵树理	Zhao Shuli

赵元任	Zhao Yuanren
赵振开	Zhao Zhenkai
郑天健	Zheng Tianjian
郑振铎	Zheng Zhenduo
正气歌	*Zhengqi ge*
真人真事	*Zhenren zhenshi*
智取威虎山	*Zhiqu Weihushan*
钟万才起家	*Zhong Wancai qijia*
中国海的怒潮	*Zhongguohaide nu chao*
中国旅行剧团	Zhongguo lüxing jutuan
中间人物	*zhongjian renwu*
中流砥柱	"Zhongliu dizhu"
周而复	Zhou Erfu
周扬	Zhou Yang
周贻白	Zhou Yibai
周作人	Zhou Zuoren
朱光潜	Zhu Guangqian
朱自清	Zhu Ziqing
准噶尔阳光	"Zhungaer yangguang"
竹马	*zhuma*
自编自演	*Zibian ziyan*
邹荻帆	Zou Difan
走私	*Zousi*
祖国	*Zuguo*
祖国啊，母亲	*Zuguo, a, muqin*
醉了	*Zuile*
罪人	*Zuiren*
组诗	*zushi*
祖师庙	*Zushi miao*

SELECTED BIBLIOGRAPHY

This bibliography contains selected materials in Western languages for further reading and reference. It includes journals, general works, anthologies that deal wholly or in part with contemporary Chinese literature and the performing arts, monographs, and articles.

Bady, Paul. "Death and the Novel—On Lao She's 'Suicide' " and "Rehabilitation: A Chronological Postscript." *Renditions* 10 (Autumn 1978): 5–14, 15–20.

———. "Pékin ou le microcosme dans *Quatre generations sous un même toit* de Lao She." *T'oung Pao* 60.4–5 (1974).

———. "Pour une histoire littéraire de la Chine moderne: quelques sources chinoises et japonaises." *Journal asiatique* (1974), pp. 445–464.

———. "The Modern Chinese Writer: Literary Incomes and Best Sellers." *China Quarterly* 88 (December 1981): 646–657.

Barmé, Geremie. "Flowers or More Weeds? Culture in China since the Fall of the Gang of Four." *Australian Journal of Chinese Affairs* 1 (January 1979): 125–133.

Bei Dao (Zhao Zhenkai). *Notes from the City of the Sun.* Translated and edited by Bonnie S. McDougall. Ithaca, 1983.

Benton, Gregor, ed. *Wild Lilies, Poisonous Weeds.* London, 1982.

Berninghausen, John, and Ted Huters, eds. *Revolutionary Literature in China: An Anthology.* White Plains, 1976. (Originally published as a special issue of *Bulletin of Concerned Asian Scholars* 8, 1 and 2.)

Birch, Cyril, ed. *Anthology of Chinese Literature,* vol. 2. New York, 1972.

———. "The Dragon and the Pen: The Literary Scene." *Soviet Survey* 24 (April–June 1958): 22–26.

———. "Fiction of the Yenan Period." *China Quarterly* 4 (October–December 1960): 1–11.

———. "Change and Continuity in Chinese Fiction," in Merle Goldman, ed., *Modern Chinese Literature in the May Fourth Era.* Cambridge, Mass., 1977.

———, ed. *Chinese Communist Literature*. New York, 1963. (Originally published as a special issue of *China Quarterly* 13 [January–March 1963].)

Cavendish, Patrick. "The Revolution in Culture." In Jack Gray and Patrick Cavendish, *Chinese Communism in Crisis*. London, 1968.

Chan, Peter. "Popular Publications in China: A Look at *The Spring of Peking*." *Contemporary China* 3, 4 (Winter 1979): 103–111.

Chen, Jack. *The Chinese Theater*. London, 1949.

Chin, Ai-li S. "Family Relations in Modern Chinese Fiction." In M. Freedman, ed., *Family and Kinship in Chinese Society*. Stanford, 1970.

———. "The Ideal Local Party Secretary and the 'Model' Man." *China Quarterly* 1 (January–March 1964): 229–240.

China Handbook Editorial Committee, ed. *China Handbook Series: Culture*. (Peking, 1982).

———, ed. *China Handbook Series: Literature and the Arts*. (Peking, 1983).

Chinese Literature (Peking), 1953–present.

CHINOPERL News (Ithaca), 1971–1975. Renamed *Chinoperl Papers*, 1976–present.

Chu, Godwin, ed. *Popular Media in China: Shaping New Cultural Patterns*. Honolulu, 1978.

———and Francis L. K. Hsu. *Moving a Mountain: Cultural Change in China*. Honolulu, 1979.

Clark, Paul. "Film-making in China: From the Cultural Revolution to 1981," *China Quarterly* 94 (June 1983): 304–322.

Denès, Hervé, ed. *Le Retour du père*. Paris, 1981.

Ebon, Martin. *Five Chinese Communist Plays*. New York, 1975.

Fokkema, D. W. "Chinese Criticism of Humanism: Campaign against the Intellectuals, 1964–1966." *China Quarterly* 26 (April–June 1966).

———. *Literary Doctrine in China and Soviet Influence, 1950–1960*. The Hague, 1965.

Gibbs, Donald A., ed. *Dissonant Voices in Chinese Literature: Hu Feng, Chinese Studies in Literature* 1, 1 (Winter 1979–1980): 3–89.

———, comp. *Subject and Author Index to Chinese Literature (1956–1971)*. New Haven, 1978.

Goldblatt, Howard, ed. *Chinese Literature for the 1980s: The Fourth Congress of Writers and Artists*. Armonk, N.Y., 1982.

Goldman, Merle. *Literary Dissent in Communist China*. Cambridge, Mass., 1967.

Goodman, David S. G. *Beijing Street Voices: The Poetry and Politics of China's Democracy Movement*. London, 1981.

Gunn, Edward M., Jr. *Unwelcome Muse: Chinese Literature in Shanghai and Peking, 1937–1945*. New York, 1980.

———. *Twentieth-Century Chinese Drama: An Anthology*. Bloomington, Ind., 1983.

Hinrup, Hans J., comp. *An Index to 'Chinese Literature' 1951–1976*. London, 1978.

Holm, David. "Hua Guofeng and the Village Drama Movement in the North-west Shanxi Base Area, 1943–45." *China Quarterly* 84 (December 1980): 669–693.

Howard, Roger. *Contemporary Chinese Theatre,* London, 1978.

Hsia, C. T. *History of Modern Chinese Fiction.* 2d ed. New Haven, 1971.

Hsu Kai-yu. *The Chinese Literary Scene: A Writer's Visit to the People's Republic.* New York, 1975.

———, ed. *Literature of the People's Republic of China.* Bloomington, Indiana, 1980.

———, ed. *Twentieth Century Chinese Poetry: An Anthology.* New York, 1964.

Huang, Joe C. "Hao Ran: The Peasant Novelist." *Modern China* 2, 3 (July–September 1976): 369–396.

———. *Heroes and Villains in Communist China: The Contemporary Chinese Novel as a Reflection of Life.* London and New York, 1973.

Index on Censorship 9, 1 (February 1980), pp. 3–48. Special issue on China.

Jenner, W. J. F., ed. *Modern Chinese Stories.* London, 1970.

———. "1979: A New Start for Literature in China?" *China Quarterly* 86 (June 1981): 274–303.

King, Richard, " 'Wounds' and 'Exposure': Chinese Literature after the Gang of Four." *Pacific Affairs* 54, 1 (Spring 1981): 82–99.

Kubin, Wolfgang, ed. *Hundert Blumen: Moderne chinesische Erzählungen.* Second volume: 1949 to 1979. Frankfurt, 1980.

——— and Rudolf Wagner, eds. *Essays in Modern Chinese Literature and Literary Criticism.* Bochum, 1982.

Lee, Leo Ou-fan. "Dissent Literature from the Cultural Revolution." *Chinese Literature: Essays, Articles, Reviews* 1,1 (January 1979): 59–79.

Leyda, Jay. *Dianying: An Account of Films and the Film Audience in China.* Cambridge, Mass., 1972.

Link, Perry. *Mandarin Ducks and Butterflies: Popular Fiction in Early Twentieth-Century Chinese Cities.* Berkeley, 1981.

Liu Xinwu, et al. *Prize-Winning Stories from China, 1978–1979.* Peking, 1981.

Liu, Alan P. L. *The Film Industry in Communist China.* Cambridge, Mass. 1965.

Loi, Michelle. *Poètes du peuple chinois.* Paris, 1969.

Louie, Kam. "Discussions on 'Exposure Literature' since the Fall of the 'Gang of Four'." *Contemporary China* 3, 4 (Winter 1979): 91–102.

Lu Xinhua, et al. *The Wounded.* Hong Kong, 1979.

Mackerras, Colin. *Amateur Theatre in China 1949–1966.* Canberra, 1973.

———. "Chinese Opera after the Cultural Revolution (1970–1972)." *China Quarterly* 55 (July–September 1973): 478–510.

———. *The Chinese Theatre in Modern Times, from 1840 to the Present Day.* London, 1975.

———. *The Performing Arts in Contemporary China.* London, 1981.

Malmqvist, Göran, ed. *Modern Chinese Literature and Its Social Context.* [Stockholm, 1977.]

McDougall, Bonnie S. "Dissent Literature and Contemporary China: Varieties of Dissent Literature in and about China in the Seventies." *Contemporary China* 3, 4 (Winter 1979): 49–79.

———. *Mao Zedong's "Talks at the Yan'an Conference on Literature and Art."* Ann Arbor, 1980.

———. "Poems, Poets, and *Poetry* 1976: An Exercise In the Typology of Modern Chinese Literature." *Contemporary China* 2, 4 (Winter 1978): 76–124.

———. "Underground Literature: Two Reports from Hong Kong." *Contemporary China,* 3, 4 (Winter 1979): 80–90.

Meserve, Walter J., and Ruth I. Meserve. *Modern Drama from Communist China.* New York, 1970.

——— and ———. *Modern Literature from China.* New York, 1974.

Mitchell, John D., comp. *The Red Pear Garden: Three Great Dramas of Revolutionary China.* Boston, 1973.

Modern Chinese Literature Newsletter (Minneapolis), 1975–present.

Monsterleet, Jan. *Sommets de la littérature chinoise contemporaine.* Paris, 1953.

Mowry, Hua-Yuan Li. *Yang-pan hsi: New Theatre in China.* Berkeley, 1973.

Nieh Hualing. *Literature of the Hundred Flowers.* 2 vols. New York, 1981.

Pollard, D. E. "The Short Story in the Cultural Revolution." *China Quarterly* 73 (March 1978): 99–121.

Prùsek, Jaroslav. *Die Literatur des Befreiten China und ihre Volkstraditionen.* Berlin, 1955.

———. "La Nouvelle Littérature chinoise." *Archiv Orientálni* 27, 1 (1959): 76–95.

———, ed. *Studien zur Modernen Chinesischen Literature.* Berlin, 1964.

Ragvald, Lars. *Yao Wen-yuan as a Literary Critic and Theorist: The Emergence of Chinese Zhdanovism.* Stockholm, 1978.

Ru Zhijuan, et al. *Seven Contemporary Chinese Women Writers.* Peking, 1982.

Scott, A. C. *Literature and the Arts in Twentieth Century China.* New York, 1963.

Sidane, Victor. *Le Printemps de Pékin, Novembre 1978-Mars 1980.* Paris, 1980.

Shih, Vincent, "Satire in Chinese Communist Literature." *Tsing Hua Journal* n.s. 7, 1 (1968): 54–70.

Słupski, Z., ed. *Dictionary of Oriental Literature, I: East Asia.* New York, 1974.

Snow, Louise Wheeler. *China on Stage: An American Actress in the People's Republic.* New York, 1972.

Ting Yi. *A Short History of Modern Chinese Literature.* Peking, 1959.

Tsai Meishi. *Contemporary Chinese Novels and Short Stories, 1949–1974.* Cambridge, Mass., 1979.

Westerly. Contemporary China Issue. University of Western Australia. September 1981.

Xiao Lan, ed. *The Tiananmen Poems.* Peking, 1979.

Yang, Richard F. S. "The Reform of Peking Opera under the Communists." *China Quarterly* 11 (July–September 1962): 124–139.

INDEX

RANDALL LIBRARY-UNCW
3 0490 0412377 /